Critical Thinking through Debate

Joseph Corcoran
Mark Nelson
Jack Perella
Santa Jose Junior College

KENDALL/HUNT PUBLISHING COMPANY
4050 Westmark Drive   Dubuque, Iowa 52002

Cover images © 2006 by Photos.com

Printed in the United States of America
10   9

CONTENTS

Preface xiii

Chapter 1
The Nature of Argumentation 1
Why Study Argumentation and Debate?.................................1
    The Meaning of Assertion and Contradiction 2
    The Meaning of Argument 3
    The Meaning of Debate 4
Rhetorical Argument: The Three Aristotelian Means of Persuasion...........5
    The Basic Unit of Rhetorical Argument: The Enthymeme 6
    Applying the Enthymematic Model 7
The Relationship of Debate to Argumentation 8
    The Protagorean Model of Debate 8
    Protagorean Model in Today's World 9
    Affirmative and Negative Defined.....................................10
The World of Debate 11
    Academic vs. Public Debate..11
    The Purpose of This Book 12
    Benefits of Academic Debate...13
    Interscholastic Forensics...14
    Your Authors' Academic Debate Experiences 15
    Forensics Organizations..16
Summary 18

Chapter 2
Analyzing Debatable Claims 19
The Claim Tree...19
    The Principle of Clarity 19
        Methods of Defining Terms...25
        Standards for Evaluating Definitions 27
    The Need for Jurisdiction 27
    The Need for Controversy 28
The Classification of Debatable Claims 29
Types of Propositions...29
    Factual Topics 30
    Value Topics 31
    Policy Topics 32

Stock Issues 33
    Stock Issues for Legal Debate 34
    Stock Issues for Fact Debate 36
    Stock Issues for Value Debate 36
    Stock Issues for Policy Debate 38
        Motive 38
        Blame 38
        Cure 40
        Cost 40
The *Prima Facie* Case 40
Summary 43

Chapter 3
The Resolution: The Focus of a Debate 45

The Nature of a Resolution: Origin and Definition 46
    The Origin of the Term 46
    The Definition of Resolution 47
    The Implicit Resolution 48
The Framer of the Resolution 48
The Assignments in a Resolution: Presumption, Burden of Proof,
    and Standard of Proof 49
    Presumption 49
        Presumption in Policy Debate 50
        Presumption for Resolutions of Fact and Value 51
    The Burden of Proof 53
        A Burden for Proof 54
        The Effect of Assigning the Burden of Proof 55
    The Burden of Clash 57
    The Game-Room Analogy 57
    The Standards of Proof 58
        Determining the Applicable Standard for Fact and Value Propositions 60
        Determining the Applicable Standard for Policy Propositions 61
        The Bowling Ball Analogy 61
        The Requirement to State the Intent of the Framer 61
Guidelines for Wording Resolutions 63
Summary 65

Chapter 4
Fundamentals of Academic Debate 67

Academic Debate 67
Distinctions Made between Parliamentary and Cross-Examination
    Debate 69

Parliamentary Debate..70
    Pros and Cons of Parliamentary Debate 70
    Topics for Parliamentary Debate 71
    Effective Utilization of Preparation Time.......................................72
    Basic Speaker Responsibilities for Parliamentary Debate..............74
        Prime Minister 74
        Leader of Opposition 74
        Member of the Government 75
        Member of the Opposition 76
        Leader of the Opposition Rebuttal..76
        Prime Minister Rebuttal 77
    Parliamentary Procedure...77
        Points of Information 77
        Points of Order 78
        Points of Personal Privilege 80
        Points of Clarification 80
        Heckles 80
        Showing Approval and Disapproval...81
Cross-Examination Debate 81
    Pros and Cons of Cross-Examination Debate 81
    Basic Speaker Responsibilities for Cross-Examination Debate....................83
    Cross-Examination in Academic Debate 85
    Preparation Time...87
        Affirmative Preparation Time..87
        Negative Preparation Time..87
        Further Suggestions for Using Preparation Time 88
    Summary 89

Chapter 5
Research: Finding Sources of Evidence 91

    A Trip to the Library 91
    Purpose of Chapter 92
    Recentness of Evidence 92
    Definition of Evidence 93
    Sources of Evidence 93
        Personal Experience and Investigation...................................94
            The Problem of Personal Examples....................................95
        Unpublished Sources Other Than Personal Experience 96
            Opponent Admissions...96
            Non-Party Unpublished Sources 97
        Published Third-Party Sources: Library Research 98

Library Research Techniques...99
    Levels of Material: The Popular, Specialist, and Scholarly Presses.............99
        The Popular Press 100
        The Specialist Press 100
        The Scholarly Press 100
    The Genre of Sources: Books, Periodicals, and Newspapers...........101
        Books...102
        Periodicals 105
        Newspapers 105
        Miscellaneous Genre 106
Summary..113

Chapter 6
The Analysis of Evidence: Evaluating Data.............................115
  The Need For Evidence..115
  The Tests of Evidence 116
    Interpretation 117
    Relevance 117
    Reliability 118
    Competence Generally 119
    Bias Generally 120
    Hearsay Generally 120
    Competence in Detail 120
        Internal Tests of Competence 120
        External Tests of Competence...................................122
    Bias in Detail 124
    Hearsay in Detail 125
  The Hierarchy of Evidence 127
    Level 1. Assertion 127
    Level 2. Judicial Notice/Common Knowledge 128
    Level 3. Lay Opinion 128
    Level 4. Expert Opinion/Consensus of Lay Opinion.....................129
    Level 5. Empirical Study/Consensus of Expert Opinion 129
    Level 6. Consensus of Studies 129
  Fact vs. Opinion 130
  Summary..131

Chapter 7
Using Sound Reasoning 133
  Deductive and Inductive Reasoning......................................133
  Deductive Reasoning..134
    Categorical Syllogisms...134

Truth and validity..135
Elementary Venn Diagrams 136
Conditional Syllogisms 138
Disjunctive Syllogisms 139
Inductive Reasoning 143
The Relationship between Induction and Deduction 144
The Importance of Induction 144
Summary 147

Chapter 8
Categorical Logic 149
Categorical Claims 149
The Standard Form of a Syllogism 151
Discerning the Mood of a Categorical Syllogism................153
Determining the Figure of a Standard Form Categorical Syllogism 154
Distribution 156
Determining the Validity of a Syllogism.............................157
Rules of the Syllogism..158
Matching the Mood and Figure 161
Drawing Venn Diagrams 162
Summary 169

Chapter 9
Types of Arguments..171
Classifications of Argument 171
Toulmin Analysis...171
Testimony Argument 174
Example Argument...176
Statistics 179
Analogy Argument 183
Causal Argument 185
Sign Argument 188
Argument by Definition 190
Summary 192

Chapter 10
Exposing Fallacies 195
The Fallacy of Example Argument 195
The Fallacy of Composition 196
The Fallacy of Division..196
The Fallacy of Mistaken Causation 196

The Fallacy of Significance 197
The False Analogy...197
A Priori Fallacy 198
Begging the Question 199
Arguing in a Circle 199
Over-Reliance on Authority...200
Reductio Ad Absurdum 201
The *Ad Hominem* Fallacy 202
Fallacy of False Consolation 202
The False Dilemma Fallacy..203
The Fallacy of Ignoring the Issue...204
The Fallacy of the Loaded Question..204
The *Ad Populum* Fallacy 205
The Fallacy of Psychological Language....................................205
The Fallacy of Equivocation 206
The Fallacy of the Straw Person 206
The Fallacy of Tradition..206
The Fallacy of Sign Reasoning 207
The Fallacy of Shifting the Burden of Proof 207
Summary 208

Chapter 11
Refuting and Rebuilding Arguments

Refuting and Rebuilding Arguments 209
Preparing for Refutation 209
The Three "Ds" of Refutation 210
    Deny the Argument 210
    Diminish the Argument..211
        Turn-around Arguments 211
        Show the Argument Is Irrelevant to the Resolution 211
        Mitigate Arguments 212
        Point Out Contradictions 212
        Demonstrate a Lack of Impact....................................213
        Argue No Links 213
    Disbar the Argument...214
        Question the Connection between the Claim and the Evidence 214
        Question Authority 214
        Question the Recentness of Evidence............................215
        Question Opponent's Logic 215
Four-step Refutation...216
Preparing for Counter-refutation 217
    Preempting Potential Arguments 218

Rebuilding Original Arguments...219
Five-step Counter-refutation 220
Point Out Errors in Opposing Refutation 221
Summary 222

Chapter 12
Cross-Examination 223
The Nature of Cross-Examination 223
The Questioner 223
Clarify Points 224
Expose Opposition Weaknesses 224
Set Up Future Arguments..225
Use Controlling Questions 226
The Respondent 228
Know the Issues...228
Avoid Traps..229
Try to Control the Cross-Examination Period 229
Summary 230

Chapter 13
Debating Resolutions of Fact 231
The Nature of Fact..231
Cross-cultural Considerations 232
Resolutions of Fact...233
The Convertibility of Resolutions 233
The *Prima-Facie* Case Elements for a Resolution of Fact....234
Definitions 234
Evidence 234
Inference 235
Chains of Inference...235
A Sample Case..235
I. Definitions and Criteria..235
II. Evidence (a reason which is an empirical observation)....236
III. Inference (the affirmative might explain) 236
IV. Opinion Evidence 237
Negative Stock Issues for a Resolution of Fact 237
Standards and Burdens..238
On-case Arguments...238
On-case Issue I. Definitions...238
On-case Issue II. Evidence 239
On-case Issue III. Inferences.......................................240
Off-case Attacks 240

A Sample Case of a Resolution of Fact 241
  Prima Facie or On-case Elements 241
An Alternative *Prima-Facie* Format Based on Syllogisms........................242
Summary 245

Chapter 14
Debating Resolutions of Value 247
The Affirmative/Government Case 247
How to Construct a Value Affirmative Case 248
  Definition of Terms 248
  Criteria for Judgment 248
  Application of the Criterion...252
  The Categorical Syllogism..253
  Outline of a Government's Case..255
Negative Strategies in Value Debate 256
Refuting the Definitive Stock Issue 256
  Prima-Facie Argumentation..256
  Definitional Arguments...257
  Topicality Arguments...258
  Argue Criteria 260
Refuting the Designative Stock Issue.....................................261
  Arguing against Dependent Contentions.....................................262
  Arguing against Independent Contentions 263
  Denying Applications to the Criterion.....................................263
Off-case Arguments 263
Summary 266

Chapter 15
Debating Resolutions of Policy 267
Traditional Policy Stock Issues 267
  Motive 268
  Blame 270
  Cure 272
  Cost...275
Policy Case Strategies 276
  Needs Analysis Case..276
  Brainstormed Policy Debate Outline..277
  Comparative Advantage Case...278
  The Goals Case 279
  The Alternative Justification Case 279
Negative Strategies 280

Defense of the Present System 280
Minor Repair...281
Counterplan 282
    Requirements of the Counterplan...................................282
    Types of Counterplans 284
Reliance on Presumption 285
Disadvantages..285
Jurisdictionl Arguments...287
The Meaning of *Should* and *Fiat* in Policy Debate.................290
Negative Fiat Power 290
Summary 293

Chapter 16
Attending a Debate Tournament

Attending a Debate Tournament....................................295
Things to Bring 295
Getting Oriented 297
    Learning Your Code 297
    Finding Your Room 298
    Getting Your Topic 299
    Setting Up 299
Evaluating the Debate 301
Elimination Rounds 302
Summary 304

Glossary 305

Selected References 313

Index...317

PREFACE

This book is a fusion of Jack Perella's book, *The Debate Method of Critical Thinking*, Joe Corcoran's book, *An Introduction to Non-Policy Debate*, and additional material by Mark Nelson. We are pleased with the outcome.

The academic and intercollegiate debate world is changing rapidly. This book attempts to translate recent trends in academic debate into a digestible format for the beginner. An argumentation teacher or debate coach should find this book helpful in preparing the argumentation student for classroom debates and preparing the novice debater for competition.

We also believe that the frst printing of this book was the first debate text to integrate the new form of intercollegiate debate in the United States: parliamentary debate. We incorporate the principles and practices of parliamentary debate throughout the text. And in this most recent printing in 2005, we have updated our descriptions of parliamentary practices to reflect the most recent evolutionary developments in that event. While fusing parliamentary debate into two previously existing debate textbooks, we feel confident that we are able to maintain a strong commitment to the cross-examination format, which has dominated argumentation classrooms and the intercollegiate circuit since the mid 1970s.

Many teachers of argumentation and coaches of debate have complained about the choices for debate texts. We do not want to malign any of those texts, but we feel that we have answered many of those complaints in the design of this book. In terms of pedagogy, we attempt to present all sides of a theoretical issue so that the beginner can understand the choices that he or she must make in the process of becoming proficient at debate.

This book also integrates throughout each chapter examples of real-world argumentation and college tournament debating. Many textbooks seem to focus on one approach or the other. We believe that there is something to be learned from both types of approaches. Additionally, as a critical-thinking textbook, we hope to help our readers become proficient consumers of argument, as well as better advocates for their own argumentative positions.

THE NATURE OF ARGUMENTATION

WHY STUDY ARGUMENTATION AND DEBATE?

One of the first questions students often ask themselves when taking a class is "how does this pertain to me?" Sometimes the courses we take might not seem, at least initially, relevant to our daily lives. The study of argumentation and debate certainly is not one of those disciplines. It is hard to conceive of a single day in our lives when we are not exposed, directly or indirectly, to arguments. Arguments, and the use of those arguments in debates, are at the core of just about all facets of our lives.

First, from an academic perspective, argumentation is truly interdisciplinary in nature. Historians, biologists, philosophers, economists, sociologists, astronomers, mathematicians, theologians, and geologists (just to name a few) construct arguments and debate issues amongst themselves in order to advance the body of knowledge in their respective fields. Regardless of your major or career choice, the ability to advance arguments, evaluate arguments, and refute arguments will almost certainly become a part of it.

Second, arguments and debate permeate virtually all aspects of our society. Attorneys debate legal matters, elected officials debate proposed legislation, scientists debate new discoveries, coaches debate strategy, military officials debate issues of defense, and labor and management debate working conditions.

Third, you may engage in argumentation and debate to personally advance your own interests. You might have to defend yourself in a small claims court, argue with the insurance company over a claim, dispute a credit card bill, contest extracurricular activities being eliminated from your child's school, or argue to your instructor why you deserve a higher grade on a recently submitted paper.

Fourth, argumentation and debate is a form of entertainment and social bonding. We spend hours having fun debating our friends, relatives, coworkers, and even acquaintances over topics of no real importance. How many of us have spent hours (sitting in a local pub, driving to destinations, or gathered around the dinner table) debating who is the best baseball player of all time, which movie deserves to win "Best Picture," or should people live together before getting married? In fact, have you ever argued for a position that you disagreed with just for the fun of it? Most

1

likely the answer is yes. The topics clearly are not the issue. The very process of debating is what we enjoy.

Finally, even if we do not advance arguments ourselves, we are constantly bombarded with arguments which we must process and evaluate. Politicians tell us why we should vote for them, commercial advertisements try to convince us to purchase their products, and newspaper editorials tell us how we should react to world events. From the moment we first learn to communicate until we die, we are exposed to arguments on virtually a daily basis.

As should be obvious by now, everyone debates. It is a pastime, an affliction, and often a necessity. This book concerns itself with argumentation and debate, but since you have made and refuted arguments all your life it is really an introduction to the formal study of argumentation. As you already know, debating can be fun when done well, a curse when done poorly, and at times a skill of great importance. It is not a foreign subject since you've been doing it since early childhood. This book just systematically explains the process of argument.

The Meaning of Assertion and Contradiction

Let's begin with an examination of an everyday dialogue. Imagine that two little kids are standing in adjacent front yards. "A" says to "B," "My daddy can beat up your daddy." "B" responds "No, my daddy can beat up your daddy!" "A" repeats his earlier statement, but with greater emphasis. They go through several exchanges. Is this an argument? Is this argumentation?

Most observers passing by would say that the kids were arguing, and they would be using the word as a lay person would use it. *Webster's* defines argument as "to have a disagreement; quarrel; dispute." Speaking as a lay person, they would be correct. However, one trained in argumentation (as you are about to be) would realize that this was not an argument in the technical sense because no reasons were given.

Each kid's statement was an **assertion,** a claim statement without a reason. Together, their dialogue would be a contradiction, not an argument. A **contradiction** takes place when two parties assert opposite claim statements without giving any reasons. Notice that when kid "A" said "My daddy can beat up your daddy" and when kid "B" responded by saying "No, my daddy can beat up your daddy" that neither kid gave any reasons to justify his/her claim. The two kids simply contradicted one another, and we must therefore accept or reject either kid's assertion on grounds other than logic. We might accept such a claim because of what we think of the person making it (this is proof based on "ethos" or ethical proof) or because emotionally we want it to be true (this is proof based on "pathos" or pathetic proof), but it is not an argument addressed to our rational faculty, our logic. Mere contradiction is not argument in the formal sense.

The Meaning of Argument

For purposes of this book, we will define **argument** as a claim supported by a reason. A **claim** is the conclusion that the arguer advances for acceptance. It is here that we should probably clarify the distinction between argument and argumentation. An argument is a single claim supported by a reason. Argumentation concerns the general theory and practice of reasoning.

Suppose that Kid "A" originally said, "My daddy can beat up your daddy because my daddy is a prizefighter." At this point we have an argument in the technical sense. A reason has been given. No longer is this statement an assertion. Note the use of the word *because* in his newer version. In English, often what precedes the word *because* is a claim (or proposition) and whatever follows the word *because* is often a reason. The word *therefore* reverses the process: the reason is given first, followed by the claim. The words *because* and *therefore* are the most important words in the language for the study of argumentation. They express the key relationship that makes a statement argumentation. The appeal is to our rational faculty, to logic.

Notice that by our definition of argument it is not even necessary for there to be disagreement. Suppose Kid "B" after hearing this argument says, "I believe you are correct; your daddy can beat up my daddy." Kid "B" has just agreed with Kid "A's" argument. Let's assume further that kid "B" also says, "I want to point out that another reason your daddy can beat up my daddy is because your daddy is stronger than my daddy." Kid "B" has now given an argument that agrees with Kid "A's" argument. Kid "A" and Kid "B" have each advanced an argument even though they agree with one another.

Also notice that by our definition the reason for the acceptance of the claim does not even have to be true or compelling. The reason might be simply a figment of a small child's wishes. It might be a strong reason or a weak one in the mind of a judge, but it is a reason nonetheless. For example, suppose that kid "A" says, "My daddy can beat up your daddy because my daddy has black hair." Most people would not find this to be a very compelling reason to accept the claim, as most people do not draw a connection between the color of one's hair and an ability to beat someone up. In fact, this is a *non sequitur* fallacy. Non sequitur means that "it does not follow," indicating that there is no logical connection between one thing (color of hair) and another (ability to win a fight). (The definition of *fallacy* will be covered in Chapter 10, but a sufficient definition for now would be a "bad argument.") Whether it's a good or a bad reason is irrelevant to our definition of argument. We may of course choose to reject the conclusion of the argument if we believe the reason is not compelling. However, the fact still remains that a reason was given to support a claim. Non-sequitur or not, an argument was made.

The Meaning of Debate

In simple terms, in order to engage in a debate, both contradiction and argument must be present. A kind of mathematical formula can be devised that says "Contradiction + Argument = Debate" (C+A=D). Suppose kid "A" says, "My daddy can beat up your daddy because my daddy is a prizefighter" and kid "B" responds by saying, "No, my daddy can beat up your daddy because my daddy is meaner than your daddy." We now have a debate taking place. Kids "A" and "B" have articulated contrary claim statements while giving reasons for their positions, thus engaging in a debate.

At this time we will formally define debate. **Debate** is the process of logically evaluating a claim by entertaining arguments for and against the claim, and then adopting or not adopting the claim as a reasonable resolution of a dispute. This definition contains some key concepts that need to be analyzed.

First, debate is a process. By process we simply mean rules which must be followed. A debate is not an uncontrolled forum where people stand up and all shout at the same time (although some PTA meetings might resemble this). Debates utilize procedures that are developed to help ensure that both sides have an equal opportunity to have their arguments heard. The rules might cover such issues as the speaking order, the number of speeches, the length of speeches, the types of evidence allowed, and the nature of cross-examination, if any, that is utilized.

Political candidates will often negotiate the processes of their debates, even down to such details as to which family members can be allowed in the audience and who the moderator(s) will be. Attorneys must learn the procedures for arguing in court, and they spend an inordinate amount of time attending law school in order to do so. They must learn what types of questions are permissible to ask witnesses, when evidence can be introduced, and when motions need to be filed. Congress uses a system of parliamentary procedures to govern its floor debates, rules which address such issues as when motions can be raised, which motions need a second, and under what situations motions can be divided. Your classroom debates will no doubt contain rules that will need to be followed. Needless to say, learning the process by which the debate will be governed is extremely important.

Second, debate relies on a logical or rational evaluation of the claim. The term **critical thinking** as used in the academic world is essentially synonymous with *logical thinking*. It has always implied that logic was to be the test of the truth or falsity of a statement. Included in this concept are the requirements that we be able to spot fallacies of reasoning, invalid reasoning, appeals to our emotions, distortions of evidence, or an inappropriate reliance on the personality of the advocate. The devices of logic are not secret. In fact, their success depends upon the opposite. The principles are widely agreed upon and understood by most educated persons. This agreement allows decision makers anywhere in the world to understand and evaluate each others' reasoning. The knowledge of these principles of logic is an entry ticket into educated discussions on most issues. This book is intended to teach a system for the broad application of the principles of argumentation as they are understood and used by an educated society.

Third, debates entertain arguments for and against the claim. Simply put, both those who support and oppose the motion are allowed an opportunity to be heard. More formal debates also attempt to ensure that both sides are allocated an equal amount of time. It would certainly be unfair if debaters on one side were given two hours to argue their side while their opponents were given only ten minutes.

Fourth, following the debate the resolution is either adopted or not adopted. All debates have as their end result only two options: to either accept or reject the resolution under discussion. There can never be a "tie." In a court of law, either the jury finds the defendant guilty or it does not. In Congress, either a proposed law is passed or it is not. In labor disagreements, either a proposed package containing certain working conditions is accepted or it is not.

Fifth, the decision to accept or reject the claim is based on a reasonable resolution of the dispute. This means the decision maker weighs the arguments presented by both sides and then makes a "reasonable" decision based upon those arguments. It does not mean that a "correct" decision was made per se. It might be reasonable given the evidence presented in a trial to conclude that the defendant is guilty of the charges. However, if later evidence is presented, it might at that time be reasonable to change one's view based upon that new evidence. Recently, many individuals convicted of murder and sentenced to death have been released as new DNA testing has shown them to be innocent. This does not mean that the juries who convicted them were being unreasonable. Given the evidence they had at the time, a finding of guilty may have been very reasonable.

RHETORICAL ARGUMENT:
THE THREE ARISTOTELIAN MEANS OF PERSUASION

In *The Rhetoric*, Aristotle states there are three means of persuasion that may be used to support or refute an argument's claim. **Ethos** is the character of the rhetor (the person advancing the argument) as perceived by the judge. We find individuals who are competent and trustworthy to be believable. In today's society no one can be an expert on everything. As a result, we are often forced to rely on the advice of others. Most of us, not being trained in medicine, normally accept what our physicians tell us and are eager to follow the treatment they advise. On the other end of the spectrum, many of us might be wary about taking the advice of an automobile sales representative when she or he advises us to buy a particular car. **Pathos** is an appeal to emotions. While most of us like to view ourselves as rational beings, the truth is we are also very emotional beings. All of us are influenced by feelings of love, fear, envy, success, power, pity or any other number of emotions. Rhetors can use these emotions as a basis for persuasion. Insurance representatives create a sense of fear in potential customers of what might happen to surviving family or damaged property if they are inadequately insured. Criminal defendants might "throw themselves on the mercy of the court," with an impassioned plea to jurors to decline the death-penalty option. The clothing industry tells us that if we buy a particular outfit we will suddenly become highly attractive to the opposite gender, provoking emotions of love and belonging. **Logos** is the utilization of rational appeals as the basis for reaching conclusions. Financial brokers try to rely exclusively on logos when making financial decisions. If being persuaded to invest in a company, potential investors will want to base their decisions on information that seems relevant to the current viability and future growth of the company.

Advocates make use of all three means, and in fact all three exist in all statements. However, since the time of classical Greece, Western civilization has believed that logic is the best way to reach a decision. Logic, of course, is not the only way. Along with ethos and pathos, many people use personal intuition or spiritual revelation as methods of reaching decisions. At the turn of the new century in the United States, however, collectively we tend to place more weight on "logical" or "reasoned" decision making. Science operates on logic, not emotion. Government and business use methods of analysis based on "logos" more than on personalities (ethos) or emotions (pathos). It is worth noting that while we often tell someone to "be logical" (assuming he will then come to the right conclusion, possibly the one we're supporting) we rarely tell anyone to "be emotional." Of course, there are times and places for spiritual, emotional, or intuitive decision making. It is not our purpose to create "logic monsters" out of our readers. Critical thinking is something that has appropriate venues. In gatherings of family, services at church, meetings with friends, and impulses of socially-sanctioned spontaneity, we suggest developing a knack for knowing when to be merely logical and when to be wholly human.

The Basic Unit of Rhetorical Argument: The Enthymeme

Aristotle believed that when people argued over probabilities rather than certainties they used what he called enthymemes (pronounced in English *EN-tha-memes*). (At www.m-w.com you can listen to the pronunciation of this word and most others.) There is nothing mystical about enthymemes just because they're "Greek." You have been using them all your life to make arguments. Now you have a word for what you've done.

The word comes from the Greek words *enthymus,* which means "in the mind," and was intended to show that an informal argument has three parts: 1) a claim (or thesis or conclusion), 2) a reason (or premise) and 3) a mental connection between the two supplied by the listener. Aristotle called this supplied step **a suppressed premise.** Modern writers call it a **warrant.** In contrast, in dialectic logic all steps were explicit and technically formed to produce certainly valid conclusions. The enthymeme may be diagrammed as shown in Figure 1.1. The diagonal line between claim and reason is the *because* connection, or **enthymematic connection.** The suppressed premise, or warrant, is in a box to indicate it is a thought linking the Claim to the Reason. It may seem

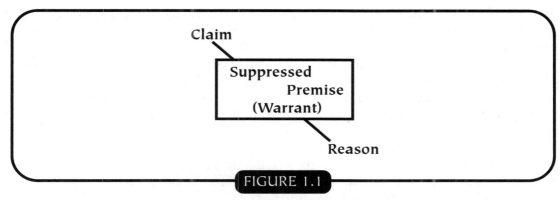

FIGURE 1.1

The Enthymematic Model of Argument

that we're now refining our definition of argument by adding the concept of a supplied premise or warrant. However, this is not the case. Remember that our original definition of an argument was "a claim supported by a reason or reasons." Whenever a claim is made and a reason is given, the suppressed premise, linking the claim to the reason, automatically exists also. You cannot have a claim and a reason without also having the supplied premise emerge. This concept will be discussed much more in depth in Chapter 9, when we discuss Stephen Toulmin's three primary parts of an argument.

Applying the Enthymematic Model

All rhetorical models of argument follow from this analysis, and these elements remain the starting point for the analysis of rhetorical logic. Figure 1.2 is a diagram of our Two Little Kids in enthymematic (en-tha-me-MA-tic) form.

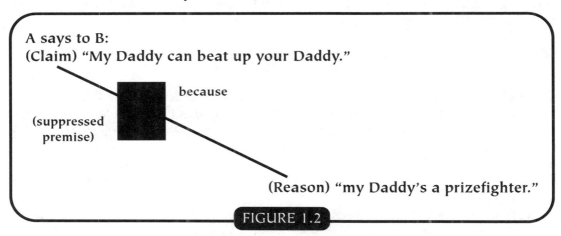

FIGURE 1.2

The Enthymematic Model Applied

The black box indicates that a belief is filled in to connect the reason to the claim. How might that belief be expressed? One could express it as "prizefighters can beat up non-prizefighters." It could also be expressed dozens of other ways, or may be a "thought" we find difficult to put into words. However the listener thinks it or phrases it, it is "enthymus" in the mind of the listener, and an argument exists.

If the listener cannot supply a belief, there is no enthymematic connection and the argument is not accepted. Suppose "A" said, "My daddy can beat up your Daddy because my Daddy has black hair." "B" might well answer, "So what if your daddy's has black hair. That doesn't mean anything." If there is no enthymus connection, that is to say there is no enthymeme, then the argument is NOT accepted. The creation of enthymemes is subjective. The conscious examination of whether or not a reasonable person should find a connection is the heart of critical thinking.

THE RELATIONSHIP OF DEBATE TO ARGUMENTATION

We earlier defined debate as the process of logically evaluating a claim by entertaining arguments for and against the claim, and then adopting or not adopting the claim as a reasonable resolution of a dispute. This is a technique of "critical thinking." It tries to reduce the complexity of decision making to a series of binary choices, to adopt or not adopt a claim. Debate is based on the belief that out of a clash of opposites the right decision is most likely to emerge. Early experts in epistemology called this **the dialectic process:** a process that arrives at relative truth through the test of debate. Correctly done, the dialectic process can help to eliminate assumptions and myths to hone an argument into a more reasonable one. You can try this yourself by arguing a position to its extremes, to see what the end product (conclusion) looks like. This process is used in many forums. For example, many group communication texts suggest that groups of people, like school boards, should play devil's advocate to make sure they come up with the best solutions possible.

The Protagorean Model of Debate

Debate is based on a principle of argument first devised by the Greek sophist Protagoras of Abdera in the fifth century BCE. Protagoras is often referred to as the "father of debate." The term "sophist" simply meant a "wise person" (from the Greek *sophia*, which means wisdom). By his time it had come to mean a teacher, particularly one of rhetoric. As today, the term has prejudicial implications and was often taken to mean "one who pretends to have knowledge he does not have" (the origin of our modern word "sophomore"). Protagoras was, however, one of the most respected men in the Greek world.

Protagoras believed that it was not possible to know "truth" with certainty. This was a significant break from previous rhetorical practice. Before Protagoras, it was believed that a speaker must have "The One Truth" on his side to win a debate of any kind. To Protagoras, a debate could be won by either side. For example, if "A" and "B" advocated different positions, one could not tell directly which was "more right" and which was "less right" unless one weighed the positions against each other. Out of this clash, either the "right" would prevail, or a new position would be found, a synthesis of the opposites presented by "A" and "B" which could be tested in further debates. Thus rose the idea of "A" and "B" debating their opposing positions for the benefit of a judge, "J," who would base his or her judgment on an evaluation of the logical strengths of the opposing positions. This Protagorean Model of Argument might be diagrammed as shown in Figure 1.3. In the original model, "A" and "B" were simply opposites. In modern debate, "A" would be the advocate of a claim or resolution and be the affirmative, while "B" would oppose the claim and be the negative. The negative debater has no duty to present a proposition of his or her own, but only to oppose the affirmative's position.

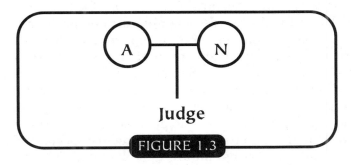

FIGURE 1.3

The Protagorean Model of Argument

Protagorean Model in Today's World

This Model of Argument is the basis of our judicial system. Our courts are a forum for carefully structured debates. It is not surprising that many of the examples used in this book will be drawn from the courts.

The same model can, however, apply to matters we are trying to decide within ourselves. Anyone who has ever consciously tried to weigh the pros and cons of an action has engaged in a debate. Your "affirmative" self ("A") has listed the "pros," while another part of your mind ("N") listed the "cons." If you phrased a proposition, and then thought of reasons to adopt it or not adopt it, your "Affirmative" self debated your "negative" self for the benefit of your final judgment. It is simply a matter of alternative roll-playing.

Your authors believe what goes on in our heads can be, or should be, debates. Most texts require different persons to advocate different positions before a neutral judge. We use the form of public debate as a model for what anyone might also do internally as a method of critical thinking. The purpose of this book prescribes our belief that in learning to debate one learns a method of critical thinking which can be applied by analogy to individual decision making and problem solving. Of course one also learns how to participate in formal debates, and that's fun.

Affirmative and Negative Defined

In any debate, there will be an explicit or implied resolution. The **resolution** is the focus of the debate. (The concept of a resolution is discussed much more in Chapter 3.) An example of a resolution might be "Resolved: That capital punishment is immoral." The party that supports the resolution is known as the **affirmative.** The party that opposes the resolution is known as the **negative.**

For now, we want you to understand that the words *affirmative* and *negative* are general terms. Different forums of debate may employ these terms or may use different terms that have the same meaning. For example, the two most dominant forms of intercollegiate debate today are **cross-examination** and **parliamentary** debate. The cross-examination organizations use the general terms affirmative and negative. However, in parliamentary debate, **government** and **opposition** are terms used instead of affirmative and negative respectively. Similarly, in criminal law the terms **prosecution** and **defense** are used while in civil law the terms **plaintiff** and **defense** are employed. In public debates the terms most often utilized are **pro** and **con.** To simplify our discussions, we will use the general terms affirmative and negative when referring to all debates, unless we are referring to a specialized forum of debate in which case we will use the terms employed by that field. Please refer to Figure 1.4 for a clear listing of the different terms used to represent affirmative and negative by different debate forums.

Type of Debate	Affirmative	Negative
Cross Examination (NDT & CEDA Policy)	Affirmative	Negative
Parliamentary	Government	Opposition
Criminal Law	Prosecution	Defense
Civil Law	Plaintiff	Defense
Public Debates	Pro	Con

FIGURE 1.4

Affirmative and Negative Descriptors

THE WORLD OF DEBATE

Whenever two people sit down at a chess board, and "white" moves, the world of chess exists. In parallel, whenever an advocate of a claim gets together with the opponent of a claim to dispute before a judge, the world of debate exists. Both of these activities draw much of their development from organized contests. The world of debate can be divided in into two halves: academic and public debate.

Academic vs. Public Debate

Public debates are debates that take place in the "real world." These may be legal debates (criminal, civil, appellate, etc.), political debates (Presidential, congressional, mayoral, city council), debates over public policy (affirmative action, social security, welfare, possible military action), scientific debates (What caused dinosaur extinction or how did life originate on earth?), theological (Is there a God or why does evil exist?), or even interpersonal debates one may have with a relative or friend (Should we have children or what movie should we see tonight?). In other words, these are debates that take place in our society on issues that will potentially affect us. In contrast, academic debates take place in high school, college, and university argumentation classes, at speech and debate tournaments, or in law schools. The outcome of these debates plays no direct role in shaping society. Thus, the purposes of academic and public debates are very different.

The purpose of **academic debate** is to teach students how to argue and debate well. Specific skills such as critical thinking, refutation, asking and answering questions, delivery, research and even professionalism are taught. The truth of the resolution is really unimportant. A resolution is announced and students may be arbitrarily assigned to defend one side regardless of how they personally feel about the topic (sometimes students may be required to debate both sides). The resolution simply exists to provide students something to debate about so that valuable skills can be developed. That is not to say that socially significant resolutions are not debated; they certainly are. And this is not to suggest that students who debate these resolutions do not want to discover the "truth" about them; many do. This just means that any topic could be chosen for an academic debate. It is an artificial selection. As long as the resolution provides fairly even argumentative ground to both teams, it is probably acceptable.

When intercollegiate academic debates are evaluated, the vast majority of critics are not deciding if they really support or don't support the resolution. They simply vote for the team which they believe did the better job of debating. The critics may adamantly oppose a resolution, but still vote for it if they believe that the affirmative did a better job of debating than the negative. The opposite is also true. Critics try not to let their personal bias for or against a resolution determine how they will decide the debate. Their aim is to be as objective as possible.

Public debate does not share these goals. The purpose of public debate is to decide the "truth" of a resolution and not to develop argumentative skills. In a court of law for example, members of a jury might think that the prosecution did a great job of presenting its case. They might believe that the attorney representing the prosecution is a superior attorney to the defense attorney in every way. They might believe that the prosecution was smoother, more dynamic, and more articulate; it asked better questions, engaged in more effective refutation, and gave a superior closing statement. They also might think that the defense attorney bordered on incompetence. However, given all of that, members of the jury still would be expected to vote for the defense if they did not believe that the evidence, regardless of how well it was presented or how horribly refuted, was insufficient to lead to a conviction.

Critics of public debates also do not always set aside their personal biases when deciding whether to vote for or against a given resolution. In other words, in public debate, you do not vote simply for the side that debated better. For example, heading into the first Presidential debate between then President Ronald Reagan and Walter Mondale in 1984, polls showed that Ronald Reagan was winning in a landslide. Following their first debate, the polls showed that the vast majority of people, including Republicans, believed that Mondale out-debated Reagan. However, polls also showed that no change took place in who likely voters said they were going to vote for. The fact that Mondale won the debate was irrelevant to whether people would actually vote for him. In other words, in public debate, the critics vote for or against a resolution based on how they really feel towards it. They don't vote based on who debated better.

The goal of this book, as its title suggests, is to help students develop critical thinking skills by participating in academic debates. As such, this book is written from an academic point of view. We are fairly confident that during your classroom debates, your instructor will evaluate your debates by how well you utilize the argumentation techniques available to you in order to advance the best case that you can. It is also our firm belief that the skills learned via participation in academic debate, whether in an argumentation & debate class and/or on a college debate team, will help students immensely when they find themselves involved in public debates.

The Purpose of This Book

Unlike chess, which has firmly established rules, academic debate has unwritten norms, which are subject to change and challenges. These loosely-guarded conventions are not strictly enforced. Many debate scholars adamantly disagree on what is and is not acceptable strategy. One of the frustrating and, at the same time, exciting occurrences is that participants may debate the logic behind the activity's current conventions. If the student believes that a traditional convention should be ousted in favor of a new perspective, the student just needs to make the necessary arguments.

While most conventions can be contested, we suggest that there are probably only three rules that are a constant in academic debate whether conducted in a classroom or a tournament: 1) the resolution, as officially stated, must be the resolution debated, 2) the official time limits per speech must be adhered to, and 3) the official speaking orders must be followed. Beyond that, just about everything else is, well, debatable. The openness of academic debate to new ideas and perspectives, while exciting, especially to the advanced debater, can be somewhat confusing to the new student. Just as soon as new students learn a convention of debate, they then learn that that norm can be challenged.

Unfortunately, while debate theory has developed rapidly, few people have consolidated this information into a digestible form for the beginning debate student. In addition, there are many controversies in the literature. This book does not attempt to resolve those controversies, but rather to identify them and offer practical advice to students. The purpose of this book, then, is to serve as a guide for the beginning debater. This book represents an attempt to collate the key debate theories developed in the past twenty years and to allow readers to make their own decisions regarding the viability of a theory or practice. Coming at the activity from a practical standpoint, hopefully the advice contained in this book can be of service to students who are just being introduced to the world of debate and who desire answers to questions. We also hope that this book will spawn many discussions between students and instructors about the nature of academic debate theory and its applicability and relevance (or lack thereof) to academic and public debate situations. The goal of this book is not to train students to be tournament debaters (although this book should be extremely helpful to students who wish to make that journey), but rather this book aims at helping students become more proficient critical thinkers which should be beneficial to them regardless of the type of argumentative situations in which they may become involved.

Additionally, this book takes the position that both parliamentary and cross-examination debate, the styles most utilized in contemporary academic debate, are valuable activities. (Chapter 4 explains these two debate formats in detail.) Of course, academic debate can be conducted in many other formats as well. The format is really quite arbitrary. Your instructor may choose to have you do a cross-examination debate and/or a parliamentary debate or your instructor may invent his or her own format. The possibilities of debate formats are endless. Regardless of the approach taken by your college, your argumentation teacher or your debate coach, this book should be helpful for you.

Benefits of Academic Debate

In the academic world, few activities compare to debate in terms of academic and personal benefits. A serious debate student acquires skills in critical thinking, research, speaking, organization, writing, cross-examination, critical listening, and leadership. The student also learns the theory and practice of argumentation and debate, a body of knowledge that has application in nearly every field of inquiry and employment.

In fact, debate as a scholastic activity has been heralded as effective training for aspirants in all fields. The prospective business person learns how to advocate an idea, just as he or she will do at corporate board meetings. The aspiring teacher learns to prepare notes and deliver well-documented speeches on the spur of the moment, a skill that will pay for itself over and over again when preparing future lectures for the classroom. The hopeful lawyer learns to prepare briefs, practice cross-examination, and (depending on the debate topic) perhaps even do some legal research. The aspiring scientist, architect, or computer programmer learns communication skills that will give them an edge over their colleagues in the job interview process. In addition, those skills will help bridge the gap between the technological and the lay world. The list of potential benefits is endless. A student with communication skills has a definite edge over his or her colleague who lacks those skills. Helen Wise, the former president of the National Education Association, observes,

> No college freshman can project twenty five years to decide what he needs to learn—subject matter is easily forgotten and in today's world, the knowledge explosion makes constant learning an inevitability. But all adults today need to be able to communicate with clarity, to articulate ideas, to reason, to separate key facts from the barrage of ideas we all are exposed to every day. No single activity can prepare one better than debating—the ability to think on one's feet, to form conclusions rapidly, to answer questions logically and with clarity, to summarize ideas are all processes which forensic (speech and debate) activities develop and develop well (Freeley, 1986, p.13).

As Dr. Wise tells us, debate is the best preparation for anyone's future, no matter what it will be. Therefore, any student interested in the best preparation for his or her future ought to think seriously about participating in debate.

Interscholastic Forensics

Most organized academic debate is part of an interscholastic and intercollegiate competition called **forensics.** High schools and colleges field **forensics teams.** These teams usually sport some type of debate, along with other kinds of speech competitions.

The word "forensic" means "in the public forum." The term is of Latin origin and is connected with the Roman Forum. Unfortunately, the etymology of the word is confounded by the fact that many things happened in the forum, and thus we have inherited a term with multiple applications. The Roman Senate met in the Roman Forum, and thus "forensic" is related to "political discussion." The Roman Law Courts were held in the Roman Forum, and thus forensics still carries a "legal" nuance. (The only place most readers will have heard the word before is in the myriad of detective novels, films, TV programs, and magazines, in which the investigators often use forensic medicine to discover important clues about a victim's demise.) At modern speech tournaments political questions form the core of discussed issues; thus, today we have "forensics tournaments" and "forensics teams," which include events from debates on political issues to poetry readings of famous authors' works. Yet, the all-inclusive term, forensics, is still used to describe all of interscholastic and intercollegiate speech and debate competition. Those readers who are on their school's forensics team know the frustration of trying to tell their friends what they do.

You may not be an International Grand Master at chess, but you can study their games to learn new techniques. You may never debate in intercollegiate debate tournaments, but the techniques practiced there have lessons to teach. Your authors all have extensive intercollegiate forensics experience, and thus some personal background is appropriate here.

Your Authors' Academic Debate Experiences

Dr. Perella debated as an undergraduate for the University of California in the early 1960s, enjoyed the activity, and had a modest competitive career. Professors Nelson and Corcoran competed during the 1980's, and also enjoyed some relative success. To each of us, intercollegiate debate, at times, seemed isolated from the rest of life. There were many artificial constraints. The resolutions were chosen by anonymous selection committees. The time format was rigid. Debaters, rushing to get in as much argumentation as possible, spoke very fast. There was so much emphasis placed on research and evidence that one had to marry the library and sound like a bibliography to win. While all of this may seem sterile, difficult, and boring, for anyone who is in college for the purpose of learning about your world, then competitive debate is for you. And there's plenty of white-knuckled excitement in a final round of any tournament, during which quick witted comments or precisely calibrated arguments can make the difference between first and second place.

As each of your authors participated in year after year of competitive debate, we noticed rather quickly that all of our other academic work became exponentially easier. Research for a term paper is a snap once you've learned how to research for a debate. Writing essay examinations is stunningly like writing a debate case. The ability to think dispassionately is often a saving grace in a world filled with passions.

Any reader now on a college or high school debate team has heard all of these descriptions. They're still true. The miracle is that debate is so worthwhile an activity that it rises above the excesses so often associated with it.

When Dr. Perella reached law school he discovered that he could find the argumentative structure in a case in half the time it took even the brightest students who hadn't debated. None of your authors could even imagine presenting lectures day after day in college classrooms, as a part of the duties as college professors, without having had an extensive intercollegiate debating career.

The core of debate was, and is, that one tries to think not just individual thoughts, but to approach a problem methodically, systematically. Debate decisions are not random but the result of an integrated method which extends from the making of a claim, to the formation of a resolution, to the construction of a case for that resolution, to supporting the case with evidence and analysis, to criticizing the case, weighing the issues raised, and arriving at a reasoned decision.

Forensics Organizations

In the United States, academic debate is a part of a larger activity called forensics. As we've discussed, the term **forensics** means, in this context, competitive public speaking. Intercollegiate forensics tournaments are held in each region of the country nearly every weekend from late September to early May. The major organizations relevant to this book are the following:

National Debate Tournament (NDT). Founded in 1920. Schools in this organization debate policy resolutions (which propose actions). The NDT has developed the debate world's theory on debating resolutions of policy. The NDT national championships are held in March or April.

Cross-Examination Debate Association (CEDA). Founded in 1971 as a response to perceived problems with the NDT, CEDA started out supporting a much more audience-friendly format for debate. However, today, there are virtually no stylistic differences between CEDA and the NDT. For much of its history, CEDA sponsored two resolutions of value per year, one in the fall and one in the spring semesters. However, beginning in 1997–1998, CEDA and NDT began sharing the same annual policy resolution. Both CEDA and NDT continue to have separate national championships, but the great philosophical split that caused CEDA to form in 1971 seems to have been eliminated.

Phi Rho Pi, Pi Kappa Delta, and **Delta Sigma Rho-Tau Kappa Alpha** are the three "forensics fraternities." Each holds national championships. Phi Rho Pi is open to two-year schools only.

National Forensics League (NFL) is the high school organization that conducts tournaments and has a national championship in June.

National Parliamentary Debate Association (NPDA). The NPDA was formed in the late 1980's by a group of college forensics coaches in Colorado. Parliamentary debate is the predominant form of intercollegiate debate found in the world. The Colorado coaches were interested in participating in the World Debate Championships, so they formed the league to be able to practice the parliamentary format used worldwide. NPDA utilizes a different topic for each 1.5 hour debate round, and usually there are between 8 and 12 rounds in any given weekend tournament. Intercollegiate debaters participating in this form of debate should thus expect to use up to 12 different debate topics in a single tournament. When NPDA first began, students were prohibited from consulting any person or resource from the moment a resolution was announced until the start of a debate (usually 15 minutes). Today, in many cases, those restrictions are relaxed, allowing for consultations with coaches and referencing of prepared materials during the 15 minutes of preparation.

Junior Statesmen of America (JSA) is a high school organization dedicated to leadership and political training. J.S A. is not a part of forensics but is instead a student-run political organization. They hold "conventions" rather than tournaments, but many individual JSA members also participate in their school's NFL program.

National Educational Debate Association (NEDA). Started in the early 1990s as a response to CEDA becoming a lot like NDT. NEDA has enjoyed modest success by the time of this writing. Its purpose is to advocate a slower rate of delivery and, what its founders believe to be, a more educational format.

American Debate Association (ADA). The ADA has been attempting to win over colleges to the policy debating world. Like many third parties and social movements in politics, the ADA may be a victim of its own success. Having convinced many educators of the advantages of policy debate, CEDA's informal commitment to value debate, at the exclusion of policy debate, has waned in recent years; thus, perhaps leading to less of a need for the ADA.

Taken together, these organizations, and the activities they sponsor, are the world of organized formal debate activity from which this book draws much of its inspiration. But these organized activities are not the "real world," they are models of it. Similarly, campus argumentation classes (such as the one we assume you're taking) try to serve as laboratories to develop skills you'll use elsewhere.

SUMMARY

This chapter introduced the basic components necessary to begin a study of the world of argumentation. Key terms including claim, assertion contradiction, argument, argumentation, and debate were defined. Assertion was defined as a claim statement without a reason, contradiction was defined as asserting a contrary claim statement, argument was defined as claims supported by a reason or reasons, argumentation as the general theory and practice of reasoning, and debate was defined as entertaining arguments for and against a claim, and then adopting or not adopting the claim as a reasonable resolution of a dispute.

The three Aristotelian proofs of ethos, pathos, and logos were discussed. The enthymematic Model of Argumentation was introduced. The model explains the relationship between the three elements which make up an argument. They include a claim, a reason, and a mental connection between the claim and the reason. Next, the Protagorean Model of Debate was discussed. The Protagorean Model of Debate consists of: the affirmative, the negative, and the judge. Finally, some differences between academic and public debate were presented, the purpose of this book explained, your authors' debate experience summarized and many forensics organizations listed. We now hope that you have a good grounding to begin a more in-depth study of argumentation and debate.

CHAPTER 2

ANALYZING
DEBATABLE CLAIMS

There are many issues to have debates about. Some are of a factual nature, some of a value nature, some of a policy nature. All debates have one thing in common: they all center on a proposition. Different propositions have different requirements of which the advocates and opponents must be aware. The purpose of this chapter is to give an overview of the basic requirements attached to each type of proposition. After completing this chapter the reader should have a basic understanding of how to debate propositions of fact, value and policy. Subsequent chapters will explore the requirements of these three different propositions in greater detail.

THE CLAIM TREE

In order to compete in any of the forums of debate, one must first have a debatable claim. The diagram in Figure 2.1 is called "The Claim Tree." It is a series of binary decision gates from the point at which a claim is made to the point at which it may be debated (a debatable claim). A claim is simply a declaration asserted for acceptance. "My dad can beat up your dad," "The Beatles were the greatest rock-n-roll band of all time," and "The United States should repeal NAFTA" are all examples of claims.

In order for a claim to be an "arguable" claim, two factors are necessary. The first requirement is clarity. Second, the claim must be within the jurisdiction of rational demonstration. Jurisdiction also implies that the parties involved are open to using rational thought when analyzing the merits of the argument.

The Principle of Clarity

Clarity simply implies that there must be agreement among the parties as to what the resolution means. Debate is a linguistic activity. While chess uses pieces (queens, rooks, etc.) to play the game, debate uses words. Unfortunately, any word can have more than one meaning. What you may think a word means may not be what someone else (like your opponent) thinks it means. Sometimes there is a genuine disagreement over the meaning of a word. Many times, however, the other side will find it strategically beneficial, for the purposes of the debate, to define a term differently.

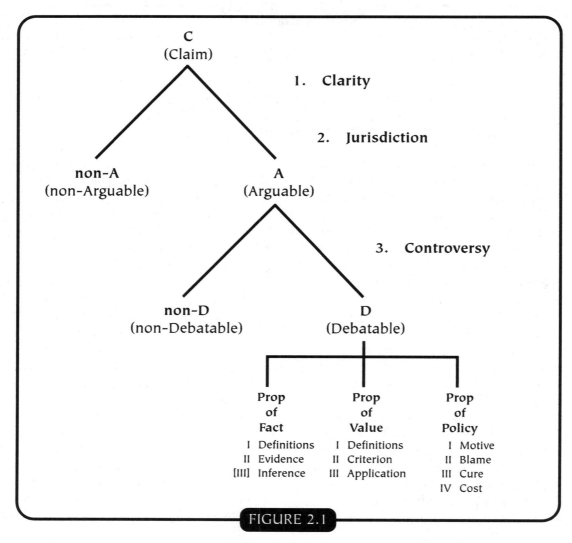

FIGURE 2.1

The Claim Tree

For example, take the resolution "Resolved: that television is to be more condemned than approved." What does the word "television" refer to? Does it refer to only the television set? Does it include the programming? If so, what programming does it include? Does it include only shows that were made by television companies for specifically airing on television? Does it include sports events that are shown? Does it include movies that were originally shown in theaters? Does it include cable and satellite programs? Does it include videos that you may rent and watch on your DVD player? Does it include video games that are designed to be played on the television? To some the term "television" may include all of the above. and to others it may include perhaps just a few (or maybe just one) of the above. Obviously, before the merits of television can be evaluated, we must first know what it is we are to evaluate. As such, the first requirement of any advocate is to define the terms of the resolution if any ambiguity exists. Arguments over definitions are known as procedural issues. **Procedural** issues are regarded as *a priori* issues, that is, they must be decided upon before the substantive arguments, which are the arguments for or against the resolution, can be entertained.

Author Nelson has a saying that "During a debate, debaters debate about what they are going to debate about so they can then debate about what they want to debate about." Definitions are important because they define what are (and what are not) topical issues. **Topical** issues are issues which are germane to the resolution under dispute. Obviously the affirmative and the negative can only advance substantive arguments that are related to the resolution under discussion. Non-topical arguments, regardless of their importance, would be of no value in a debate. Think of the resolution as a box. The resolution's terms make up the box. The broader the definitions become, the larger the box, and hence the greater the amount of relevant issues that may be introduced into the debate. Narrower definitions create a smaller box, subsequently limiting the relevant areas that can be introduced.

The first thing the affirmative should always do is to define any terms that need clarification. One of the conventions of debate is that the side which defines a term first claims presumption on that term. This means, all else being equal, the definitions that were advanced first will be used unless good reasons are given for using other definitions. Since affirmative debaters always give the opening speech they have the first opportunity to define terms. If affirmative debaters fail to define terms in their opening speeches, then the negative team should seize the opportunity to define terms in its opening speech.

After the affirmative team defines terms in its opening speech, the first thing the negative should always do is to evaluate whether or not the affirmative's substantive arguments fall inside the box created by the definitions. For example, suppose the affirmative while debating the above television resolution defines "television" as just the "television set" and then argues that television programming is violent and harmful to children. In this case the negative should be prepared to point out why the affirmative's substantive arguments (violent programming) fall outside the box created by its own definition of television and hence is not **topical**. ("Not topical" means that the arguments do not support the debate "topic" or resolution.) Of course most affirmatives will not make this mistake, but it does happen. However, it is still possible for a negative to win a **topicality** argument even if the affirmative's substantive arguments do fall within their own definitional box. The negative need only justify narrower counter-definitions which would effectively place the affirmative's arguments outside of the smaller newly created box. For example, assume the affirmative defines "television" to include all programming and shows how this programming is violent and harmful to children. The affirmative would so far be topical since their substantive arguments fall within their definitional box. However, if the negative successfully counter-defines television as only the "television set" then the affirmative's substantive arguments are no longer topical. This is known as "defining the affirmative out of the round."

There are times, however, when a negative will want a broader definition than that offered by the affirmative. For example, assume the negative wants to argue that television can be highly educational. However, the affirmative has defined television as just the "television set" (and perhaps made arguments on how the radiation hurts the eyes). Under the affirmative's definition, a negative argument about the benefits of television programming is not topical and would be dismissed by the affirmative. The negative debaters will need to counter-define with a broader definition that includes programming to allow them to introduce this argument.

In a debate there are four conventions regarding disputes over definitions. First, the affirmative debaters are allowed to define terms in their opening speech, and these definitions become the "presumed" definitions for the debate. Second, the negative may counter-define terms but must give reasons why the alternative definitions are superior to the affirmative's original definitions. Third, the negative team must show how its definitions have a substantial impact on the debate. A counter-definition that says essentially the same thing as the affirmative's definition and does not change the size of the definitional box is of little use to the negative. Fourth, if the affirmative debaters fail to define any terms in their opening speech, then the negative team may usurp that right for its opening argument. If this occurs then the negative's definitions are given presumption, and the process for challenging those definitions reverses. It thus behooves the affirmative team to define all relevant terms in its opening speech. Definitions are often crucial to deciding who wins a debate. It is often said, and with great truth, that the party who controls the definitions controls the debate.

The Monica Lewinsky-Bill Clinton controversy illustrates how important definitions are to an argument. In the Paula Jones case, President Clinton was asked in his deposition if he ever had an affair with Monica Lewinsky. His response was "I have never had sexual relations with Monica Lewinsky. I've never had an affair with her." However, according to the August 15, 1998, *San Francisco Chronicle*, Monica Lewinsky later testified before a Grand Jury that she "had performed sex orally and manually on the President on several occasions." Then, on August 17, President Clinton addressed the American people (after testifying before the Grand Jury earlier that day), and admitted to having had inappropriate relations with Monica Lewinsky but said his actions did not constitute "sexual relations." So, did President Clinton tell the truth or did he lie in his deposition? To answer that question we must know what is meant by the term "sexual relations." In the Paula Jones case, that definition was debated by the attorneys representing Paula Jones and those representing President Clinton. The definition of "sexual relations" that was submitted to US District Judge Susan Webber Wright by Jones' attorneys was a three part definition.

"For the purposes of this deposition, a person engages in 'sexual relations' when the person knowingly engages in or causes:

(I)   contact with the genitalia, anus, groin, breast, inner thigh or buttocks of any person with an intent to arouse or gratify the sexual desire of any person;

(II)   contact between any part of the person's body or an object and the genitals or anus of another person; or

(III)   contact between the genitals or anus of the person and any part of another person's body. 'Contact' means intentional touching either directly or through clothing."

Clinton's attorneys argued that the definition was too broad and could include all kinds of benign contact, including shaking hands. After some back and forth debating, Judge Wright agreed that the definition was too broad and excluded sections II and III from the definition leaving only section I as the acting definition. It has been maintained that even if the President did engage in oral or manual sex with Monica Lewinsky that such actions, strictly speaking, would not meet the narrow definition of 'sexual relations' as defined by Judge Wright. Of course the more important question is "what is the definition the President had in his own mind when he used the term sexual relations?" That is something that can probably never be substantiated.

Perhaps the most famous definitional argument raised by President Clinton concerned the meaning of the word "is." Figure 2.2 recounts that testimony (for purposes of space and relevance the Grand Jury Testimony has been edited).

These examples should illustrate how important definitions are to an argument. It also demonstrates why definitional arguments must be adjudicated prior to evaluating the substantive arguments. It is only after we know what is meant by "sexual relations" or "is" that we can determine if President Clinton lied on any of these issues.

AUGUST 17, 1998

QUESTION: Mr. President, I want to go into a new subject area, briefly go over something you were talking about with Mr. Bittman.

The statement of your attorney, Mr. Bennett, at the Paula Jones deposition—counsel is fully aware—it's page 54, line 5. Counsel is fully aware that Ms. Lewinsky is filing, has an affidavit, which they were in possession of, saying that there was absolutely no sex of any kind in any manner, shape or form with President Clinton. That statement was made by your attorney in front of Judge Susan Webber Wright.

CLINTON: That's correct.

(continued)

FIGURE 2.2

President William J. Clinton's Testimony (edited) before the Grand Jury

QUESTION: Your—that statement is a completely false statement. Whether or not Mr. Bennett knew of your relationship with Ms. Lewinsky, the statement that there was no sex of any kind in any manner, shape or form with President Clinton was an utterly false statement. Is that correct?

CLINTON: It depends upon what the meaning of the word is means. If is means is, and never has been, that's one thing. If it means, there is none, that was a completely true statement.

QUESTION: You're the president of the United States, and your attorney counseled the United States District Court judge that there's no sex of any kind or any way, shape or form whatsoever. And you feel no obligation to do anything about that at that deposition, Mr. President?

CLINTON: I had told you, Mr. Wisenberg—I will tell you for a third time—I am not even sure that when Mr. Bennett made that statement that I was concentrating on the exact words he used. Now, someone had asked me on that day, are you having any kind of sexual relations with Ms. Lewinsky—that is ask me a question in the present tense—I would have said no. And it would have been completely true.

QUESTION: Was Mr. Bennett aware of this tense-based distinction you were making?

CLINTON: I don't—I don't . . . Kendall: I'm going to object to any questions about communications with private counsel.

QUESTION: I just want to make sure I understand you correctly. Do you mean today that because you were not engaging in sexual activity with Ms. Lewinsky during the deposition that the statement Mr. Bennett made (OFF-MIKE)?

CLINTON: No, sir. I mean that at the time of the deposition, we had been—that was well-beyond any point of improper contact between me and Ms. Lewinsky. So that anyone generally speaking in the present tense saying that was not an improper relationship would be telling the truth if that person said there was not, in the present tense—the present tense encompassing many months. That's what I meant by that—not that I was—I wasn't trying to give you a cute answer to that.

I was obviously not involved in anything improper during the deposition. I was trying to tell you that, generally speaking in the present tense, if someone said that, that would be true.

FIGURE 2.2

Continued

What follows next is a fairly detailed discussion about definitions. If you are reading "The Claim Tree" for the first time, you may wish to skip from this point to the section on "Jurisdiction." You might then return here after you have the total "Claim Tree" concept in mind.

Methods of Defining Terms

There are many ways to define terms for a debate. The most popular way is to use a **general dictionary definition.** A simple *Webster's* or *Oxford English* definition is fine for most purposes. After a brief introduction (usually a serious quotation or humorous anecdote) and a verbatim reading of the resolution, simply list the key terms of the resolution with their dictionary definitions. Key terms usually involve words that may bring controversy. Obviously, words, such as "a" and "the" usually do not need to be defined. More and more, however, debaters are finding the need to define the various forms of the verb "to be," such as "is." Often, the time-frame of the resolution becomes an issue. For instance, should one be able to argue past or future harms if the resolution says, "is detrimental?" That is an issue that needs to be resolved by the debaters during the debate, starting with the first affirmative. It is also important to realize that many critics will not allow debaters to define a term after their side's first speech. Therefore, if there is any question at all that a term's definition may become an issue, the term should be defined in the affirmative's opening speech. Besides ordinary dictionaries, there are **specialist dictionaries** for almost every profession and subject area: journalism, law, politics, language, philosophy, etc. Using those dictionaries can be a valuable asset. For instance, on the media-coverage-of-terrorism topic, journalism dictionaries helped immensely in finding just the right definition. A note of caution, though, is that you should avoid using a certain type of dictionary unless it truly applies to the topic at hand.

While dictionary definitions are the most common, there are other ways to define terms. If the resolution is a policy topic it may be appropriate to define the "policy" terms of the resolution **operationally.** In other words, if the "policy" terms of the resolution suggest the policy of "a unilateral freeze," then it is often enough to simply state how you use that phrase in your speech. For example, you may want to define a unilateral freeze as a temporary challenge to the rest of the world, or you may want to define it as a permanent freeze. Nowhere in a dictionary will you find either of those definitions. Therefore, an operational definition may be appropriate. You will still have to defend the definition as the most appropriate for the topic at hand, but only if the negative argues against it. An operational definition simply demonstrates how a policy "operates."

A third way to define a term is to say what it is not, to define by **negation.** For example, in the illegal-immigration topic, some debaters tried to distinguish illegal immigration from illegal immigrants who later were granted status as refugees. A definition may read as follows: "By illegal immigration we do not mean immigrants who come to America illegally but later are granted refugee status. We mean the bulk of illegal immigrants who come here, not fleeing political tyranny, but seeking American's jobs." Such a definition gives clear ground against which the debate can be judged or the negative can argue. A definition by negation can, of course, be supported by other evidence or definitions. Alone or in conjunction with other definitions, the definition by negation helps give a clear delineation when needed.

A fourth way to define terms is to quote **field-specific authorities** on the subject. Often scholars or commissions set up to study an issue will offer a definition in their books or reports. Often, those definitions are helpful in finding how the term is being used in the public debate on the issue. Furthermore, these "studied" definitions are often more accurate and more helpful than any you can find in a dictionary.

A fifth way is to use an **etymological** definition. This simply means defining the word based on its original root meaning. Suppose that someone said a movie they watched was pathetic. Most of us would take that to mean the movie was of poor quality, as that is the current usage in many parts of the United States. According to *The Merriam-Webster Unabridged Dictionary*, the etymology of the word, "pathetic" is as follows:

> Etymology: Middle French or Late Latin; Middle French *pathetique,* from Late Latin *patheticus,* from Greek *pathētikos* capable of feeling, sensitive, pathetic, from *pathtos* subject to suffering, liable to external influence (from *path-,* stem of *paschein* to experience, suffer) + *-ikos* -ic, -ical – more at pathos.

This definition seems to parallel the definition of pathos we offered in the previous chapter, as "being liable to external influence by something that makes us capable of feeling emotion." While it's likely that linguists would haggle over such a pieced-together definition from centuries of mutation, it still certainly seems to parallel Aristotle's use of *pathos* in *The Rhetoric.* Let's return to the example of a friend telling you that a certain movie was a "pathetic" movie. While most of us would assume the movie in question is just a bad movie, this etymological approach to the term proves that untrue. While the etymological definition of "pathetic" may be closer to the actual current-day definition found in dictionaries, it certainly does not seem to be the case for actual usage in everyday conversations. Therefore, convincing those watching a debate that the etymology is a preferred method of defining any term if it goes against current usage may be difficult, if not impossible. Yet, armed with the history of a term, you may be able to say that *West Side Story* was a very pathetic movie, in the sense that it evoked emotions in its viewers. Of course, *West Side Story* is also of extremely high quality, having won eleven academy awards, including best picture. Most of us would not describe *West Side Story* as "pathetic," because to do so would be ambiguous at best. It seems etymology is helpful, but rarely is it precise enough to serve as an unaided definition. It may tell us where a word has come from and how it was originally employed, but not necessarily how it is used in contemporary society. While that is true, there are of course exceptions to that rule. For example, if a debate concerns past events or classical literature, certainly resorting to such etymological investigations may be fruitful. And for some words on some topics, the etymological definitions may reflect more accurately the intended meaning of the resolution's framers.

A sixth way to define is by using an **analogy.** This is an especially effective technique when one wishes to introduce a new term that as of yet has no formal definition. Using an analogy allows you to define terms by comparing the unknown term at issue to a known term. Thus, if you wished to propose holding "National Olympic Games" you might define them by saying "they would be like the regular Olympic Games, but held each year and for the United States only." If the judge is familiar with the original term, definition by analogy works well since it makes it easy to envision the new term in a concrete way.

There are many other ways to define terms, but these should give you a good start. When trying to find the best definition to fit your case, think of how a reasonable person with no debate experience would probably define the term. Usually, that is your best hint as to which definition of many to use. It often may be your best defense, as well.

Standards for Evaluating Definitions

There has been a long standing controversy over the standard used to judge definitions. Practice, at present, seems to allow the affirmative to get away with any reasonable definition. However, there is a big push now to adopt the *best*-definition standard. In other words, the best definition in the debate is the one that should win. Therefore, affirmatives should be aware that some critics may expect them to have the best definitions in any round. That should be incentive for affirmatives to find the best and most appropriate definitions available.

There are many standards used to evaluate definitions. Some argue that field contextual definitions (from the experts) are best because they demonstrate more expertise; and some conversely argue that objective dictionary definitions are best because they don't fall victim to the bias of the field definitions and are more in line with how most of society uses the term. Some argue that the most precise definition is best because it gives focus; conversely, some argue that the broadest definition is best because the breadth of educational opportunities is expanded. In the end, it is up to the advocates to justify why their definition should be used if challenged.

The Need for Jurisdiction

The second requirement for a claim to be arguable is **jurisdiction.** Jurisdiction may be defined as the willingness of the parties to submit the claim to logic and presumably abide by the result. The term is borrowed from law. If a court does not have jurisdiction over a case, it can't decide it, regardless of its merits.

Jurisdiction involves two concepts. The first is that the claim itself must be one that is susceptible to analytical argument. If the claim falls outside the boundaries of rational demonstration it is unarguable. For example, consider the claim that "the entire universe and everything in it just popped into existence ten seconds ago." This claim falls outside the jurisdiction of rational demonstration. No rational argument could be made to either prove or disprove such a claim. Suppose you were to argue against this claim by arguing that you yourself are clearly biologically over ten seconds old and that you have memories dating back more than ten seconds. The proponent could just maintain that when the universe popped into existence ten seconds ago everything that exists was given the artificial appearance of seeming to be older than ten (now probably twenty) seconds, including your biological appearance and your memories. This may or may not be true. If the deception were impenetrable, there would be no way to test the truth of such a claim. Clearly, no analytical demonstration could possibly prove or disprove such a claim.

Assuming the claim is one that falls within the jurisdiction of rational consideration, the second element of jurisdiction must also be present before a claim can be considered arguable. The second part of jurisdiction applies to the parties involved in the presentation and/or evaluation of the argument. The parties must be willing to think rationally about the claim being analyzed. If the parties are unwilling to think critically, no one can make them do it. They must "grant" jurisdiction.

While this may seem elementary, it is a major reason why some claims can't be resolved by reason-giving. Many individuals hold beliefs that they simply can't or don't want to consider logically. One fundamental requirement of argumentation is that the parties involved have an open mind concerning the claim being considered. If one has a "closed mind" and refuses to even listen to the reasons (or will listen to them but has no intention of really considering them) then jurisdiction is not being granted and the augmentation process comes to a halt. For instance, perhaps the parties are too emotionally attached to one side of the issue. This is one major reason why the pro-lifer and pro-choicer cannot agree. Both sides are emotionally attached to their major premises concerning abortion. One side emotionally adheres to privacy and free choice; the other to the sanctity of human life. Due to their emotional attachment to disparate world views, neither side is likely to concede "jurisdiction" to a "logical" argument made by the other side. Another example is the parents who refuse to accept that their child did something horrendous regardless of the amount of evidence to substantiate the claim. They will not grant logical jurisdiction over the claim, and therefore arguments on it will not be listened to. Statements like "no matter what you say I will never change my mind" or "you are wasting your time, my mind is made up" are indications that jurisdiction is not being granted. The granting of jurisdiction does not mean that one will accept the claim. It simply means that one has an open mind to evaluating the evidence in a fair manner and then accepting or rejecting the claim as the evidence would suggest.

The Need for Controversy

If a claim is clear, and the parties involved are willing to grant jurisdiction over the claim, then we may say that we have an arguable claim. This does not mean that a debate ensues. One might write out an argument on an issue no one would contest. For example, in the early twenty-first century no one would seriously contest that the Earth is approximately spherical (yes, we know about the Flat Earth Society, but we'd contend they are unwilling to grant jurisdiction). One can develop an essay proving logically what we already believe. This may be a fine argumentative exercise, but it is not a debate.

Thus, a claim is non-debatable if no reasonable person could hold a contrary belief. As explained in Chapter 1, the Protagorean Model of Argument assumes that there will be a clash of opposites. Obviously, if there are no opposites, there is no debate. The process of debate demands that there be at least two sides. These sides might be created artificially by a devil's advocate or by a genuinely held contrary position, but if there is no opposition, there can be no debate.

THE CLASSIFICATION OF DEBATABLE CLAIMS

The next step after determining that a debatable claim exists is to determine which type of debatable claim it is. Debatable claims are often called propositions. As used here, the terms are synonymous, but this will be clarified later. You will notice in the Claim Tree diagram the words "fact," "value," and "policy." These three words identify the three types of debatable claims. Each of the three different types of propositions has different requirements of proof. You will notice there are Roman numerals below each of the three types of propositions. The Roman numerals represent the stock issues which create a *prima facie* case for each type of proposition. The stock issues for a proposition of fact are definitions, evidence, and inference. The stock issues for a proposition of value are definitive (which has two components: definitions and criterion) and designative. The stock issues for a policy proposition are motive, blame, cure, and cost. The tree types of propositions and their stock issues are explained in more detail later in this chapter as well as in Chapters 13, 14, and 15.

TYPES OF PROPOSITIONS

Propositions are traditionally classified into one of three categories: fact, value, and policy. Whether you are participating in academic debate (CEDA, NDT, or NPDA styles) or in public debate, knowledge of the different types of resolutions will make you a better debater. Whether a resolution fits into a particular classification is often debatable, meaning that arguments can be made in a debate round as to whether the topic should be considered a fact, value, or policy. This is especially true in parliamentary debate where metaphorical topics are often used. Therefore, it's not only important to understand the basic rules of classification, but it's also important to understand how to defend and argue your interpretation and classification.

Factual Topics

Factual resolutions deal with statements that determine whether something is true or false or whether something exists or does not exist. Factual questions also concern themselves with relationships between phenomena, such as in the determination of causes, effects, and dilemmas. Theoretically, a factual question can be answered in an objective manner. By theoretically objective we mean there is an empirical answer behind the controversy; although, sometimes obtaining objective verification is impossible because it lies outside humans' ability to directly observe phenomena, such as our inability to see dark matter or subatomic particles. Most of our universe is unobservable or imperceptible simply because of time-related restrictions or spatial constraints (we cannot go back in time to observe human macro-evolution occurring, nor can we travel across the galaxy to determine whether intelligent life exists elsewhere). Factual resolutions are perhaps the most difficult for beginning students to understand. Because the word "fact" is used, there is a tendency to think that factual resolutions deal with questions for which the answer is already known. This is not the case. If the answer were already known then the requirement for controversy would be lacking and there would be no need for a debate. For example, the resolution "Resolved: That the US possesses weapons of mass destruction (WMDs)" is a factual resolution. It is either true or false. However, this is a non-debatable resolution because we know the answer—The United States does in fact possess WMDs.

Compare that to what had been debated earlier this decade, when a serious controversy existed: "Resolved: That the Iraqi regime of Saddam Hussein possessed weapons of mass destruction." This is also a factual statement. Iraq at that time either had such weapons or they did not—an empirical answer existed; this question was controversial because a certain answer was beyond the scope of United Nations weapons inspectors and United States intelligence at that time. The United States decided to unilaterally disarm Iraq of its alleged stockpile of WMDs, without waiting for UN inspectors to conclude their work and without ensuring that confirming intelligence was accurate. At the writing of this book, the world's experts are pretty much convinced that a decade of severe economic embargos imposed on Iraq prior to Operation Iraqi Freedom disabled Saddam's WMD program. In 2003, when the US attacked Iraq, current wisdom is that Iraq had no stockpile of WMDs and no active WMD program, except perhaps at the very thinnest theoretical levels of planning. While today the controversy is all but settled, in 2003, the jury was still out, and thus the resolution debated by the world met the standard for controversy. From the beginning of the discussion of the Iraqi threat immediately following 9/11 until the final concession by the Bush administration, the topic of Iraqi WMDs was a controversial and debatable resolution.

While the Iraqi WMD topic would have been a present-day controversy during that crisis, actual resolutions may deal with past, present, or future controversies. Here are some examples of each type of factual resolution:

Past:

- Lee Harvey Oswald did not act alone when he assassinated John F. Kennedy.
- In the 2000 Presidential Election, Democrat Al Gore had enough popular votes to have been awarded Florida's electoral votes and thus the US Presidency.
- Life on earth originated, at least partially, through means of intelligent design.

Present:

- There is enough oil in the Alaskan National Wilderness Refuge to meet US energy demands for the next 50 years.
- Capital punishment deters murders.
- Acupuncture cures disease.

Future:

- Hillary Rodham Clinton will be the first female US President.
- Lowering interest rates will lead to more consumer spending.
- The Boston Red Sox will win this year's World Series.

Factual resolutions are intriguing for two almost paradoxical reasons. First, some factual resolutions may never be empirically proven and thus may be debated for all eternity. We may never know with certainty if Lee Harvey Oswald acted alone when he assassinated President Kennedy; thus, debates over this issue may always exist. The opposite is also true. Factual resolutions have the possibility, and in many cases, the certainty, of being empirically verified and thus becoming non-debatable issues, such as the Iraqi WMD question discussed above. Additionally, propositions over who will win next year's World Series or who will win the next US Presidential election will almost certainly be answered. Here is another very good example of this actually occurring: Following the bombing of Saddam Hussein's bunker at the beginning of the most recent US-Iraqi conflict, there were reports that Saddam had been killed. Other reports claimed he was still alive. For months, the proposition "Saddam Hussein is dead" was a hotly debated topic. However, once Saddam was captured, this instantly became a non-debatable issue.

Value Topics

While factual resolutions deal with theoretically-objective issues of truth or falsehood, value resolutions deal with subjective evaluations of good or bad. Unlike factual statements where an empirical answer exists, value statements have to do with making judgments over statements where no empirical answer exists. If you think of a value topic as *a topic in which an evaluation is made* you'll probably avoid the problem of misinterpreting the ambiguous word *value*. Notice that the root word of *evaluation* is *value*. Think of the old adage that beauty is in the eye of the beholder. Consider the following:

- Abortion is immoral.
- *Gone with the Wind* is the greatest movie of all time.
- The US military operation to overthrow Saddam Hussein was unjustified.
- Jackie Robinson is the greatest American sports Figure in the last one hundred years.
- The USA Patriot Act is an unwarranted intrusion on civil liberties.
- It is better to fight fire with fire.

You should have quickly discerned from examining the above propositions that they are subjective in nature. There is no empirical answer waiting to be discovered. These are evaluations with which people may disagree.

A more complex variation on the traditional value resolution, where only one item is the focus of evaluation, is the **comparative-value resolution.** In this type of resolution, two things are compared to each other to determine which has more "value" than the other. Consider the following propositions:

- That protection of the environment is more important than satisfaction of American energy demands.
- That protection of the public safety is more important than the protection of individual civil liberties.
- First Amendment rights are more vital than Sixth Amendment rights.
- It is better to have loved and lost than never to have loved at all.

These types of topics present many problems for affirmative debaters because they are asked to evaluate the relative worth of two things instead of one. These topics also give the negative the option of arguing that the two competing values are of equal worth.

Just as with factual topics, controversy must exist. Resolutions such as "dropping out of high school to become a crack addict is bad" or "the US torturing of Iraqi war prisoners was immoral" probably fail to be debatable topics as nearly everyone would already agree with such positions. However, topics like "abortion is immoral" or "capital punishment is unjustified" do possess controversy, thus making them debatable topics.

Policy Topics

Advocating a course of action is within the purview of the policy topic. A proposition of policy proposes that some *agent* or *agency* (which may be a person, group, or institution) do something. *Doing*, in this case, means going beyond an internal attitude or belief and manifesting that belief by acting. For example, the proposition "Capital punishment is unjustified" does not require an act. Someone could hold this belief her/his entire life, and no one might ever know it. In contrast, the proposition

"The state of California should abolish the use of capital punishment" proposes a manifest act. The latter topic is a policy topic because it advocates performing an action: that action is inherent in the active verb *abolish*. In this context, a judge voting for or against a resolution does itself not constitute the type of action needed to classify all resolutions as ones of policy. All propositions seek their end in a judgment or vote. The proposition of policy mandates some further action as a result of the vote on the resolution. The following are examples of policy propositions:

- The US should implement a flat tax.
- California should abolish the initiative process.
- The United Nations should authorize military action against country 'X'.
- The Supreme Court should overturn Roe v Wade.
- Santa Rosa Junior College should build a parking garage.

The use of the auxiliary word *should* has caused great confusion. Many people have confused "the bath water as the baby" and assumed if the word should is present the proposition must be one of policy. Admittedly, noticing the word should is a good starting place because nearly all policy topics include the word, as do the ones listed above. However, it is NOT always the case that a sentence with the word should in it is one of policy. In fact, the word should is always used in conjunction with some verb. If that verb requires an action, the proposition is one of policy. If that verb describes an evaluation, it is probably one of value. For example, the proposition "Capital punishment should be considered unjustified" is still a proposition of value because *consideration* does not require a manifest act. The correct question to ask is whether or not the verb requires that an overt action be taken.

Once again, controversy over the proposed policy must exit. Policy propositions like "California should execute all people found guilty of petty theft" or "The US should invade Canada" would rightfully fail to merit much serious consideration.

STOCK ISSUES

Understanding how to classify each different type of resolution is important; otherwise, an advocate will not know how to defend or refute the resolution in a particular debate round. This is especially important for the newer forums of debate that switch topics often, such as parliamentary debate.

For each type of resolution a different set of requirements is placed upon the advocates. Those requirements involve standard questions relative to each resolution's classification. In other words, policy resolutions have different requirements than do value resolutions. Not only must an advocate know how to classify a resolution, but she or he must be able to live and breathe the standard requirements for each classification. These standard requirements are called *Stock Issues*. What follows is a brief explanation of the stock issues for fact, value, and policy propositions. These stock is-sues are explained in much greater detail in Chapters 13, 14, and 15 respectively.

Stock Issues for Legal Debate

Before getting to a specific discussion of fact, value and policy stock issues, it is important to explain stock-issue analysis. Let's look at a subset of factual proposi-tions, the legal proposition, to determine how stock-issue analysis works.

Let's start with a set of **stock issues** related to a criminal trial. Stock issues are standard or universal questions that need to be answered when attempting to prove a proposition true. Stock issues are much like a shopping list for a specific recipe; you cannot make the white clam sauce for your pasta dinner, unless you have each of the ingredient sets. If you forget to buy the clams and clam juice, fresh parsley and gar-lic, white wine and cream, roux mixings, or pasta, the dinner fails completely. For those readers who are chefs, notice how missing even one of those five ingredient sets, without a viable substitute, would make the sauce unrecognizable as white clam sauce over pasta, if not completely unpalatable. Although legal stock issues are not the focus of this book and will not be discussed in later chapters, looking at how a courtroom works can shed a great deal of light on academic debate. Actually, a lot of what is done in academic debate was borrowed from the legal system. In a criminal case, before a case is allowed to go to trial, a district attorney will have to present a *prima-facie* case that addresses each of these four legal stock issues: suspect (who commits the crime), crime (whether a crime occurred), opportunity (was the suspect at the scene of the crime when it took place?) and means (did the suspect have the physical and mental means to commit the crime?). A good way to understand the Latin phrase *prima facie* is to substitute the word "complete"; a complete case (a *prima-facie* case) is one that successfully addresses ALL four stock issues. A judge will not allow a case to go to trial unless each of these stock issues is addressed. Motive (why the suspect committed the crime) is normally not a stock issue that must be proven. However, it is usually unofficially treated as one since many juries are hesi-tant to convict unless they are given a reason which explains why the defendant would have committed the crime. Motive may also be relevant to a person's compe-tence to stand trial, a determination that often examines a defendant's mental state or motive during and/or after the crime. Technically, if the motive were nothing more than a mental illness manifesting itself, the defendant may not be required to face a criminal trial on the matter.

Once the trial begins, and in applying stock-issue analysis, the defense or nega-tive only need show reasonable doubt on one of the stock issues to win. (For our clam-sauce analogy, if one of your key ingredients is of dubious quality, your dinner may be still become ruined, even if you have the correct materials at the start of preparations.) The prosecution or affirmative needs to win all of the stock issues in order to win the debate. Why is that true? Because the affirmative and prosecution have the burden to prove the resolution is probably true in its entirety. For example, during the O.J. Simpson criminal trial, reasonable doubt could have existed on at least three of the stock issues. On the suspect stock issue, was O.J. Simpson the person who actually committed the murder? Questions had arisen during the criminal trial about whether the police planted evidence, whether the glove fit O.J., and whether O.J.'s blood was missing from the amount collected from him during the investigation. These questions combined with the racist comments made by LA Police Detective Mark Fuhrman made the jury a little nervous about convicting such a big celebrity. What if the police had planted evidence? O.J. may not have committed the crime. If the jury had a reasonable doubt on the suspect stock issue, it could have voted not guilty on that one stock issue alone, even if the prosecution won all of the other stock issues. However, there were questions about other legal stock issues, as well.

The means stock issue asks whether O.J. had the means to commit the crime. Questions had arisen as to the health of O.J.'s hands and knees. The fact that the killer must have been strong enough to wrestle with a fairly bulky Ron Goldman put into question O.J.'s physical ability to commit the crime. Again, the jury could have voted not guilty on the means stock issue alone; although, that was not the key stock issue for the defense.

The opportunity stock issue asks whether the suspect had enough time at the murder location to commit the crime. In this case, the prosecution's own timeline had to be adjusted during the trial, thus casting some doubt on the credibility of the prosecution's case. At least one jury member mentioned the timeline being unclear to her, thus being a factor in her decision. Again, reasonable doubt on this one stock issue is enough for the defense to win.

The key point to understand regarding stock issue analysis is this: The affirmative has to win all of the stock issues and the negative has to win but one of the stock issues. The O.J. Simpson criminal trial is a good example of how reasonable doubt on one stock issue can win the trial for the defense. As many readers may know, the plaintiffs in the civil trial seemed to do a better job building a case against Simpson. Of course, they had the advantage of seeing how the criminal trial went, as well as not having to establish as high a level of proof. Nevertheless, the quality of the explanations and the quality of the arguments can have a lot to do with the outcome of a trial. Many readers may feel that O.J. Simpson did commit the crime, and may wonder how a jury could have acquitted him on the murder charge. However, a discussion of reasonable doubt regarding just one stock issue can make the trial's outcome seem more understandable.

And here's just a note on the stock issue of motive: As mentioned earlier, motive is not a stock issue that must be established in North-American jurisprudence. Christopher Darden, during the closing arguments for the prosecution in the Simpson criminal trial, acknowledged that motive is not necessary to prove. Nonetheless, the prosecution spent much time trying to establish motive because while not technically required it is still very helpful.

Stock Issues for Fact Debate

As Chapter 13 will demonstrate in great detail, the three stock issues for factual debates are **definitions, evidence,** and **inference.** The first requirement is to define any unclear terms of the resolution. Former President Clinton was accused of lying when he asserted that he had never been alone in the White House with Monica Lewinsky. This is clearly a factual statement. Either the two of them were alone at one time or they were not. However, before we can answer that question we must first define, in this context, what "alone" means. Those who accused Clinton of lying pointed out that he and Lewinsky were alone together in the Oval Office for long periods of time. The Clinton defense team countered that other individuals including secretaries, security guards, and maintenance workers were also in the White House (but not in the Oval Office) while he and Lewinsky were alone in the Oval Office. Hence, they were not alone "in the White House." So, was Clinton alone in the White House with Ms. Lewinsky? It all depends on the definition. But once we define what "alone in the White House" means, the answer is either a yes or no.

The second requirement is to introduce your lines of argument. Suppose you are debating the proposition "Saddam Hussein possessed weapons of mass destruction in 2003." This is a proposition of fact for either he did or did not possess them. The first requirement would be to define the key terms. Secondly, the advocate must present the lines of analysis to support why they believe he possessed these weapons.

Advocates might argue firstly, that during the first Persian Gulf War Saddam owned chemical weapons, secondly, Saddam had used chemical weapons against the Kurds in the past, and thirdly, UN inspections of banned weapons were inadequate to ensure these weapons were destroyed. Figure 2.3 illustrates an outline of an affirmative case addressing the stock issues for a resolution of fact. Of course, we know today that Iraq did not possess WMDs; however, at the time these were the arguments presented by the United States. Please note that inference is not perfect, as is the case here; however, at the time it was defensible and debatable, which is the point we are trying to relate to our readers.

Stock Issues for Value Debate

The stock issues for value debate are **definitions, criterion,** and **application.** The first part involves defining the terms of the resolution. Just as in factual debate, any unclear terms need to be clarified.

The second stock issue is the presentation of a criterion for judging the debate round. A criterion can be a goal, a standard, a value, or the conclusion to a philosophical treatise. Usually the criterion is on a higher level of abstraction than the proposition itself. For instance, a criterion often deals with economic, social, or political values. The criterion is used to measure the extent of benefit or detriment asked for by the resolution. In other words, a criterion is like a litmus test. Imagine that you

Resolved: That Saddam Hussein possessed weapons of mass destruction in 2003

Definitions: A) Possessed: to have in supply, to own.
              B) Weapons of mass destruction: chemical, biological, or nuclear devices capable of killing thousands of individuals

Contention I: Fact. Saddam possessed chemical weapons during and after the Gulf War
    A) US solders were issued gas masks to defend against chemical attacks (evidence/analysis)
    B) Iraqi officials said they had and would use chemical weapons (evidence/analysis)

Contention II: Fact. Saddam possessed chemical weapons in the past
    A) Saddam used chemical weapons against the Kurds (evidence/analysis)
    B) Thousands of Kurds were killed with these weapons (evidence/analysis)

Contention III: Inference. There is no proof that these chemical weapons were ever destroyed
    A) Saddam had strong reasons for keeping such weapons (evidence/analysis)
    B) UN inspections to enforce chemical weapons ban were inadequate (evidence/analysis)
    C) During the 2003 US invasion small traces of banned chemicals were found (evidence/analysis)

FIGURE 2.3

Affirmative Case Addressing the Stock Issues for a Resolution of Fact

are driving to a particular destination and have the choice of two routes. You decide the first route is better because it is quicker. In that case "quickness" is the criterion. However, someone else may decide route two is more desirable because, while it takes more time, it offers more interesting sights to see. Hence, maybe "pleasure" is their criterion.

The third stock issue in value debate is the application of the designative stock issue. This stock issue simply involves the application of the criterion to a specific case. In the above example, the first advocate would need to substantiate that the first route is indeed quicker. They might establish that it is the route with the fewest miles. The negative might accept the affirmative criterion but argue the affirmative application fails to uphold the criterion. For example, the negative could argue that while the route outlined by the affirmative is shorter in distance, the windiness of the road makes the route actually take more time to travel. On a more substantial level one debating the proposition, "Resolved: That illegal immigration into the United

States is detrimental to the United States," might use a social value, such as the lack of crime, as the criterion. In the application, one might prove that illegal immigrants are significant contributors to crime in the US. Or, on the same topic, one might offer a political value as a criterion: full employment for US citizens. By applying that criterion, one might find that illegal immigrants take jobs that Americans want. If the job displacement is widespread, it could be significant enough to justify the *detrimental* phrase in the resolution. The negative could argue that the jobs that illegal immigrants are taking are jobs that most Americans refuse to accept therefore the criterion of "employment of US citizens" is not being harmed.

Regardless of the actual application, more and more debate critics are requiring that affirmatives show that their application is significant. For instance, if illegal immigrants only contributed to a fraction of one percent of the crime in the US, then even though the criterion was applied successfully, the small amount of crime might not justify the resolution. Of course, if the affirmative could prove that the small amount of crime is significant (e.g., many illegal immigrants are potential presidential assassins), then it may be debatable.

The most important point here is the relationship between the two stock issues. A value advocate must integrate the stock issues so as to have the application match the criterion. In other words, if the criterion is justice, the advocates must show how the illegal immigrants subvert justice. This is definitely easier said than done, as you will see if you are asked to debate questions of value.

One final note. The criterion of "cost-benefit analysis" is widely misunderstood. Many beginning students confuse it with net benefits. A criterion of net benefits is where all of the advantages are weighed against the disadvantages. However, cost-benefit analysis is purely an economic consideration. In other words, if the financial expense is greater than the financial income, cost-benefit analysis would suggest a deleterious condition exists. Figure 2.4 illustrates an outline of an affirmative case addressing the stock issues for a resolution of value.

Stock Issues for Policy Debate

Policy propositions ask the critic to determine if a particular proposal should be implemented. For example, "Resolved: That your college should build a new parking garage" is a proposition of policy. In order to justify a change in policy, the advocate is usually called upon to uphold the stock issues of motive, blame, cure, and cost (the stock issues of motive and blame can be reversed in their order of presentation).

Motive

In the **motive** section, the affirmative is asked to demonstrate that a need for change exists. Just as one would not undergo medical surgery without good reason, so a society does not implement change without good reason. If your college has adequate parking facilities then it would be hard to justify spending money on a new

Resolved: That illegal immigration into the United States is detrimental to the United States

Definitions:
- A) Illegal immigration: entering a foreign nation without legal authorization
- B) Detrimental: negative or harmful

Criterion: cost-benefit analysis

Contention I: Illegal immigration causes an economic drain on social services
- A) Illegal immigrants don't pay taxes
- B) Illegal immigrants drain publicly funded services
  - 1) Children are allowed to attend public schools
  - 2) Medical services must be provided
  - 3) Children born in the US whose parents are illegal immigrants receive welfare

FIGURE 2.4

Affirmative Case Addressing the Stock Issues for a Resolution of Value

parking garage. However, if your college does not have adequate parking facilities then spending money on a new parking garage might be warranted.

Blame

In the **blame** section, the affirmative is asked to demonstrate that the problem indicated in the motive section is inherent. That is, the status quo is incapable of solving the problem. The affirmative would need to show that given the present number of parking spots and the number of students and faculty driving to school that the parking problem will be an ongoing situation.

The negative might argue that the reason the parking lots are overcrowded is because the college presently does not vigorously enforce an existing policy disallowing non-college-related parking in the facilities. As a result, perhaps people who work in places close to the college are using the college's parking facilities, thus leading to the overcrowded situation. All that need be done is for the college to enforce the existing parking regulations and the problem will be solved without the need for a new garage. If the negative were to win the status-quo enforcement argument, the negative would win the debate based on this stock issue alone. The advocates for change must demonstrate that nothing short of implementing their policy, in this case building a new parking garage, will solve the problem. They must prove that enforcement of existing policies is not enough. If the affirmative were able to prove that only ten non-college related cars were actually parking on campus and the need is for 500 more spaces, then the negative status-quo enforcement argument, outlined above, would be inadequate by 490 spaces. Thus, the advocates of change would win the inherency issue.

Cure

In the **cure** section, the affirmative outlines the mechanics of the plan. In the **mandates,** the affirmative specifies exactly what is to be done (what type of parking garage and where will it be built). The affirmative must also indicate the **agency** that will be used to carry out the plan (in this case it is the college itself and the construction company it hires). In the **funding** plank the affirmative must demonstrate that they can pay for the proposal (how much the garage will cost and how it will be paid). Finally, in the **enforcement** plank, the affirmative demonstrates how the plan will be enforced. (If the plan will only allow college students to park in the new garage, will more campus police be hired to patrol the new garage?)

Cost

In the **cost** section, the affirmative debaters must demonstrate that their proposal will solve the problem without accruing any significant disadvantages. The affirmative would obviously need to demonstrate that a new parking garage would alleviate the parking problem. The negative could try to demonstrate that the new garage would not solve the parking problem. Perhaps a new garage would simply encourage those who are now car pooling, riding their bikes, taking public transit, etc. to start driving their own cars. The negative might also argue that even if the new garage solved the parking problem it does so at the cost of creating even bigger problems. Perhaps in order to pay for the new facility, faculty will be laid off, course offerings will be cut, a new computer lab will not be created, and athletic programs will be reduced.

It should be kept in mind that the affirmative is usually required to prove all of the stock issues. The negative need only disprove one of them. Figure 2.5 illustrates an outline of an affirmative case addressing the stock issues for a resolution of value.

THE *PRIMA FACIE* CASE

Having examined stock issues, we can now continue our discussion about what is known as a *prima-facie* case. The concept of the ***prima-facie*** case is central to debate. The goal of an advocate is to prove a *prima-facie* case for his or her cause. If this were a sport, the *prima-facie* case would be how one scored. Without such a case, one cannot win. With it, one might still lose if the opponent scores more points, but without a *prima-facie* case there is no chance of winning.

The term *prima-facie* comes from the Latin words meaning "on first face" or "at first appearance." It refers to the fact that a *prima-facie* case is one which, on first appearance, is a complete case for the proposition. There are at least two definitions of

Blame: College "X's" current parking situation is inadequate
    A) Ratio of parking spots to students is too low (structural)
    B) Students don't like to car pool or take public transit (attitudinal)

Motive: Inadequate Parking is disadvantageous
    A) Students late to class
    B) Students choose not to attend the college

Cure: Planks of plan
    A) Mandate: Build a two story garage with an additional 1,200 spots
    B) Agency: Parking committee will oversee the process
    C) Funding: Monies will come from a bond initiative and new sales of parking permits
    D) Enforcement: Cars will be ticketed and towed if parked in garage without a permit

Cost: Implementation of the policy is beneficial
    A) Students won't be late, or not attend the college (solvency)
    B) Added revenue from increased attendance can be used to update library holdings (advantage)

FIGURE 2.5

Affirmative Case Addressing the Stock Issues for a Resolution of Policy

a *prima-facie* case. The first is the traditional definition and the second is the "organic" definition.

The traditional definition of a *prima-facie* case is a case which, without refutation, would convince a reasonable person to adopt the resolution. This definition requires that at the end of the affirmative case, the judge be compelled to adopt the resolution. If after hearing the arguments in favor of the resolution, the judge is not compelled to vote for it, then the affirmative has not met its *prima-facie* obligation and the negative would win by default. The traditional definition of *prima facie* is usually applied in informal debate settings: debating with a spouse, with a co-worker, or in a small group setting (a church-council meeting, for example). The more formal debate settings tend to apply a more technical definition which we term the organic definition.

The organic definition of a *prima-facie* case is a case which substantiates the stock issues required for that type of a proposition. As we have just seen, propositions of fact, value, and policy have different stock issues associated with them. Using the organic definition, the affirmative (in a policy debate) would have presented a *prima-facie* case if they were able, in their opening presentation, to present sufficient reasons to prove the policy stock issues of motive, blame, cure, and cost. If the affirmative had failed to address one of these issues, or failed to give sufficient reasons to support one of these issues, they would have failed to present a *prima-facie* case. In other words, had the affirmative proven motive, cure, and cost, but failed to address the cure issue, they would not be *prima facie*. This would be true regardless of how well the other three stock issues were developed. In theory, the negative could just point out that the affirmative had failed to address the cure issue, sit down, and win the debate.

In fact, in law this is done all the time. Following the prosecution's opening case the defense will move that the case be dismissed on *prima-facie* grounds by claiming that the prosecution has failed to prove one or more of the legal stock issues (suspect, crime, motive, means, and opportunity). If the judge agrees, the defense wins. The O.J. Simpson defense team made such a motion which Judge Lance Ito rejected. The defense was then compelled to put on its defense. As should be apparent, this then is an all-win, no-lose position for the negative. If the negative debaters are able to win the *prima-facie* argument, they win the debate. If they lose the *prima-facie* argument, it simply means they must argue their case.

Another way to understand this organic definition of *prima-facie*, as we explained above, is to substitute the word, **complete.** In policy debate, the affirmative is *complete* or *prima-facie* if reasonable arguments are presented on each of the policy stock issues: motive, blame, cure and cost. In value debate the affirmative team is complete or *prima facie* when the definitive and designative stock issues are addressed in a reasonable manner. When debating a factual proposition, the *prima-facie* elements, which make the arguments in favor of the new belief complete, are of course definitions, evidence (and inference if required).

The traditional and organic perspectives on *prima facie* have similarities and differences. It is possible that someone, unaware of the stock issues for a proposition, might nonetheless find the affirmative case compelling enough to vote for even though technically all of the stock issues had not been addressed. Hence, the traditional definition would have been met while the organic definition would not have been. Of course, people are fooled by fallacious arguments daily. That is why you're taking this class: so that you will know a "complete" argument when you see one. To get a truly complete argument, you must use the organic definition.

It is your authors' collective opinion that many of the poor decisions made in our society stem from using the traditional, rather than the organic, definition of *prima facie*. City councils adopt land-use plans which do not address serious disadvantages, like the disappearance of agricultural tax dollars or the elimination of open spaces. Voters pass propositions that have unworkable plans. School boards adopt new curricula and throw out the old, when the old curriculum was working well. (This happened when whole language took over for phonics. The answer was to keep phonics AND add whole language to the existing reading curricula, but many children's lives were damaged because of this one non-*prima-facie* decision.) And people move their families to new cities, hoping for a better way of life. Later, they find that there was no inherent reason for the existence of their perceived problems in the old city. In fact, things could have been just as good with some minor tinkering with the *status quo,* and they could have avoided the trauma and cost of moving halfway across the country. Not all traditional *prima-facie* arguments meet with such tragedy, but the chances of tragedy are greatly increased when the organic definition is not used. The rest of this book will explore the importance and illustrate the uses of this organic definition of *prima facie.*

SUMMARY

The purpose of this chapter was to analyze the components of debatable propositions. The Claim Tree was used to illustrate the requirements for a debatable resolution. These requirements include clarity, jurisdiction, and controversy. Three different types of propositions were identified. These were propositions of fact, value, and policy. Each of these propositions was defined and their stock issues discussed. The stock issues for propositions of fact are definitions, evidence, and inference. The stock issues for propositions of value are definitions, criterion, and designative applications. The stock issues for propositions of policy are motive, blame, cure, and cost. Finally, the traditional and organic definitions of a *prima-facie* case were presented.

THE RESOLUTION:
THE FOCUS OF A DEBATE

Let's return to our two little kids. Assume "A" issues the debatable claim "My daddy can beat up your daddy" [Claim 1]. "B" responds "My daddy's a good daddy" [Claim 2]. Between Claim 1 and Claim 2 one of two things has happened. The first possibility is that "B" has accepted "A's" Claim 1, a proposition of fact, and now proposes Claim 2, a proposition of value, as a further topic of discussion. The second, and more likely possibility, is that Claim 1 is still disputed, but the debate is about to wander into irrelevant issues.

In either event, the critical thinking process has stopped. In the first case (acceptance of Claim 1) it has stopped because neither "A" nor "B" has acknowledged that a "resolution" to a question has been reached. If they both understand this, the fact that neither party has forced the issue explicitly probably makes no difference (and indeed, may preserve neighborly relations). If they don't realize this, both will continue on as though Claim 1 were still contested but drift into irrelevant issues. If Claim 1 has indeed been granted, the debate should now shift to what is relevant to Claim 2. Recognizing the resolution keeps a debate focused on what is disputed and sorts the relevant from the irrelevant.

A claim may or may not be argued in a given debate. If the claim creates no controversy among the advocates in a given debate then it is not debatable. However, your authors believe that although any claim may be debated, it depends on the context as to whether it *should* be debated.

For example, in most contexts, debating whether the object you're sitting on actually exists or not would be a waste of time. However, if you're a professor of subatomic physics at a major university, just such a debate may be relevant. Among physics professors, there is a reasonable and healthy debate about whether matter exists at any level. As scientists discover smaller and smaller pieces of an atom, the discoveries seem to blur the distinction between matter and energy; thus leading some scientists to conclude that matter may not exist and that energy may be the common denominator if there even is a common denominator at the quantum level at all (Davies, 1983). Additionally, an atom is made up of more than 99% empty space, so what you're sitting on is really a firm shell of electrons and nothing more.

Debating whether a sentence is grammatically correct may be a waste of time in some contexts, but, if precision is deemed to be an important context, grammar may be an issue which should be debated. When advocates believe that a claim is debatable and it is put forward for debate, it becomes a resolution. The resolution is the focus of any debate. This chapter explores the purpose of having a resolution, the nature of resolutions, the assignments within a resolution, and what makes a good resolution.

The Nature of a Resolution: Origin and Definition

We have all been in conversations which started out considering one issue, which reminded us of another issue, which reminded us of another, and so on. When this free association occurs we may have fun, but seldom is anything resolved.

To promote the critical thinking process one states a resolution in order that a question may be resolved. The resolution may be explicit, as in a formal debate, or implicitly recognized by the participants. In either event it provides a focus for the critical thinking process, so that at the end of the process the participants will sense that their argument has accomplished something by adopting or rejecting a specific idea.

The Origin of the Term

The term resolution is derived from the traditional form of presenting a motion. Most of us have seen bills or proclamations in the form:

Resolution
Whereas,   [reason 1] and
Whereas,   [reason 2] and
Whereas,   [reason 3] therefore, be it
Resolved: that . . .

Our modern term resolution is a vestige of this form. It means that the proponent of this bill wants us to accept this resolution of the question or issue.

The grammar creates problems. One cannot say "therefore resolve. . ." after a series of whereas clauses. But since the whereas clauses are not normally read aloud, except in proclamations, we have the past tense (Resolved) referring to something we want the judge to do in the future at the end of the debate. Speakers have been remarkably inventive in circumventing this grammatical thicket. The most common phrasing is "I therefore ask you to join me in standing resolved that. . . ." It is the job of the affirmative advocate to work backwards from the resolution, finding the whereas clauses or reasons that she or he feels will be the most effective in defeating all potential negative attacks. Thus by debate's end, the critic, whose job it is to assign a winner, will be convinced by the affirmative that the resolution should be adopted.

Of course, to continue with the temperament of this book, not everyone agrees that the traditional view of the resolution is necessarily the purpose of academic debate. In other words, many feel that the resolution is NOT actually adopted with the affirmative ballot; rather the resolution is merely the boundary in which the game of debate is played. That debate is a game does not necessarily mean that it is NOT educational. There are many games which are educational: Chess for example. What resolution-as-boundary simply says is that the critic at debate's end votes for whoever does the better job of debating, and that may or may not mean that the resolution is actually adopted, even in a hypothetical sense.

The Definition of Resolution

Today, the term resolved is a code word meaning that the phrase that follows is a special type of proposition intended for debate. Various other parallel terms are also used to refer to resolutions presented for debate. These include question, proposition, and topic. Each is subtly different from the others, and they derive from various backgrounds. The differences are largely semantic, but worth noting.

The word *question* is drawn from parliamentary procedure and refers to the issue to which a vote is an answer. Thus, the stock phrase: "Call the Previous Question." (Translation: "I want to vote on the main motion now.")

"Is there an objection to putting the question to the House?" (Translation: "Does anyone object to voting now?")

A *Proposition* is something to be proven. The term is used in geometry and philosophy to mean something proposed to be true, but not yet demonstrated. The proponent then presents his demonstration to show that the proposition is valid.

A *topic* refers to a subject matter. It does not refer to any special form of phrasing, and simply means "this is what we're going to talk about." Thus, assume you are debating the resolution "Resolved: that the federal government should abolish the minimum wage." If a stranger asked you what you were debating you would probably answer simply "the minimum wage." Phrased thus, it is just a topic since it describes the subject matter under discussion but does not take a position on it. The term topic is, however, used as a synonym for the resolution in at least one context worth noting here, and that is the issue of topicality. Topicality will be discussed at length later, but it should be noted that this term refers to an evaluation as to whether the affirmative is arguing within the boundaries of the resolution. Topicality should more accurately be called *resolutionality*, but more on that later.

For this chapter, we will use the term proposition to refer to claims we are considering, and resolution to refer to a class of propositions intended for public debate. The word resolution is a term of art in debate. It may be in either way as follows:

Resolution: a debatable claim which is proposed by the affirmative for adoption by a judge at the conclusion of a debate.

Resolution: a single, declarative sentence which serves as the boundary for a debate.

The first definition suggests that the resolution is actually or hypothetically adopted as belief, value, or policy at debate's end. This definition suggests also that the debate critic is serving as a hypothetical world dictator essentially deciding what course of action or belief system is best. The second definition suggests that the resolution is not adopted in any form but serves simply as the boundary in which the game of debate is played. In the second forum, the critic usually plays the skills judge or argument critic, deciding who does the best job of debating.

This chapter will focus on the first definition, but the two definitions are not necessarily mutually exclusive. In other words, a critic could look at who does the best job of playing the game of providing the best argumentation for or against resolution-adoption.

The Implicit Resolution

The model of critical thinking that we are following was developed in debate tournaments, where resolutions are always explicitly stated. In non-tournament situations, resolutions are usually implicit, and therefore are propositions and not really resolutions at all. Most people do not say to a friend "Resolved: that we should go to the movies." While this is an absolutely accurate rendering of the decision desired, this is not how people talk. One would normally say, "We should go to the movies." (which is a proposition of policy). A dispute may follow which would sound very much like a debate.

The critical thinking model developed in intercollegiate debate is a good one, and there is benefit in mentally applying the same rigor to everyday decisions. The first step in this process is to recognize "the resolution that is implicitly under discussion." An *implicit resolution* is a statement recognized by at least one of the parties as the focus of a debate. This is obviously more subjective than the explicitly stated resolution of a formal debate. But, it is advantageous for the party that recognizes the implicit resolution. In the Two-Little-Kids hypothetical example, "A" could readily respond to "B," "I'm not saying your daddy's not a good daddy, I'm just saying mine could beat him up." In so doing "A" can control and channel the dispute. If one can keep sight of what is being proposed by phrasing it mentally as a resolution, one can remind the other parties "I thought what we were trying to decide was 'X.' Likewise, in an internal dialogue, we can bring ourselves back to our focus.

THE FRAMER OF THE RESOLUTION

Obviously, resolutions have to be created by someone or some group. The framer of the resolution is the party wording the resolution. The framer may be the affirmative, the judge, the instructor in an argumentation class, a topic selection committee in a debate league, and even on rare occasions the negative. There are differences, advantages and disadvantages to each of these origins, but whomever the framer is he or she should do two things to provide a good focus for a debate: 1) assign the duties of the resolution correctly, and 2) state the desired decision. We now turn to examine each of these in turn.

THE ASSIGNMENTS IN A RESOLUTION: PRESUMPTION, BURDEN OF PROOF, AND STANDARD OF PROOF

There are three interrelated factors that help frame any resolution: A) presumption, which in turn produces a B) the burden of proof, and a wording that sets C) the standard of proof. Together these may be spoken of as the assignments of the resolution since they in turn tell the affirmative and negative what they must do. An argument is won when the party with the **burden of proof** meets the standard of proof necessary to overcome presumption. Thus the concepts of burdens, presumptions, and standards, while not identical, are closely related. The burden answers the question of who has the task of proving an issue, presumption rests automatically with the party that doesn't have the burden, while the standard is the degree of certainty to which the claim must be proven.

Presumption

The first step in phrasing or analyzing any resolution is to determine the status quo, which in turn tells you what presumptions exist. **Presumption** is the belief that the status quo should continue until there is a reason to change it.

While the phrase **status quo** has been defined as "Latin, for the mess we're in," it may more technically be defined as what will happen if the resolution is not adopted. It has also been defined as the absence of the resolution. In short, the status quo is simply "the way things are now" or "the existing state of things." Present policies or present beliefs are the status quo. On the issue of abortion, the status quo is that abortion is legal. The status quo belief is that although it may be immoral, it is a choice of the woman in question. Morality, therefore, in the status quo, has an individual and situation-based component. Most people believe that the woman has the right to make the choice and that she may define morality for herself.

Fundamental to understanding presumption is to understand the following principle. **Not to decide is a decision.** Presumption is not just a trick of logic or a technicality of debate. It is a vital step in critical thinking because it forces the one framing the resolution to consider what will happen if there is no resolution. It may be that what will happen is what one wants, and therefore there is no reason to debate. Whenever a proposition is submitted for debate as a resolution, it must seek to change things. It may change a belief, an attitude, or a policy, but it must change the existing state of things (the status quo) or there is no reason to debate it. If everything is already going the way you want it to go, why should you change it? You might want to test your beliefs by listening to arguments for a change (an affirmative case for the resolution), but if you do not adopt the resolution things will continue as they are. We call "things as they are" the status quo, and the support we give to things as they are is presumption.

The status quo is determined objectively or subjectively. It is objectively determined in policy debate because anyone framing the resolution should place presumption in the same place, based on an analysis of existing policies. On the other hand, in resolutions of fact and value, because no one can see a belief or attitude, different framers may arrive at different determinations of the status quo.

In practical terms, as applied to academic debate, presumption is the mindset that the resolution under consideration should not be adopted until good reasons are provided for its adoption. That is, the mindset of the critic upon first hearing the resolution is one of rejection. Assume two debate teams enter the room and sit down. The critic is there and ready for the debate to begin. Instead of debating, the two teams simply look at each other and smile at one another. Neither team says a word. After a while both teams get up and leave. Nothing has been said. Who wins the debate? The answer is that the negative wins. Why? Because of the presumption which exists against the topic. The mindset of the critic upon entering the room is to reject the resolution. Since nothing was said to alter that original mindset, the resolution is not adopted.

Presumption in Policy Debate

If a policy is being debated, the status quo can, and should be, determined by an objective examination of the present policies of the resolution. These policies are the status quo, and a properly phrased resolution of policy will always seek to change them. For example, assume you are in the US Senate and you believe the United Nations is a good organization and deserves our support. You know there are other members of the Senate who do not feel that way. You could, of course, propose a bill that says, "we should stay in the United Nations." But since that is the status quo we'll do it even if your bill is not introduced. What do you have to gain by such a debate? Let the opponents of the UN propose their bill to have us withdraw from the UN. You favor the status quo, and presumption is on your side. Keep it there.

Sometimes, the framer of the resolution must deal with what is referred to as "The problem of a discontinuing status quo." In some policy situations it is difficult to tell what will happen if the resolution is not adopted. It is difficult to know what decision one has made in not making a decision. Consider any election. Who has presumption when candidates are debating each other? If one of the candidates is an incumbent, one might say that the incumbent is the status quo, but this is inaccurate. A fixed term of office expires. If no one voted, the incumbent would not remain in office (unless appointed out of desperation, which would entail action). What if neither candidate is the incumbent? Consider the parallel case of advertising. What happens if you choose not to buy? Clearly both candidates and soap flake manufacturers are debating policies. Both voting and buying are manifest acts. Each candidate is the affirmative for "Resolved: that you should vote for me." Each manufacturer is the affirmative for "Resolved: that you should buy my product." But the agent indicated in the resolution (us) doesn't have to do anything.

The best answer seems to be that the *status quo* is not voting or buying. Each candidate and manufacturer is the affirmative for his resolution, and the negative to each opposing candidate's or manufacturer's case. The advocate must not only convince us to vote (at all) or enter the marketplace, but also to vote for his cause/product. Fortunately, as a practical matter in an election, somebody will always vote (at least the candidates), so there will always be a decision. A candidate is therefore able to argue that the voter should help make the right decision. Soap flake manufacturers are not so fortunate.

Presumption for Resolutions of Fact and Value

While one can objectively determine the status quo or presumption on propositions of policy, one cannot always determine what facts are believed or values held. Public opinion polls, when available, simply point to the ephemeral nature of this quest. On controversial issues, the writer of the resolution could be put in the position of being an amateur pollster.

A better position is that for propositions of fact and value, the status quo may be determined subjectively, in order to reverse the belief or opinion the judge presently holds, whether or not anyone else shares the judge's belief. If the judge frames the resolution, she need only ask herself what she believes or what attitude she holds. If the framer is someone other than the judge, it is only necessary that the framer of the resolution ask himself what he wishes the judge to use for the status quo, and construct a resolution which tests this belief. This type of psychological presumption is difficult to manage in a debate forum, unless the purpose of the debate is actually to dissuade a judge or framer from holding a certain belief or value.

In tournament debate, the resolution is written by a committee. The individual judge in the round is asked to assume what that committee believes is the status quo as the starting point for the debate. However, when framing resolutions for classroom debates or future tournament debates, the best rule for presumption is to tie the value to existing policies in order to assign presumption. For example, take the issue of abortion. Many Americans believe that abortion is immoral, while many feel abortion is moral. In this case, how should the resolution be worded? Which party should enjoy presumption and which party should carry the burden of proof? The simplest answer is to make the value and factual resolutions correspond with current policy. In this case, the resolution should be worded, "Resolved: that abortion is immoral." Abortion is now legal, thus the value topic would be worded in correspondence to the current topic. Presumption would rest with abortion, causing the affirmative to prove the current values wrong.

Factual topics should be worded accordingly. "Resolved: that human life begins at conception" would be the correct wording for the factual resolution on the same topic. This would cause the anti-abortion advocates to prove a statement contrary to present policies. It would give pro-abortion advocates the presumption; thus, keeping the debate closer to how it must actually play out in society. Therefore, this is how the issue would look with presumption correctly placed on each of the three types of claims:

- Policy: Resolved: that the US Congress and/or the State legislatures should amend the US Constitution to prohibit abortion, except in the cases of life threat, incest, or rape.
- Value: Resolved: that abortion is immoral.
- Fact: Resolved: that human life begins at conception.

Note that as you move up the hierarchy, the presumption stays consistently with the status quo policy of abortion on demand. If you're writing resolutions for your classroom debates, deciding resolutions for parliamentary tournaments, or suggesting resolutions for national debate topic committees, keep these suggestions in mind.

Value topics pose another interesting problem. How to word a proposition when there is is no clear or even suggestive status quo belief to challenge? For example, assume we want to debate which animals, dogs or cats, make better pets. Which animal enjoys presumption? There probably is no correct answer.

Unfortunately, topics are not always worded with presumption correctly placed. Except in the infrequent instances in which the affirmative would want to claim presumption (this will be discussed later), poorly worded topics require a simple rule be applied. And that rule is that, until argued otherwise by the affirmative, the negative has presumption.

With the advent of parliamentary debates, the number of resolutions with presumption poorly placed is legion. Topics like "what goes up must come down" or "don't put the cart before the horse" are problematic. Clichés and proverbs are not always true, but most often they are at least assumed true. Therefore, it's easy to see how things could get somewhat confusing. Instructors, parliamentary topic writers, and others should try to word the resolutions differently, so that that the government is not given the advantage of defending status-quo beliefs. On the *what-goes-up-must-come-down* topic for example, not many opposition teams were able to overcome the government's clear tactical advantage. For debate, this creates the following:

Unless argued otherwise, presumption is always against the resolution.

This standard for presumption is called artificial presumption. In other words, we artificially assign presumption to the negative as a rule in debate. For example, the presumption of innocence is a standard of jurisprudence in US law; however, many systems of law work well with a presumption of guilt. Neither standard is natural as far as the status quo is concerned. Under American law, an accused is considered innocent until proven guilty. When George comes to court for the murder of Martha, it is not up to George to prove that he is innocent until someone (the prosecutor) sets out to prove him guilty. Thus, phrased as a resolution, the charge is Resolved: that George is guilty of murder. Note that the possible verdicts are guilty (the affirmative wins) or not guilty (the negative wins). The defense/negative does not have to prove George innocent, but only show that guilt has not been proven. This is because the defense (the negative) started with presumption.

In many countries, the legal system is based on the Napoleonic Code. In such countries presumption is reversed, and the accused is considered guilty until proven innocent at the trial. Mexico uses the Napoleonic Code as the basis for its law. Consider what this does to the concept of bail. In the United States we favor bail because no accused is guilty until so proven at trial. Thus one bails out an innocent person. In Mexico, bail is rare because the courts would be freeing a guilty person who can only be proven innocent at trial. Both systems are logical. Each has assigned presumption differently. We learn from this that many times presumption can be placed any way one wants, but the resolution must always overcome it.

Under either legal system, the assignment of presumption is arbitrary. The writers of the United States Constitution wanted a system that followed English Common Law, which gives the defendant presumption in order to restrict the power of the state. The Napoleonic Code placed a presumption of correctness on the prosecutor's judgment. Both systems work to further the values which spawned them.

Similarly, for a judge-created resolution of fact, if a judge wishes to test the accuracy of his belief that extraterrestrial intelligent life does not exist, he would phrase the resolution as "Resolved: that extraterrestrial life exists." Otherwise an affirmative would only be confirming its own presumptions and prejudices and not testing them. Thus the concept of presumption and the related concept of the burden of proof allow the framer of the resolution to assign burdens and presumption in the many situations in which such assignment is arbitrary (as in the legal system). The founders of the republic wanted a system which would favor the defendant, and so assigned presumption and burdens accordingly.

In any given situation, the status quo will continue as it is unless the judge decides to change it by adopting the resolution. Therefore, if no decision is made to adopt the resolution, there is an implicit decision that the status quo should continue.

The Burden of Proof

The reverse of enjoying presumption is having the burden to establish good reasons for adopting the resolution. This burden is termed the *Burden of Proof.*

If the party with the burden of proof does not accept that burden the status quo prevails. One of the most elementary statements of debate theory is: **The party that asserts a claim must prove it.** At the start of the debate the affirmative asserts the resolution. Therefore, by the end of the debate, the affirmative must prove the resolution, or lose the debate.

If there is a tie between the affirmative and the negative at the end of the debate, the judge would vote for the negative because the affirmative had the burden to prove the resolution true and could not do it. A tie goes to the party with presumption. Remember that having presumption is the opposite of having the burden of proof. For example, if proof was quantifiable, and each party submitted 100 points worth of proof, the party with presumption would win because it has 100 points plus presumption. Thus, at the start of a debate, before a word is spoken, the negative is ahead because it starts with presumption.

A Burden for Proof

Whereas the affirmative has the burden of proof in the entire debate, both the affirmative and the negative have a burden to prove their specific claims. This is called a burden of proof. When a debate begins, only the affirmative has a burden of proof. They must substantiate the specific claims that they put forward as justification for adoption of the resolution. In theory, the negative does not have a burden of proof which they must meet, because in theory the negative doesn't have to put forward any arguments. If after hearing the affirmative argumentation in favor of a resolution the critic is not convinced, the result would be a *de facto* negative win.

For example, assume the resolution is "Resolved: That the United States should ban the use of chlorine in all industrial operations." The affirmative has The Burden of Proof to prove the resolution should be adopted. To help prove that resolution, the affirmative might claim 1) that chlorine use destroys the ozone layer and 2) chlorine use poisons drinking water. The affirmative would then have a burden of proof to demonstrate that these two claims are true. They simply can't assert that they are true. Let's further assume that the negative claims that the evidence used by the affirmative to prove the first claim is biased and the evidence used to prove the second claim is based on a flawed study. The negative would then assume a burden of proof to substantiate those claims. They must give reasons why we should believe the affirmative's first claim is supported by a biased source and the second is based on a flawed study. They too could not just assert these arguments. Now let's assume that when the debate ends the negative has failed to convince us that the evidence used by the affirmative to support the first claim is biased. But let's further assume that the negative is able to demonstrate that the evidence used to support the second claim is from a flawed study, therefore leaving that claim unproven. We now have a situation where the affirmative has won one and lost one of its two claims. In respect to the first claim, it can be said that the affirmative met the burden of proof; while, with respect to the second claim, it can be said the affirmative failed to meet the burden of proof. Notice also how the affirmative can lose an individual claim and still meet the burden-of-proof requirement. It could be that just destroying the ozone layer is enough reason for banning chlorine. Also notice that the negative in refuting the second claim did not put forth an argument against the resolution per se. They simply pointed out that the affirmative evidence being used to prove the claim was inadequate.

While it is true that in theory the negative does not have to introduce a single argument against the affirmative case and/or the resolution, most negatives will want to do so. Some of the arguments that the negative will initiate are called off-case arguments and will be discussed in detail in later chapters. For now, it is important to know that on these arguments the negative now takes on a burden of proof to substantiate them and the affirmative has presumption. Therefore, a tie on any of these issues goes to the affirmative and usually becomes a non-factor in the overall decision. (In other words, the affirmative will not win a debate just because one of many negative arguments results in a tie.)

Instead of just trying to poke holes in the affirmative arguments, the negative might want to "take the offensive." The negative may argue an off-case argument or a disadvantage to the plan. The negative might argue that the ban of chlorine would lead to the spread of water-born bacterial diseases, like cholera, and the suffering and death from cholera would outweigh the advantages gained from chlorine prohibition. The point here is that the negative would assume a burden of proof to demonstrate that a chlorine prohibition would result in an increase of the bacterium, *vibrio cholerae*, and thus an increase in US cholera cases. If the judge has a doubt at the debate's end as to the truth of this argument, then he or she should not vote for the negative on this argument. It becomes an unimportant argument in the outcome of the debate. However, the negative still might win the debate on another argument.

The Effect of Assigning the Burden of Proof

Thus it is obvious that the Burden of proof is indeed a burden. Debates on issues that are difficult to prove are often determined by who has the burden of proof and who enjoys presumption. A good example of the effect of assigning the burden of proof, as well as the on-case/off-case distinction, is found in the insanity plea in criminal law. It is very difficult to prove whether a defendant was sane or insane at the time the crime was committed. Most jurisdictions agree that if a defendant was insane, he should not be held criminally accountable for his actions.

Under federal law, the burden of proof is on the prosecutor to prove that the defendant was sane. It is thus part of a *prima-facie* case for murder and an affirmative burden. However, under California law, the burden is on the defense to prove that the defendant was not sane. It is thus an off-case argument for which the defense has the burden and the prosecutor holds presumption. You may remember the case of Richard Hinkley, who was accused in Federal court of attempting to murder President Reagan. The federal prosecutors were unable to prove that Hinkley was sane, and thus he could not be convicted of attempted murder. In a California court, the verdict might have been otherwise for no other reason than that he would be presumed sane until proven insane.

What happens when an initial burden is met?

There are two theories. One is referred to as the bubble burst theory, and the other as the theory of shifting presumption.

Under the bubble-burst theory, presumption is like a bubble, which bursts once the initial burden is met. After this point, there is no further presumption and the judge would somehow have to avoid a tie.

Under the shifting-presumption theory, presumption never vanishes, but the burden/presumption positions shift. Once the initial burden is met, the party which originally held the burden of proof now enjoys presumption, and the party which originally held presumption now has the burden to prove that the now presumed position is wrong. Some books have gone so far as to call this shifted presumption the burden of rebuttal, indicating that after the initial burden is met the party that initially held presumption now has a burden to rebut the newly-established position.

This is an older theory of debate that does not now enjoy popularity. Debate ballots used to be written so that the judge kept a record, rather like a slowly played tennis game, on which was recorded whether the speaker effectively hit the ball over the net. The team holding the ball at the end of the debate would lose, as they were unable to meet their burden of rebuttal and send the tennis ball back to their opponents.

The top perhaps 2% of all debates do tend to have this feeling of back and forth. We have all watched several debates in which the participants were so good that we were ready to assign the ballot after each speaker was through. However, most debates do not comprise speeches in which each speaker seems to hit an ace, to continue the tennis metaphor. (An ace occurs when the opponent cannot even reach the ball, let alone hit it back.) Most debates, even good ones, have a lot less clarity in terms of the eventual outcome.

Overall, we prefer to see debates as a set of mini-debates occurring simultaneously. The debaters must clarify the importance of each issue in the eventual outcome of the debate and clarify why it is that they may be winning a given position. Each debate probably boils down to 3–6 key issues, all of which must be weighed by the judge or judges. In multi-judge rounds, it's not unusual to see one judge vote for the negative on topicality, a second judge vote for the negative on the disadvantage, and a third judge vote for the affirmative on plan solvency. So to reduce a debate to a bursting-bubble or a tennis-game analogy is too simplistic. Really, there are a number of tennis games occurring simultaneously, and it takes a critical and well-trained eye to watch them all at once.

The Burden of Clash

No matter which theory we use to explain the role of presumption and burdens, the negative cannot simply rest on its presumption and await victory. Once the party with the burden of proof has set forth an initial argument, the opposing party must respond to the argument or it is considered granted. The burden of clash is the burden to respond to an opponent's argument, or by silence grant it. This burden of response or clash grows out of one of the oldest principles of argumentation: **Silence means consent.**

The rule means that if 1) an opponent has made an argument and 2) you do not respond to it, it is assumed granted. The fact that you hold mental reservations is irrelevant; the judge cannot read your mind. For an argument or response to be considered by the judge it must be articulated. Your silence allows the judge to assume that you do not have an answer.

In intercollegiate debate, this rule is carried one step further. In tournament debate we find: **You must respond at your first opportunity.**

In a debate, the speeches alternate between the affirmative and the negative. If either party delayed its response, the opposing debaters may claim that, by implication, a concession has occurred. The only exception, in current practice, is that the second speaker for the negative in cross examination format or the member of the opposition in parliamentary debate may refute part of the affirmative's or prime minister's original case in their respective constructive speeches. Generally, however, at first opportunity you must respond to an argument raised by your opponent.

The Game-Room Analogy

Many of these rules about presumption and burden of proof may seem cumbersome. Be at ease; all difficult games, bridge, chess, *etc.*, require not only an understanding of the rules but also a watching of the game being played. Most likely, your instructor will take you through a learning process that will include 1) seeing a debate live and/or on videotape, 2) walking through a hypothetical classroom debate, and 3) participating in a practice or walk-through debate. If you've ever learned a difficult board or card game you went through the same process: you read the rules or had a friend explain them to you, you watched someone else play the game, you played a couple of practice rounds, then you played the game for real, referring to the rules now and then for guidance. Eventually after playing the game for a period of time, the once complicated rules became second-hand and even seemed fairly simple. Debate is no different. In fact, it would be absurd to think that you could learn to debate by simply reading a book, just as it would be absurd to think that you could learn to play bridge by reading a book on bridge. Reading the book is an important part of learning, but it is by no means the only part.

The Standards of Proof

So far in this chapter we've discussed how the resolution grants one party presumption and places on the other party the burden of proof. Once there is a burden of proof, the next issue to consider is how thoroughly the burden must be carried to win. This refers to the standard of proof. The standard of proof is the degree of certainty to which a claim must be proven in order to warrant its adoption by the judge. In a debate, since the affirmative is asserting the resolution, it is the degree of certainty to which they must prove their case in order to win.

Common standards of proof in English are found in terms such as possibly, plausibly, probably, and certainly. The British logician Steven Toulmin (in different editions of his theory) calls these terms qualifiers or modalities. Such terms indicate the "degree of certainty with which the claim is presented." As qualifiers they set the burden of proof for the advocate of a claim. Similar concepts in mathematics are shown by such symbols as ~ (approximately), ± (equal within a range of error, i.e. probably), and = (meaning exactly equal). In each case the advocate of the claim has set the standard for which he is responsible. In each case, the advocate has the burden. Now consider how different the burdens are in proving each of the following:

1) It is *possible* that intelligent extraterrestrial life exists.
2) It is *plausible* that intelligent extraterrestrial life exists.
3) It is *probable* that intelligent extraterrestrial life exists.
4) It is *certain* that intelligent extraterrestrial life exists.

In fact, the concept of standards of proof are as finely graded as language (or mathematics) will allow. Consider the gradations in the following terms (separated by the mathematical sign < for is less than):

> just possible < possible <very possible < plausible
> <very plausible < probable <highly probable < certain

Each of these terms suggests a degree of certainty greater than that to its left and less than that to its right. Parallel terms, such as "it is our consensus," or "it's conceivable that" are almost infinite.

However, for convenience, we may group them into four categories.

Standard 1: Possibility.   This is the lowest standard of proof and hence the easiest to uphold. Imagine one is playing bridge. In bridge each of the 52 cards are dealt out to four players. What is the likelihood that all of the clubs will be dealt to the first player, all of the diamonds to the second player, all of the hearts to the third player and all of the spades to the fourth player? The answer is, is that this is not very likely at all. The odds of this occurring are extremely remote. If one were to keep dealing out all of the cards and had an infinite amount of time, then at some point this would happen. But I don't suspect that I will ever see this occur in my bridge playing days. However, it is possible.

Referring back the extraterrestrial life resolution, the advocate has a low standard to meet because he must only show that a reasonable person should consider intelligent extraterrestrial life, by some definition, a possibility. This burden is so low that possible resolutions are rarely debated. Perhaps this is because a reasonable person with an open mind would consider just about anything possible.

However, within resolutions with higher degrees of cogency an issue of possibility may become important as a minor issue. For example, a debate on nuclear power might include an issue being raised about the degree of risk (possibility) that a meltdown would occur. While it is only possible that a given nuclear plant may meltdown, it may still be important when considering the overall net-worth of the nuclear-power industry.

Standard 2: Plausibility.   This standard suggests that the claim has a relatively good chance of being true, but one that still is less likely than likely to be true.

Assume a standard set of 52 cards. There are 13 clubs, 13 diamonds, 13 hearts, and 13 spades. Now, take out one of the clubs, one of the diamonds, and one the hearts leaving all of the spades in the deck. Shuffle the cards and select a card at random. Will it be a club, diamond, heart, or spade? Because there are more spades in the deck than another suit, this is the most likely suit. However there is still a better likelihood that a spade will not turn up then that one will. Remember there are only 13 spades in the deck and 36 cards of different suits. Spades is the most plausible suit you will draw, but it is still a relative long shot. Plausibility, if it could be quantified, might fall between the 20% and 49% level of likelihood.

Standard 3: Probability.   The classic phrasing of this standard is that the judge must consider the claim to be "more likely true than not true."

The probable standard would literally require only that the claim be true "more probably than not." This is the classic standard of proof relevant to civil cases at law. To show how finely this line might be drawn, assume one has a pack of playing cards (suits only, no jokers, literal or metaphorical). One could not prove that it is probable I will draw a black card because the chances of drawing a black or red card are exactly equal. However, take from the deck just the 2 of hearts (a red card) and it is now probable that one will draw a black card because there are more of them in the deck than there are red cards. Technically, this is all that it means to say something is probable. I suspect, however, that most people asked to quantify the term would express probability as 60%, 70%, or more.

Most debate resolutions assume a high degree of probability as their starting point. In other words, possibility is not enough, nor is certainty normally required.

Standard 4: Certainty.   The fourth standard of certainty is expressed in criminal cases at law as proof "beyond a reasonable doubt and to a moral certainty that the accused committed the alleged crime." With no pun intended, we might say that believing something to be certainly true is a conviction in which we have considerable faith.

As examples of certainty, most of us are convinced to a standard of certainty that the earth is round and that human life exists. To return to our pack of cards, absolute certainty of drawing a black card could only be gained if we took away all the red ones. Suppose we left just the 2 of Hearts. Now our chances are literally 1 in 27 of drawing a red card. Is this certainty? Each of us must determine what certainty is for the claim offered. In a criminal trial, the witnesses could all be lying. In a debate on extraterrestrial life, the data could all be falsified, or subject to some error of perception so fundamental to Twentieth Century Western Culture that we cannot detect it.

It is worth mentioning that the phrase "beyond a shadow of a doubt" is never used in law. The theory is that no reasonable person would be certain to this degree unless he/she had personally witnessed the acts alleged. Therefore, convictions would not be possible. When we consider that "a reasonable person might consider anything possible" and "a reasonable person would always entertain doubts" one might fairly conclude that uncertainty is the price of an open mind.

Determining the Applicable Standard for Fact and Value Propositions

For simple propositions of fact and value, the standard of proof is usually assumed to be one of probability. Unless the issue is susceptible to statistical analysis, probability is ultimately a subjective judgment. However, we can at least determine the appropriate standard: The implied standard for a proposition of fact or value is probability unless some other standard is stated or implied.

Certain types of propositions of fact and value state not only the fact to be acknowledged or attitude to be justified but set the burden for proving this relative to something else. This example is a resolution of relative fact, or arguably of relative value, "Resolved: that the theory of creation is as worthy of belief as is the theory of evolution." It would be fact if the accepted empirical standards of science were applied to both theories, value if creation is argued as worthy of belief on theological rather than empirical grounds.

In this resolution an affirmative could win by simply proving both theories are true only to a level of possibility. The affirmative does not have to prove that creation is the correct theory. Thus, the burden on the affirmative is set by the level of proof possible for evolution.

Consider this example: "Resolved: that modern art is more to be condemned than approved" (a balance proposition of value). In this resolution, the attitude proposed is not just condemnation (which would be a proposition of simple value) but that the arguments against modern art outweigh those in favor of modern art. Again, the burden on the affirmative is set by the arguments the negative can produce.

The standard of proof in both these examples remains probability, but the burden is lessened. Thus, one must show that the theory of creation is probably more worthy of belief than the theory of evolution, but the burden set by the resolution is limited to proving a relative truth.

Determining the Applicable Standard for Policy Propositions

In dealing with propositions of policy, a slightly more precise formulation is possible. The automatic standard of proof for any policy may be phrased thus:

The standard of proof for the adoption of a policy is the risk incurred in taking the proposed action. The risk is the product of the (1) magnitude of the possible disadvantages, (2) the likelihood of their occurrence, and (3) the difficulty of correcting the disadvantages (such as, the difficulty in reversing the entire proposition, if necessary) if they do occur. Formulated mathematically, it would be $R = S \times L \times C$ (Risk = Significance of Disadvantages × Likelihood of Occurrence × Difficulty of Correction). For instance when one has a resolution such as "Resolved: that we should go to the movies," the standard is determined by the certain disadvantage that it will cost money, which cannot be reversed once it is paid.

Thus, there are three essential requirements for any resolution. First, it must be clear to parties in the debate. Second, it must correctly delineate the assignments of the resolution. Third, it must state the intent of the framer.

The last of these is the least technical and the most difficult. It simply asks "did the framer say what he meant."

The Bowling Ball Analogy

Imagine a bowling alley. The bowling ball is sent down the alley toward the distant pins. The presumption is that it will hit the pins unless deflected. The bowling ball will obey Newton's First Law of Motion: objects in motion tend to remain in motion unless acted upon by an outside force. The bowling ball has painted on it the words status quo. Its inertia as it rolls down the alley is presumption. At some point along the alley, a foot reaches out to push the ball off its course. On that foot is painted the word the affirmative. The burden is on the foot to change the course of the ball. The amount of force necessary to change the ball from its course is the standard of proof. If the affirmative does not succeed in deflecting the course of the status quo it will go on its previous course and continue down the alley.

The Requirement to State the Intent of the Framer

A resolution may be clear, but not say what the framer of the resolution intended to say. If the framer is the affirmative in a formal debate he cannot escape by saying "but that's not what I meant." The negative and the judge have the right to take the framer at his word. Judges and negatives cannot read minds and should not be expected to.

In personal critical thinking, one should likewise try to put one's thoughts into words for the sake of clarity. A basic part of argumentation is the process of making feelings explicit, and therefore susceptible to analysis. Note that even in psychotherapy the patient is encouraged to talk out his feelings in order to understand them.

Thus the simplest, least technical, and most difficult task involving resolutions is standing back from the resolution one has just written, and ask "Is this what I wish to decide?"

An early assignment in our own argumentation classes is for students, either in groups or individually, to write a number of resolutions which 1) are debatable claims, 2) assign the duties of the resolution correctly, and 3) state the intent of the writer.

Consider the following resolution, which turned out not to represent the intent of the framer.

Resolved: that we stop using nuclear energy.

When asked to clarify "we" the response was "all of us." When asked to clarify "nuclear energy" the response was "all kinds." What this person meant to say was "Resolved: that the federal government should phase out the use of nuclear power for the generation of electricity." But that isn't what was said, and consider the problems. Under the resolution the student phrased:

1. We don't know whether the resolution is meant to predict that we will stop using nuclear energy (a proposition of future fact) or that we should stop using it (a proposition of policy).

2. We don't know whether this action is to be taken by each individual consumer, (who would then have to shut off his power lines if they're supplied by a nuclear power plant), the State government, the Federal government, or some worldwide organization. Consider how different the arguments would be for each of these agents.

3. We would immediately have to stop. The word stop is unmodified. This means that power plants would have to shut down the minute the resolution is passed. The disruption to society would be staggering. Just in terms of investment, billions of dollars would be lost.

4. The term "nuclear energy" is unmodified and is very broad. As phrased, it would encompass not only power stations (which was all that was intended), but also the use of radio-isotopes in medicine, the power plants on nuclear submarines (which would have to be immediately dry-docked), and technically includes solar power (since the sun uses fission to produce light).

The student had simply never stopped to think what the words explicitly meant. As stated, the resolution was so vague that it allowed legitimate interpretations that collectively would have put the affirmative in a hopeless position. The moral is that when you put the word Resolved: in front of a debatable proposition you take on the task of wording the resolution so that it says to another what you think it says to you.

GUIDELINES FOR WORDING RESOLUTIONS

1) Determine the nature of the underlying question. If you merely want to know whether or not some statement is true, phrase it as a proposition/resolution of fact. If you want to determine your attitude towards something, phrase it as a proposition/ resolution of value. Only if you want to evaluate a potential action is a policy resolution necessary.

You might simply want to determine whether or not Elvis Presley is alive. If so, the question would be one of fact and the resolution would be "Resolved: that Elvis Presley is alive." If you wish to shape an attitude but not pass a law, the question would be one of evaluation, and the resolution might be "Resolved: Elvis Presley is/was a great musician." If you wish to seek something done, the question would be one of policy, and possible resolutions might be "Resolved: that the alleged body of Elvis Presley should be exhumed to determine its identity" or "Resolved: that Elvis Presley's birthday should become a national music holiday."

2) Keep the resolution as simple as possible, but be prepared upon request to clarify any term. If you want to debate nuclear testing as policy, you might have the wording Resolved: that nuclear testing should be made illegal. The phrase "made illegal" implies government action, and you should be prepared to clarify which government you mean. You may mean "the United Nations or the federal government if they'll do it, or the state government if they won't," but plug that into the resolution proper and one gets, "Resolved: that the UN or federal government, if they'll do it, or the state government, if the UN and feds won't, should make nuclear testing illegal." At the very least, the phrasing is awkward.

You will later find that many concepts which would be unclear in the resolution are clarified by the affirmative providing definitions early in the debate. In legislatures, an anti-nuclear testing bill might require dozens of pages of technical language, and that whole bill would be "the resolution as defined." In any case, the resolution in a debate round must be simple. Determine the status quo first. Let's say that you find that nuclear testing is already illegal, but you find a loophole that says computer testing is okay. So you may word a resolution: "Resolved: that the US federal government should ban computerized nuclear testing."

3) Avoid combining separate ideas unless that combination is uniquely desired for very specific reasons. For example, "Resolved: that the federal government should ban abortion and create a national adoption agency" combines the concepts of "banning abortions" and "creating a national adoption agency." Clearly it is possible to implement either one without the other. If one only wishes to debate the banning of abortions, the concept of a national adoption agency does not need to appear in the resolution. On the other hand, if a framer wants both to be debated and feels they should be considered together, combining the ideas is okay under unique circumstances. Those circumstances may involve debating both ideas in front of a club or organization that wants to hear a debate on both issues at once or perhaps there is a bill before Congress that addresses both issues and your argumentation teacher wants both debated within the same resolution. Of course such a resolution now carries a double burden of proof. The best resolution entertains only one central idea because debaters are not allowed to divide the question into its two parts, as they may if they were engaged in a meeting using parliamentary procedure.

4) **Avoid overemotional or biased language.** It clouds thinking. Resolutions need to be written using neutral terminology. The wording of the resolution should be acceptable to both the affirmative and the negative. If one is debating the issue of abortion, it would not serve fairness, sensitivity, or education to phrase the resolution "Resolved: that the butchering of unborn babies should be stopped." Even if you believe that is what abortion amounts to, it would be fairer to word it: "Resolved: that the federal government should ban abortion, except to save the life of the mother." For an additional example, it is also biased to write a resolution which says, "Resolved: the illegal slaughter of Iraqi people in the name of oil that the Western media calls the Iraq war is totally unjustified." Instead, it should be worded "Resolved: that the most recent US war against Iraq was unjustified."

5) **Keep the arguments balanced on both sides.** Another way of looking at this is that the resolution should provide fair argumentative ground to both sides. If a resolution is worded in a way that a reasonable person would not be able to defend one of the sides of the resolution, it fails to be a debatable resolution. Remember, to be debatable, a resolution must contain controversy. Thus, the purpose of writing a resolution should be to keep the arguments on each side of the resolution somewhat equal. A resolution, such as, "Resolved: That poverty is extremely beneficial" or "Resolved: that the sun rotates around the earth" fails this test. It would be very difficult for the affirmative to argue in support of such topics. The national topic committee for CEDA goes to great lengths to do a literature check to ensure that arguments on each side of the resolution are balanced.

However, without the scrutiny of a committee of debate scholars, it is easy to form a resolution that favors one side over the other. A resolution such as "Resolved: That the US federal government should adopt the policies of Karl Marx and Frederick Engels" is one such resolution. There would be very little written in the unbiased literature that would aid an affirmative team in its research. That's not to say that this wouldn't be a fascinating debate; however, there would be a stronger presumption for the negative than is fair. While debate should be about questioning assumptions, the resolution's wording is not usually the place for such overt questioning to occur. However, many intercollegiate debaters will argue on many resolutions issues like socialism, world government, anarchy, and so on, but forcing all debaters to argue such issues in every round would be unfair.

6) Correctly place the burden of proof and presumption. We have spent much of this chapter on this point. Remember that the affirmative must propose a change in the status quo. A resolution like "Resolved: that the United States should keep the Electoral College" is incorrectly worded. This resolution gives the affirmative the advantage of defending the status quo (i.e., presumption) and has given the negative the burden of proof of showing why we should not keep the Electoral College. The resolution should have been worded "Resolved: That the United States should abolish the Electoral College," as this forces the affirmative to argue for a change in the status quo and allows the negative to defend the status quo.

7) Don't include the rational for adoption of the resolution in the wording. A resolution should only consist of what the writer wishes to see adopted, not why they think it should adopted. The reasons for adopting the resolution will be raised in the debate. For example, the resolution "Resolved: that the war against Iraq was unjustified because it led to the deaths of many Iraqi civilians" is incorrectly worded. It should simply state, "Resolved: That the war against Iraq was unjustified." Affirmatives could raise the deaths of Iraqi civilians as part of their case if they desired.

Summary

Before this chapter you should have been able to distinguish the technical use of the term argumentation from the lay term argument. You should have understood what is meant by debate. You should have understood the meaning of the reasonable-person model. You should have been able to start at the point at which someone makes a claim and trace it to the point at which it can be called a debatable claim.

In this chapter we saw that when one intends a debatable claim to be the focus of a debate, one converts it into a resolution. It has been seen that the resolution provides the focus for the debate. Any resolution is largely a matter of assigning presumption and burdens and setting the standard of proof. These are the most important technical matters to consider in proposing a resolution. Any resolution must also state the desired decision.

CHAPTER 4

FUNDAMENTALS OF ACADEMIC DEBATE

This chapter attempts to explain how academic debate is currently being practiced at intercollegiate debate tournaments. This is not to suggest that this is how you will debate in your argumentation classes. However, many instructors of argumentation classes are current debate coaches, former debate coaches, or former tournament competitors. As such, many of them will adopt the current tournament practice for your classroom. For example, many of you may end up debating the current CEDA or NDT (cross-examination) topics in your classroom, utilizing almost the identical format that would be used in a debate tournament. Others of you will end up debating NPDA (parliamentary) style using similar tournament rules. Some of you may do both. However, not all argumentation instructors are current or former debate coaches and/or competitors. And even if they are, it does not automatically mean they will use a tournament model for their classroom debates. Therefore, some of you will be introduced to your instructor's own format, which might be very similar or very different from those used at academic debate tournaments.

Since there are an endless number of formats your instructor could use for your classroom debates, it would be impossible for any text to cover them. That is why this chapter is devoted to discussing the most dominant formats being used in the current academic debate community. If your instructor does choose to use a tournament Model of Debate you will then find this chapter extremely helpful. Even if your instructor uses a different format, this chapter should still be very helpful because the principles, techniques, and strategies discussed herein should overlap easily with whatever format your instructor may choose.

ACADEMIC DEBATE

Our present tradition of interscholastic debating goes back to the Oxford and Cambridge Debate Unions in Britain. These were, and are, modeled on the House of Commons and give the best students in the Commonwealth an opportunity to develop their thinking and leadership skills.

Academic debate, as presently practiced in colleges, universities and high schools, is a highly structured competition between individuals (Lincoln/Douglas debate) or two-person teams (team debate). A debate may use any number of different formats, including a cross-examination format or a parliamentary format. This book attempts to integrate both formats. A typical debate round lasts anywhere from one hour to two hours, depending on time constraints. College debaters need to be prepared to debate both the affirmative and negative sides of a resolution. A **resolution,** the focus of a debate, is a declarative statement of fact, value, or policy, worded in unbiased terms. An example of a resolution is "Resolved: That the American judicial system has overemphasized freedom of the press." An affirmative advocate or team would support that resolution; the negative side would refute the affirmative's case. In a parliamentary format, the government supports the resolution, and the opposition, as the name indicates, refutes the government's case. Figure 4.1 lists the different time constraints for speakers in each of the different types of debate. As you

CROSS-EXAM	L/D CROSS-EXAM	PARLIAMENTARY
1AC 9 minutes	1AC 9 minutes	PM 7 minutes
c/x 3 minutes	c/x 3 minutes	
1NC 9 minutes	1NC 13 minutes	LO 8 minutes
c/x 3 minutes	c/x 3 minutes	
2AC 9 minutes		MG 8 minutes
c/x 3 minutes		
2NC 9 minutes		MO 8 minutes
c/x 3 minutes		
1NR 5 minutes		LO 4 minutes
1AR 5 minutes	1AR 6 minutes	PM 5 minutes
2NR 5 minutes	1NR 6 minutes	
2AR 5 minutes	2AR 4 minutes	

KEY

A C	Affirmative Constructive	1__	First
N C	Negative Constructive	2__	Second
N R	Negative Rebuttal	c/x	Cross-Examination
A R	Affirmative Rebuttal	L/D	Lincoln/Douglas
PM	Prime Minister	LO	Leader of the Opposition
MG	Member of the Government	MO	Member of the Opposition

FIGURE 4.1

Traditional Speaking Order and Time Constraints

will note, in team debate each speaker gives one constructive speech and one rebuttal speech. In Lincoln/Douglas (LD) debate, the same is true except that the affirmative speaker gives two rebuttal speeches to compensate for the longer negative constructive (12 minutes). In the parliamentary format, there are no formal questioning periods; instead the debaters may raise points of information during opponents' presentations. During those points of information, advocates ask questions. Additionally, note that the parliamentary format has only two rebuttals. The Prime Minister and the Leader of the Opposition give the only rebuttals.

In all three formats, the main purpose of a constructive speech is to build arguments. The main purpose of a rebuttal speech is to refute an opponent's arguments and rebuild your original ones.

Finally, debate is a contest that is judged by an impartial third party. In intercollegiate competition, that third party is usually a forensics coach, a speech communication professor, a graduate student, or a former debate competitor. In the argumentation classroom, that third party is the instructor, a guest lecturer, and/or your fellow students. Most critics, as well as debaters, take comprehensive notes on what are called flowsheets. Normally, a flowsheet is nothing more than a pad of paper with each of the speeches in the debate written in shorthand in columns side by side, starting with the first affirmative constructive (1AC) and ending with the second affirmative rebuttal (2AR). In parliamentary debate, the contest begins with the Prime Minister's constructive and ends with the Prime Minister's rebuttal. The critic evaluates the debate based on his/her notes. A failure to respond to an argument appears as a blank spot on the flow-sheet corresponding to the speaker who is guilty of dropping the argument. Usually, a failure to respond results in an opponents' advantage on that particular issue. The critic also evaluates his or her notes to see which debater or team had better reasoning, analysis, and evidence on each of the other issues in the debate. The debater or team that he or she feels did the better job of debating wins the debate. Speaker points are based on the critic's evaluation of a debater's delivery, reasoning, organization, poise, and content.

DISTINCTIONS MADE BETWEEN PARLIAMENTARY AND CROSS-EXAMINATION DEBATE

The debate world is changing rapidly. What may be true today of academic debate may not be true tomorrow. For example, there is nothing in Cross-Examination Debate Association's rules that require use of quotations. Therefore, shortly after publication of this book, CEDA could begin sponsoring parliamentary-style debate. Conversely and just as unlikely, the NPDA could begin allowing use of prepared material.

Therefore, in the context of this book, we will be making a fairly artificial distinction between the two formats of debate. Parliamentary debate will refer to the lay-audience-centered debate format that prohibits the use of prepared material.

Cross-examination debate will refer to a specialized-audience, quotation-based form of debating. We realize that these distinctions are artificial and that one could find parliamentary debates that are not lay-audience centered. And one could find cross-examination debates that are highly enjoyable, lay-audience events. However, it is our experience that a median debate from each format would match our descriptions.

Throughout this book we will be integrating these generalizations in discussions of each of the major topics. We do this so that the argumentation teacher or forensics coach, who has a predisposition toward one format over the other, will be able to use this book to help his or her students learn the art of debate. In fact, the authors of this book feel very strongly that both formats of debate are extremely beneficial.

At the same time that we're making this artificial distinction, much that is true of one form of debate is true of the other. Therefore, at times we will draw a distinction between parliamentary and cross-examination, and at times we will assume similarity. For example, at times the word *affirmative* is synonymous with the word *government*, and the word *negative* is synonymous with the word *opposition*. When we want to make a distinction, we will do so overtly.

PARLIAMENTARY DEBATE

Parliamentary debate is molded after the type of debate that theoretically takes place in a house of parliament. This style of debate places a high emphasis on the use of whit, humor and rhetorical skill. The National Parliamentary Debate Association (NPDA) is the intercollegiate association most closely associated with this style of debate. Following will be a discussion of the pros and cons of Parliamentary debate followed by a description of the currently practiced rules, guidelines and procedures that are now being utilized.

Pros and Cons of Parliamentary Debate

There are many reasons for students to compete in parliamentary debate. First, as currently practiced, intercollegiate parliamentary debate is easier for the novice or beginning student. The National Parliamentary Debate Association, the intercollegiate organization that sponsors parliamentary debate, began several years ago with a philosophy of making debate more accessible to all students. CEDA and NDT debate, as currently practiced, seem to encourage a type of debate that rewards extremely rapid rates of speaking and extensive researching of the topic. Such debate emphasizes the content of the message. There are many benefits to debating NDT and CEDA, but accessibility of the beginner is not one of them.

Parliamentary, on the other hand, takes the emphasis off of rapid speaking and extensive research and asks its competitors to be more communicative instead. Rather than look at debate as an activity with emphasis on content, parliamentary debate chooses to view debate as an activity with emphasis on public speaking. Parliamentary competitors do not have to spend as much time as their NDT and CEDA counterparts researching a topic or learning to speak rapidly. In fact, current rules in intercollegiate parliamentary debate prohibit the use of prepared material by debaters. Additionally, each 55 minute round requires a new resolution, meaning that intercollegiate competitors argue dozens of different resolutions throughout the course of a season. Thus, accessibility to the beginner and diversity of the topics are advantages of parliamentary debate. Add to those the perk of a good debate format that lay audiences tend to prefer.

The first disadvantage of parliamentary debate involves substance rather than form. It's sad to say but generally true that many of our college students are not knowledgeable about philosophy, current events, political science, history, and cultural diversity. This makes watching some novice parliamentary debates truly demoralizing for any serious educator. On the upside, it does gives educators a clear barometer of what students need to know in order to function in our world. Clearly, anyone who wants to be successful in parliamentary debate must research, read, and understand the basics of each major discipline, some of which are mentioned above.

A second disadvantage of parliamentary debate is that, because of the 15-minute limitation on preparation time and the evidentiary restrictions promulgated by many tournament directors, it is difficult to know whether the government or the opposition has the better grasp of the facts. A key ingredient of most other intercollegiate debating forums is the verifiability of evidence. In parliamentary debate, providing for the verifiability of the evidence is often difficult, making the discernment of the truth on a given issue nearly impossible. In fact, at the world championships, some teams were so fond of the limitations on evidence that they were said to "lie like rugs." Of course, unethical behavior, such as purposefully lying, is prohibited by every code of forensics ethics ever written. However, this just goes to show how problematic the limitations on verifiable evidence can be. A debater may refer to *The Grapes of Wrath*, for example, but he or she may not bring in a copy to read aloud in a parliamentary speech. That is prohibited by most tournament rules.

Topics for Parliamentary Debate

The student engaging in Parliamentary debate must be cognizant of two critical characteristics of the event. The first is that the resolution for each debate round will be different and the second is that no source material is allowed during the debate. As a result, debaters must keep themselves familiar with current events. Students should be reading current event magazines (*Time, Newsweek, The Economist, Foreign Affairs*, etc.), daily newspapers (*Christian Science Monitor, LA Times, NY Times*, etc.) and watching television news shows (*The News Hour with Jim Lehrer, Cross Fire, The McGloughlin Group*, etc.). Students should not just be familiar with what is happening, but should also be cognizant of the different perspectives on why they are happening and their implications on society. Students should also be reading works on political science, philosophy, and other such disciplines. The more informed students are the better success they will probably experience in parliamentary debate.

At the beginning of each debate round, the critic will state the resolution for that particular round. Currently there are two ways this is done. The first is the single-topic method. The judge has one topic and simply reads it. The second method is the three-topic method. The Judge will have three topics for the debaters to choose from. The Government and Opposition will each strike one of the three topics, with the remaining topic being debated. As of the writing of this book, topics can usually be classified into one of three categories: current event policy, current event value/fact and metaphor.

As its name suggests, current-event policy topics require the Government to advocate a policy change. Examples include "This house should abolish affirmative action" and "The United States should pass term limits for Congressional Representatives."

Current event value/fact resolutions make up the second category. Possible resolutions include "This house disapproves of current US foreign policy toward China" and "The Green Party cost Al Gore the 2000 Presidential Election."

Metaphors make up the third category and are usually the most troublesome for students new to debate. Examples include "This house would rage against the machine" and "Canyons are preferable to mountains." Metaphorical topics are difficult because they are vague. After all, what does "this house would rage against the machine" mean? When faced with a topic such as this, the Government will usually parametracize the topic. That is, they will interpret the topic to mean one concrete idea. For instance, maybe "this house" means the United Nations, and maybe "rage against the machine" means to abolish North Korea's nuclear capacity. As long as the Government's interpretation provides fair ground, the Opposition will usually be required to accept the Government's interpretation.

Effective Utilization of Preparation Time

After receiving the topic from the judge, the debate teams will have a specified amount of preparation time, usually 15 minutes, to prepare their arguments. Depending on the tournament (or classroom) rules, you may or may not be able to consult with individuals other than your partner or reference outside materials. During the preparation period, both the government and the opposition should try to accomplish a few things.

First, they should decide who will speak first. Remember that while each debater will give a constructive speech, only the first speaker for the government, called the Prime Minister and the first speaker for the opposition, called the Leader of the Opposition, will give a summary speech. There are several variables that might influence who will speak first for each team. Some considerations might include who is more familiar with the resolution, who has the most debate experience, and who is the better speaker.

Second, the debaters should determine if the resolution, as interpreted, is one of fact, value, or policy. This should help guide the debaters as to what might be the most appropriate and effective arguments to raise. If the resolution is of a factual nature the debaters will want to develop the stock issues of definitions and application. If it is a value resolution the definitions, criterion and application stock issues should be developed. And of course if it is a policy resolution the stock issues of motive, blame, cure and cost should be explored. These stock issues were discussed in Chapter 2, and are covered in much greater depth in Chapters 13 (factual propositions), 14 (value propositions) and 15 (policy propositions).

Third, the debate teams, especially the Government, must decide on the resolution's interpretation. This of course is crucial when the topic is a metaphor. While the Government gets to decide on the case area to be debated they must be careful to provide fair ground for the Opposition. If they interpret the resolution too narrowly or too obscurely, the Opposition might be able to convince the judge that the Government's interpretation is unfair, insignificant, or too limiting and thus win the debate. The Opposition really is at a disadvantage on metaphorical topics. While the Government knows exactly what they will debate, the negative can only "wait and see." However, the Opposition can do at least two things to get ready. First, they can try to anticipate the case area the Government might choose. Think about the major current topics that seem most appropriate. There is a good chance the affirmative will select one of these. Second, think of some generic philosophical objections to the topic as a whole. For instance, on the "rage against the machine" topic, the Opposition might develop arguments on how "rage" implies a loss of emotional control like when someone losses their temper. They might then argue why taking any actions under such a state of mind is undesirable. Such a line of analysis would probably link to any government case.

One intriguing, though rarely chosen, option open to the Government is to advance a **temporal-displacement** (or time-warp) case; that is, the Government can for the purposes of the debate, shift the debate to a different era—past or future. The debaters are then to debate the resolution as if they were in that era. Hence, only information that people of that era would know about can be used in the debate. For example, if the Government moved the debate to the 1800s then references to the United Nations would be invalid since the United Nations did not exist until 1945. The Government can also shift the debate to the future so that the debate is taking place on the bridge of the Enterprise (a spaceship highlighted in the popular and fictional *Star Trek* series, but which for the purposes of your debate could become a real spaceship of the future). In this scenario, arguments based on warp speed (faster-than-light-speed) technology and alien threats (Borg, Klingon, or other) would be valid. The Government may not use temporal displacement cases to create an unfair advantage over the negative. The negative must still have reasonable ground. This means that the Government may NOT select narrow interpretations of the future that disallow any other possibilities.

Fourth, specific arguments that support your side of the resolution should be developed. All arguments and examples must be within the scope of common knowledge.

Finally, all four debaters should anticipate the arguments that they think their opponents will raise and think of counter arguments. When the preparation time expires, the debate begins. Once the debate begins, debaters should be aware that there is no preparation time between speeches. When one debater relinquishes the floor, the next debater should be up and speaking within 15 seconds.

Basic Speaker Responsibilities for Parliamentary Debate

The following is a brief description of the basic responsibilities for each debater. While there are no set rules on what each speaker must do, the following should serve as a good basis for what is usually done and what most critics usually expect. There of course can be exceptions based on the idiosyncrasies of any particular round.

Prime Minister

The Prime Minister (PM) begins the debate. In this opening constructive the PM should do a few things. Traditionally, the PM will begin by thanking all those present. This includes the Opposition team, his/her partner, the Speaker of the House and any audience members. These remarks communicate respect for all those involved, reaffirm a feeling of collegiality, and make it clear that the topic (not the opposing team) is the focus of the arguments. After thanking everyone, it is sometimes effective to begin with an opening device which sets the tone for the Government's case. This may consist of a narrative, quotation, rhetorical question, or other effective device. Third the PM should state the resolution and his/her support for the resolution. Fourth, the key terms of the resolution should be defined. Fifth, a criterion should be introduced if a value is being debated. Finally, a series of well structured arguments in favor of the resolution should be made. Each argument should be supported by reference to common knowledge information. The more organized this opening speech is, the better the debate will be. Try to incorporate a little whit and humor while still maintaining a serious and professional demeanor. This speech sets the tone for the entire debate.

Leader of the Opposition

The Leader of the Opposition (LO) speaks after the PM has finished. Like the PM, the LO should begin by thanking everyone present. There are three classifications of arguments for the LO to advance: procedural, case refutation, and off-case arguments.

Procedural arguments should be introduced first. If the Opposition believes that the Government's interpretation is not relevant to the resolution, they should immediately argue a topicality argument. Carefully 1) explain your interpretation of the resolution, 2) why you believe it is a superior interpretation than the Government's and 3) demonstrate how the Government's case is not relevant under this interpretation.

The second procedural argument to consider is significance. Here the Opposition argues that the Government interpretation simply is not a large enough "slice of the pie." For instance, assume the topic being debated is "That US foreign policy should be condemned" and the Government is able to demonstrate the North American Free Trade Agreement is harmful. The Opposition might argue that NAFTA is just one of numerous foreign policies and that it is unwarranted to generalize to all US foreign policy based on one isolated example. The third procedural argument to consider is moral-ground abuse. Moral Ground Abuse occurs when the Government's interpretation, while perhaps being topical and significant, places the Opposition on morally untenable ground. An example of this would be if the Government's interpretation would require the Opposition to defend racial segregation laws. Finally, the Opposition might challenge the Government's criterion and offer a new one.

Next, the LO will want to address the specific substantive arguments presented by the PM. These are known as the case arguments. It is usually best if the LO can follow the same structure as that laid out by the PM. Remember that if you fail to address an argument advanced by the PM, many critics will consider it granted. Try to say something against the major issues presented by the PM. Even if you grant an argument, try to point out why it is not that important to the debate as a whole.

Finally, the LO should present the opposition arguments by giving well organized and structured arguments against the resolution. These off-case arguments usually do not directly deny arguments made by the PM but are arguments against the resolution as a whole. For example, on the "US foreign policy should be condemned" topic, the Opposition should try to give positive examples of US foreign policy to counter the NAFTA example.

It is important for the LO to put out a number of different types of arguments. Think of the PM's speech as making up the hull of a boat. The job of the LO is to drill as many holes into the bottom of the hull as possible to help sink the ship. Some arguments may represent larger holes than others. Indeed, one argument might be so large that it alone could sink the ship (like topicality). However, in most cases, it will take an accumulation of holes to bring down the affirmative. The more holes that are drilled into the boat, the more difficult it becomes for the Government to patch them up.

Member of the Government

The Member of Government (MG) needs to both defend their team's original position and refute the Opposition's case if one was introduced. To extend the boat analogy, the MG must patch up all of the holes drilled by the LO. If the opposition challenged the Government's interpretation of the resolution, the MG must show why the Government's interpretation is superior. If the criterion was challenged, then it must be defended. If a disadvantage was introduced, it must be mitigated. In simple terms, the MG must respond to all of the arguments presented by the LO. Remember, if an argument is not responded to, that argument is normally granted. Failure to respond to one critical argument (like topicality) could cost the round. It is best to follow the same structure as that presented by the LO.

Member of the Opposition

The Member of the Opposition (MO) is the final constructive of the debate. It is also one of the most strategic speeches of the debate. The MO has two general strategies. The first is to try and cover all of the original arguments presented by the LO and show why the MG's arguments were not sufficient to patch the holes. The advantage of this strategy is that it can overload the Prime Minister's summary speech making it hard for the PM to cover all of the issues in only five minutes. The disadvantage of this strategy is that it prevents the MO from developing in great depth any one particular argument. The analysis tends to be more superficial.

The second strategy is to select only a few of the LO's arguments and to explain in great depth the importance of those arguments and why the Opposition is winning those arguments. Utilizing this strategy, the MO analyzes the responses made by the MG and then decides to go after only those issues which they believe the MG did not handle well. The remaining arguments are dropped out of the round. For example, the MO might decide to go after only topicality and one disadvantage and not address other arguments introduced by the LO. Of course, if the LO only introduced a few arguments, it would make sense to cover all of them. This strategy works best when the LO introduces numerous arguments with the intent of overloading the MG. If only a few arguments are introduced by the LO it is fairly easy for the MG to cover them. But introduce six, seven, or eight distinct lines of argument and things get much tougher on the MG. As the old saying goes, the LO throws a lot of mud against the wall and sees what sticks. The MO then focuses only on those arguments poorly handled by the MG.

One final strategy is for the MO to introduce entirely new arguments (like a new disadvantage, counterplan, etc.) than those presented by the LO. Be very cautious with this strategy as it is usually frowned upon. Many critics believe it is unethical for new issues to be introduced in this speech because the only chance the Government has to respond to them is in the Prime Minister's summary. In essence the MG has been silenced on these issues. The other reason to be very cautious about introducing new arguments in this speech is because the PM will be allowed to make new arguments against them as it is their first chance to respond. A good PM will try to turn these arguments in his or her summation. And remember, the Opposition will be out of speeches with which to respond!

Leader of the Opposition Rebuttal

This is the last speech for the Opposition in the debate. During this speech the LO summarizes the major Opposition's key arguments. No new arguments are allowed although new examples to extend existing arguments are sometimes allowed. During this speech the LO should try to put all of the arguments which have been presented into some context for the critic. What arguments are the most important and why? What are the implications of certain arguments being won or lost? How should the critic weigh competing value interests? The LO should attempt to answer these questions for the critic. In other words, it is the LO's job to put all of the pieces of the puzzle together. It is often a good idea to outline key voting issues for the judge to consider. You might open by saying "There are four key issues to this debate." Clearly go over each of those areas and explain the importance of those issues and why you believe you are winning them.

Prime Minister Rebuttal

This is the last speech of the debate and probably the most difficult. The Prime Minister must respond to two back-to-back Opposition speeches. No new arguments are allowed; although, new examples to extend existing arguments are sometimes allowed. The Prime Minister should also be aware of any new arguments presented by the MO. Since the Government has NOT had an opportunity to address these new arguments, the Speaker of the House usually gives a lot of leeway to the Prime Minister to make new arguments. If the LO has outlined their voting issues make sure that you address them. You don't want to lose a debate because you granted a voting issue by your silence! Point out why these Opposition voting issues are not key to the debate and/or why the Opposition is not winning those arguments. Next, outline your own set of voting issues. Don't get bogged down in a bunch of small, isolated arguments. In this last speech, the PM should try to draw the big picture for the critic.

Parliamentary Procedure

One of the intriguing aspects of parliamentary debate is the interaction that can take place between the Government, Opposition, Speaker of the House and even the audience. Debaters engaging in parliamentary debate thus need to have a fairly solid understanding of the basics of parliamentary procedure. There are four different areas of parliamentary procedure of which the debater should be aware. They are Points of Information, Points of Order, Points of Personal Privilege, and Points of Clarification. Closely related are the procedures for heckling and showing approval and/or disapproval. Effective Parliamentary debaters are able to use Parliamentary procedure to their advantage during the debate. The following section should give the beginning debater a fairly solid understanding of the different rules of parliamentary debate and how and when to utilize them during the debate. The following rules are based on current practice at most intercollegiate tournaments. Your instructor may choose to modify them for your classroom debates.

Points of Information

Points of Information take place when the debater holding the floor, that is, the person who is presently speaking, is asked a question by a member of the opposing team. For example, during the Prime Minister's opening speech, both the Leader of the Opposition and/or the Member of the Opposition may ask questions of the Prime

Minister. The following are some rules and guidelines for using points of information successfully.

First, only members of the opposing team may ask a Point of Information. Team members may not question one another. The critic, referred to as the Speaker of the House, nor audience members are allowed to ask questions either.

Second, points of information may be asked only after the first minute and before the last minute of a constructive speech.

Third, no points of information may be asked during rebuttals.

Fourth, to ask a point of information, simply stand up (if the Speaker of the House does not see you, simply say, "point of information," in order to get the speaker's attention) and then wait to be recognized by the debater holding the floor. The debater holding the floor has the right to decide whether to accept a point of information. If accepting the question, he or she will say, "Yes sir/madam," after which the opposing debater may ask her or his question. If the debater holding the floor does not wish to accept the question he/she will say "No thank you sir/madam," after which the opposing team member must sit down without asking a question.

Fifth, points of information must be asked within a limited amount of time (about 15 seconds). This is because the time it takes to ask and answer a Point of Information is deducted from the speaker who is holding the floors total speaking time. Only one question may be asked per Point of Information.

Sixth, after a Point of Information has been asked, the speaker asking the question then sits down. The speaker holding the floor then needs to answer the question and then continue with their speech.

Seventh, the debater holding the floor needs to be judicious in handling points of information. If a debater refuses to accept any points of information he or she might be perceived as lacking confidence in the arguments made. If debaters accept too many points of information they run the risk of not being able to deliver a fluent or cohesive speech. Usually, accepting two or three points of information strikes a good balance.

Eighth, the team not holding the floor must also be judicious in the number of points of information they ask. If they fail to ask any questions they let the speaker holding the floor go unchallenged. If they ask too many questions they appear to be overly aggressive. Once again, asking two or three points of information strikes a good balance. Also, it is a good idea to make sure that not just one person asks all of the points of information for the debate.

Points of Order

Points of Order are objections which are raised when one side believes that the speaker holding the floor has committed a procedural violation. Unlike points of information, points of order may be raised at anytime during the debate. Also, unlike points of information which are directed to the speaker holding the floor, points of order are directed towards the Speaker of the House. These are analogous to an objection in a court of law.

There are generally three violations which may occur during a debate. They are violations of common knowledge, new issues raised in rebuttals, and misconstruing of an argument.

Regardless of the specific point of order being raised, the procedures guiding them are the same. If an opposing team believes that the debater holding the floor has committed a violation, one of opposing debaters needs to stand up and say, "point of order." The debate will then stop. The critic will ask what the point of order is over. The person raising the point of order will then explain the objection. Normally, the Speaker of the House will also let the speaker holding the floor a brief rebuttal of the charges. The Speaker of the House will then respond in one of three ways. The Speaker of the House may say "Point well taken" which means he/she agrees with the objection. The Speaker of the House may say "Point not well taken" which means he/she disagrees with the objection. Finally, The Speaker of the House may say "Point taken under consideration" which means s/he will make a decision on the issue after the debate has concluded. Regardless of the decision, it is vital to remember that there is no arguing with the Speaker's decision!

If the Speaker of the House upholds the Point of Order, then the time it took to adjudicate the point is deducted from the debater's speaking time. If the Point of Order is not upheld by the Speaker of the House, then the time is not deducted from the debater's time.

Violations of Common Knowledge

All arguments introduced in Parliamentary Debate must be based on general common knowledge. It is impossible to define exactly what the boundaries of common knowledge are. Some issues are black and white while others are gray. Normally, it is best to think of common knowledge as knowledge that a well informed college student should be expected to have. If you believe that an argument raised by your opponent is not based on common knowledge then you should advance a Point of Order. To initiate a challenge, simply stand up and say, "Point of Order, the following claim is not within the scope of common knowledge and should be stricken from the round."

Violations of Raising New Issues in Rebuttals

Once the debate moves into rebuttals, neither side may raise new issues that were not raised in the constructive speeches. If you believe that during a rebuttal speech, the debater (Prime Minister or Leader of the Opposition) has raised an issue which was not raised in any of the constructive speeches simply stand up and say, "Point of Order, this is a new argument."

Violations of Misconstruing an Opponent's Argument

Misconstruing an argument occurs when the speaker who has the floor applies an argument made by their opponents in a way not intended by the original initiator

of the argument. If you believe that an argument you have made is being misconstrued by the opposing team, simply stand up and say, "Point of Order, that argument is being misconstrued."

Points of Personal Privilege

Points of Personal Privilege are raised when someone believes that they are being personally slandered, either directly or indirectly, by the other team. This is a
fairly serious charge and should not be raised without due consideration. If you believe that you have been the object of a slanderous comment, simply stand up and
say, "Point of Personal Privilege," and within 15 seconds explain your objection. The
Speaker of the House will then render his/her finding.

Points of Clarification

Points of clarification are initiated when one when does not understand something that has just been said. For example, assume the debater who has the floor says,
"Sixteen people were arrested at a demonstration last weekend." But suppose the debater said it in such a way that it was unclear if they said "sixteen" or "sixty." A debater on the other side has the right to stand up and say "Point of clarification, did
you say "sixteen" or "sixty?" The speaker holding the floor must then clarify this
point. Points of Clarification can be raised anytime during the debate.

Heckles

Heckles are comments made by the team not holding the floor meant to make
light of the speaker holding the floor. In the most basic sense, heckles are a form of
verbal harassment which should be done in good fun. Heckles are not personal attacks, but instead are comments usually made in response to something the speaker
has just said. To illustrate this concept, an often told story of what occurred when an
American debate team was debating an English debate team will be recounted. The
resolution dealt with the privacy rights of political figures versus the people's right
to know. The American team was arguing that the people's right to know was more
important then the political figure's privacy rights. The English team was defending
the privacy rights of political figures. During the debate, the American debate team
asked the English team how they would like it if a photograph of their Queen "using
the john" were published. The English debater responded with a humorous quip
stating that that scenario could never happen as their queen did not "go to the john."
Seizing the moment, the other American debater blurted out, "yeah, we can tell."

Heckles, if used judiciously, can score a telling point for the team issuing them,
but can become an irritation if overly utilized. It is probably a good idea not to heckle
more than two or three times during a debate. Heckles can take place any time during the debate.

Showing Approval and Disapproval

The showing of approval and disapproval of the debater holding the floor is common in parliamentary debate. If the speaker makes a good point or says something your strongly agree with, it is customary to show your approval by pounding on the table and/or saying, "hear, hear." This is true even if the speaker is on the opposing team. Likewise, it is also customary to show your disapproval of a comment by hissing, booing, or saying, "shame, shame." The showing of approval or disapproval can take place anytime during the debate. Debaters should be aware that the audience and the Speaker of the House are also allowed (and encouraged) to show approval and disapproval.

CROSS-EXAMINATION DEBATE

Cross-examination style debate as it is academically practiced is sponsored by two different organizations: The NDT (National Debate Tournament) and CEDA (Cross Examination Debate Association). The NDT traditionally sponsors only policy debate topics. CEDA has recently moved to sponsoring policy debate topics after years of sponsoring value debate topics. Simply stated, this format calls for a cross-examination after each constructive speech, but that distinction is arbitrary, because the norms of the activity are really the defining characteristics: a heavy emphasis on research and well-prepared, briefed-out arguments.

Cross-examination style debate differs from parliamentary debate in two important respects. First, cross-examination debate uses the same resolution all year long. Debaters will debate three times for and three times against the same resolution at every tournament they attend for the entire academic year. In fact, NDT and CEDA now use the same topic and essentially have merged for all pragmatic considerations! The second major difference is that while Parliamentary debate forbids the presentation of prepared evidence, cross-examination debate thrives on it. The student participating in cross-examination debate should be well researched on both sides of the resolution.

Pros and Cons of Cross-Examination Debate

The advantages of such a format involve the following: First, each debater researches the topic for the entire year developing research skills and an in-depth topic comprehension. This helps avert, but doesn't eliminate, the parliamentary problem mentioned above, in which debates occur with wholly uninformed advocates. The evidence requirement presupposes that the advocates will research and write a debate case before attending a classroom or tournament debate.

Second, cross-examination debate gives you something substantive to discuss in between debates. A parliamentary format limits most inter-debate discussions to discussions of form, rather than content. Cross-examination debate invites ongoing academic discussions about substantive political and social issues.

Finally, cross-examination debate eliminates a variable in the win-loss decision. Parliamentary debate offers a new topic each round, thus making the topic a factor in who wins and who loses the debate. For instance, if the government knows more about a topic than does the opposition, the government is more likely to win the debate. Or sometimes a topic might tend to favor one side over the other as written. A cross-examination format, on the other hand, makes research and planning more of a variable than an elusive and chance advantage on a parliamentary topic.

There are several disadvantages to cross-examination, evidence-based debate. As currently practiced, rapid rates of speaking and hoards of research are required to be successful. Most argumentation students or forensics competitors do not have time to learn how to listen and speak at 200-plus words-per-minute. (The average person speaks at around 125 wpm.) Additionally, some estimate that a nationally competitive debater will do a masters-thesis worth of research in one academic year. While your coach or teacher may prohibit fast talking or reams of research, the vast majority of evidence-based debate seems to evolve (some would say devolve) to fast talking to get in as much information as possible. Classroom and tournament-novice-division debates, however, do not usually exhibit as much fast talking as do the upper levels of college-tournament competition.

A second disadvantage is that evidenced-based debate is not usually audience friendly. Although it certainly could be a slow and persuasive event (CEDA was originally created with this idea in mind), most evidence-based debates as currently practiced are unappealing to the lay audience who may be listening. It should be noted that not many in the cross-examination debate world would dispute this list of disadvantages. Far from being a disadvantage they would maintain that these practices are actually advantageous. Let's use the Indianapolis 500 race as an analogy to understand this position.

At the Indianapolis 500 drivers drive very fast. The situation is rigid and artificial since all they do is drive around in a big loop while under severe time pressures. The cars they drive are built for this specific situation, and no other. They'd look strange in a supermarket parking lot, but the Indianapolis 500 is a functioning laboratory of automotive design and driving techniques.

When an Indy driver drives to the market the day after the race, his individual life is made better by what happens at Indianapolis. The brakes, suspension, and other technical features of his car were pioneered there. Methods of driving defensively or controlling skids were perfected under racing pressure. He would never drive 120 mph to the store, but he benefits from the skills he learned in pushing his driving abilities to the limit.

Cross-examination debate, it is argued, develops critical thinking skills under intense pressure, in a controlled, laboratory situation. Debate tournaments are a functioning laboratory for critical thinking skills and presentation techniques. The skills learned in the lab have direct application in the real world.

Basic Speaker Responsibilities for Cross-Examination Debate

The following is a brief description of the basic responsibilities for each debater. Since cross-examination debate, as currently practiced by both the NDT and CEDA, are utilizing policy topics, the following description will outline the basic speaker responsibilities for policy debate. The following descriptions are only guidelines. There are many ways to divide up speaker responsibilities. However, the following suggestions should at least give the beginning debater a basic idea of how to begin.

First Affirmative Constructive (1AC):   In this opening speech, the debater needs to present a *prima-facie* case. In policy debate, this means that the stock issues of motive, blame, cure, and cost must all be developed in the opening speech. The opening speech should be very organized and structured. A piece of evidence should be used to substantiate all claims that are made. This speech is normally delivered from a manuscript in outline form.

[Cross-examination by the Second Negative Speaker]

First Negative Constructive (1NC):   There are many options for this speech depending on the affirmative case. Normally the 1NC and the 2NC will split the negative responsibilities with the 1NC arguing against the cure and cost stock issues and the 2NC arguing against the motive and blame stock issues.

If any procedural issues are to be addressed, they must be introduced by the 1NC. For example, if the negative wishes to challenge the affirmative definitions and interpretation of the resolution it must be done in the 1NC. Topicality arguments, critiques and counter plans must also be initiated in the 1NC. More and more critics are expecting any negative disadvantages to also be initiated in the 1NC. Normally the 1NC will give what is known as a disadvantage shell. That simply means that 1NC will present a briefly evidenced disadvantage that will be further developed by the 2NC.

[Cross-examination by the First Affirmative Speaker]

Second Affirmative Constructive (2AC):   The major responsibility of the 2AC is to refute all of the issues raised by the 1NC. Thus, this debater must be very familiar with all of the possible negative arguments which could be raised against their case and know how to refute them. If the 1NC raised a topicality argument then the 2AC must respond to it. If the 1NC introduced a counter plan then it must be refuted. If the 1NC advanced two disadvantages then both of the disadvantages must be responded to. The bottom line is, what ever the 1NC argues, the 2AC needs to respond to. If there is still time remaining after responding to all of the 1NC positions, then case arguments can be extended and additional evidence can be introduced.

[Cross-examination by the First Negative Speaker]

Second Negative Constructive (2NC):   This is the beginning of what is known as the negative block. The negative block consists of the 2NC and the 1NR which are presented back to back. As such, the 2NC and the 1NR should divide the arguments up between them.

First, the 2NC should argue the motive and the blame stock issues if they wish to contend them (remember that the 1NC probably did not argue these stock issues, the 1NC has probably only argued the cure and cost stock issues). If these issues are to be contended and if they have not as yet been contended, then they must be argued by the 2NC. Even though the 1NR speaks immediately following the 2NC, the 1NR would not be allowed to initiate arguments on these issues because technically the debate would then be in rebuttals and no new arguments may be raised in rebuttals.

Next, the 2NC should select a few of the existing issues and argue them while leaving the remaining issues for the 1NR. For example, suppose that there have been five different major issues raised in the debate: topicality, a counter plan, arguments denying the affirmative advantage and two disadvantages. These five issues should be divided up. The 2NC might deal with three of them (say the topicality, counter plan and affirmative advantage) and the 1NC should deal with the remaining two issues (the two disadvantages).

[Cross-examination by the Second Affirmative Speaker]

First Negative Rebuttal (1NR):   This is the continuation of the negative block. Notice how the negative team has two speeches back to back. No new issues may be raised in this speech. The 1NR should extend any issues not dealt with by the 2NC. The goal of the negative block is to try and make it very difficult for the 1AR to cover all of the issues raised in the negative block. Remember that the 1AR will only have six minutes to respond to the 14 minute negative block. One error that many novice debaters commit during this block is to double cover. This means that the 1NR argues the same issues that the 2NC just argued. This is very poor strategy. Remember that the affirmative has not responded to the 2NC arguments yet, so there is very little value in repeating them. Double coverage usually happens because the negative debaters have not divided the issues amongst them prior to the 2NC speaking.

First Affirmative Rebuttal (1AR):   This is regarded by many as the most difficult speech in the debate. That is because the 1AR must respond to all of the arguments raised during the negative block. To put this in perspective, the negative has just spoken for 14 minutes and the 1AR has only five minutes to respond. As such the 1AR must be very concise. Do not try and argue every point, instead try to group arguments and try to deal with them in a general manner. Also, read as little evidence as possible. You simply don't have the time to be reading more than two or three pieces of evidence. Arguments that are not covered by the 1AR become conceded. Hence, the 2AR is limited to what they can argue by what the 1AR says. This is because the negative team will not have a chance to respond to arguments that were not argued by the 1AR but then raised by the 2AR. For example, if the 1AR failed to respond to a topicality argument, then that issue becomes granted and the 2AR will not be allowed to respond to it, and the debate will probably be won by the negative. (Remember that there is no 3NR). Keep in mind that it is often said that the job of the 1AR is not to win the debate; the job of 1AR is not to lose the debate.

Second Negative Rebuttal (2NR):   This is the last speech for the negative in the debate. The 2NR should extend and develop only those issues that they believe they are winning. For example, if they believe they are losing the topicality argument, the harm issue, and one of the disadvantages, they would be wise in dropping those issues and concentrating on the issues they believe they are winning. Also, if the 1AR dropped (failed to respond) to key arguments then the 2NR should point this out to the critic and tell why the drop is important. Don't just say, "the 1AR dropped the counter plan"; rather, the importance of this drop should be briefly explained as well. It is also a good idea to remind the critic that they should not listen to any arguments that 2AR might bring up on the dropped issue since they will not have a chance to respond (this is known as protecting the negative). Finally, the negative should give the big picture as to how all of the various arguments tie together in a way that negates the resolution.

Second Affirmative Rebuttal (2AR):   This is the last speech of the debate. The 2AR must contend with any issues extended by the 2NR. If the 2NR dropped out of any issues, then those issues need not be addressed. However, if the negative dropped out of an argument that you believe you are winning you might want to remind the critic of this and perhaps even resurrect the issue. For example, let's say that 1AR turned a disadvantage (showing that a perceived disadvantage is really an advantage) and the 2NR dropped out of the disadvantage. In this case the 1AR should not let the disadvantage drop out of the round but should instead remind the critic of the turn and why this issue really should be weighed in the affirmative's favor. Finally, the 2AR should give a summary as to why they believe they have won the round. They too should explain how all of the various arguments tie together in a way that supports the resolution.

Cross Examination in Academic Debate

One of the unique contributions by CEDA to academic debate was the development of the cross-examination format. The NDT soon followed CEDA's lead and also now uses cross-examination. After each constructive speech during a debate, the constructive speaker must be cross examined by a member of the opposing team. There are no written rules concerning which speaker of the opposing team must question the previous speaker. However, the most common method is for the speaker who *does not speak next* to do the questioning. For example, once the first-affirmative-constructive speaker finishes his or her presentation, the second negative speaker does the questioning. The first negative speaker, who speaks next, then may use the cross-examination period to listen to the cross-examination and/or prepare for 1NC. The logic behind this method is that the next speaker will have more preparation time. In the typical debate, second negative questions first affirmative, first affirmative questions first negative, first negative questions second affirmative, and second affirmative questions second negative. (See Figure 4.2.) Notice that each speaker both asks and answers questions once each.

Most tournament and classroom formats limit the cross-examination period to three minutes. There are a few things that you can do to make your questioning easier. First, before the debate begins, you can prepare a list of generic questions on both sides of the topic. If all else fails, at least you will have something to say during your three minutes. Second, while the other team is delivering a constructive speech, be sure to jot down some possible questions that you may wish to ask. Third, as your first question, ask an open question, such as, "Could you explain your plan to me?" While the respondent answers, you will have time to get your thoughts together. Finally, whether you are the questioner or the respondent, feel free to use humor when appropriate. Being facetious, for instance, can be a way out of a difficult situation.

During cross-examination the questioner and respondent face the audience, not each other. Cross-examination is as much for the benefit of the audience as for the debaters. Some judges allow what is known as tag team cross-examination. That is where the two members who are not officially involved in the cross-examination become involved by either asking questions for their partner or answering questions for their partner. Most judges will allow limited tag teaming in a debate. For example, if you are not involved in the cross-examination period but want an argument clarified you can usually interrupt and ask the respondent directly or instruct your partner to ask the respondent to clarify. Conversely, if you are the respondent but do not know the answer to a question, but your partner does, it is usually permitted for your partner to answer. However, partner involvement should be the exception, not

CONSTRUCTIVE	RESPONDENT	QUESTIONER
First Affirmative	First Affirmative	Second Negative
First Negative	First Negative	First Affirmative
Second Affirmative	Second Affirmative	First Negative
Second Negative	Second Negative	Second Affirmative

FIGURE 4.2

Typical Cross-Examination Format

the rule. The best thing to do is to ask the critic before the debate how she or he feels about tag-team cross-examination and then adhere to the feedback you get.

Please see Chapter 12 for a detailed discussion of cross-examination strategies.

Preparation Time

Most debate formats allow a limited amount of preparation time between speeches: usually five minutes total for each team. The team that speaks next is charged with prep-time use. For instance, if 2AC uses one minute of preparation time, the affirmative team will have four minutes left. Critics will usually announce the amount of prep-time remaining; however, just to be sure, you should ask them to do so.

Affirmative Preparation Time

Most affirmative teams attempt to save the bulk of their preparation time for the first affirmative rebuttal. The reason for this is obvious. 1AR has to answer twelve to thirteen minutes of negative argumentation in one-third of the time. Additionally, second affirmative constructive should already be prepared for their presentations, and second affirmative rebuttal is not as crucial as 1AR. Ideally, with a five-minute preparation rule, 2AC should not need more than one minute of preparation time. Remember, 2AC has three minutes of cross-examination time after 1NC in order to prepare. 1AR requires at least three minutes, and, if possible, save approximately one minute for second affirmative rebuttal. Figure 4.3 lists the suggested prep-time use for affirmative as well as negative teams.

Negative Preparation Time

Normally, first negative constructive will argue topicality, counter plan, and perhaps a disadvantage. These positions generally are created prior to the debate. Most often, 1NC merely needs to listen to the affirmative's case and make adjustments to the briefs, which are sometimes called shells. Therefore, as currently practiced, the first negative speaker should not need more than a minute of preparation time. Second negative constructive and first negative rebuttal should require but a brief one-minute strategy session going into the negative block. This will allow the negative debaters to make sure they are not double covering arguments. In other words, if 2NC takes on the disadvantage, then 1NR should not. If 1NR takes on the topicality, then 2NC should not. Any new positions or case refutation that need to be developed can be done so during other speakers' cross-examination or preparation time, and those new arguments MUST be given by 2NC, as that is the last constructive. 1NR needs no prep time because it can be prepared during 2NC. The first negative speaker should not be covering the same ground as the 2NC arguments, so there should be no need to listen as carefully. That time can be used instead to prepare for the next speech. 1NR should be ready to speak by the end of 2NC, however. At times,

BASED ON AN EIGHT-MINUTED LIMIT PER TEAM		
NEXT SPEAKER	AFF. TIME USED	NEG. TIME USED
First Affirmative Constr.	Not applicable	
First Negative Constr.		One minute
Second Affirmative Constr.	Two minutes	
Second Negative Constr.		Four minute
First Negative Reb.		Zero minutes
First Affirmative Reb.	Four minutes	
Second Negative Reb.		Three minutes
Second Affirmative Reb.	Two minutes	
Total	**Eight minutes**	**Eight minutes**

FIGURE 4.3

Suggested Use of Preparation-Time

opposing questioners may prematurely end the questioning of 2NC if 1NR is still preparing during the cross-examination. The final three minutes of negative preparation time then can be used for second negative rebuttal.

Further Suggestions for Using Preparation Time

Most critics prefer that you do not use all of your preparation time if you don't really need to. Of course, you should always use your preparation time if you need it. Occasionally, however, the opposite occurs, and a team runs out of preparation time early in the debate. A speaker then may have to speak without having adequate time to prepare. Fortunately, there are some things you can do to mitigate the effects of such a tragedy. First, during the course of the debate, think of things you'll want to say during your rebuttal. Write those ideas on the far right side of your flowsheet: that way, at the end of the debate, at least you will have something to say.

Second, practice taking an adequate flowsheet, so that you can speak easily from it. If you do not have time to write out your responses, you will be able to read earlier arguments with ease. Thus, you can refute opponent's arguments and extend yours without having to write out everything. Truthfully, even with judicious use of preparation time, you will probably never be able to write out all of your responses anyway. Through trial and error, debate forces you to learn the skill of thinking while you speak. Taking a good flow-sheet is the first step toward developing that skill.

Finally, what you do before the debate can also help you deal with lack of preparation time. Sit down with your partner and write out some stock responses for each of the rebuttals, especially 1AR. Write the arguments on index cards and keep them with your evidence. Also, the more you prepare and practice the less you will need to use prep time. Know your arguments, as well, so that you can summarize them without really having read your flowsheet. And, make sure that your evidence file and brief folder are in order, so that you don't have to waste time looking for that one perfect piece of evidence.

SUMMARY

The goal of this chapter was to give an overview of academic debate and its relevancy to other fields of debate. Procedures for how academic debate is currently conducted were examined including traditional speaking orders and time constraints.

The different types of academic debate were discussed. There are three major intercollegiate debate organizations. National Debate Tournament (NDT), Cross-Examination Debate Association (CEDA) and the National Parliamentary Debate Association (NPDA). CEDA and NDT currently sponsor debate on policy topics where research is required. The NPDA sponsors debate on a variety of topics and prohibits the reading of evidence during the debate. The pros and cons of each style of debate were discussed along with the basic format and responsibilities for each style of debate.

RESEARCH:
FINDING SOURCES OF EVIDENCE

A TRIP TO THE LIBRARY

Evidence can be found anywhere, including your memory, a bookstore, a garage sale, the internet, or a library. Most of you will be using the latter at some time during your argumentation or forensics class. One of the most overlooked parts of research is being prepared for your trip to the library. The following is a list of things you will need to bring:

1. A pencil, eraser, and pen,
2. Post-it notes (so you aren't tempted to write in the publications and so you easily can keep track of important pages),
3. A notebook (for writing down call numbers, ideas, search terms, first drafts of briefs),
4. At least a dozen newer dollar bills and/or change and/or copy payment cards (to pay for computer printing and/or photocopying),
5. Two 3.5 inch floppy disks (one pre-formatted for Macintosh and one for an IBM Compatible for downloading data),
6. Your student I.D. (so you may check out material),
7. Your email address to which you may need to send full-text articles,
8. A few hours to spare, and a full stomach (so you're not distracted).

Even though these suggestions seem obvious, we're always surprised by the number of students we escort to the library who do not have any of the above. Going to the library unprepared can be frustrating and more time-intensive than necessary. For example, we've done computer data searches in libraries ourselves, only to find, as we're ready to print, that the computer's printer is broken, and we need a disk to save the data. No disk and an hour's searching are all but wasted.

Purpose of Chapter

Evidence, like gold, is where you find it. Both evidence and gold are valuable, but only evidence can be submitted in a debate. The focus of this chapter will be to aid the debaters involved in the cross-examination format find research to support their cases. However, it is our contention that parliamentary debaters should also research key areas in current events, philosophy, history, foreign policy, economics, psychology, political philosophy, and any other field you or your teacher deems important.

Rules in parliamentary debate prohibit prepared materials. However, in informal interviews with many debate coaches now involved in parliamentary debate, including one of NPDA's founders, this prohibition does not exclude evidence; rather it merely prohibits "reading paragraphs straight out of books and magazines." This means that a parliamentary debater should be allowed to refer to great works in literature, religion, philosophy, political theory, psychology, or to major current events and the opinions about them.

For example, in a debate an issue may arise over an interpretation of Thoreau's *Walden* or of Dante's *Divine Comedy*. The test during parliamentary debates is whether the reference should be common knowledge for a college-educated person. It is our contention that the standard for common knowledge should be high; in other words, we should expect college students to have read the classics in the Western and Eastern traditions, including writings from all of the world's key religions and cultures. A college student should know the major events in history, including major battles in major wars. A college student should know the major players in science, and a college student should know the recent findings of physicists and cosmologists about the nature of our physical universe. Hopefully, you get our point: college students should be expected to be educated and up-to-date on all major issues and in all major disciplines. As was discussed in Chapter 4, a parliamentary debater has the right to make a point of order, to ask the judge to rule against a team citing information which is not common knowledge.

However, the judge (called The Speaker of the House in parliamentary debate) should not rule against a team unless the reference is so obscure, so trivial as to be beyond any scope of what a college student should know. For example, a reference to a major part of Marx and Engel's *Communist Manifesto* would be legitimate, but a reference to Karl Marx's interchange with a friend over lodging arrangements may not be common knowledge. Hopefully, the parliamentary debater will be as interested in a search for evidence and for knowledge as the cross-examination debater.

Recentness of Evidence

As you do your library search, keep in mind that you're generally looking for the most recent evidence available. We suggest that you limit your search to the past two years. Obviously, there are exceptions to this rule. If you're researching the United States Civil War it may be better to get information that was written during the war itself. However, for most issues the most recent is always better. The real question becomes, "has anything changed since publication that would make this evidence suspect?" If the answer is "No" then the evidence is probably fine, but if the answer is "Yes" then the evidence is of little value. The world is changing fast. Periodicals referring to the prospects for Middle Eastern peace, if written prior to 2004, may be so ludicrously irrelevant as to be not only useless in a debate but actually highly inaccurate. Obviously the removal of Saddam Hussein in Iraq has drastically altered the landscape of that region. Analysis about the prospects for peace in the Middle East would be of little use if that change were not taken into consideration. However, essays written in the 1800's that argued for the elimination of the Electoral College are probably valid today. Many of those articles pointed out that under the Electoral College a Presidential candidate who did not receive the most popular votes could still be elected President. Since nothing in the Electoral College process has been changed to preclude this from occurring—as the 2000 Presidential attests—evidence published in the 1800s which point this possibility out is still relevant today.

DEFINITION OF EVIDENCE

Evidence consists of opinions or empirical observations offered to support a claim. The phrase *observations* and *opinions* exhaust the classes of evidence. Everything you will ever submit as evidence is an observation or an opinion, or a combination of the two.

Observations are what a lay person calls facts. It is a statement based on personal empirical observation. The observer saw, heard, tasted, touched or felt the phenomenon in question. All eye witnesses at trials are offering their observations. To say that a particular painting hangs in a particular museum is a fact. **Opinions** are not empirically verifiable; although, they are normally based on facts. To say that the painting is beautiful is an opinion.

The distinction between observations and opinions will be explored later. For now, one need only understand that all evidence can be classified into these two types, and that observations, when available, are considered more reliable than opinions. This chapter deals primarily with where and how you find evidence. Crudely, this means research, but not just library research.

SOURCES OF EVIDENCE

All of the evidence you will use in a debate will be written or spoken by you or by someone else. Many readers may dismiss the importance of personal observation, but in any debate format an advocate's own resources are much more important than they may appear at first glance. In a parliamentary format, this is especially true. So let's begin our discussion with personal experience and investigation.

Personal Experience and Investigation

The first and most obvious source of opinions and observations is your own personal experience. If you are thinking critically about the resolution Resolved: that I should buy a new car, your own experience with your present car—"it didn't start yesterday"—is an observation. The non-empirical inferences you have about your car—"I own a really bad car"—are opinions.

On occasion, you might investigate some phenomenon in order to observe or form opinions about it. Investigation differs from experience in that experience is passive, while investigation is intentional and active. **Investigation** is an intentional experience for purposes of acquiring evidence. When an anthropologist does field work he or she is observing another culture, and her or his recorded observations become the basis of opinions. If you want to evaluate an unfamiliar car, you drive it. This is an investigation consisting of observations (how it looks and performs) upon which you will base an opinion of the car.

In many instances, our own experience may be the only evidence available. If the discussion centers on your car or your health, you may be the only one who knows very much about it. Each of us places great weight on our own experience. Personal experience is, for most people, the strongest evidence. Unfortunately, there are at least two problems with using personal experience as evidence. First, we may not in fact be telling ourselves the truth. The human capacity for rationalization is well known. Second, we may not be competent to interpret our experience and form a reliable opinion. Even when we experience something, such as medical symptoms, we may not know what it means.

When we present a debate to a third party judge, our personal experience or investigation may be of limited value. This is certainly true of an opinion we hold. If you have the burden of proof, and you assert your opinion as evidence, your opponent can simply assert the contrary and win. Since your opponent started with presumption, he or she has an opinion whose value is equal to yours plus the weight of presumption. Therefore, if all an affirmative debater has for support is her or his own opinion, that debater will almost always lose.

In parliamentary debate, more so than in cross-examination debate, personal experience is viewed as a viable form of argument. In the least, it's an example, and examples compromise evidence. Secondly, the genius in being able to generalize from personal observation and experience is well documented in people like Socrates, Jesus, Copernicus, Einstein, and Freud. So whereas a debate can turn into an example war in which the government never wins, it's also possible that you can develop arguments from example that strike a cord in your judge, much like a good poem, in which your observations seem valid because they are consistent with the experience of your judge.

In Parliamentary debate, where no evidence is allowed to be read, the reliance on personal examples is very tempting. When using personal examples in parliamentary debate one should rely on universal examples. A universal example is an example where the experience can be generalized to most everyone. For example assume the resolution "Resolved: that he or she who hesitates is lost." Assume the Government in attempting to support the resolution draws on the example that she had in a college class where she was given an assignment to write a paper. The debater argues that she personally kept putting the paper off until just a few days before it was due and when she finally did write the paper it was rushed and not as good as she had hoped. This she argues is an example of where hesitation leads to a poor outcome. Now the Opposition might feel inclined to advance a Point of Order on the basis that such a personal example is not common knowledge. How is the negative to know that this occurrence ever even happened? The judge in this situation would probably not uphold the Point of Order even though the particulars are not common knowledge or verifiable. This is because the Government is relying on a universal example. Whether the example is true or not, all of us can probably relate to the underlying principle which the example illustrates. We have all probably experienced, or know of someone who has experienced, delaying school work until the last minute and then being disappointed (but not necessarily surprised) when the finished product is not of great quality.

The Problem of Personal Examples

First, the party with presumption on a particular argument (i.e. the party who does not have a burden of proof) can usually defeat an opponent's opinion by simply asserting the contrary. If the debaters are equally qualified the party with presumption wins. If a lay-person were debating an auto mechanic on the worth of a car, the opinion of the auto mechanic would have more weight than a lay opinion and therefore could not be defeated by the assertion of the contrary, unless both debaters were auto mechanics.

However, over-reliance on authority is also a fallacy. Just because someone is an auto mechanic does not mean he or she is always to be believed. Remember; argumentation is based on reasoning, so anything is debatable. One might argue that auto mechanics also have been known to lie about car problems, so that they can make more money from you. In the least, you would have to wonder about the bias of the auto mechanic, since she or he stands to gain from a pessimistic diagnosis.

The same is not true of statements that are observations. If you have observed the performance of a car, your report of that performance is observational evidence so long as you're speaking in empirical terms: such as miles per gallon, acceleration, etc. An opponent that has not had an opportunity to observe the phenomenon by driving the car cannot simply assert the contrary without calling you a liar.

However, while an advocate may be reporting an observation, that report can be considered biased. Every advocate is presumed biased in his own cause. Thus a debater's own observation is evidence, but there is no way to check it, and it is presumed to be a biased account.

When a scientist reports the results of an experiment, she or he is reporting a personal observation. The check on accuracy rests in part on the scientist's reputation, but more on the fact that another scientist should be able to repeat the same experiment and get the same result. When an eyewitness testifies at a trial, the witness is reporting first-hand observations. The check on honesty is the penalty for perjury. But consider the difference between a defendant testifying on his or her own behalf and a neutral witness putting the defendant at the scene of the crime.

A second problem with the advocate using his or her own experience is that the debater is often not qualified to make an evidentiary observation or opinion. If you are debating the existence of extraterrestrial life your own opinion would be that of a lay person, an untrained person, unless you happen to be trained in exo-biology or astronomy. Therefore, you need to bring before the judge the opinions and observations of others who have greater expertise.

Taken together, this analysis means that in a debate judged by a third party, personal observations and opinions are of some value, but should not serve as the entirety of a debater's evidence arsenal.

Thus, because the advocate always is considered biased in his or her own cause, but while his or her own observations and opinions are certainly evidence, an advocate should use personal observations and opinions in conjunction with other evidence. One must therefore usually go in quest of the observations or opinions of others, or at least try to show how personal experiences are consistent with the experiences of others. In parliamentary debate, you must try to build an ethical (as in ethos or credibility) connection with the judge to convince him or her that you are accurately representing empirical facts and expert opinions.

Unpublished Sources Other Than Personal Experience

If your own opinion is biased and your observations suspect, the next logical step is to find someone else's opinions and observations. The best possible source is your opponent.

Opponent Admissions

A commonly overlooked source of evidence is your debate opponent. It is common in a debate for an opponent to make a statement that damages his or her own case. It may be a careless statement, or an honest admission of some limitation. Once said, it is a stipulation. For purposes of the debate it becomes evidence. The classic case is found with any statistic. If an opponent says that 6% of workers are unemployed, you can always respond that 94% of workers are employed, and your evidence is your opponent's statement. Let's look at a Martial-Arts Analogy. In many martial-arts or self-defense strategies, the black belt will use the efforts of opponents against them. If an opponent lunges forward the Black Belt may side step their opponent and push him or her to the ground, thus taking advantage of their opponent's effort. In debate, if you can use an opponent's effort to support your position, then you may be able to win the debate much easier. A black belt will rarely take an opponent's blow head on, and so, in debate, if you can partially agree with your opponents or use their evidence against them, you ought to do so. For parliamentary debate, this is especially important, since there is a prohibition against prepared material. In order to do this effectively, one should consider, almost as a first order of business, how an opponent's argument may be used for your advantage. Like a martial-arts duel, you will be able to use less effort to achieve the same result.

If an advocate is considered biased in his own cause it must follow that he is biased against the opposing position. Therefore opponent admissions are very strong evidence since it represents something which is granted even by a hostile party. The most common use of cross-examination in debate is to elicit damaging admissions from an opponent.

Non-Party Unpublished Sources

Another common source of evidence is something said by third party sources to an advocate, but not published. Interviews fall into this category, as do a student's lecture notes, questions asked of teachers, mom and dad's opinions, and anything else that has been said but not published.

A great division in non-party evidence is between verifiable and unverifiable statements. If you have an interview with an authority on a subject, the statements made are certainly evidence but the judge has no way to know what was in fact said other that what you tell him or her. There is also no way to ascertain the context in how it was said. Was the interviewee talking off the record? Was the interviewee being sarcastic? Are you reporting word for word what was said or are you paraphrasing? If so, might you have misinterpreted what the interviewee meant? These are all relevant questions which cannot be answered in a debate and thus lower the probative value of the evidence. Technically, you are reporting your own observation of what someone else said, and all the limitations of your own observation are present.

On the other hand, if the statement is recorded in some way, and the recording of the statement is submitted, the statement can be verified. Thus, personal letters are unpublished, but can be shown to the judge, and thus the statements made in them can be verified. Photographs that you took, tape recordings, notes made of an interview, and anything else that preserves the statement independent of the debater's memory raises the value of unpublished third party evidence.

Published Third-Party Sources: Library Research

This is research as you have come to know it, and either loathe or love it, in your other classes. So just what makes a library so wonderful? As a source of evidence, a library may be thought of as a massive collection of opinions and observations, recorded over all of human history, and verifiable as having been said because they are in writing. Notice that this verification doesn't mean the statements are all true, but it does mean that someone, someplace, said them. That *someone* is often an eminent authority. It is no wonder that libraries are such powerful research tools. If evidence is gold, the library is the mother lode.

The word *publication* means literally "to make public." Thus, the views expressed in books are available to anyone. The verification for debaters' research is similar to the check on scientists' veracity. Any researcher looking at the same book should find the same statement. If the debater is unwilling or unable to help in such verification, the judge is justified in suspecting the evidence. A debater must be able to verify the fact that a published source quoted by the debater made the statement presented in the debate. Most commonly this means, which upon request by the opponent or the judge, the debater must either be able to produce the work itself, a photocopy, or a complete bibliographic citation. This is parallel to a scientist being believable because another investigator could duplicate his work.

This does not mean that the debater has the burden of proving that the source told the "whole truth and nothing but the truth," only that the quotation is in fact imprinted in the document in question. All of the rules for quoting and paraphrasing that you learned in English classes apply here. Quotations are indicated by quotation marks, and indicated when reading aloud either by saying, "quote" and "unquote," or by indicating non-verbally that you're quoting someone other than yourself. As in any other kind of research, paraphrases are fine, but you must make clear that you are paraphrasing and the paraphrase must be an honest representation of the original statement.

It is with the paraphrase that parliamentary debate has some salvation. A student who is well read and who has a reasonably good memory should be able to paraphrase segments from books or even articles from magazines or newspapers. Those sources could be verified at a later time by all parties. Such verification would not be part of the decision, however. But at least there could be some standard that allows enforcement of common academic mores associated with such citations.

The phrase "I read somewhere that . . . ," or its functional equivalent, is not verifiable evidence and enters the debate as the advocate's own opinion or observation. This is a basic principle of modern scholarship. This is why books that require external sources, such as books in history and the social sciences, commonly include a vast number of footnotes. On the other hand, works that are essentially the author's own opinion, such as works of philosophy (or debate texts) commonly have few footnotes. Because of the scope of material available, and the ease with which it can be verified, library research is the bread and butter of debate research.

Again, we want to emphasize that parliamentary debate is not exempt from the use of published material. A debater may paraphrase last Sunday's *New York Times*; however, she or he will not be able to prove the information is verifiable because of the absolute prohibition on verifiable evidence. Of course, your argumentation instructor may allow prepared and thus verifiable evidence in a parliamentary format debate. The best insurance for the viability of parliamentary debate is to make sure our judges and debaters are well read.

LIBRARY RESEARCH TECHNIQUES

Library research is changing so fast, with the advent of computer technology, that it is our belief that devoting pages of a book to *how-to-research* would become anachronistic the day it was written. Therefore, we will focus on the more universal principles of reviewing the literature. A literature review is done by scholars who endeavor to understand the status of knowledge (and thus also the limits of knowledge) of a particular subject. For example, a biologist would review what is known about a particular species of bird before endeavoring personally to study that species with field observation or scientific experimentation. Similarly, a social scientist would review the literature with regard to elderly care before conducting a study in several nursing homes.

A debater will do a similar, if truncated, review of literature by finding and reading books (or significant parts of books), scholarly publications, magazines, and newspapers. Government documents, non-print media, pamphlets, and web pages also comprise several of the genres available to the student. At this writing, most of the above are available through both computerized and non-computerized indexes, archiving, and retrieval. The best computerized sources, like Lexis-Nexis and Dialogue, have full-text archival and retrieval, meaning that in one step you can get the citation and the entire article. Any internet service can link you to newspaper services, for example the *New York Times*. Through the use of your internet browser and an internet connection, you can sign up for all kinds of newspaper services. For example, *The Los Angeles Times* has its own website; with a credit card number, a student can sign up for full text web searches for a relatively small amount of money.

While the specific research tools available at each library or with each computer service will differ, there are certain constants. We'll discuss these in terms of A) the level at which material is written, B) the genre of the material, and C) the indexing methods through which it is retrieved.

Levels of Material:
The Popular, Specialist, and Scholarly Presses

Published research material is written on one of three levels. **Popular press** material is intended for reading by the general public with no special knowledge of the subject. The **specialist material** is written for those who already possess above average knowledge in the field. The **scholarly press** is written to further knowledge of some subject rather than for commercial gain. Each has its advantages and disadvantages for the debater.

The Popular Press

Popular press material is exemplified by all mass-sale books, magazines, and newspapers that one sees daily. For example, *Time, Harpers,* and *Parade* are written so that anyone can read them. They define unfamiliar terms, use many diagrams and illustrations, and choose subjects of general interest. When starting research on an unfamiliar area, it is best to use the popular press until you have a grasp of the subject. But as soon as you are able, you should jump to the specialist or scholarly press.

The Specialist Press

The specialist press assumes a general working knowledge of the subject. There is a good chance that you are already familiar with some specialist publications if you have some hobby. *Runner's World* is a specialist publication for joggers. *Road and Track* is a specialist publication for auto buffs. *The Wall Street Journal* is a specialist newspaper focusing on finance. *Scientific American* is a specialist magazine for those interested in science.

The analysis in the specialist press is much deeper than in the popular press and often approaches the best of the scholarly press. Often issues will be discussed among specialists for years before they become popular issues.

The popular and specialist presses are alike in that they are commercial enterprises. They are crudely but effectively identified by the large number of advertisements they carry. The larger the percentage of ads is, the more commercial the publication. The nature of the ads is also revealing. If most of them are for specialized products, as they might be in *Runners World*, one can assume the publication is specialized. If most of them are for cigarettes and soap flakes while the articles are on the Mddle East, one may assume the magazine is intended for popular consumption.

The Scholarly Press

The scholarly press differs from the popular and specialist press by motivation. The reason most popular and much specialist material is printed is commercial. The scholarly press editor does not have the same constraint. The principal motive for publication is to expand knowledge. Much of the scholarly press is heavily subsidized by universities, professional associations, or foundations.

Almost all of the scholarly press is also specialized. Typical scholarly press materials are the journals and quarterlies of various academic disciplines. For example, in the study of argumentation, the principal publication is *Argumentation and Advocacy,* published by the National Communication Association.

An easy way to identify scholarly press materials is to ask a teacher of a subject what sources he or she relies on for current professional information. Also, the scholarly press seldom carries advertising, and the ads it does carry are usually for academic institutions or for scholarly materials such as books.

The advantage of using the scholarly press is that it is the best source of evidence. Its articles and books are in greater depth and follow the conventions of scholarship rather than the conventions of the market place. In the scholarly press, before an article is published, it most often must pass a rigorous blind review, in which other scholars read the article to decide the merits of it. Thus, the reasoning in the scholarly articles passes a tough review by the writer's peers, a group knowledgeable on the subject matter, before the article ever sees the printed page. Scholarly books or articles will normally be footnoted and have bibliographies for further reading. Generally, scholarly articles are less biased than articles in the popular or specialist press; although, some may argue that the bias may just be more difficult to see.

The scholarly press is commonly the source of information for the specialist and popular presses. Note in your own reading how often a popular-press article is based on a scholarly article or report. This means that the scholarly press usually discusses issues in advance of the time they appear in the popular press. For example, many of the medical breakthroughs reported by newspapers are first published in the scholarly publication, *The Journal of the American Medical Association*, which is nearly unreadable to the lay person.

Incomprehensibility is the first disadvantage of using the scholarly press. The writings are often difficult to understand for the lay person, and they place great demands on an advocate to make them understandable to the debate critic. For example, if the respected journal *Foreign Affairs* does an article on the same subject *Time* writes about, *Foreign Affairs* will assume the reader has significant background knowledge on people, places, and events; thus, someone lacking the basics about world politics or even simple geography will have a much more difficult time understanding the professional journal. Additionally, language use in a scholarly article is usually laden with jargon, making it difficult for the lay person to digest. A second disadvantage is lack of availability. Because of the specialized nature of scholarly periodicals, smaller libraries may not have any but the best-known sources. Of course, if your college has limited library facilities, this disadvantage may be overcome if a major university near you allows limited public access. You can check that by simply phoning the library in question. For example, here at Santa Rosa Junior College, the better students will travel up to an hour or two away to use libraries of the University of California and the California State University in the San Francisco Bay Area.

The Genre of Sources: Books, Periodicals, and Newspapers

Research materials can be divided not only by level but by genre into 1) books, 2) periodicals (or magazines), 3) newspapers and 4) miscellaneous. Each has its advantages and disadvantages. This duel classification is better illustrated in Figure 5.1, rather than in words.

Books

To a librarian a book is something published less often than twice a year and permanently bound. This includes yearbooks, almanacs, and annual reports. The key word is permanent. A book is considered to be a statement of a subject of more than passing interest. Each library today has its own cataloging system, usually involving some type of computerized system. If you are computer literate at all you should be able to follow the simple menu program. If not, ask; librarians are there to help. Although universally bookish and seemingly unfriendly, librarians are really smiling inside.

The **advantage** of using books is that they are the most complete statement of a subject, and all other things being equal are the preferred type of source. They represent a considerable time investment by the author and usually a financial commitment by a publisher. At the very least books are a considered exposition of the authors concerns. Physically, books normally have indexes which are a great aid to research.

The **disadvantage** of using books is that as wonderful as books are they have a glaring shortcoming: they are out of date as soon as they're printed. It commonly takes twelve to eighteen months from the time an author finishes his or her manu-

	Books	Periodicals	Newspapers
scholarly	Text books	Foreign Affairs	Chronicle of Higher Education
specialist	Specialty Books	Scientific American Runner's World	Wall St. Journal
Popular	Popular Paperbacks	Harper's feature stories Times	The NY Times news stories

perspective ———————————————— currency

FIGURE 5.1

The Relationship between Levels and Genre of Sources

script until a book is on a library shelf. The moment you pick up a brand new book with that year's copyright, it represents the facts as they were a year ago. A second but lesser disadvantage is that books are long. The time one spends reading one book will give you one author's view. The same time spent with magazine articles will acquaint you with the views of several authors.

Evaluating books.   All of the above does not mean that anything between two hard covers is automatically worthy or unworthy.

The Lack of Controls on Content.   The First Amendment guarantees that anyone can publish almost anything—accurate or not. Contrary to popular opinion, there is no practical legal control on the accuracy of what is said in a book. The only real controls are libel suits and prosecutions for publishing national security information.

Libel suits are almost impossible to win if the party libeled is a public Figure. Only a living person who has been damaged by a statement can sue for libel. The vilest untruths about Mohandas Karamchand (Mahatma) Gandhi or Elvis Presley are not legally actionable. If the statement isn't about a person, there is no libel at all. One could publish incredible stories about extraterrestrial beings and there would be no one to bring suit, although Dana Scully and Fox Mulder (*X-Files* characters) may want to investigate. Prosecutions for violations of national security laws are almost unheard of. When spies are tried, it is for giving the information to an enemy agent, not for publishing it. Fortunately there are ways to check the worth of a book. These will be discussed as internal and external tests.

Internal Tests are the tests you can use based on looking at the book itself. The most important test of any book is its author. The qualifications of the author will usually be given on the title page or dust jacket. Authors commonly are qualified because of training or experiences they have had. The tests of competence and bias are discussed later. Signs indicating a serious scholarly intent are footnotes, a bibliography, and an index. In the preface, an author usually states his intent in writing the book.

The role of the publisher is vital and little understood. Contrary to popular belief all one needs to get published is money. The money is normally that of a publisher but can be the author's own. This is particularly true in this age of desktop publishing and inexpensive offset presses. Anybody can write anything, go to a local printer and pay for them to run off a few thousand copies. One has then published.

Publication by a recognized publisher is another matter. Any publisher has an interest in his own reputation. A reputable publisher will not publish a book that will hurt that reputation. The basis of a publisher's reputation is therefore at issue. If the publisher publishes primarily for commercial gain the book may have no greater insured accuracy than a popular magazine article. Publishers such as Signet, Dell, Ballentine and similar houses are very successful commercial publishers of books for the popular market. Their books are often of great interest and useful, but they are not directed at the scholarly market.

At the other end of the spectrum are the university presses and scholarly book publishers. Oxford University Press, for example, has a centuries-long tradition of publishing significant scholarly works. It reviews manuscripts for accuracy before the book is published. While O.U.P. is delighted to make money, that is not their primary purpose and, like other scholarly publishers they have distributed many books that don't have the remotest chance of breaking even.

Text book houses fall somewhere in between. Publishers such as Scott-Foresmen, Wadsworth, McGraw-Hill, and all the others you've seen stamped on the spines of your class books publish books which they hope teachers will adopt. Therefore, they have to review material before publication with academic interests in mind. They are still commercial enterprises, but their market is more demanding.

There are specialist publishers which produce books for very limited and often very knowledgeable markets. In aviation history, Aero produces fine books which deal only with that one subject. Oak Publishers is a subsidiary of Folkways Records and publishes nothing but books and monographs on folk music.

Your authors wish there were a reference work that discussed and evaluated different publishers, but we don't know of one. You can do some such evaluation yourself by noting what publishers produced which books you've found valuable and which produced ones you thought useless. In short, simply start paying attention to the name at the base of the book spine.

A look at a publisher's catalog will quickly reveal whether they are a specialist house or a general commercial publisher. A university press may be assumed to be a scholarly publisher. The specialist house is aiming at a more knowledgeable market and must make sure that its books will be taken seriously by that market.

External Tests. Fortunately books get reviewed. Book reviews are evaluations of a book by people knowledgeable about books. They are often written by scholars of the subject. The easiest way to find book reviews is through *Book Review Digest*. This series comes out annually. It publishes short excepts from reviews of major works and tells you where the whole review may be found. We especially recommend it to any debater planning to base his case on one particular book. There are few feelings so humiliating as finding out in the debate that your opponent looked up the reviews you didn't, and discovered that your author is thought by authorities in the field to be a jerk.

The Old Book.   In some cases older books, or newspapers or periodicals for that matter may be better. There are at least two conditions which prompt this analysis.

Whenever you want a sensory impression of past events more than you want perspective, the eyewitness account is preferred, no matter how old it is. The accounts of historic travelers such as Pausanias or Marco Polo are better sources of what ancient Greece or China were like than those of any modern expert. *They are valued for their empirical observations.

The second case is the *classic*. The thoughts of a wise person can transcend her or his own time. Generations have found Plato, Buddha, Machiavelli, or Thomas Jefferson useful not because of the time in which they wrote but because of the ideas they proposed. They are valued for the wisdom of their opinions. If an *old book is still in print, in indicates that some publisher thinks it is still important.

Periodicals

Periodicals are the most commonly cited sources in debates because they are more current than books, represent a greater diversity of views, and are often more succinct in their statements. To a librarian, a periodical is *something published more than twice* a year. If it's published less often it's a book or a pamphlet and cataloged as such.

Since you often don't know the author, you are relying on the editor's judgment that the article is worthy. Libraries have a variety of ways to access a periodical. They should have the more traditional, hard-bound indexes, like *The Reader's Guide to Periodical Literature*, or the computerized searches including network connections. For the latter, most libraries are requiring that you bring a 3.5 inch floppy disk with you. Rather than actually print out the articles, you will copy the files onto your disk.

Evaluating Periodical Articles. Fortunately, evaluating a magazine is relatively easy. In addition to the internal tests discussed earlier there is Katz and Katz *Magazines for Libraries*. This incredibly useful book is a *Michelin Guide to Magazines*. It lists, discusses, and evaluates virtually any magazine you will ever need to cite. If your library has it, any magazine unfamiliar to you should be checked. If your library doesn't have it, there is a second test.

You can find out where the magazine you've found is indexed. Most magazines will tell you, on the page that has the table of contents, where they are indexed. If it is indexed only in *Readers Guide* and the *Magazine Index* you may assume it is not considered scholarly. Scholarly periodicals will be indexed in the appropriate specialized periodical index. For example, if a law review is not indexed in the Index to Legal Periodicals it is suspect.

Newspapers

Within their limits, newspapers are excellent sources. Newspapers are snapshots of the events of a given day or week. They may also, however, contain feature articles which more closely resemble magazine articles than news stories. In fact the weekly news magazines like *Time* resemble weekly newspapers as much as they do monthly periodicals.

The advantage of newspapers is their currency. If you are debating a resolution that just became a news story they may be your only source. The disadvantage of a newspaper story is that it lacks perspective. It can be so caught in the rush of events that the reporter has little time to evaluate what he's reporting.

Evaluating a newspaper story. In evaluating a newspaper story one should note the source of the story. Most newspapers do not originate most of their stories but reprint reports from the major wire services: UPI, AP, Reuters, Tass, Argents Francais, Knight News Service, etc. It is really these services that one is quoting. The local paper is just a conduit. In fact, the proper way to cite a wire service story in a debate is, for example, "UPI dispatch, London, June 15, 19xx, as printed in the *Podunk Gazette*." Clearly a story originating from Tass will have a different viewpoint that one originating from UPI.

A by-line usually indicates that either the reporter is well known enough to deserve one or that this particular report is especially worthy. Also note the dateline. Did the reporter file the story from a location indicating he personally observed what he reported? For example, it is common in war reporting to file stories from a country's capital and base the story on press releases rather than first-hand observation. A good reporter wants to get into the field, but often this is not allowed by local authorities. Consider the language of the story. Do the words and phrases indicate that the reporter has interjected his own views, or are they a neutral report of observations?

Evaluating a newspaper as a whole.   Only in the largest cities do you have a choice of newspapers. In most localities, there is one dominant newspaper and everybody takes it. For research on national issues, however, certain papers have achieved enduring stature. A parallel to Katz and Katz is the *Newspapers for Libraries* which evaluates the daily press. There are five newspapers that are generally considered to be national newspapers even though published in a particular city. They are *The New York Times, The Wall Street Journal, The Christian Science Monitor, The Washington Post*, and *The Los Angeles Times*.

Miscellaneous Genre

There are some types of materials that are not books, periodicals or newspapers. The average student rarely consults these sources, but they are particularly valuable to debaters.

Government Publications.   Government publications are not so much a matter of level as of intent. The United States Government is the largest publisher in the country. It publishes material at every level from popular pamphlets on the national parks to treatises on nuclear power plants that only engineers can understand. Most are not published as commercial ventures and will never make money. They are normally published either because 1) the government itself needs this information to reach its decisions, or 2) to keep Americans reliably informed on subjects of interest. In depth and breadth of coverage they are amazing. You have paid for every one of them through your tax dollars. The least you can do is to take advantage of them.

The **Hearings** published by the House and Senate are some of the most important sources of evidence for serious tournament debate. The reports of various agencies and commissions have often been prominent parts of our national history. One need only recall the *Warren Commission Report* on the assassination of President Kennedy.

Hearings usually call as witnesses the best experts in the country and from a variety of biases. The Congressional Hearing therefore is a great place for cross-examination debate research, but we believe its also a great place for a parliamentary debater to get a scholar's view of a topic. Hearings occur on anything from the exclusionary rule, to endangered species, to earthquake preparedness.

Not all libraries have access to government documents. Usually one library within a congressional district will be dubbed the government depository. In that library, a fairly complete holding of all relevant documents are kept. Technically, any citizen of the United States should be able to check out a government document, regardless of whether you have a library card for the library in question. Some libraries have restrictions on use, but should not. Please check with your local congressional representative to find the depository in your congressional district.

Printed Debates.   It is obvious that a valuable source for a debater would be other debates on the same subject. There are a number of publications that print just such material.

The most famous is *Congressional Digest.* Each month the *Digest* prints pro-con debates by members of Congress on a contemporary issue. The format is literal. The pro (affirmative) arguments are on the left hand page and the con (negative) arguments are on the right hand page.

Several publishers, most notably Greenhaven Press, produce bound collections of articles exploring the arguments on a popular issue. These collections are excellent places to see the issues early in your research. These books are so diverse that only your reference librarian can tell you which ones are available in your library.

Most libraries also have publications similar to the *Opposing Viewpoints* series, which catalogues written debates on most major issues, from the legalization of drugs to the treatment of immigrants. These sources are usually kept in the reserve or reference section of the library, meaning that you will not be able to check them out, but merely may make photocopies of relevant material.

Congressional Publications.   Congressional Hearings were discussed earlier under government publications. It is the most profound but not the only way to find evidence on current bills.

The *Congressional Record* is the official daily record of what happens in Congress. When a major floor debate is held on a bill the arguments for and against that bill can be very useful in finding arguments you may wish to use.

Also related to the Congress, but far easier to use than the *Congressional Record* itself, are the publications of *Congressional Quarterly.* CQ is a private publishing company greatly respected for its summaries of Congressional work. CQ produces *CQ Weekly* and the *CQ Annual.* Each is well indexed, quick to use, and provides an outstanding summary of whatever Congress has done (or not done) on any issue before it.

The Computer Search.   Most of the above indexes and sources involve manual searches, but as time goes on much of the information is being stored in some kind of computer format. Internet and the world-wide web are becoming more and more available. Any college student, as we enter into the twenty-first century, should have a computer at home and an internet connection of some sort. Many of the nation's newspapers and magazines can be accessed from any web connection. Most local internet providers can get you on the web for monthly fees of less than $20.00 per month. With the advent of the new internet computers, a student should be able to find a new or used computer with modem, for well less than $1000.

A **descriptor** is a word that describes what a book or article is about. It is used in the same way as a subject heading. Any given book or periodical article might have a dozen or more descriptors describing its contents. These descriptors are not necessarily the same ones you or I would use when discussing the same subject and data bases have to publish thesauruses to give the searcher the term the computer will recognize.

Boolean logic gives the relationship between descriptors. Thus, if you were researching extraterrestrial life, the search would be for "extraterrestrial life." The computer would then list all of the sources in its data base which had both of these descriptors. A search of a large data base, such as the Magazine Index could provide hundreds, if not thousands, of articles with both descriptors. You would probably then have to find other descriptors to narrow the field.

Programs like Lexis/Nexis have very complicated truncation language, which once learned, helps immensely in doing computer research. Most libraries with access to computer data searches will have brief descriptions to help you get started. If using the web, any web browser will allow you to simply type in your starting topic, and then by simply clicking on the hypertext with your computer mouse, you can move all over the world gathering data all along the way.

Any library can be linked to any of the major information service companies which compile data bases. Whole articles can be printed by transmission if necessary. For the first time in the history of our planet small libraries have access to virtually unlimited collections. This is a very exciting time for students, the youngest of whom have no idea how much the world of research has changed in just the past 20 years.

All of the above sources, indexes, references and techniques only scratch the surface of what is available. As mentioned at the start of the chapter, technology is having such an impact on libraries that the best index available this year may be replaced by a better one next year. Any student planning to do much library research would be well advised to take a course in library research (many colleges have self-paced programs), or get to know a reference librarian, or both.

Most often you should try to work within the confines of your college's online library links. Your library should subscribe to full text services like Proquest or Lexis/Nexis, and with a password everything should be easily accessible from any internet connection. Contact your library for further information.

Evaluating Web Pages.

However, there is also a lot of valuable information in general on the World Wide Web. From any browser, simply type in the URL of any of your favorite search engines, such as yahoo.com or google.com. (URL stands for Uniform Resource Locator, and it is basically the same thing as a website address, such as http://www .google.com/). Into the search engine, type in your search term and parameters, and you will be given a list of websites. Once you have a decent list of sources, you can click on any that seem relevant.

At first, just try to get a sense of the page: Why does the group or individual have a website? For personal satisfaction? To advance the cause of the group? To get you to buy or do something? For altruistic or selfish motives? By no means at first do you need to read the entire page; just kind of glance through it. If you find any site offensive, don't read it. Click back on your browser and try again. If it looks like a credible source and a helpful page, you can save it in your bookmarks (also called favorites). Create a new bookmark folder if needed and title it for the type of information for which you are researching. Be sure also to change the name of the webpage before saving it, especially if its name is just a list of numbers or meaningless terms, so that you can easily recognize it for quick retrieval.

Internal versus External Page Links: As you do your research, you will need to learn the difference between internal page links and external page links. Sometimes it's hard to know the difference. Therefore, watch the URL as you click through the links on any website. As you're evaluating a site, stay within the internal links, until you get a good sense of that site and whether it will be helpful to your purposes. If you jump to an external site with an entirely different URL, then click "back" on your browser. If your browser's back button is not working, that means the link probably opened a new browser window automatically. Simply close that page or browser window if possible and go back to your original discovery.

Reading the URL. The URL itself can help you understand what type of website you have found. Additionally, your new-found understanding will help you evaluate the information in the site. URL stands for Uniform Resource Locator. Also called a web address, a URL is the long string of protocols, servers/domain, directories, and file names that helps you locate a web page. For example, the URL for the National Aeronautics and Space Administration (NASA) reads:

http://www.nasa.gov

Let's break this apart, so that you can see how this works. Let's start with the protocol, usually "http". This simply means "hypertext transfer protocol," and is simply telling your computer what to show on the screen. Next is WWW, which stands for World Wide Web. Next, is NASA, which in this case is the same as the initials for the agency: National Aeronautics and Space Administration. "Gov" stands for government, and is telling you what type of site you have found.

What have we learned from this breakdown? Well, most importantly, we have learned that right in the URL may be the source for a given site. Of course, this isn't always the case: "freespace," "geocities" or other generic domains are sites on which people can get their own web page for absolutely no cost. This is especially important to know because in many cases you have no idea who wrote a given page (on geocities for example). Secondly, we learned that the suffix on the basic information tells us what kind of site it is. In NASA's case, it's a government site. What other kinds of suffixes might we find?

- gov = government
- edu = education
- com = commercial
- biz = business
- org = organization
- net = network

We have to be careful about making blanket assumptions about these suffixes, but some clues are helpful to note. Government sites are usually trustworthy in terms of the information presented, but we also know the type of biases a government site may have. In the least, an agency, like NASA, is going to be fairly likely to include laudatory information about itself, and fairly unlikely to indict its own programs. So with any .gov site, you will want to keep that in mind.

An institution of education, like a university, with the suffix "edu," is likely to include accurate information, as well as chronicle the scholarship of its faculty, but you have to be careful that you haven't located the website of an undergraduate student who just happens to be hosting a webpage on a university computer.

A commercial or business site with the suffix "com" or "biz" is likely to be selling you something, directly or indirectly. Or the site could just be hosting someone else's site, which is the case with a large number of websites. Anyone can purchase a web domain name and host a webpage with virtually any suffix, so caution is warranted. However, most people who are offering products or services for sale prefer the .biz or .com domain suffixes. These sites may or may not contain valid information. Steering clear of commercial and business sites with biased sales information is obviously wise. However, if the site is selling online and daily newspapers and magazines, like www.nytimes.com, then obviously it's a worthwhile read.

An organization, like Earth First!, will usually have the suffix "org," but not always. A domain name is usually more expensive than a personal name, so some organizations may not have the suffix "org," simply due to cost. However, when it's present, it is usually a good idea to find out a little about the organization. However, try not to dismiss information simply because a website's organization is biased. Some organizations with apparent biases may still have valuable websites. For example, your authors have been impressed by www.aclu.org, a website obviously biased in favor of civil liberties. The American Civil Liberties Union fights for the rights of people against aggressive law-enforcement tactics, yet its website is laced with accurate facts and information about the legal system in the United States. While you may want to take with a grain of salt ACLU's claims against law enforcement agencies, you can probably trust its listing of facts, such as the demographics of our prison population or the number of women on death row for killing abusive husbands.

Network, with the suffix "net," is usually just an indication that someone has purchased space on a computer, or the computer network company itself could be hosting its own webpage, like www.altavista.net. A lot of local internet service providers (ISPs) have .net suffixes, as do all of their customers. Evaluations of .net sites probably vary as greatly as any domain suffix, with some highly credible sites with viable news pages all the way down to some sites that are just hosted by a bunch of web bloggers. That is why looking at the suffix is just the start of your evaluation. There are many other ways to investigate the credibility of websites you have located on the net.

Occasionally, the author of a given webpage will be listed directly on the visual part of the homepage for a given site; with credentials of the author and a date of on-line publication, you have a complete citation, viable for a debate round, as long as the citation is accurate. However, determining accuracy can be difficult; many students have been fooled by parodies, hoaxes, and outright jokes. Urban legends seem to live a much livelier, albeit shorter, existence now that the internet is around to spread the word. Checking with your instructor or a librarian is a good way to verify a site's authenticity. If the author's name and qualifications are not listed on a given site, viewing the page source can be an alternative way to determine authorship. To view page source on Internet Explorer, click "view" and "source" on your browser. You will have to scroll through some html code, but if listed the author or webmaster's name will be found within the heading or first few lines of the source. If this does not work, look for a link back to the site's homepage; there you might find a sitemap, navigation bar, or other table-of-contents function to help you determine authorship, sponsorship or some other clues to a website's credibility.

A mailto link or email icon can also be a way to track down authorship. Sometimes simply emailing a webmaster can get you the information you're looking for, at least enough to fill in your bibliography. Also, consider the links into and out of a given site. If you're getting to a site from another reputable site, you may be able to rely on the veracity of the second site's information, for example, or even use the linked sites to gather information about the website you're investigating. Common in .org or .edu sites, often the author's name will be imbedded into the URL itself. For example, in the following fictitious URL, the author is listed in the directories of the website:

http://www.bmxu.edu/evolution/professorclaudiadiaz/
cambrianexplosion.html

Our pretend professor, Claudia Diaz, may be found perhaps in the campus directory of our hypothetical BMX University. You may be able to reach the professor by email, phone, or snail mail to help you determine the background of the webpage's information. If there is neither contact information for BMX University nor a link for an index or homepage, then go back through the URL, one forward slash at a time.

A forward slash looks like this: /

It is a marker that delineates between directories on a webpage. Starting at the right of the URL, eliminate one directory at a time, by backspacing your cursor through the current directory up to the last forward slash, and then hit return on your computer's keyboard. If that tells you little, then try eliminating the next directory and so on, until you find the homepage.

For example let's say your browser tells you that you're at the following fictitious website:

http://www.bmxu.edu/evolution/professorclaudiadiaz/ cambrianexplosion.html

To go back to the root directory, place your cursor to the right of the "l" of "html". Back space on your keyboard until you see this:

http://www.bmxu.edu/evolution/professorclaudiadiaz/

Then, push "enter" on your keyboard. Look around in the new directory for information about the source. You should be at our pretend professor's home directory at BMX University. Her contact information, credentials, research background, etc. may be listed there.

If that produces no results, then go back one more directory level.

http://www.bmxu.edu/evolution/

And so on . . .

http://www.bmxu.edu/

Until you find the homepage and hopefully more information about the web source. In our last step, you should be viewing the homepage for our hypothetical university. There, you should be able to find faculty listings, research interests, etc. Sometimes, investigating the credibility of websites can be frustrating, sometimes fruitless, but often extremely helpful in finding that one piece of evidence that can win that key debate round.

Evaluating websites is almost as much an art as it is a science. It's very difficult sometimes to determine whether a website is legitimate, a hoax, or simply lacking credibility. It's always better to work within the confines of your college's legitimate library sources, whether those are online or not.

However, of course venturing out onto the world-wide web may be required by your college's lack of online resources or your need to find quick information prior to a debate. In either case, it's imperative that you're able to find out whether a website is legitimate and credible. Any errors in source credibility can cost you a debate round at any time. Sometimes the world-wide web can be a source of excellent debate material, if one is able to navigate away from the land mines of blogs and parodies.

SUMMARY

You need to find data to support claims. Sometimes that data can come from your own experience, but your own experience is of limited value when speaking to a third party judge. Evidence is opinions or observations offered to support a claim. In a denotative sense, this is the same as data. Connotatively, evidence usually means the opinions or evidence *of others* and that in turn means research.

The unpublished statements of others can provide evidence, but unless verifiable they are suspect. Most research will center on libraries and the published sources they contain. The first step is to select the library available to you that is most likely to have a good collection on the topic you're researching. This may involve a law library which uses techniques unique to legal publications.

Material you will encounter will be written on three different levels: the popular, the specialist, and the scholarly. The popular level is the best for you to start with if you are unfamiliar with the subject. You should progress to the specialist and finally the scholarly levels as soon as possible. The scholarly level is preferred over the others as a source of evidence.

There are four genres of sources: books, periodicals, newspapers, and miscellaneous. Books are the most complete sources but have a significant time delay in production. Periodicals are more current and succinct. Newspapers are the most current, but lack perspective. Miscellaneous sources are treated in the same way you would treat whichever of the first three they most resemble. The published debates of others on your subject are particularly useful. There are ways to find and evaluate each genre of source.

After one has found evidence, the next step is to check its relationship to issues likely to appear in your debate.

THE ANALYSIS OF EVIDENCE:
EVALUATING DATA

It is common for someone to challenge the claim of another by saying, "You have no evidence for that." What is usually meant by this is that the advocate of the claim has only his personal opinion as evidence. In argumentation, most judges will require more than the debaters personal opinion if the claim is to be accepted. To be sure, a personal opinion is evidence. **Evidence** is an opinion or empirical observation offered to support a claim.

As discussed in the previous chapter, it's not usually very convincing evidence unless it can be demonstrated that it has some external validity. Similarly, you could say that evidence is equivalent to the facts upon which an argument rests, but one must realize that some of these facts are actually opinions.

As we are using the term evidence, any data/reason would be evidence, but in debates before a third-party judge we usually mean the observations and opinions of others. However, for parliamentary debates, both sides are prohibited from using the verifiable opinions of others, so evidence must not only be cogent but it should be defensible as well. In other words, you must be ready to defend your interpretation of Thoreau's opinion about economics or Eisenhower's view of war.

This chapter provides a step-by-step procedure for determining the value of any evidence, even one's own opinions. After a discussion of the need for evidence, three tests will be proposed: relevance, reliability, and the hierarchy of evidence.

THE NEED FOR EVIDENCE

A claim without evidence or analysis is an **assertion.** In a debate no claim on which an advocate has a burden of proof can be proven by an assertion. So with this definition, it would be incorrect to say that parliamentary debate uses no evidence. Rather, it uses no prepared material. If any reasons at all are given, then technically those reasons comprise evidence. All elements necessary to present a prima facie case, and all negative off case arguments, must be supported by evidence. The less likely a claim is, the more one needs evidence to support it.

Eventually a chain of reasoning reaches facts which a judge will grant as self-evident. The point at which this is reached determines what we call the fill factor. In effect, the judge is filling in something he or she is willing to accept on common knowledge. If this did not happen, we would have to start every debate with what philosophers call first principles, that is, a statement which all reasonable beings would accept as certainly true. When one considers that philosophers have debated for the past 2,500 years what acceptable first principles are, the problem becomes apparent. In practice, audiences in agreement with a speaker's position may fill in a lot, and thus lower the evidentiary burden on that speaker. If a judge disagrees with a speaker's position, more support will be required. A large part of Burden of Proof doctrine is determining what must be evidenced. This creates the requirement that all elements of a *prima-facie* affirmative case and all off case arguments must be supported by evidence.

Usually an advocate will go beyond his/her minimal burden and present more evidence than is strictly necessary in order to strengthen his/her position. Obviously a reasonable judge should want to consider as much evidence as possible. Thus, all relevant and reliable evidence should be considered, unless there are strong policy reasons to the contrary.

This statement exactly parallels the Common Law rule that "all relevant and reliable evidence should be admitted," with the added clause that sometimes there are good reasons for not listening to everything. The major "strong policy reason to the contrary" in courts of law is the exclusionary rule which keeps from the jury any evidence seized in violation of Constitutional rights. Also, however, courts exclude any evidence that is "substantially more prejudicial than probative." Thus juries are often not shown photographs of the bloody victim in a murder trial.

In ordinary debate, the major "reasons to the contrary" are the imposed time limits. Most debaters have far more relevant and reliable evidence than they can possibly present in a debate, but to keep the discussion within limits, a judge should consider only that evidence actually chosen for presentation by the advocate. Thus the advocate should present all the relevant and reliable evidence that time and good presentation/delivery technique allows. Of course, with parliamentary debate, advocates are asked by rule not to present reams of evidence, but rather to present quality evidence and to explain it well. Therefore, a parliamentary debate is much like a criminal trial in which prejudicial or illegally-obtained evidence is excluded from consideration. In such a case, the legal advocates would have to find another way to refer to the facts. Such is the challenge for the parliamentary debaters. It is our contention that the more a parliamentary debater knows about history, great books, and current events, the better she or he will be able to explain relevant evidence. The contrary is that evidence which is not relevant or not reliable should not be considered.

THE TESTS OF EVIDENCE

All evidence is susceptible to the three-stage test of 1) interpretation, 2) relevance, and 3) reliability.

Interpretation

Before asking about relevance, we need to do a quick check about whether the evidence seems accurate, especially in parliamentary debate. This can be done without challenging the ethics of your opposing advocates. Rather than call your opponents liars, you may simply challenge their interpretation of the facts. Intelligent people may disagree on the overall message of a book, for example. One may feel that *Huckleberry Finn* is a book that cuts through racial boundaries by showing the friendship between Jim and Huck, while other reasonable interpretations might find the book to be racist since it uses derogatory language, albeit the language of the time period in which the story is set, to refer to African Americans. This is a debatable issue. No one needs to be accused of misrepresenting the facts or of outright lying. Advocates can simply present their viewpoint and give reasons for preferring their interpretation.

Additionally, we should ask whether the evidence is consistent with a conclusion the author argues elsewhere. An opponent may have inadvertently taken a quotation from an early part of a book without realizing that the book concludes differently. We are asking all debaters to completely avoid making ethical accusations against your opponents. Such accusations usually serve to embarrass all players in a debate, and the disagreement can almost always be handled without the personal attack. One can confront the accuracy of the quotation simply by stating, "The author concludes otherwise." Then give your reasons or quote the author's end-of-the-book conclusion. There's no need to present questions of accuracy in any other way. One need not question the ethics or motives of an opponent. (However, an advocate should avoid purposefully taking a quotation out of context.) Intelligent people can disagree over the intent of an expert's quotation or a purpose of an author's book.

The step of discerning accuracy is usually skipped in a debate. Normally, advocates do not have the knowledge or evidence to question the accuracy of a quotation or reference. In this case, if you're not sure, you should assume that your opponents have presented the evidence fairly. When you're in doubt, always give your opponents the benefit of that doubt.

Relevance

Once the issue of accuracy is addressed, we then ask if the evidence is relevant. In the debate, if you believe your opponent's evidence is irrelevant, you would simply tell your critic why the evidence is irrelevant and present a reason that you believe that is so. In cross-examination debate, you would explain what the opponent's evidence is saying and then explain why that evidence does not make a relevant point. If the argument is presented by the affirmative, the negative team may need to offer a topicality argument to prove irrelevancy.

In parliamentary debate, the opposition offers a Point of Order to the speaker of the house (critic or judge), and the speaker rules immediately on the Point of Order. For example, let's say you're the opposition in a parliamentary debate, and the resolution is *an apple a day keeps the doctor away.* In this debate, one of the government's arguments is that a correct diagnosis and prescription can cure a patient. A person debating for the opposition, in such a case, would stand up and say, "point of order." At that point, the government advocate should be silent, and then the Point of Order would continue: "This argument is irrelevant because a doctor gives a prescription and the pills are a cure rather than a type of prevention. The resolution is asking the government to discuss prevention that precludes having to see a doctor."

At this point, the Speaker of the House (your debate critic) will say one of three things:

1)   Point well taken. (Meaning the Speaker agrees the argument is irrelevant.)
2)   Point not well taken. (Meaning the Speaker disagrees that the argument is irrelevant.)

In this case, *a prescription* would probably be ruled irrelevant, and the Speaker would say, "point well taken." At this moment, the government would need to abandon the irrelevant argument and go on to the next point.

In a cross-examination format, the judge or critic does not rule during the course of the debate, which means that arguments about irrelevancy may continue from the beginning to the end of the debate. At that time, the judge will decide on topicality and other issues concerning an argument's pertinence.

If, however, an argument is to some degree relevant, we must evaluate it to determine how much weight we should give it. We are thus concerned in this chapter with how reliable a piece of evidence might be.

Reliability

Reliability can most easily be measured by three standards: **competence, bias and hearsay.** The declaration of observation or opinion must be made by someone competent to make it. The source should have as little bias as possible so that he or she can accurately report the fact or opinion. Finally, we should be close enough to the original source to believe that what the judge is hearing is what was said. These three dimensions, competence, bias, and hearsay, will serve to organize the analysis. The relationship between competence, bias, and hearsay is illustrated by the following diagram (Figure 6.1):

The vertical axis represents bias, and the horizontal axis represents competence. The third element is hearsay. The theoretically perfect source is represented by position A, completely competent with no bias, with the declarant speaking directly to

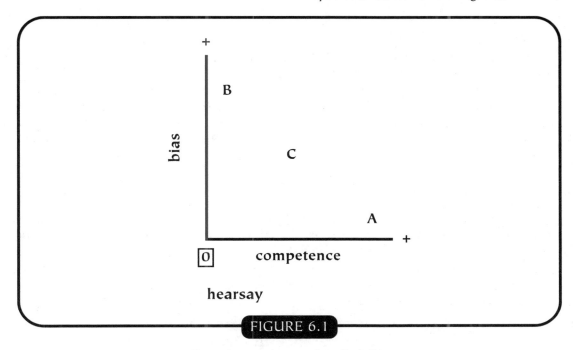

FIGURE 6.1

The Dimensions of Reliability

the judge. The worst possible source is represented by position B, completely biased with no competence, at the end of a long chain of rumors and repetitions. Most sources will fall in range C, with some degree of competence and some degree of bias, and at least some distance from the judge. We will generally define each axis and hearsay, and then discuss each in detail.

Competence Generally

Competence may be defined as the background, training, or experience which qualifies the advocate to make the statement. Thus most individuals would be competent, from their experience, to recognize members of their family. A trained expert in art could recognize the brush strokes of a Rembrandt as opposed to those of a forger. (What exactly constitutes training as distinguished from experience is a fine point we need not discuss here.)

To be competent does not of course mean that one will accurately convey what one has observed. For example, an accused person is competent (from experience) to say whether or not he or she committed the acts charged. However, few accused persons, who actually committed the crime, will accurately reveal what they know. They are biased.

Bias Generally

Bias may be defined as a predisposition, usually created by self-interest, to interpret or report observations and/or opinions in favor of a particular interest. All human beings are biased to one degree or another. Even the completely disinterested objective scientist is biased in the direction of objectivity. Thus, bias is always a question of degree. In examining for bias, one attempts to indict bias so great that the accuracy of the declaration may be seriously questioned.

Hearsay Generally

The word hearsay comes from the phrase "I heard someone say . . ." **Hearsay** may be defined as the distance between the advocate and the judge. Distance means the number of repetitions through which it has had to pass before it is heard in the debate. The accuracy of a citation is inversely proportional to the number of parties repeating it. Anyone who has ever played the parlor game of *Rumor* knows the rule. As a story proceeds around a circle of players, whispered from one to another, it changes.

Competence in Detail

Competence may be measured by internal and external tests. Internal tests rely on the plausibility of the declaration itself. External tests rely upon the stated authority, including compurgation of the declarant. Thus, internal tests rely upon the sense the statement makes independent of the declarant's training and experience while external tests rely upon an acceptance of that training and experience to produce credibility.

Internal Tests of Competence

In classical logic, only internal tests were relevant, and evidence (premises) could not be accepted upon authority alone (this is the basis of the classical fallacy of Appeal to Authority). This distinction has not been found as tenable in the modern world because knowledge has become so specialized that we must, like it or not, rely on the judgment of specialists. However, over-reliance on authority could be considered a fallacy. In this sense, it can become at least related to other fallacies, such as a circular fallacy, as follows:

> Our automobile has 5,000 miles to live.
> Why?
> Our mechanic said so.
> Why did our mechanic say so?
> Well, it's simple. Our automobile has 5,000 miles to live.

Here, we can see that over-reliance on authority puts the advocate in a trap from which there is no escape. One of the good points about parliamentary debate is that it avoids the trap because *whether someone else said something* is only one reason among many for believing a claim. The advocate must also be able to explain the reasons given within the evidence. This means that *competence plus an assertion* is not much better than an assertion alone. While an expert may just give his or her opinion that opinion should be based on reasons. If asked for those reasons, the expert should be able to explain those reasons. When quoting or referring to evidence therefore, one should remember to include the reasons given by the source or at least be able to produce them if requested. Thus, you avoid the begging-the-question or circular fallacy, both of which will be explained later.

For example, if the President of the United States were to say tomorrow, "We will all die in a nuclear attack within the next two years," people would ask the President why and most would not believe the President until some reasons were given. Even though the President may have high credibility among a slight majority of people in the USA, we would be unlikely to believe him or her until explanations were advanced.

Further, if your doctor told you that you were going to die in 6 months but refused to give you a reason, you would most certainly seek a second opinion. You then would not be satisfied until a reason was given for or against the original opinion.

Finally, in Israel's early recorded history, prophets would appear from time to time declaring God's wrath upon the people. Occasionally, the prophets were believed, but only after giving reasons. Those reasons usually included the "sinfulness of the people." In this case, the reasons, rather than the legitimacy of the prophet, are what were believed. Each person hearing the reason could review the Hebrew law to determine whether he was following it. Seeing that the prophet's reason seemed legitimate (i.e. he was not following the law), he affirmed the reason. Very little persuasion has occurred in human history merely because an authority "said so," even if the reason were merely coercive in nature. We must remember this context as we continue to review the rules for evidence reliability. An assertion, even from authority, does not constitute a good argument.

Typical internal tests would rely upon two factors. The first deals with the consistency of the statement. One should determine if the statement is consistent in itself. If a source said, "It was a cold winter day with the temperature in the mid-seventies," the statement is not internally consistent and is suspect. The second test deals with the vocabulary employed by the author. Does the advocate use the vocabulary one would expect of an authority on the subject? If in discussing baseball, the speaker keeps talking about "the guy who throws the ball" instead of saying "pitcher" one has a right to be suspicious. Internal tests are of limited value because virtually any cited source will meet these tests.

External Tests of Competence

The major external test is found in the theory of Compurgation. **Compurgation** is the acceptance of the accuracy of a declarant's statement based on the parties attesting to his/her competence. It is derived from an ancient Anglo-Saxon legal practice. This practice is best understood by a hypothetical example.

Assume that you are in a Saxon village in the Eighth Century. While in a field you have a fight with another villager. There are no witnesses. The party who threw the first punch will be guilty of battery while the other party may recover damages. When the case comes before the magistrate, you will bring all of your friends who are willing to swear that you didn't start it. Let us assume there are seven of them. These seven would compurgate your story by swearing that you didn't start the fight even though they didn't see the incident. The other party will bring his six friends to compurgate his story. You will win because you have seven compurgators and he only has six. Simple! Also, obviously flawed (Consider how hard this mode of proof must have been on strangers!). Note that these compurgators are in effect character witnesses because they're testifying to your credibility.

From this theory we borrow the term compurgation to stand for all those parties who, directly or indirectly, attest to the competence of a source. To see how this works in practice, consider the following:

To Prove (claim): That extraterrestrial intelligent life exists.

Evidence (datum): Smith says that in his opinion it does.

So stated, the validity of the claim relies entirely on Smith's opinion. Assume for the moment that we consider his/her opinion relevant. How much weight should we give it? We don't know Smith and thus cannot judge how competent or biased he/she is. Consider how the following additions would serve as compurgation.

1) Dr. Smith says . . . We now know that somebody at some place at some time gave this person a doctorate, and therefore he/she presumably has some intelligence. In effect, some degree-granting body someplace thinks Smith is knowledgeable in something and is willing to serve as his compurgator. Of course we don't know what his doctorate is in, so the degree may not even be relevant.

Be cautioned. There is no law governing the use of the title Doctor (or for that matter, Colonel, Judge, Professor, or anything else). You could walk out of the room at this moment and start referring to yourself as such. There is nothing to stop you unless you start accepting money offered you because of your title (accepting money under false pretenses) or until you try to treat a medical patient (practicing medicine without a license). Since society respects the opinions of doctors or professors more than those of ordinary mortals, the world is full of charlatans who adopt titles to which they have no legitimate claim.

2) Same facts, but assume **Professor Smith says . . .** The title professor adds the compurgation of some college someplace that thinks Smith is qualified to teach something. Most audiences will consider professor a higher qualification of competence than doctor.

3) Same facts, but assume the citation is **"Smith, in her book Extraterrestrial Life, says . . ."** Designating Smith as an author lends authority to her statement, but one might ask "why?" All it takes to publish a book is money. Any person, no matter how incompetent, can pay a printer to publish his/her book on subject X. It might not receive much distribution or recognition, but it is nonetheless a book, and most people will consider the author competent to say something on the subject. I am always amazed by how much credibility is given to citations with no more qualification than is shown in example 3.

Examined rationally, publishing a book should bring increased compurgation because the soundness of the ideas presented has been considered by some publisher someplace. But, as discussed earlier, publishers vary greatly in their sense of scholarly responsibility.

4) Same facts, but the citation is **"Smith, in his recent article in *Exo-Biology Journal* says . . ."** The analysis here is similar for that of a book citation, except that here the compurgation added is that of the periodical in which the article is published. (Obviously periodicals lend their imprimatur only to their articles and not to letters to the editor.) Thus if *Exo-Biology Journal* is a respected scientific publication, Smith's credentials are boosted. If it is a sensationalistic pop periodical, his credentials would suffer. Of course some authorities are so recognized that they would compurgate the periodical rather than the other way around. For example, Carl Sagan could publish in any journal he wished, and it would be his authority rather than that of the magazine that would count.

Compurgation flows from the known to the unknown. The whole purpose of compurgation is to lend authority to someone who is not known on the basis of how many known sources agree with him/her. Thus if Sagan is known and the journal is not, compurgation flows from the writer to the journal. If the journal is known and Sagan is not, compurgation flows from the journal to the author. If both are known, they compurgate one another (an incestuous but strong form of evidence). If neither is known, there is no compurgation and no credibility is added. In this last case, however, it is curious how much carryover there is from the relatively meaningless fact that it was published someplace.

5) Same facts, but assume the citation given is **"Smith, Professor of Biology at Prestigious University, says . . ."** Here the additional compurgation is that of a University. If one doesn't know Professor Smith but does know the university he/she teaches at, the prestige of the college transfers to the Professor. (Here again, mutual compurgation often occurs. Does John Kenneth Galbraith gain prestige because he holds a chair at NYU or does NYU gain because he holds a chair there? Both are correct.)

One could go on to endless permutations of the above pattern, but the general technique should be clear. If a judge does not know the declarant, the judge will look for something she/he does know to lend compurgation. The credibility of the declarant is therefore largely determined by the compurgation provided.

External Competence by Demonstration. The second way in which competence is determined externally is by demonstration. This means that the source is able to demonstrate directly to the judge that he/she "knows what he's talking about."

For example, a friend of author Perella is a breeder of Gordon Setters. He trains these dogs to hunt. He has no relevant professional training, and could not have since he invented most of the techniques he uses. He is accepted by courts in our area is an expert witness on canine behavior despite his lack of degrees. His competence stems not from compurgation (the testimony of another who believes in him) but from the fact that his dogs win most of the hunting contests they're entered in. No one ever told his pack that college degrees are needed, and so they just follow his commands. Watching them is demonstration of competence.

A demonstration of competence is superior to compurgation.

Judges will trust their own senses more than they will trust third parties. This is good news for parliamentary debate as practiced in intercollegiate forums. If you debate well, if you confidently present your interpretations of great works and historical events, and if you present facts consistent with other known facts, you can demonstrate competence to your judge. This means that both of the predominant forms of academic debate should have equal legitimacy in terms of the arguments being presented. Of course, all debates depend on the actual competence of the debaters. Debaters must be prepared for their debates and have studied current issues related to their topic.

Bias in Detail

Remember that bias is a predisposition which would cause the declarant to make a certain statement. The fact that a statement is biased does not mean that it is wrong. An accused would be biased in favor of their innocence, and may actually be innocent. It has been found that most debaters think they won their debate. Many of them must be right. What we are therefore concerned with is a level of bias which would cause the statement to be unreliable.

While there are many causes of bias, we will group them under two headings: self-interest and emotion. Self-interest may be defined as what the declarant would want for himself, one close to him, or a cause he believes in. Emotion means an emotional state of sufficient intensity that one cannot interpret perceptions accurately. Thus one might and should feel the emotion of pity when considering the plight of starving babies, but if one is still able to consider the issue as a reasonable person the emotional state would not be sufficiently intense to cause the statement to be disregarded.

As with competence, there are both internal and external tests.

The principal internal test of bias is the use of **emotional language.** Statements with hot language are properly suspect.

The principal external test of bias is consistency with **self-interest.** First, of course, one must try to determine what the self-interest is and in what direction it might be working. If the accused says, "I didn't do it," we would realize that he/she has a self interest in acquittal. If an ad says, "this product is great," the self-interest in selling is obvious. In both cases the self-interest would work to possibly distort the statement. However, if a neutral witness says, "he didn't do it," or Consumers Union says, "this product is great," there is still self-interest present, but it is towards objectivity—the same self-interest the reasonable person has.

The Statement Against Interest. Sometimes, declarants make statements against their self-interest. If the accused says, "I did it.", the statement carries great weight. This is a Statement against Interest, and has enormous evidentiary weight. Suppose a debate is taking place over whether oil drilling should be allowed in the Alaskan National Wildlife Preserve. The affirmative, anticipating the negative will argue that oil drilling will be harmful to the environment, finds two sources which both state that oil operations will not cause significant environmental harm. One of the statements comes from the President of an oil company who has drilling right in the area. The second comes from the President of an environmental organization. Which of these two pieces of evidence would be the most persuasive? It seems rather obvious that the second piece of evidence is the most powerful. The first piece of evidence could be easily dismissed by the negative as being a biased statement. However, the second statement would be more difficult to refute. That is because we would not expect an environmental organization to say something was not harmful to the environment if in fact it were. A statement against interest is the least biased and most powerful source possible.

Hearsay in Detail

Let us return to our two little kids. First kid says to second kid "My daddy can beat up your daddy because my daddy's a prizefighter. I know my daddy's a prizefighter because he told me so last night." The second little kid is the judge, and now there is distance between him and the declarant (Daddy). He can't know the context in which the statement was made (were they playing a game?), he can't ask Daddy what was meant, and he doesn't even know that the first little kid is accurately repeating Daddy's literal statement. There is no issue of competence; Daddy would clearly know whether or not he was a prizefighter. There may be some bias, but so would there be if Daddy were standing with the two kids. The unreliability of this evidence is the result of the third factor: hearsay.

Hearsay might be thought of as a chain, stretching between the declarant and the judge who is to evaluate the declaration. Consider the following: "Penny told Maxi who told Hazel who told me what I'm telling you."

Penny	Maxi	Hazel	Brian	You
declarant	link 1	link 2	link 3	the judge

Assume that Penny is saying something relevant, that she is competent to say it, and she has no detectable bias. The judge might still validly question the reliability of the evidence simply because he or she is so far removed from it. If this sort of chain seems unlikely, consider the following statement which might appear in any debate: "Expert said X, which was reported in *Obscure Scholarly Journal,* an excerpt of which was reported in this paragraph from *Time* magazine, which is now read into the debate.

Expert declarant	Journal link 1	Time link 2	Debater link 3	You the judge

Thus, all evidence should be examined internally and externally for signs of bias. If excessively biased, it should not be considered. If worthy of consideration the probable affect of the bias on the statement should also be considered. Upon such slender threads of hearsay is most debate evidence based. The rule in such cases is simple: Hearsay is a chain, and a chain is only as strong as its weakest link.

In the Penny example above, the judge may well feel that this is simply a rumor, and disregard the statement, no matter what it says. In the expert example, a judge would be justified in accepting the evidence because links 1 and 2 are professional repeaters of information and likely to be accurate, and a debater is unlikely to distort a citation from such a commonly available source as *Time* for fear the other side will note the discrepancy.

Hearsay and Demonstrations. You will remember that when we discussed compurgation it was pointed out that competence could be shown by compurgation (the testimony of others) or by demonstration. It was noted that proof by demonstration was superior. This same principle applies to all types of evidence and is related to the Hearsay problem.

If a judge is shown directly some phenomenon there is still an observation or opinion and it is still evidence, but it is directly the observation or opinion of the judge, and is not the testimony of another.

A demonstration places a phenomenon before the judge and asks the judge to directly make an observation or form an opinion. Obviously there are no hearsay issues with a demonstration. There are, however, the same issues of relevance and reliability which we find with any piece of testimonial evidence. The difference is that now it is the competence and bias of the judge that is being measured.

Assume again our little kids, but the first kid offers to prove that his daddy is a prizefighter by taking the second little kid to the next fight. The second little kid goes. The fight is evidence, but it is a demonstration rather than testimony. The second kid observes what happens directly. He might ask 1) "Is the fact that my neighbor's daddy is in the ring relevant to prove that he's a prizefighter?" Clearly yes. 2) "Is my observation reliable? Am I competent to know what I'm seeing and unbiased enough to draw a fair conclusion?" If all that is to be proved is that Daddy's a prizefighter, the kid can make the judgment. All he has to do is watch a fight and see that a prize is awarded. In fact, Daddy doesn't even have to win. The claim is only that he's a prizefighter, not that he's a good one. On the other hand, if the claim were that *Daddy is a good prizefighter,* little kid two is probably not qualified to draw such an opinion. Note that the first question is an observation fact while the second one is an opinion.

Only the judge can assess his/her own bias, but it is from a concern over bias, or the appearance of bias, that courtroom judges will disqualify themselves from some cases. It is fair to say, however, that most judges in debates will place heavy weight on demonstrations because they can assess their own bias and competence and compensate for them.

Do not feel that this is the full legal concept of hearsay. Courts are much fussier than debate judges and the rules for hearsay much more strict and complicated. At root, however, the same question is being asked. Is there a justification for hearing something other than a first-hand account because we think the repetitions are reliable?

THE HIERARCHY OF EVIDENCE

Thus we can analyze whether evidence is accurate, relevant, and reliable. Assuming that these three hurdles are crossed, there is still a lot of evidence left. How are we to weigh the evidence of various types? There seems to exist in evidence the same kind of hierarchy that exists in poker. Just as a flush beats a straight, so likewise some types of evidence will beat other types of evidence. The superior evidence is that which is least susceptible to subjective judgment.

This hierarchy can be described according to the following levels from highest (best) to lowest (poorest). We will describe these levels from poorest to best.

6. Consensus of Studies
5. Empirical Study/Consensus of Expert Opinion
4. Expert Opinion/Consensus of Lay Opinion
3. Lay Opinion
2. Judicial Notice/Common Knowledge
1. Assertion

Level 1. Assertion

An assertion is a claim without a datum, literally "asserted for acceptance." This is not logical proof at all, but relies entirely upon the ethos (credibility) of the speaker. If an affirmative advocate asserts a *prima facie* element by saying that that "X is true," the negative can usually nullify this by asserting the contrary. Because the negative starts with presumption, the negative has an assertion plus presumption while the affirmative has only an assertion. Thus the negative usually would win, unless the affirmative team is more credible, or successful arguments elsewhere are seen to compensate for the assertion.

Level 2. Judicial Notice/Common Knowledge

Technically these two concepts are different. *Judicial Notice* is a rule of evidence in legal proceedings, while common knowledge is what is generally known. However they are alike in that they are a substitute for evidence. Courts have long found that if advocates were required to prove everything, nothing would ever get done. Thus, courts evolved the rule that formal evidence need not be offered if the fact could be confirmed by consultation with a recognized reference work (including statute books) or if it was generally known in the community. Thus, in a court, a lawyer would not have to prove that Christmas falls on December 25th. This would be granted on judicial notice.

A similar standard exists outside of courtrooms if the fact submitted is:

1) generally known in the community and
2) non-controversial.

Thus, a fact may be generally known but subject to controversy (*i.e.*, nuclear power plants are unsafe) and thus not admissible common knowledge. Obviously disputes might arise on "What constitutes 'the community'?" The standard that would pertain at the local "Anti-Nuclear Power Plant Association" would be different than that of the community at large. Also, the opposing advocate always has the right to show that the purported fact is indeed the subject of controversy, and therefore requires formal proof.

Level 3. Lay Opinion

Lay opinion is the opinion of a person with no formal training in the subject of the claim. Thus, a lay person might look at fingerprints and know only that they were fingerprints, while an expert could tell you whose they were. By and large, lay opinion is of little value. However, courts have long recognized that some matters are such common human experiences that a lay person might have a fit opinion of them. In courts lay persons are allowed to identify the handwriting of an acquaintance, identify faces they have seen, judge the speed of an automobile and state if a person exhibited symptoms of drunkenness. This standard seems sound, and providing that a lay person has had sufficient opportunity to experience the phenomenon and make observations of the specific event in question, a lay opinion is certainly worthy of consideration.

Level 4. Expert Opinion/Consensus of Lay Opinion

An expert is one qualified by background, training or experience to make a judgment on the subject of the claim. Such opinions are usually accorded more weight than a lay opinion. There are as many levels of expert as there are experts but again they can all be analyzed by competence and bias.

One particular aspect of competence worth noting here is the opportunity to observe. Since an expert is rendering a subjective opinion on some phenomenon, he/she must have had adequate opportunity to observe the phenomenon. For example, if a psychiatrist is testifying that the defendant was insane when he/she committed the crime (and this is of course a subjective judgment), it should be shown that he/she had an opportunity to observe the defendant (possibly during a period of hospitalization).

Consensus of Lay Opinion means that a majority of lay persons sampled hold a particular opinion. Public opinion polls are common examples of such evidence. The Consensus of Lay Opinion differs from Common Knowledge in that with Common Knowledge there is no controversy. The subjects of Lay Opinion may divide the public sharply. Such evidence seems to have about the same weight at the opinion of as single expert.

Level 5. Empirical Study/Consensus of Expert Opinion

If one expert opinion is good, several in agreement are obviously better. Thus, the consensus of opinion level simply means that most, or a majority, or the best, or whatever number of experts in this field agree with the claim.

At about the same level of proof is the empirical study. The empirical study is not an opinion. It is a report of sensory observation. Thus, if we are debating whether or not a rat can find a way through a maze, one side might offer several opinions from rat trainers saying that it can't, while the other side offers a report from some experimenter who watched a rat go through such a maze. At this level, the proofs are about equal since the empirical finding may be isolated.

Level 6. Consensus of Studies

This highest level of proof is found when many observers reporting the same empirically observable phenomenon report the same finding. Thus, if eight out of ten studies which observed rats in this maze found that they could find their way through it, the charge of isolation which could be raised at level 5 is dispelled, and the consensus of studies would beat the opinions of experts.

This continues the rule that the higher evidence is that which is less susceptible to subjective judgment. Empirical studies by their nature reduce subjectivity to a minimum. Testimony by ordinary eye (as opposed to expert) witnesses is at the empirical study level because what each witness is required to do is report their sensory experiences. Courts are very careful not to let in lay opinions (with the exceptions noted in level 3) as opposed to a witness's observations. What makes an expert witness different is that the expert is allowed to report their expert opinions.

FACT VS. OPINION

Much is made of the difference between facts and opinions. In reality, the distinction is simple, and it's consistent with the analysis we have already discussed. *A fact is subject, at least in theory, to empirical verification; an opinion is not.* That's it. Remember our basic classification of propositions. A fact must be something which could be proven by a proposition of fact. An opinion is a proposition of value. An opinion is the attitude towards something which is expressed.

Assume that Mr. Able is selling a painting to Mr. Baker. Mr. Able makes several statements which we can classify as fact or opinion. "This painting is for sale." Fact. It either is or isn't. "This is a beautiful painting." Opinion. Beauty is not empirically provable. In fact, this is a special kind of opinion called a seller's opinion. A seller is allowed to have any opinion, inflated or otherwise, about the things being sold. The technical term is puffery, and at law a seller will not be held accountable for his opinions. He would, however be held responsible for misstatements of fact. If there is "an intentional misrepresentation of a material fact," there is fraud. This would include rolling back and later lying about the odometer reading on a car when it is sold.

"You will be very happy with this painting." Although stated as a future fact it is an opinion, since it is not subject to empirical proof at this time.

"I bought this painting for $10,000. It has appreciated $5,000 in the last year." First part fact. Dollars may be counted. The second statement is hard to classify. If the seller means "I think it's worth $15,000," it's a seller's opinion. If he means that it has been appraised by someone else at $15,000, it's a fact. An appraisal is of course the opinion of the appraiser, but the fact that the opinion was offered is empirically verifiable.

Thus in any statement one of three conditions must exist: 1) It is a report of an empirical observation and is a fact, 2) It is not a report of an empirical observation and it is an opinion, or 3) Until the statement is further clarified, it cannot be classified.

One final area needs attention. Because any advocate would like to make his evidence sound empirical (and therefore scientific), one often encounters evidence which, while sounding like an empirical study, is not anything but opinion evidence. It really does not matter how much opinion evidence one has; it does not amass to some critical threshold after which time it magically becomes empirical.

SUMMARY

Claims must be supported for argument to occur. This chapter considered evidentiary support which in turn is of two types: testimony and demonstration. Demonstrations are those situations in which the judge becomes the percipient witness. All other cases are testimony. All evidence, testimonial or demonstrative, can be tested by the elements of 1) accuracy, 2) relevance, and 3) reliability (which in turn consists of competence, bias, and hearsay). Finally, evidence can be placed on a hierarchy to determine its weight relative to other relevant and reliable evidence. In order of strongest to weakest, the hierarchy is: consensus of empirical studies, empirical study/consensus of expert opinion, expert opinion/consensus of lay opinion, lay opinion, judicial notice/common knowledge, and assertion.

CHAPTER 7

USING SOUND REASONING

Debaters must be able to use sound reasoning. Failing to do so can harm any chances of winning a debate. Conversely, debate helps an advocate develop critical-thinking skills. While the ability to think critically may seem like an innate quality, actually, it is something that can be learned. And debate enhances learning. This chapter will introduce the basic concepts of inductive and deductive reasoning. The next chapter will focus on a more in depth understanding of categorical logic.

DEDUCTIVE AND INDUCTIVE REASONING

An understanding of **deductive and inductive reasoning** can help develop your ability to reason effectively and to debate more easily. Some logicians feel that all argument is basically deductive, and some say that all argument is basically inductive. However true either of these positions may be, making a distinction between these two types of reasoning can help an advocate develop sound arguments.

Many texts in the communication discipline define induction as specific to general arguments and define deduction as general to specific arguments. However, these definitions are incomplete at best and inaccurate at worst. Ray and Zavos explain,

> [I]n deduction the conclusion is required by the premises, or reasons, whereas in induction it is not. In other words, in deduction the conclusion states no more than what is stated in the reasons taken together; in induction the conclusion goes beyond what is stated in the reasons.
>
> The definitions often given for deduction and induction make the two processes parallel and exactly opposite: deduction is defined as reasoning from general statements to particular statements, and induction is defined as reasoning from particular statements to general statements. These definitions are inadequate. For one thing, it is clearly possible to reason from general statements to other general statements: for example: "All periods of high employment are followed by periods of inflation, all periods of inflation are followed by periods of high unemployment; thus, all periods of high employment are followed by periods of high unemployment." It is also possible to reason deductively from particular to particular; for example: "A is taller

than B, B is taller than C; thus, A is taller than C." It is also argued by some that many inductions involve reasoning from particular statements to other particular statements.

Deductive Reasoning

Deductive reasoning is often described as any argument that develops from a general premise to a specific conclusion. That definition is inadequate as explained above; a more accurate definition is one offered by Howard Kahane, in his book, *Logic and Contemporary Rhetoric:* "if its premises are true, then its conclusion must be true." Formal proof of deductive arguments is made through syllogisms. There are three types of syllogisms: categorical, conditional (sometimes called hypothetical), and disjunctive.

Categorical Syllogisms

The categorical syllogism is the classic type of deductive argument. It is also the most complicated. Chapters 7 and 8 are dedicated to a very thorough discussion of categorical syllogisms. However, for this introductory chapter only, the basic concepts will be introduced.

Categorical syllogisms get their name because they are composed of three categorical claims. Categorical claims are statements that show a relationship between two different categories. The statements "All men are mortal" and "No reptiles are mammals" are examples of categorical claims. A categorical syllogism is a three part explicit argument that includes a **major premise** which is usually a general observation, a **minor premise** which is usually a specific application, and a **conclusion** which is the point the syllogism is trying to make. A categorical syllogism introduces three terms each of which is used twice. The categorical syllogism is easier to illustrate than explain. The following (Figure 7.1) is an example of a categorical syllogism.

Major Premise:	All men are mortal
Minor Premise:	Socrates is a man
Conclusion:	Socrates is mortal

FIGURE 7.1

Categorical Syllogism

Truth and Validity

All syllogisms are evaluated on two levels: truth and validity. Unfortunately, these two terms are often used interchangeably by lay persons when discussing arguments and often are used incorrectly. To say that an argument is true is very different than saying an argument is valid.

The standard of truth is met if the premises and the conclusion are all true. In the syllogism presented in Figure 7.1 the two premises and the conclusion all happen to be true, that is, they are accurate representations of reality. Thus, that syllogism is considered to be true. Unfortunately, determining if a statement is true is not always easy and indeed may at times be impossible. For example, is the statement "most politicians are corrupt" a true statement? Obviously that is a very difficult statement to label as true or false.

Although determining the truth of a syllogism is often subjective, determining the validity of a syllogism is not. Validity is a clear-cut issue. Either the syllogism is valid or it is not. A syllogism is considered valid if the premises are structured in such a way that they force the conclusion. The truthfulness of a syllogism is completely irrelevant to its validity (and vice versa). The syllogism presented in Figure 7.1 is valid since its conclusion must follow from the premises.

With truth and validity as the two tests for a syllogism, there are then four possible outcomes when evaluating a syllogism. They are as follows: first, true and valid; second, true but invalid; third, untrue but valid; and finally, untrue and invalid (Figure 7.2). For a syllogism to be considered true, all three components (major

	VALID	NOT VALID
True	All cars are motorized vehicles (True) All Ford Mustangs are cars (True) All Ford Mustangs are motorized vehicles (True)	All cars are motorized vehicles (True) All Ford Mustangs are motorized vehicles (True) All Ford Mustangs are cars (True)
Not True	All motorized vehicles are cars (False) All Ford Mustangs are motorized vehicles (True) All Ford Mustangs are cars (True)	All cars are Ford Mustangs (False) All cars are motorized vehicles (True) All motorized vehicles are Ford Mustangs (False)

FIGURE 7.2

The Four Possible Determinations for Syllogisms

premise, minor premise, and conclusion) must be true. If any part is not true, then the syllogism as a whole is considered not true. The four syllogisms represented in Figure 7.2 give an example of each. If a syllogism is both true and valid, it is referred to as a sound syllogism. The following formula must be applied to all syllogisms: **Truth + Validity = Soundness.**

Elementary Venn Diagrams

One way to demonstrate the validity (or non-validity) of a syllogism is to construct Venn diagrams. Venn diagrams are graphs which utilize circles to show the relationship between the two premises of a syllogism for the purpose of visually checking the validity (or non validity) of the syllogism's conclusion. There are different ways to construct Venn diagrams. For this chapter, a more elementary but less comprehensive format will be introduced. In chapter 8 a more sophisticated style of Venn diagramming which is preferred by philosophers will be introduced.

To construct any Venn diagram, it is best to first substitute letters (symbols) for the terms in the syllogism. If "A" = man; "B" = mortal and "C" = Socrates we can express the syllogism presented in Figure 7.1 using these symbols (Figure 7.3).

Major Premise:	All men are mortal	[All A are B]
Minor Premise:	Socrates is a man	[All C are A]
Conclusion:	Socrates is mortal	[All C are B]

FIGURE 7.3

Letter Substitutions

The letters or symbols "A," "B," and "C" are arbitrary. Any letters or other symbols could be used. In Chapter 8 the letters "S," "M" and "P" will be used instead of "A," "B," and "C." There is a rationale for using these other letters but you will need to read the next chapter to find it out. However, for our introductory discussion, "A," "B," and "C" are probably easier to remember and work just fine.

The first step is to diagram the first premise. The first premise instructs us to place all of circle "A" into the circle "B."
    (All "A" are "B.")

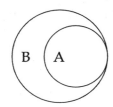

Step two is drawing the second premise, which in this case instructs us to place all of circle "C" into circle "A."

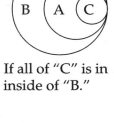

(All "C" are "A.")

The final step is to determine if the final drawing forces the stated conclusion (All "C" are "A"). As should be obvious, the completed diagram visually illustrates the validity of the syllogism. If all of "C" is in "A" and if all of "A" is in "B," then it has to follow that all of "C" is inside of "B."

For comparison, notice how the next example, while also true, is not valid.

> All men (A) are mortal (B)
> Socrates (C) is mortal (B)
> Socrates (C) is a man (A)

Step one is do diagram "All A are B"

Step two is adding the second premise "All C are B."

As can bee seen, there are three locations where "C" may be placed to conform to the premise that "All C are B." Circle "C" could be placed completely in circle "A," or placed completely outside of "A," or placed partially in "A." Since it is possible to diagram "All C are B" without being forced into the conclusion that "All C are A" the syllogism is invalid. The key to remember is that while it is possible to place all of "C" inside of "A" to complete the second premise it is not required. To be valid the premises must force the conclusion, not simply allow it as a possibility.

Let's do one more.

> No men (A) are mortal (B)
> Socrates (C) is mortal (B)
> Socrates (C)) is not a man (A)

Once again, step one is to diagram the first premise "No A are B."

Step two is adding the second premise "All C are B."

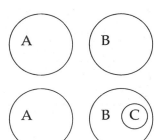

Finally, we determine if the finished diagram forces the conclusion. Since the conclusion that "No C are A" is inescapable, the syllogism is valid. Once again notice that while the syllogism is valid, it is not true as both the first premise (No men are mortal) and the conclusion (Socrates is not a man) are both false. This example should clearly illustrate the difference between the truth and the validity of a syllogism.

Conditional Syllogisms

So far the categorical syllogism has been discussed. However, there are two other types of syllogisms that are worthy of mention. The conditional syllogism is an "if-then" argument. A conditional syllogism has two parts to the major premise. They are the antecedent (P) and the consequent (Q). The antecedent is always listed first in the major premise while the consequent is always listed second in the major premise. Think of a poker game. You must first "ante" up before you confront the "consequence" of either winning or losing the pot of money. There are only two valid forms to this syllogism (Figure 7.5). The first is referred to as the **modus ponens.** The second valid form is referred to as the **modus tollens.** Notice that the minor premise must either affirm the antecedent or deny the consequent. When this occurs the conclusion must also be an affirmation or a denial.

If any other format is used, then the syllogism is invalid. The following are examples of invalid conditional syllogisms.

Invalid

Major Premise:	If P then Q	(If you hit John, then he will feel pain)
Minor Premise:	Q	(John is feeling pain)
Conclusion:	P	(Therefore you must have hit John)

Valid (modus ponens)

Major Premise:	If P then Q	(If you hit John, then he will be in pain)
Minor Premise:	P	(You hit John)
Conclusion:	Q	(Therefore John is in pain)

OR

Valid (modus tollens)

Major Premise:	If P then Q	(If you hit John, then he will be in pain)
Minor Premise:	Not Q	(John is not in pain)
Conclusion:	Not P	(Therefore you did not hit John)

FIGURE 7.5

Valid Structures of the Conditional Syllogism

OR

Invalid

Major Premise:	If P then Q	(If you hit John, then he will feel pain)
Minor Premise:	Not P	(You did not hit John)
Conclusion:	Not Q	(Therefore John is not feeling pain)

These syllogisms are invalid because the major premise sets up a condition which indicates one way, but not necessarily the only way, in which John will feel pain. For instance, someone else may have hit John, he could have fallen, been hit by a car, or have a toothache.

Finally, conditional claims may also be used to create a pure conditional syllogism (Figure 7.6). These are called "pure conditional syllogisms" because all three claims are complete "if-then" statements. In order to be valid the conclusion must again either affirm both the antecedent of the major premise and the consequent of the minor premise or deny both the consequent of the minor premise and the antecedent of the major premise.

	If P then Q	[If it gets windy then the ocean will get rough]
	If Q then R	[If the ocean gets rough then Mitch will get sea sick]
Therefore	If P then R	[Therefore, if it gets windy Mitch will get sea sick]
		OR
	If P then Q	[If it gets windy then the ocean will get rough]
	If Q then R	[If the ocean gets rough then Mitch will get sea sick]
Therefore	If not R then not P	[Therefore, if Mitch does not get sea sick then it did no get windy]

FIGURE 7.6

Pure Conditional Syllogisms

Disjunctive Syllogisms

The final type of syllogism is the **disjunctive syllogism.** The disjunctive syllogism is a deductive argument in which the major premise sets up two options and the minor premise forces the acceptance of one of the two options by eliminating or affirming one of them. The following is an example of a disjunctive syllogism.

Either Tom is a liar or what he said really happened	[Either A or B]
Tom is not a liar	[Not A]
Therefore what Tom said must have really happened	[B]

A disjunctive syllogism has two parts to the major premise. They are simply disjunct one (A) and disjunct two (B). The disjunctive syllogism has two forms that are unconditionally valid and an additional two forms that are conditionally valid. Many logicians accept only the two unconditionally valid forms. However, we will discuss all four forms.

Unless specifically stated to the contrary, the word "or" is always thought of as being inclusive rather than exclusive. Think of the "or" in the disjunctive syllogism as including an implicit "and" (A and/or B). The possibility of the "and" can be ignored only if we have knowledge that it cannot be included as a possibility or artificially rule out that possibility in advance. However, knowing that both disjuncts cannot co-exist requires knowledge that goes beyond the information contained in the premises. When the disjuncts are thought of as being inclusive there are only two valid forms. The minor premise must deny one of the disjuncts and the conclusion must affirm the other disjunct (Figure 7.7). If the reverse were to occur (that is, you affirmed one disjunct and denied the other disjunct), then the argument would be invalid.

Imagine your friend, Juanita, is holding out two closed fists in front of you. You are given truthful information that Juanita has a coin in either her left or right hand. What information does this major premise provide you? The major premise tells you that one of three situations is true: 1) Juanita has a coin in her left hand but not in her right hand, 2) Juanita has a coin in her right hand but not in her left hand, or

Deny One Disjunct and Affirm the Other:

Major Premise: Either A or B	(Either coin in left or right hand)
Minor Premise: Not A	(Coin not in left hand)
Conclusion: B	(Therefore, coin in right hand)

OR

Major Premise: Either A or B	(Either coin in left or right hand)
Minor Premise: Not B	(Coin not in right hand)
Conclusion: A	(Therefore, coin in left hand)

FIGURE 7.7

Valid Disjunctive Forms Assuming Inclusive Disjuncts

3) Juanita has a coin in both hands. Many times people overlook this third option. The key here is that nothing inherently prevents this third option from existing. Clearly, nothing prevents Juanita from having a coin in both hands. The statement "either one hand or the other" actually means that Juanita has a coin in **at least** one of her two hands. If Juanita has a coin in just one of her hands then the major premise would contain truthful information. Additionally, if Juanita has a coin in both hands, the major premise would still be providing truthful information. "Or" can mean "and." Now assume that Juanita opens up her left hand, and there is no coin. You can then safely conclude that the coin must be in her right hand. However, assume Juanita opens up her left hand and there is a coin. Could you then conclude that there is not a coin in her right hand? The answer is obviously "no." Therefore, as is clearly demonstrated, affirming one disjunct does not force the other disjunct to be denied.

However, if the syllogism sets up disjuncts that are known in advance to be exclusive rather than inclusive (either naturally or artificially), then, along with the two forms just presented, there are two additional forms that become valid. Consequently, for disjunctive syllogisms in which the disjuncts are known to be exclusive there are four valid forms (Figure 7.8).

Deny One Disjunct and Affirm the Other (Unconditionally Valid):

Major Premise:	Either A or B	(Either Pat is male or female)
Minor Premise:	Not A	(Pat is not male)
Conclusion:	B	(Therefore, Pat is female)

OR

Major Premise:	Either A or B	(Either Pat is male or female)
Minor Premise:	Not B	(Pat is not female)
Conclusion:	A	(Therefore, Pat is male)

Affirm One Disjunct and Deny the Other (Conditionally Valid):

Major Premise:	Either A or B	(Either Pat is male or female)
Minor Premise:	A	(Pat is male)
Conclusion:	Not B	(Therefore, Pat is not female)

OR

Major Premise:	Either A or B	(Either Pat is male or female)
Minor Premise:	B	(Pat is female)
Conclusion:	Not A	(Therefore, Pat is not male)

FIGURE 7.8

Valid Disjunctive Forms Assuming Exclusive Disjuncts

The hit television show *Saturday Night Live* had a very famous ongoing skit that later became a movie named *Pat*. Pat, played by Julia Sweeny, was a person whose gender could not be determined by appearance. Each skit consisted of people trying to trick Pat into revealing her/his gender. (Presumably it would have been too rude to simply ask Pat, "Are you a man or a woman?") This would meet the standard of having disjuncts which are exclusive. Clearly, Pat cannot be both male and female (yes, we know about hermaphrodites, but even hermaphrodites are legally classified as male or female).

Notice that the first two forms consist of the minor premise denying one disjunct and affirming the other disjunct. Also notice how these two forms were also considered valid when the disjuncts were considered to be inclusive. That is why those two forms are considered unconditionally valid. They are valid regardless if the disjuncts are inclusive or exclusive from one another. The last two forms consist of the minor premise affirming one disjunct and denying the other disjunct. The key to these two additional valid forms is that the major premise must deal solely with a condition in which it is known that the disjuncts are exclusive from one another. That is why they are considered conditionally valid. *War or peace* presents another such situation (these disjuncts would be by definition exclusive). The coin in the hand example would also meet this standard if we knew in advance (not necessary to make the first two forms valid) that the person only had one coin.

Further Explanation for Unconditionally Valid Forms. Almost all scholars of logic believe that the English word <u>or</u> is naturally inclusive. This means that a statement like "either cloudy or sunny" actually means "either cloudy and/or sunny." Thus, the common phrases we hear and read almost daily that include <u>and/or</u> are actually redundant because <u>or</u> means <u>and/or</u> already. To distinguish the conditionally valid syllogism from the unconditionally valid, many scholars use phrases like these:

> Major Premise: Either only light or else only darkness. (Either only A or else only B)
> Minor Premise: Only light. (only A)
> Conclusion: Not darkness. (not B)

Here, the syllogism is worded in a way that makes A and B mutually exclusive: that one cannot exist if the other is present. This is still conditionally valid even if worded as such. Validity is contingent upon the truth of the major premise: that light and darkness are in fact mutually exclusive. This exclusivity may be actual or artificial. Actual mutual exclusivity means that in natural conditions the two disjuncts are mutually exclusive; for example, if light is present, darkness cannot be present. Artificial mutual exclusivity works in the following example:

> Major Premise: Buy either only PC or else only Mac. (Either only A or else only B)

Minor Premise: Buy only PC. (Only A)
Conclusion: Not Buy Mac (Not B)

Technically, someone could buy both a Personal and a Macintosh Computer; therefore, real mutual exclusivity is NOT present in this dilemma. However, artificial mutual exclusivity may be a result of a specific situation: Juan, a medical student at Harvard, has only enough money to buy one computer. He has no way of buying or owning a second computer. Therefore, the choice of Mac versus PC is artificially mutually exclusive, the situation demanding that one and only one be purchased.

INDUCTIVE REASONING

"If it's not a deductive argument, it must be an inductive one" is a statement that may not be too far from the truth. Inductive reasoning is the use of some evidence to infer a conclusion, but inductive reasoning is not conclusive.

Many logicians prefer to describe inductive reasoning as a patterning. If you look at events or people in a number of circumstances, patterns develop. Early humans no doubt made use of induction to make sense of their world. They noticed that patterns formed in nature. They observed for example that every day a long period of light was followed by a long period of darkness. They noticed that the weather and temperature changed on a fairly normal basis. Those living along the Nile River observed flooding that would take place every year.

Like our early ancestors, we too learned to rely on induction from a very young age. We learned that when we were hungry and cried, that our mothers came, we learned that if we let go of our bottle it would fall to the floor, and we learned that if we touched a hot stove we would experience pain. Most everything we learn has a basis in induction. We may not be able to explain why something happens, but we can nonetheless recognize that patterns develop. Early humans might not have been able to explain why day and night occurred, but they certainly knew they did occur and would most likely occur again and again. As children, we might not have been able to offer a scientific explanation about the rules of gravity to explain why our bottles always fell if we let go, but we soon learned that it would fall.

We (as well as our early ancestors no doubt) also soon learned that many events, while following a pattern, did not always occur. When we cried our mothers did not always come. The Nile River did not always flood or sometimes it flooded at times when it wasn't supposed to. In other words, we soon learned that some inductive patterns are very strong while others are very weak.

Francis Bacon believed that the ability to use this type of patterning is at the root of genius. For example, Sigmund Freud, the father of modern psychology, observed his few children and patients to find patterns in human nature. Those patterns, as described by Freud, now serve as the basis for an entire discipline. The patterning we find in nature also forms the basis of all of modern science.

While deduction provides for certainty, induction does not. While we say that a deductive argument is valid, we say that an inductive argument is strong. A **strong** inductive argument is one which has a high probability of being true. A **weak** inductive argument is one that has a lesser chance of being true. Scientists may be right about theories built through use of induction, but at best they can make a case for a high probability of truth. Even if every instance of an observed phenomenon has followed the same pattern, we can still not be certain that the conclusion that follows will be true. For example, Lucky Seven may have won every single horse race he has ever been entered in, but we cannot be certain that he will win the next one.

The Relationship between Induction and Deduction

The fact that induction does not provide for absolutely certain conclusions sometimes causes students to view it as a flawed way of thinking. This is not the case. Not all things can be known with certainty. Sometimes deduction is not possible. In those cases, induction is all we have to go on. In fact, it can be argued that deduction is really just an extension of induction. For instance, earlier in this chapter we analyzed the following deductive syllogism:

Major Premise:	All men are mortal
Minor Premise:	Socrates was a man
Conclusion:	Socrates was mortal

We said that given the truth of the premises, the conclusion must follow. This is true. But ask yourself this question: How do we know that the major premise is true? The answer is, we don't really. There is just a very high degree of probability that it is true. That is because the major premise "all men are mortal" (and I guess women too) is reached by induction. Every person we know of has at some point died. Julius Caesar, George Washington, Copernicus, Martin Luther King Jr., Mahatma Gandhi, James Baldwin, *etc.* have all followed this pattern. We know of no human who has not followed this pattern. Every example we have supports this conclusion. We therefore consider it to be very strong argument. Yet, there are many people alive in the world today. Might one of them be immortal? Could be, but we doubt it.

The Importance of Induction

Induction then, instead of being thought of as deduction's imperfect twin, should be thought of as the basis for deduction itself. The major premises of most of our deductive arguments, as we has just seen, are based in induction. It is important to check our major premises inductively because failure to do so all but guarantees poor reasoning. For instance, one of the sources of prejudice and stereotyping is the failure to check the truth of the major premise. The following unchecked syllogism demonstrates the harm that may result:

Major Premise:	All Americans are lazy
Minor Premise:	John is an American
Conclusion:	John is lazy

Notice that this syllogism is a valid but untrue one. The reason it is untrue is because the arguer failed to check his or her major premise inductively. Had that double-check been done, the stereotype could have been avoided, because many counter examples of workaholic Americans could be found. You could substitute Americans in the above example for any given race or religion or human classification and come up with the same results.

The fact of the matter is every one of us engages in stereotyping. To avoid insanity, we must generalize. Otherwise, every time we opened a can of corn, we'd have to study every kernel to determine if it fits a book's description of a corn kernel. Every time you walked into a college classroom, you would wander around until someone told you to sit down, take out some note-taking material, face the teacher, and listen to him or her. So our ability to generalize is necessary in order to function. However, where it matters (when human beings are involved for instance) we must double-check our major premises inductively. Every time we are confronted with disconfirming information we must make an effort to cross check it with any general premises we now have about the particular classification. The ability to think critically depends greatly upon our ability to adapt to new information. Ralph Waldo Emerson once remarked that "consistency is the hobgoblin of little minds," meaning that human beings must be able to change their minds if data dictate doing so.

Unfortunately, human beings are not extremely adept at knowing what disconfirming information is. Information is often misinterpreted and forced to fit existing hypotheses or major premises. For example, if a racist individual were to see disconfirming information about a prejudged race, that person would see what he or she wanted to see. An instance of this would be if a Black person were to exhibit intelligence and dynamism, a racist person would still see stupidity and lack of charisma. A related alternative would be to create a subgroup or to deny that the Black person were actually Black. After a discussion about this in an argumentation class, a Hispanic student told the class that his fraternity brothers thought he was Hawaiian, not Hispanic, simply because he didn't exhibit the stereotypical characteristics of Hispanics, such as having an accent and being poor. Abraham Kaplan, in his book, *The Conduct of Inquiry*, explains, "We see what we expect to see, what we believe we have every reason for seeing . . ."

Failing to fall into this trap is really a key to thinking critically. As Howard Kahane says, "failure to bring a world view [major premise] into conformity with experience renders cogent reasoning less likely . . ." Darley and Gross completed a study that was done with grade-school children. The conclusion of that study showed that regardless of how well welfare children performed various scholastic tasks, people perceived the welfare children to be less skilled than their upper-middle class counterparts. In other words, if a behavior does not fit into someone's hypothesis (or major premise) of how a member of a certain group should perform (all welfare children perform poorly in school), the biased individual subconsciously alters his or her perception of the behavior (excellent work is perceived as mediocre) to fit the stereotype (existing major premises).

Even college students are not exempt from this trap. Numerous studies have been done proving that college students have cluster beliefs about various races, religions, and other classifications. For example, Gergen and Gergen in 1981 reveal that many African Americans as well other college students believed the following cluster beliefs about African Americans: that they are "superstitious, lazy, happy-go-lucky, musical, and ostentatious." Believing that "all African Americans are lazy" is hardly a belief for a college-educated person to have.

This little digression hopefully convinced the reader of the importance of the inductive side of reasoning. Clearly, it is important for us to check the truth of our major premises. That concept should be employed by the beginning advocate in debate when supporting criteria and building affirmative cases. An unsupported criterion or inference in non-policy debate is a *prima facie* issue for the simple reason that valid-but-untrue claims can be advanced otherwise. Unsupported criteria come in other ways besides the basic assertion. Often, debaters will propose the on-balance criterion. On balance is not a standard or criterion, but it is merely a means by which to "weigh" or evaluate a standard. *On balance* in terms of what? Human life? Health? National security? The on-balance criterion is nothing more than a failure to understand the true purpose of a criterion. Therefore, if you're debating anything other than a policy resolution, you must consider carefully the ways you present criteria.

For policy debate, the impact to a given argument really serves the same purpose as the criterion in non-policy debate. That purpose is to serve as the major premise for an argument. For example, one might argue that a certain course of action may lead to war. Why is war bad? That's where the impact (major premise) comes in. The more detailed an explanation, the more likely we are to accept the major premise that war is bad. If we hear from the advocates that innocent civilians die, that soldiers contract mysterious diseases, and that many children are left orphaned, we are more likely to accept the major premise.

SUMMARY

A debater must know how to identify and use sound reasoning. This chapter covered deductive and inductive reasoning. Deductive reasoning is defined as an argument where given the truth of the premises the conclusion is certain. There are three types of classical deductive arguments. They are the categorical syllogism, the conditional syllogism and the disjunctive syllogism. All types of syllogisms can be checked for their truth and validity. A syllogism that is both true and valid is referred to as a sound argument.

Inductive reasoning can be defined as an argument, where given the truth of the premises, the conclusion is probable but not certain. An inductive argument that has a high probability of being true is known as a strong argument. An inductive argument that has a low probability of being true is known as a weak argument. The method of induction usually is used to establish the major premise of a deductive argument.

CATEGORICAL LOGIC

Chapter 7 discussed deductive and inductive logic. Deductive logic is normally structured in the form of a syllogism. There are three types of syllogisms: categorical, conditional, and disjunctive (conditional and disjunctive syllogisms are not discussed in this chapter but are covered in Chapter 7). Of these, categorical syllogisms are by far the most complicated to understand but are also perhaps the most interesting and most commonly used. The intent of Chapter 7 was to provide the reader with a cursory understanding of categorical syllogisms. However, to really understand the categorical syllogism in depth necessitates a chapter all unto itself. This chapter is devoted entirely to discussing categorical logic.

CATEGORICAL CLAIMS

Categorical syllogisms get their name because they are composed of three categorical claims. Categorical claims are statements that show a relationship between two different categories. "All men are mortal" is an example of a categorical claim. An example of a categorical syllogism is:

All men are mortal.
Socrates is a man.
Therefore, Socrates is mortal.

While categorical claims can be composed in a number of ways, philosophers have recognized four standard forms that a categorical claim can take. These are called moods. Each of the four standard moods were named after a vowel in the alphabet and hence are referred to as either an "A," "E," "I," or "O" claim (Figure 8.1). Utilizing all four moods, there are 256 different configurations of categorical syllogisms.

Mood	Claim	Example
A	All S are P	All college professors are well-educated individuals.
E	No S are P	No submarines are vehicles that can fly.
I	Some S are P	Some computers are laptops.
O	Some S are not P	Some children are not well-behaved individuals.

FIGURE 8.1

Moods

Sometimes categorical claims are not stated in standard form. All categorical claims that are not in standard form must be restated so they are in standard form. Figure 8.2 illustrates the conversion of statement from nonstandard into standard form.

The purpose of categorical claims is to show the relationship between the two identified categories. In order to do this, all categorical statements contain five key elements. These components are not always explicitly stated but nonetheless are present (Figure 8.3).

The five components are 1) the quantifier, 2) the subject, 3) the copula, 4) the predicate and 5) the quality. *Quantifiers,* as the word suggests, simply give the quantification of the subject. When the quantifier refers to the entire subject category ("all" or "none") it is said to be universal. If the quantifier refers to less than the entire sub-

Non Standard Form	Standard Form
An Alligator is a reptile	All alligators are reptiles
Bears do not make nice pets	No bears are animals that make nice pets
Most carnivals are fun to attend	Some carnivals are places fun to attend
Not all politicians are corrupt	Some politicians are not corrupt

FIGURE 8.2

Conversion of Nonstandard Form Statements into Standard Form

	QUANTIFIER	SUBJECT	COPULA	PREDICATE	QUALITY
A	All (universal)	S	are	P	affirmative
E	No (universal)	S	are	P	negative
I	Some (particular)	S	are	P	affirmative
O	Some (particular)	S	are not	P	negative

FIGURE 8.3

Components of a Categorical Claim

ject category ("some"), it is said to be particular. The *subject* is the first category mentioned in the claim. Thus, in the claim "No snakes are whales" "snakes" would be the subject. The *copula* is the present form of the verb "to be" and links the subject to the predicate of the claim. Technically, this is the only verb that can be used in a syllogism. The *predicate* refers to the category which appears second in the claim, thus "whales" would be the predicate term in the above example. Finally, the *quality* of the categorical statement can be classified as being affirmative or negative. A claim is said to be affirmative if the subject is included (completely or partially) in the predicate term. A claim is said to be negative if the subject is excluded (completely or partially) from the predicate term.

THE STANDARD FORM OF A SYLLOGISM

Syllogisms may be presented in standard or non-standard form. Because syllogisms are checked for validity by having them in standard form it is important to know when a syllogism is or is not in standard form. If the syllogism is not in standard form, then it should be restructured so it is in standard form. The standard form for all categorical syllogisms is listed in Figure 8.4.

1. Quantifier _____   Copula _____   [Major Premise: Contains major term]
2. Quantifier _____   Copula _____   [Minor Premise: Contains minor term]
3. Quantifier _Minor Term_   Copula _Major Term_   [Conclusion]

FIGURE 8.4

Standard Form of a Syllogism

As Figure 8.4 demonstrates, to be in standard form a syllogism must be structured so that the major premise is listed first and the minor premise is listed second. It is therefore important to be able to discern the major from the minor premise. In order to do this we must first learn how to discern the various terms used in a syllogism. Remember that all syllogisms have three terms known as the minor term [S], major term [P], and middle term [M]. While we mentioned these term earlier, we did not discuss how to identify them. We will do so now since identifying them is the key to discovering the major and minor premises.

The **minor term** is always the subject (first term) of the conclusion while the **major term** is always the predicate (second term) of the conclusion. As Figure 8.4 illustrates the minor and major terms are always predetermined in the conclusion. (However, where they are placed in the major and minor premises varies and will be discussed later.) The **middle term** is always the term that appears in the two premises but not in the conclusion. (Once again, the placement of the middle term in the major and minor premises varies.)

No fish are cats	No P are S
All lions are cats	All M are S
No lions are fish	No S are P

In the above syllogism the minor term is "lions" (since it is the subject or first term mentioned in the conclusion), the major term is "fish" (since it is the predicate or second term mentioned in the conclusion), and the middle term is "cats" (since it is the term mentioned in the two premises but not in the conclusion).

Knowing how to identify the major, minor, and middle terms allows us to identify the major and minor premises. The major premise is simply that premise which contains the major term, while the minor premise is simply that premise which contains the minor term. As we stated earlier, to be in standard form the major premise must be listed first and the minor premise listed second. You should notice therefore that the syllogism is in standard form since the major premise (containing the major term [P], in this case "fish") is listed first while the minor premise (containing the minor term [S], in this case "lions") is listed second.

In some cases a syllogism will be presented in nonstandard form. That is, the syllogism will be constructed so that the minor premise is listed first and the major premise is listed second. For instance, examine the following syllogism.

All U.S. Senators are politicians
No individuals who want a bad public image are politicians
No U.S. Senators are individuals who want a bad public image

First, make sure to properly identify the major and minor terms. Remember the minor term is always the subject of the conclusion, while the major term is always the predicate of the conclusion.

All U.S. Senators [S] are politicians [M]	All S are M
No individuals who want a bad public image [P] are politicians [M]	No P are M
No U.S. Senators [S] are individuals who want a bad public image [P]	No S are P

You should have noticed that the above syllogism is not in standard form. According to the conclusion, "individuals who want a bad public image" is the major term since it is the predicate of the conclusion. Thus, the premise which contains this term is the major premise and must be the first premise listed in the syllogism. As can be seen, the major premise is listed second and the minor premise (which contains the minor term "US Senators") is listed first. The syllogism needs to be restructured by switching the major and minor premises. Doing this would result in the syllogism being in the correct standard form, as shown below.

No individuals who want a bad public image are politicians	No P are M
All U.S. Senators are politicians	All S are M
No U.S. Senators are individuals who want a bad public image	No S are P

DISCERNING THE MOOD OF A CATEGORICAL SYLLOGISM

As we saw earlier, there are four moods that a categorical statement can take (A, E, I, O). Since each standard form categorical syllogism must make use of these statements, it follows that each line of the syllogism can be labeled by one of these moods. Therefore, the combination of categorical statements utilized to construct a categorical syllogism makes up the overall mood of the syllogism. At this point, we can now give the moods to the syllogisms we have already utilized.

A	All dogs are mammals	(All S are P)
A	All collies are dogs	(All S are P)
A	All collies are mammals	(All S are P)

Thus, the above syllogism's mood is referred to as "AAA." The first listed letter always refers to the major premise, the second listed letter always refers to the minor premise and the third letter always refers to the conclusion. Let's look at another syllogism we have already discussed and determine its mood.

E	No individuals who want a bad public image are politicians	(No S are P)
A	All U.S. Senators are politicians	(All S are P)
E	No U.S. Senators are individuals who want a bad public image	(No S are P)

As can be seen, the above syllogism's mood is "EAE." (You should now also see why it is important to have the syllogism in standard form. You will remember that originally this syllogism was not in standard form and thus might incorrectly have been labeled an AEE syllogism.)

DETERMINING THE FIGURE FOR A STANDARD FORM CATEGORICAL SYLLOGISM

Not only does each syllogism have a mood, it also has a figure. The figure of a syllogism is determined by the location of the middle term in the major and minor premises. The middle term can appear in the major and minor premise in four different configurations. These are listed in Figure 8.5.

As can be seen from Figure 8.5, the placement of the minor term (S) and the major term (P) in the conclusion is a constant. However, their placement in the major and minor premises depends on the placement of the middle term (M) in the premises.

One way to help remember the different middle term figures is to envision the placement of the middle terms as creating 2 check marks facing one another. Begin on the left with Figure 1 and move right through Figures 2, 3 and finally ending with Figure 4 on the right. First, notice how the placement of the middle term in Figure 1 (as the subject of the major premise and the predicate of the minor premise) creates the diagonal line of the first checkmark. Second, notice how the placement of the middle terms in Figure 2 (as the predicate of the major premise and the predicate of the minor premise) creates the vertical line to complete the first checkmark. Third, notice how the placements of the middle term in Figure 3 (as the subject of the major premise and the subject of the minor premise) create the vertical line to begin the second checkmark. Fourth, notice how the placement of the middle term in Figure 4 (as the predicate of the major premise and the subject of the minor premise) creates the diagonal line to complete the second checkmark. Also notice that after the two checkmarks are created there is an empty corridor between them. This should help you not to confuse Figures 2 and 3. If you confuse Figures 2 and 3 there will be letters in the corridor between the checkmarks, and that would be incorrect. Another way to remember is to think of Figures 1 and 4 as creating the outside of a funnel and Figures 2 and 3 as creating the vertical passage of the funnel.

	FIGURE 1		FIGURE 2		FIGURE 3		FIGURE 4	
Major Premise	M	P	P	M	M	P	P	M
Minor Premise	S	M	S	M	M	S	M	S
Conclusion	S	P	S	P	S	P	S	P

FIGURE 8.5

Figure Placements of the Middle Term

Let's once again apply this concept to the syllogisms we have examined.

A	All dogs are mammals	All M are P
A	All collies are dogs	All S are M
A	All collies are mammals	All S are P

As can be seen, the middle term (dogs) appears as the subject in the major premise and as the predicate in the minor premise and is therefore a Figure 1 placement (Notice how when a line is drawn connecting the middle terms it creates the diagonal of the first checkmark). We have already determined the mood of the syllogism as AAA. We can then combine the mood and figure. Thus, this syllogism is an AAA-1 syllogism. Now let's look at the second syllogism.

E	No individuals who want a bad public image are politicians	No P are M
A	All U.S. Senators are politicians	All S are M
E	No U.S. Senators are individuals who want a bad public image	No S are P

Since the middle term (politicians) appears as the predicate in the major premise and as the predicate in the minor premise it is a Figure 2 placement (Notice how when a line is drawn connecting the middle terms it creates the vertical line of the first checkmark.) Thus, this syllogism is properly labeled as an EAE-2 syllogism. Let's look at a few more. Try to determine both the mood and figure.

1. No P are M	2. All M are P	3. All P are M	4. No M are P
All S are M	Some S are M	No M are S	All M are S
No S are P	Some S are P	No S are P	Some S are not P

You should have arrived at the following answers

1. EAE-2.	2. AII-1	3. AEE-4	4. EAO-3

We have just learned how to determine the mood and figure of any given syllogism. This process can also be reversed. Given the mood and figure, a syllogism can be constructed. Let's take the syllogism AIO-4. To create this syllogism, the first step is to create the skeletal mood that corresponds to each line of the syllogism. It is often helpful to list the moods in vertical order.

A	All _____ are _____	[AIO-4]
I	Some _____ are _____	
O	Some _____ are not _____	

The second step is to place the middle term into the major and minor premises as directed by the figure. Since the Figure 4 is used in this example the middle term must appear as the predicate in the major premise and as the subject in the minor premise. Placing the middle term in those locations, the syllogism now appears as follows.

A   All _____ are M   [AIO-4]
I   Some M are _____
O   Some _____ are not _____

The third step is to place the minor and major terms into the conclusion. Remember that the minor term always appears as the subject in the conclusion and that the major term always appears as the predicate in the conclusion. Placing these terms makes our syllogism appear as follows.

A   All _____ are M   [AIO-4]
I   Some M are _____
O   Some S are not P

The fourth and final step is to place the major and minor terms into the premises. Remember that the major term appears in the major premise and that in a standard form categorical syllogism the major premise is always listed first. Similarly, the minor term appears in the minor premise, which is always listed second in standard form. Thus, our finished syllogism looks as follows:

A   All P are M   [AIO-4]
I   Some M are S
O   Some S are not P

DISTRIBUTION

The final component of a syllogism that must be addressed before validity can be checked is that of distribution. The terms of a statement can either be distributed or undistributed. A term is distributed when the proposition asserts something about every member of its class. A term is undistributed when the proposition does not assert something about every member of its class. Each of the standard moods distributes none, one, or both of their terms (Figure 8.6).

Notice the patterning of the distributed terms. You begin on the top left of the "A" claim where only the subject is distributed and end on the bottom right of the "O" claim where only the predicate is distributed. In between, the "E" claim distributes both of its terms while the "I" claim does not distribute either of its terms.

In "A" claims, the subject is distributed while the predicate is not. Take the claim "All humans are mortal." This statement tells us something about the entire subject (humans), namely that they are all mortal. However, the claim does not tell us something about all of the predicate term since not all things mortal are human.

A	All $\boxed{S}$ are P	(subject distributed, predicate not distributed)
E	No $\boxed{S}$ are $\boxed{P}$	(subject distributed, predicate distributed)
I	Some S are P	(subject not distributed, predicate not distributed)
O	Some S are not $\boxed{P}$	(subject not distributed, predicate distributed)
	[Boxed terms are distributed]	

FIGURE 8.6

Distribution Patterns of Categorical Claims

In "E" claims both the subject and predicate terms are distributed. As can be seen in the statement "No dogs are cats," both terms are distributed. The statement tells us the entire subject (dogs) is not part of the predicate (cats). It must follow then that the reverse is also true. That is, all of the predicate term (cats) cannot be part of the subject term (dogs).

In "I" claims, neither the subject nor predicate terms are distributed. For instance, take the claim "Some tall people are actors." In this case, we know that some, but not necessarily all, tall people are actors; hence, the subject term is not distributed. The claim also reveals that some, but not necessarily all actors are tall; hence, the predicate term is also not distributed.

Finally, "O" claims distribute only the predicate term. In the statement "Some chess pieces are not rooks" the subject is not distributed while the predicate is distributed. Clearly, nothing about all chess pieces is stated, only that some of them are not rooks. However, the statement does reveal that all rooks are not part of the other chess pieces. Thus, something about all of the predicate term is revealed.

DETERMINING THE VALIDITY OF A SYLLOGISM

We can finally turn our attention to discovering how to discern valid from invalid syllogisms. A valid syllogism is one in which the premises force the conclusion. As we have already discovered, there are four moods of categorical statements (A, E, I, O claims). Since each standard form categorical syllogism is composed of categorical moods, there are 64 possible moods ($4 \times 4 \times 4 = 64$). Also, since there are four different Figures, there are 256 different permutations of mood and Figures ($64 \times 4 = 256$). Of these 256 permutations, only 15 are considered unconditionally valid by traditional logic, while another 9 are considered conditionally valid depending on whether or not a concept called existential import (a concept beyond the scope of this book) is granted. Since most logicians seem to grant existential import, we will too. Thus, if a syllogism fits any of these 24 patterns it will be considered valid. As is evident, the number of valid syllogism is fairly small. Less than 10% of the possible 256 syllogisms are valid. That leaves a lot of room for much of what you read or hear about to be invalid. That is why learning about them is so important!

There are three ways to check if a standard form syllogism is valid. The first is to check if it adheres to the required rules of logic. The second way is to check if the mood and Figure pattern corresponds to one of the 24 accepted valid syllogisms. If it does, it is valid. If it does not, then it is invalid. The third way is to construct a Venn diagram. We will discuss all three approaches.

Rules of the Syllogism

In order to be valid, there are four rules to which a syllogism must adhere (Figure 8.7). If a syllogism violates any one of these four rules it is considered invalid.

Rule 1 says that all syllogisms must consist of exactly three terms and each of those terms must be used exactly twice. If a fourth term is introduced or a term is used more than twice, the syllogism is invalid.

No	conservatives are environmentalists	[EIO-4]
Some	environmentalists are radicals	
Some	radicals are not liberals	

1. Exactly three terms must be used, each being used twice, with no term appearing twice in the same claim.

2. The number of negative claims in the premises must match exactly the number of negative claims in the conclusion.

3. The middle term must be distributed at least once in either the major or minor premise.

4. If a term is distributed in the conclusion, then it must also be distributed at least once in the premises.

FIGURE 8.7

Rules of Syllogisms

Even though this syllogism is an EIO-4 syllogism which is a valid form, it is nonetheless invalid because it violates rule one. The conclusion introduces a fourth term "liberals." The terms "conservative" and "liberals" (each of which are used only once) are not synonymous. Thus, the syllogism is invalid since no inference between the categories is possible.

Rule 2 states that the number of negative claims in the premises must correspond exactly to the number of negative claims listed in the conclusion. There are actually three different permutations of this one rule. Many texts list these three permutations as three distinct rules since each permutation carries a different rational for why violating its tenets causes a syllogism to be invalid. Those permutations are as follows:

Sub-rule 2.1: Two negative premises are not allowed.

Sub-rule 2.2: If the conclusion is affirmative then both premises must be affirmative.

Sub-rule 2.3: If the conclusion is negative then exactly one premise must be negative.

Since each of the above permutations are all similar in that the number of negative claims in the premises must end up matching the number of negative claims in the conclusion they can be thought of as creating one overall rule. However, an explanation for each permutation will be provided.

Sub-rule 2.1: Two negative premises are not allowed.

[OEI-2]	[EEE-3]
Some mammals are not dolphins	No cows are carnivores
No insects are dolphins	No cows are sharks
Some insects are mammals	No sharks are carnivores

The syllogisms listed above both violate sub-rule 2.1. The OEI–2 Syllogism has an affirmative conclusion while the EEE-3 syllogism has a negative conclusion. However, in both cases the syllogisms each consist of two negative premises. The rationale for why a syllogism is invalid if two negative premises are present is identical regardless if the conclusion is affirmative or negative. The reason is as follows. If the M class is separate either completely (E-claim) or partially (O-claim) from the S class, and the M class is separate either completely (E-claim) or partially (O-claim) from the P class, then nothing is established about the relationship between the S class and the P class. The S class and the P class might be completely distinct, partially related, or identical. There is no way to tell.

Sub-rule 2.2: If the conclusion is affirmative then both premises must be affirmative.

No reptiles are dogs   [EII-4]
Some dogs are collies
Some collies are reptiles

The above EEI-4 syllogism violates rule 2.2 because the conclusion is affirmative, while one of the premises is negative. The reason for this is that an affirmative conclusion always asserts the S class is contained either completely (A-claim) or partially (I-claim) in the P class. But the only way this can be accomplished is if the S class is contained either completely (A-claim) or partially (I-claim) in the M class while the M class is completely contained (A-claim) in the P class. In other words, it takes two affirmative premises to accomplish this objective. Therefore, any negative premise would make the syllogism invalid.

Sub-rule 2.3: If the conclusion is negative then exactly one premise must
               be negative.

All cats are felines   [AAO-4]
All felines are mammals
Some mammals are not cats

The AAO-4 syllogism violates rule 2.3 because the conclusion is negative while both premises are affirmative. Remember that a negative conclusion always asserts the S class is separate either completely (E-claim) or partially (O-claim) from the P class. But logically the only way this can be accomplished is for one of the premises to assert class separation either completely (E-claim) or partially (O-claim). But since both premises assert class inclusion the syllogism must be invalid.

Rules 3 and 4 both deal with distribution. Remember that a term is distributed when something about the entire class is revealed. It is a good idea to underline the distributed terms in order to check these two rules.

Rule 3 states that the middle term must be distributed at least once.

Some sharks are man eaters   [IAI-1]
All Hammerheads are sharks
Some Hammerheads are man eaters

This syllogism violates rule 3. The middle term, sharks, is not distributed in either the major or minor premises. The reason that the middle term must be distributed is because the middle term is always the category that is being used to provide common ground between the major and minor premises. Therefore, it is required that we know something about the entire middle category in order to make any valid connections. For example, it should be clear that if a premise states that some sharks are man eaters one cannot conclude that all or even some hammerheads are man eaters. The reason for this limitation is because the middle term, which is being used to provide common ground between the categories of "Hammerheads" and "man eaters," asserts knowledge about only part of the class of sharks. Clearly, if the middle term stated that all sharks are man eaters one could then conclude that Hammerheads are man eaters since the premise would then be asserting knowledge about all of the shark class.

Rule 4 states that if a term is distributed in the conclusion it must also be distributed in the premise.

> Some spiders are poisonous animals   [IEE-1]
> No <u>snakes</u> are <u>spiders</u>
> No <u>snakes</u> are <u>poisonous animals</u>

This syllogism violates rule 4. The term "poisonous animals" is distributed in the conclusion but not in the major premise. This syllogism thus commits the fallacy of the illicit major (there is also the fallacy of the illicit minor).

Remember that distribution is a positive attribute. When a term is distributed, knowledge about the whole class is asserted. Therefore if a term is distributed in the conclusion but not in the premises the conclusion claims more knowledge than that offered in the premises and is therefore invalid. Of course, it is perfectly acceptable for the premises to claim more knowledge than that asserted in the conclusion. Therefore it is permissible for a term to be distributed in the premises but not in the conclusion.

While these rules may seem complicated they are really fairly easy to apply. With just a little practice, you will easily be able to determine if a syllogism is valid or not valid. Remember, to be valid all four rules must be adhered to. If one rule is broken, then the syllogism is invalid. Of course, a syllogism might break more than one rule.

Matching the Mood and Figure

As was stated earlier, there are 24 syllogisms out of 256 possible permutations that are considered valid. Figure 8.8 lists the 24 valid syllogisms. Remember, for purposes of this book, those syllogisms that are listed as conditionally valid will be considered valid. In other words, the required conditions which would be necessary to have them be valid will be presumed to exist.

Given the above table, all one needs to do is to determine the mood and Figure of a syllogism and then see whether that configuration appears on the table. If it does, it is valid. If it does not, it is invalid.

Using the table, determine if the following syllogisms are valid or invalid.

1. Some radicals are nice people
   All nice people are suckers
   Some suckers are radicals

2. No criminals are model citizens
   Some criminals are not shop lifters
   Some shop lifters are not model citizens

VALID CATEGORICAL SYLLOGISMS

UNCONDITIONALLY VALID

FIGURE 1	FIGURE 2	FIGURE 3	FIGURE 4	
AAA	EAE	IAI	AEE	
EAE	AEE	AII	IAI	
AII	EIO	OAO	EIO	
EIO	AOO	EIO		

CONDITIONALLY VALID

FIGURE 1	FIGURE 2	FIGURE 3	FIGURE 4	REQUIRED CONDITION
AAI	AEO		AEO	S exist
EAO	EAO			
		AAI	EAO	M exist
		EAO		
			AAI	P exist

FIGURE 8.8

Valid Syllogisms

The first syllogism has an IAI mood and is a Figure 4. Thus it is an IAI-4 syllogism. Since this configuration appears in the table, it is a valid syllogism. The second syllogism is an EOO-3. Since this syllogistic configuration does not appear on the table, it is invalid. [Note: this syllogism violates rule 2, since the number of negative premises in the conclusion (1) does not match the number of negative premises (2).]

Drawing Venn Diagrams

Another way to check the validity of a categorical syllogism is to draw Venn diagrams in order to visually illustrate whether the premises force the stated conclusion. Each of the four categorical moods has a corresponding Venn diagram (Figure 8.9).

The Venn diagram representing the A-claim shows that every member of the subject category (dogs) is contained within the predicate category (mammals). The E-claim shows that none of the subject category (dogs) is contained in the predicate category (reptiles). The I-claim shows that at least one of the subject category (mammals) is contained within the predicate category (dogs). The "x" in the overlap of the

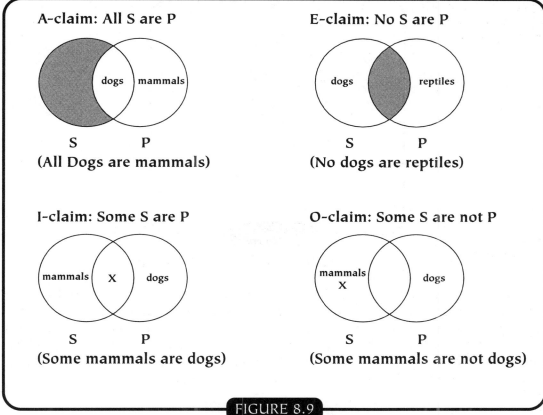

A-claim: All S are P

dogs | mammals

S   P
(All Dogs are mammals)

E-claim: No S are P

dogs | reptiles

S   P
(No dogs are reptiles)

I-claim: Some S are P

mammals | X | dogs

S   P
(Some mammals are dogs)

O-claim: Some S are not P

mammals X | dogs

S   P
(Some mammals are not dogs)

FIGURE 8.9

Drawing Venn Diagrams

subject and predicate circles visually illustrates that at least one thing which is S is also P. Finally, the O-claim illustrates that at least one member of the subject category (dogs) is not a member of the predicate category (mammals). The "x" appearing in the part of the subject category which does not overlap with the predicate category visually illustrates that at least one thing which is S is not P.

Since each categorical syllogism has three terms, three overlapping circles are used. The first two circles drawn represent the subject and the predicate (as shown in Figure 8.9). Next the circle representing the middle term is attached. The completed Venn diagram has seven sections (Figure 8.10).

Before drawing a Venn diagram, make sure to label the major term (P), the minor term (S) and the middle term (M). The following syllogism has been so labeled.

> All Birds [M] are animals which have feathers [P]   [AAA-1]
> All canaries [S] are birds [M]
> All canaries [S] are animals which have feathers [P]

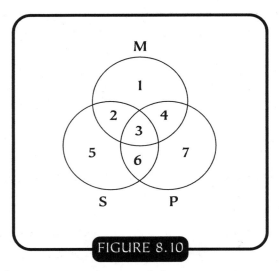

FIGURE 8.10

The Seven Sections of the Venn Diagram

Normally, the first step is to diagram the major premise. (However, if the major premise is particular while the minor premise is universal it is better to start with the minor premise.) In this case, both premises are universal so it is best to begin with the major premise. When this is done, the Venn diagram appears as in Figure 8.11. You will notice that all of the "M" circle which is not part of the "P" circle (areas 1 and 2) has been shaded out. This drawing therefore shows that "All M are P."

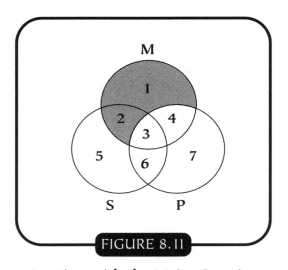

FIGURE 8.11

Starting with the Major Premise

The second step is to diagram the minor premise "All S are M." You will notice the entire "S" circle which is not part of the "M" circle (areas 5 and 6) has been shaded out (Figure 8.12)

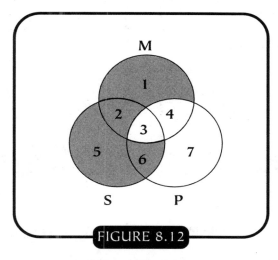

FIGURE 8.12

Minor Premise

The final step is to determine whether the Venn diagram accurately reflects the conclusion. In this case, the conclusion is "All S are P." As the Venn diagram shows, the entire remaining (non-shaded) portion of the "S" circle (area 3) is also part of the "P" circle. In other words, there is no part of "S" which is also not part of "P." Thus the syllogism is valid. You might also notice that none of the five rules of constructing syllogisms has been violated.

When the major premise is particular while the minor premise is universal, begin the Venn diagram with the minor premise and then add the major premise. Examine the following syllogism.

> Some M are not P   [OAO-3]
> All M are S
> Some S are not P

You will notice that if you started with the major premise "Some M are not P," there would be doubt as to where to place the "x" since it could be placed in either area 1 or 2 (Figure 8.13). However, if the minor premise "All M are S" is diagrammed first then area 1 is shaded out leaving only area 2 as the possible location of the "x" (Figure 8.14). Remember that an "x" can only be placed in a non-shaded area.

The last step is to determine if the completed Venn diagram forces the conclusion, in this case that "Some S are not P." The finished diagram shows that the "x" is

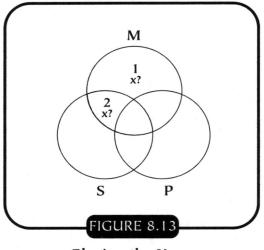

FIGURE 8.13

Placing the X

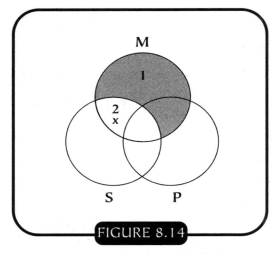

FIGURE 8.14

Do Not Place the X in a Shaded Area

located in area 2 which is in the class of "S" but not in the class of "P." Thus the syllogism is valid.

Unfortunately, the above stated strategy does not always work. There are times when it is still unclear where the "x" should be placed even after the universal premise has been diagrammed. Examine the following syllogism.

All P are M   [AII-2]
Some S are M
Some S are P

You will notice that even after the major premise "All P are M" is diagrammed there is still doubt as how to diagram the minor premise "Some S are M." The "x" could be placed in area 2 where only the "M" and "S" circles overlap; or the "x" could be placed in area 3 where all three circles overlap (Figure 8.15). Where should "x" be placed? The rule is that if an "x" can be placed in two different areas, it is placed on the line separating the two areas. This indicates that we are unsure if the "x" belongs to just one or both of the possible areas. Thus, the minor premise would correctly be drawn with the "x" on the line that separates the two possible correct areas (Figure 8.16).

The final step is to determine if the completed Venn diagram forces the conclusion. The conclusion for the above syllogism states "Some S are P." For this to be valid there would have to be an "x" located completely in the area where "S" and "P" overlap. Since there is no "x" located entirely in the area that "S" and "P" share, the syllogism is invalid. The above diagram simply tells us that that there is some "S" which may or may not be part of "P." Remember that if an "x" appears on a line separating two areas, the syllogism is always invalid (Notice that the syllogism violates rule three as the middle term is not distributed in either the major or minor premise).

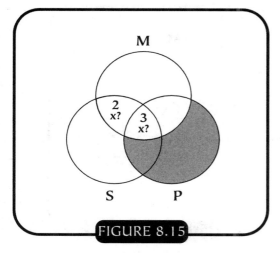

FIGURE 8.15

Doubtful X Placement

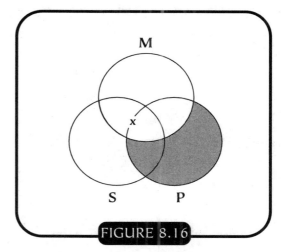

FIGURE 8.16

Place the X on the Line

So far we have considered syllogisms that are not affected by any existential assumptions. Remember that of the 256 possible syllogisms, 15 are unconditionally valid. These 15 are valid whether or not existential assumptions are made. Another 9 syllogisms are conditionally valid. These 9 are valid only if existential assumptions are made. That is, they are valid only if we assume that the major, minor or middle terms refer to classes of things that actually exist (like dogs) as opposed to things that do not really exist (like unicorns). For example examine the following syllogism.

    All P are M   [AEO-2]
    No S are M
    Some S are not P

Figure 8.17 shows the completed Venn diagram after the major and minor premises have been diagrammed. For the syllogism's conclusion "Some S are not P" to be valid, there would have to be an "x" located in a non-shaded area of the "S" circle that does not overlap the "P" circle. You should notice that no "x" even appears in the completed diagram (Figure 8.17) as neither the major nor minor premises instructs as to place an "x" anywhere. Thus, this syllogism is invalid from the Boolean standpoint.

However, if we assume that the universal premises refer to things that actually exist then the syllogism may or may not be valid from the existential standpoint. If we assume that "S" is not an empty class, then obviously at least one thing must exist in "S." Inspection of the diagram shows that only one area of "S" is left non-shaded. Therefore, the "x" representing the thing(s) in "S" that we assume to exist must be placed in that non-shaded location (Figure 8.18). The circle around the "x" indicates that we are making assumptions about "S" not being an empty class. When

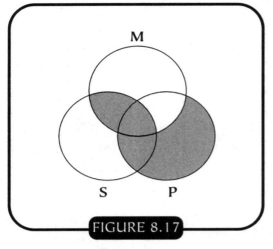

FIGURE 8.17

Major and Minor Premise

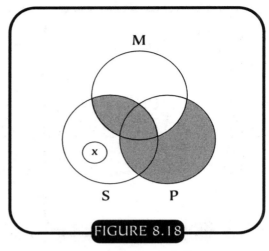

FIGURE 8.18

Existentially Valid

the existential assumption is made, it becomes clear that there is at least one thing that is part of "S" but is not part of "P." Thus, from the existential standpoint, the syllogism is valid.

SUMMARY

A debater must know how to identify and use sound reasoning. This chapter covered deductive and inductive reasoning. Deductive reasoning is defined as an argument where given the truth of the premises the conclusion is certain. There are three types of classical deductive arguments. They are the categorical syllogism, the conditional syllogism, and the disjunctive syllogism. All types of syllogisms can be checked for their truth and validity. A syllogism that is both true and valid is referred to as a sound argument.

Inductive reasoning can be defined as an argument, where given the truth of the premises, the conclusion is probable but not certain. An inductive argument that has a high probability of being true is known as a strong argument. An inductive argument that has a low probability of being true is known as a weak argument. The method of induction usually is used to establish the major premise of a deductive argument.

For categorical syllogisms there are four mood statements. The "A" claim asserts "All S are P," the "E" claim asserts "No S are P," the "I" claim asserts "Some S are P," and the "O" claim asserts "Some S are not P." All categorical statements distribute none, one or both of their terms. A term is distributed if the claim asserts knowledge about its entire class. "A" claims distribute only their subject, "E" claims distribute both their subject and predicate, "I" claims do not distribute either their subject nor their predicate, and "O" claims only distribute their predicate.

All categorical syllogisms are composed of three categorical statements. There are also four possible Figure placements of the middle term in the major and minor premises. Therefore there are 256 possible categorical syllogisms of which only 15 are unconditionally valid and nine are conditionally valid. There are three ways to determine the validity of a syllogism. The first is to determine if the syllogism violates any of the four logical rules. There rules are 1) the syllogism must use three terms, 2) then number of negative statements made in the conclusion must match exactly the number of negative premises 3) the middle term must be distributed and 4) if a term is distributed in the conclusion it must be distributed in the premises. The second way to determine validity is to compare the mood and Figure arrangement of the syllogism and check to see if it appears on the list of valid syllogisms. Finally, a Venn diagram can be composed to visually illustrate the validity of the syllogism.

TYPES OF ARGUMENTS

CLASSIFICATIONS OF ARGUMENT

In Chapters 7 and 8, deductive and inductive reasoning were examined. Now that you have a better understanding of deductive and inductive reasoning, a discussion of the types and tests of argument is necessary. Some of these classifications of argument may at times be deductive, at times inductive, and at times a little of both. Additionally, just because the questions asked about each type of reasoning seem objective the answers are not necessarily so. For argument types that use inductive reasoning, the application of the tests may be debatable. That is why you need to be able to defend your arguments as good ones. For instance, someone may argue that you haven't a sufficient number of examples. You must be prepared to argue that you do have a sufficient number and be able to provide additional examples.

TOULMIN ANALYSIS

In order to discuss the types of argument, an understanding of Toulmin analysis is helpful. Stephen Toulmin is an English philosopher whose main purpose in developing his model was to find application for logic outside the realm of the philosopher's P's and Q's. While he has failed to convince many of his philosophy colleagues, his ideas have found a home among rhetoric and argumentation scholars. The main purpose of the Toulmin model as used in argumentation is to demonstrate the structure of any given argument. The purpose of the model is not to determine validity. Toulmin analysis is analysis in its literal form: to separate an argument into its component parts. Toulmin argues that there are six elements present in any wholly explicit argument. However, only three of the components, claim, data and warrant, are primary features of all arguments (Figure 9.1).

The first primary element, the **claim,** is the conclusion that the arguer is trying to advance. Statements such as "Birds evolved into dinosaurs," "The United States should institute a military draft," and "My boyfriend is a jerk" are all examples of

FIGURE 9.1

Primary Components of the Toulmin Model

claims. There are three basic types of claims advanced in a debate: fact, value, and policy. These have all been defined in Chapter 2.

The **data (or grounds)** are the support for that conclusion. In the statement, "My boyfriend is a major jerk because he didn't call me on my birthday," the data is "he didn't call me on my birthday." Recall also our discussion from previous chapters when we covered the different concerns about evidence. That support can come in the form of testimony, examples, statistics, analogies, causes, signs, and definitions. Later in this chapter, we'll discuss the tests for each of the different forms of data. All of those concerns apply when discussing data in this context.

The **warrant** is the logical connecting link between the data and the claim. More often than not the warrant is implied, not stated, by the arguer. The warrant is the underlying assumption that one must accept in order to agree with the argument's conclusion. The warrant for the "my boyfriend is a major jerk because he did not call me on my birthday" example is simply the assumption that it is very poor behavior for a male not to call his significant other on her birthday. The completed argument, put into syllogistic form, would be as follows:

> All boyfriends who don't call their girlfriends on their birthdays are major
>   jerks (unstated warrant).
> My boyfriend is a boyfriend who did not call his girlfriend on her birthday
>   (data).
> Therefore, my boyfriend is a major jerk (claim).

Remember, the warrant represents the arguer's assumption, not yours. If you disagree with the assumption, that disagreement may not be voiced by you until the Toulmin analysis is completed. For inductive reasoning, the warrant helps make the inference to the conclusion. Usually, the inductive warrant will simply assume the argument meets the key tests for that particular type of argument. For instance, the warrant for example argument is almost always the same: that the data are sufficient and typical enough to justify the claim. (Discovering whether there are sufficient and typical examples is the key to testing example argument.) On the other hand, for a deductive argument, often the warrant is simply the major premise to a syllogism. In looking at the Socrates syllogism studied in Chapter 7 (All men are mortal, Socrates is a man, therefore Socrates is mortal), the conclusion to the syllogism is the claim, *Socrates is mortal;* the minor premise is the data, *Socrates is a man;* and the major premise is the warrant, *All men are mortal.* When human beings speak, however, we usually do not speak in complete syllogisms. We normally speak in what are called **enthymemes,** which are bits and pieces of syllogisms. Often, the major premise and, less often, other parts of the syllogism are left out. Therefore, performing a Toulmin analysis on an enthymeme is often more difficult than a full syllogism. Additionally, for an argument by definition, which is basically deductive, the definition itself becomes the warrant.

The last three parts of the Toulmin model, the qualifier, reservation, and backing are the auxiliary parts of the model. When completing a Toulmin analysis, these elements only need to be included if the author includes them him or herself. However, the refuter may want to introduce these elements if the arguer fails to verbalize them. One, two or all three of these auxiliary components might be introduced in an argument. Figure 9.2 illustrates the Toulmin model containing all six components.

The **qualifier (or modality)** establishes the degree of cogency of the argument, as explicitly stated by the arguer. The qualifier manifests itself usually as one word or phrase, such as probably, certainly, perhaps, more than likely, possibly, plausibly, rarely, hardly ever, by no means, and so on. In the statement "by boyfriend is without doubt a major jerk" the qualifier is the term "without doubt."

The **backing** is support for the warrant. If challenged, the advocate often has to provide backing to maintain a high degree of cogency with regard to a particular argument. The girlfriend might argue that in American culture the recognition of one's birthday by their significant other is an important part of dating. The girlfriend might

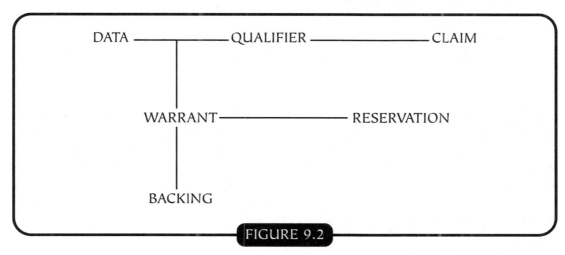

FIGURE 9.2

Fully Diagrammed Toulmin Model

also include testimonial support from a relationship councilor who states that such behavior is not appropriate.

The **reservation (or rebuttal)** is a specific exception to the claim. In the boyfriend example the reservation might be "my boyfriend is without doubt a major jerk for not calling me on my birthday unless he was hospitalized and not able to call." ". . . unless he was hospitalized and not able to call" is the exception (reservation) to the claim, "by boyfriend is without doubt a major jerk."

TESTIMONY ARGUMENT

An argument from testimony is an argument that uses as its support the authority of another person. If someone were to say, "Mr. Jones said that it will rain tomorrow," the support for that argument is Mr. Jones' authority. Therefore, that argument is an argument from testimony or authority.

Testimony argument is by nature secondary. A person other than the primary source is using a quotation or paraphrase as grounds for a particular claim. Let's look at a complete version of the above argument:

> Mr. Jones says that it probably will rain tomorrow unless the wind picks up. Mr. Jones has predicted correctly the weather the past 100 days straight.

The Toulmin analysis is as follows:

Claim:	It will rain tomorrow.
Data:	Mr. Jones says so.
Warrant:	Mr. Jones is an expert on the subject and is unbiased.
Qualifier:	Probably.
Reservation:	Unless the wind picks up.
Backing:	Mr. Jones has predicted correctly the weather the past 100 days straight.

Notice that the arguer stated everything explicitly except for the warrant. Remember, the warrant is the underlying assumption that the arguer makes, and it is usually not stated. The other five elements must be explicitly stated in order to be included.

The warrant for any testimony argument is basically the same as the one listed above. In order to determine the warrant for an argument, you must first classify the argument. In this case, that is given to you: This is a testimony argument. The second step, in this case, is to assume that the argument meets the key tests for that particular type of argument. The tests for testimony argument are as follows:

1. Is the source an expert?
2. Is the expertise relevant on the subject being discussed?

3. Is the source unbiased?
4. Is support available?

Once you identify the warrant, you need to evaluate those tests and answer them for yourself. Remember, answering the questions on your own is not a part of Toulmin analysis *per se*. For the first test listed above, an advocate must determine whether the source has the expertise necessary even to be considered. Often, in a debate round, an opponent may quote a law-school student or a graduate student. Of course, your opponent may not readily admit the fact that his or her evidence was written by an apprentice. That's why you need to ask to see the qualifications of any unqualified evidence. Occasionally, an opponent will read evidence from an obscure newspaper or magazine with little or no journalistic expertise. In either of these cases, the testimony fails to meet the first test for testimony argument. Of course, your opponent may be ready to defend the evidence as presented, and the defense may be justified. Remember the caution listed above: Just because the tests seem objective does not mean the answers are necessarily so. In other words, it is arguable whether a law-school student lacks expertise. On the one hand, he or she is still studying and hasn't completed an education nor received proper credentials. On the other hand, a second-year law school student who has an article published in the *Yale Law Journal* can hardly be considered a lay source. These tests are not scientific litmus papers that will turn a certain color if a person is an expert or unbiased or whatever. These tests merely provide a format for evaluating a line of argument. They are not meant to end all controversy.

If, however, you do establish that the source is an expert, you must then ask the second question. The second test for testimony argument is to ask whether the expertise is related to the claim. In other words, we may accept the law student's expertise in the area of law and other related fields, but the claim may be dealing with whether there would be a nuclear winter after a missile exchange between two countries. Obviously, the credentials, law, have nothing to do with the claim, effects of a nuclear war. There may be other cases however where the answer of relevance is not so clear. For example, if a lawyer works for the nuclear energy facility she may be very educated in the workings of a nuclear power plant. Although she may not have any formal education in nuclear power plant design, her legal work in the area would certainly dictate that she have a fairly good understanding of how a nuclear plant operates. While not technically being a nuclear power plant design expert by trade, she certainly would have much more expertise than lawyers who specialize in some other unrelated area.

It is also the case that the level of expertise can vary. For example, a civil rights attorney is certainly much more qualified to discuss legal matters that relate to civil rights than is an attorney who specializes in bankruptcy. Also, an attorney who has a law degree from Harvard may be perceived as being more of an expert than an attorney who has his law degree from a small town law school, even if they both specialize in the same type of law. Other factors such as experience and years of practice can also tend to make one more qualified.

The third test for testimony argument is to ask whether the source of the information is unbiased. Realize, again, that bias is not a black/white issue. There are degrees of bias, so whether a source is too biased to be acceptable can be argued in a debate round. Take the issue of whether communist countries harm human rights. Say you have two sources each saying that communist countries do not harm human rights: one from a member of the communist party and one from a liberal democrat in the US Senate. Obviously, the communist party member would be viewed as much more biased than a liberal democrat. Yet both have clear biases. Although the politician is biased, an advocate could make a case for him or her more easily than for the communist party member.

On the other hand, if a source goes against a perceived bias, then that evidence may be even more valuable. Say a conservative republican was to state that gay marriages should be legalized. We would expect a conservative republican to be biased against gay marriages. By using evidence that goes against a perceived bias, therefore, we may actually strengthen our position. Of course finding such evidence is usually much more difficult.

The final question deals with whether the person testifying has a reason for believing what he or she is saying. The reasoning in this type of argument is sometimes omitted, such as when a doctor tells you what type of illness you have. The question becomes this; can the expert supply a reason if asked for one? If there is no reason available, then it is not an argument, but just an assertion. If an expert testifies only to a material fact, this may not be as great a problem. However, if the expert is giving an opinion (for example, solar power is better than tidal power), then a reason must be available for the opinion. Otherwise the evidence is weakened due to the fact that it is merely an expert's assertion. In Chapter 10, a related fallacy, the Fallacy of Over-Reliance on Authority, is discussed. With the great popularity of Parliamentary debate, this renewed fallacy has taken on greater consideration by debate scholars. Since Parliamentary debaters are normally prohibited from presenting prepared material, people have begun to ask the question about how much should we rely on expert opinions.

EXAMPLE ARGUMENT

Example argument provides the patterning process that is inductive argument. As mentioned, when supporting major premises, often you want to use example argument to do so. **Perfect induction** comprises looking at all of the examples within a given classification or population in order to find the patterns or similarities within the grouping. Often, however, perfect induction is not possible. But even when it is available, perfect induction does not guarantee a conclusion. For example, just because a boxer might have won all of his fights, it does not guarantee that he will win the next one.

When perfect induction is not possible, certain rules must be applied to the data to determine if they are acceptable. The tests for example argument are as follows:

1. Are the examples relevant to the claim?
2. Are there a sufficient number of examples?
3. Are the examples typical?
4. Are counterexamples insignificant?
5. Is the claim qualified?

Note that the first question deals with relevancy. This is a question that is asked about a number of different types of argument. It is a more general question than the rest. It is simply asking if the data and the claim are related enough even to consider. If you answer "no" to the first question, there is little reason to ask the other questions.

For instance, an advocate may advance an argument that says that many politicians are corrupt. As data, the advocate provides the example of a US Senator's support of a congressional pay raise. One may be able to advance the argument that support of a pay raise is indicative of a politician's greed and thus corruption. However, just because you ask for a raise does not mean that you are corrupt. Therefore, the example (a senator asking for a pay raise) is not relevant to the claim (many politicians are corrupt). Another factor in determining relevancy is the issue of time. For instance, an advocate could argue that moral decay exists in US society. As data, the debater may offer the example of the sexual revolution. Arguably, however, the sexual revolution is irrelevant because it occurred in the 1960s; therefore, there is a lack of relevance based on the timeframe alone.

The second question (*are there a sufficient number of examples?*) is a question that cannot be answered with any surety. Statisticians have developed formulas to determine a sufficient sample size for a given population. Outside the realm of statistics, the answer to this question, then, is subjective, and should be considered at the same time as the third question, *typical examples.* For instance, an advocate may advance the claim that the forest service harvests too much timber on US national forests. As support for the claim, the advocate offers the example of Lassen National Forest in northeastern California. In answering the question about sufficient numbers of examples, on the surface, this one example out of all of the National Forests in the country would seem insufficient. However, you must also ask the question about whether the example is typical, because, if all of the other national forests harvest the same percentage of timber, then one example may be sufficient. There are two ways to determine whether an example is typical. One way is to use example argument in conjunction with general testimony argument. For instance, you might use the example of the Lassen Forest with a quotation from a US senator saying that the forest service harvests too much timber from the national forests. A second way to indicate an example is typical, of course, is to provide more examples. So the relationship between sufficiency and "typicality" becomes apparent. One example is sufficient if it's typical, but often we don't know if it's typical unless we look at numerous examples. Hence, using simple example argument often puts the advocate in a dilemma. The best option is to use example argument in conjunction with general testimony argument, as suggested above.

The fourth question (*are the counterexamples insignificant?*) is related to the last two questions as well. Rarely will you find a classification or population with 100% similarity or patterning. Of course, that means that there will always be a counterexample, even with a seemingly sound example argument. Therefore, as you are trying to defend your examples as sufficient and typical, you also must be able to refute any counterexamples raised by your opponents. In the above instance, your opponent may point out that in the Mendocino National Forest, timber harvests were cut in half last year. Your duty, then, is to prove that Mendocino is not a typical example. In this instance, you may be able to find evidence that says that the spotted owl population in the Mendocino Forest is unusually large, and court battles have prevented many timber sales there; therefore, the Mendocino Forest counterexample is atypical. You must be aware of as many possible counterexamples, such as this, so that you can quickly dismiss them.

The final question (*is the claim qualified?*) refers to the fact that, even with perfect induction, let alone imperfect induction, example argument cannot provide 100% certainty. The best we can expect, then, is an argument that establishes a high degree of probability. Therefore, qualifiers (such as *probably, more than likely, many,* or *most*) ought to be affixed to a claim established by example argument. This again goes back to the issue of stereotyping. Any black/white views that we have about the world ought to be suspect simply from the standpoint that we cannot know everything.

The warrant for an example argument assumes that the examples meet the above tests. Remember that the listener is not making that assumption; the arguer is. Once the Toulmin analysis is completed, you may then evaluate the warrant, which may call for backing. Let's look at the following example:

> The US national forests are probably being over harvested. Look at Lassen National Forest; they take way too much timber out of that place. And Lassen is of average size and use of most forests in the national forest system. Well, I suppose this is all true unless Lassen has some kind of one-time harvest plan going.

The Toulmin analysis should look like this:

Claim:	The US national forests are being over harvested.
Data:	Look at Lassen National Forest; they take way too much timber out of that place.
Warrant:	Lassen is a typical and sufficient example to prove the claim.
Qualifier:	Probably.

Reservation:	Unless Lassen has some kind of one-time harvest plan going.
Backing:	Lassen is of average size and use.

Notice that again that the warrant is not stated by the arguer. The warrant, as implied by the arguer, merely assumes that the argument meets the key tests for example reasoning. Once the Toulmin analysis has been completed, however, you may then evaluate the warrant. In this case, you may in fact find the assumption faulty. Indeed, Lassen may be atypical.

STATISTICS

Statistics involve the use of numbers: conclusions to studies, results of opinion polls, or total numbers of people or objects within a certain classification. The one thing that you should gain from any discussion about statistics is that debate advocates ought to know the methodology of any study or poll that they use. Sometimes that is difficult, however. Often, a study's conclusion is found in a magazine or in some other secondary source. Whenever possible, look for the primary source, so that if you are challenged, you may defend a particular methodology. In the course of your research, you may come across hundreds of studies found in secondary sources. Obviously, you may not have the time or the inclination to locate the primary source for each study; however, the studies that seem important to you or that you use for an affirmative case or negative position really ought to be located and read.

There are two basic types of statistics: descriptive and inferential. **Descriptive statistics** are numeric representations of an entire class of something. For instance, the percentage of people who voted in the last Presidential election, the total number of people raped during the last year, the total number of TWA airline accidents, and the numbers of houses sold during a given month are all attempts to describe an entire category. While it is desirable to be able to account for every instance in a category, it is not always possible or easy to do so. Luckily, there is a way to use statistics without having to account for every instance in a category; this method is known as inferential statistics. **Inferential statistics** are numeric representations of some, but not all, of the instances of a category from which a generalization of the entire category can be made. For instance, election polls are attempts to determine how an entire category of people voted by questioning only some of them. Debaters raise four common issues with regard to inferential statistics: the degree of cogency assigned by the study's author(s), the sampling technique used in the study, the means employed to find central tendency, and whether the conclusions are compared to other figures.

In the first case, those who perform studies usually have a good idea of what they want to say about the data. Often a conclusion to a study might include a caution, such as, "the data are useful only for the population under study and should not be generalized." Such a statement means that the study's conclusion is extremely limited. Use of such a study for debate evidence must be considered carefully. During the third-parties in presidential elections topic, some affirmative teams used inoculation theory to prove that more participation by third parties will cause the general public to reject them. Inoculation theory is a medical analogy that says that unless we have been inoculated against a diseased argument, we may fall victim to it when we are weakened and exposed. Thus, affirmatives argued that third party participation is beneficial because it eliminates the possibility that in times of crisis a radical third party candidate would be elected to the presidency or to any other office. Negative teams quickly armed themselves with indictments against the inoculation studies, saying that the studies were not able to be generalized. Many affirmative teams were not ready for the indictments and had not read their own studies. Had they done so, they would have realized that inoculation theory was intended to be generalized for the cultural truisms that third parties threatened, but not for other matters.

A second consideration when using statistics is the sampling technique employed in the study. A sampling technique should attempt to ensure that a **representative** sample is collected. A representative sample is one that gathers information in a non-biased manner to ensure that the results are typical of the whole category. News programs are infamous for asking callers to phone a 900 number in order to give their opinions on various subjects. However, the programs usually offer the qualification that the survey is not scientific, but only represents the opinions of the callers who decide to participate. If a debater attempted to cite the conclusion to a 900-number survey and then infer its results to the entire nation, the opposing team should point out that such a survey does not generate a representative sample of the population and thus may not be used as evidence.

To help ensure a representative sample is collected, the researcher will usually collect the information in a non-biased manner. For example, suppose we wanted to know how students at your college feel towards the college library's new computer data research capabilities. We could simply stand by the computer and ask students who use it what they think about it. This however would not be a very representative sampling of the entire student population. We would probably expect students who use the computer to have different views than those who do not. One way to gather a representative sample would be to survey every student at the college and obtain a descriptive statistical result. However, surveying every student may not be realistic. Therefore, the researcher would probably need to rely on inferential statistics.

One way to ensure a representative gathering of data using inferential statistics is to conduct a simple random sample. A **simple random sample** suggests simply that each person in a given population has an equal chance of being selected. For example, we could have a computer randomly select names of those students currently enrolled at your college and then survey those students. Some studies take that a step further to obtain a **stratified random sample.** To do that, certain segments of the population are isolated, and the survey ensures that it obtains a proportionate amount of responses from each segment. For instance, suppose you wanted to determine if there is a difference among how freshman, sophomores, juniors, and seniors at your college feel towards the college library's new computer data research capabilities. To find this out you would need to guarantee that you had a relatively proportionate number of people from each class level respond to your survey. Of course, you would still want to randomly select students from each class level.

Sample size is also a consideration. If a poll only contacted 13 people out of a population of one million, obviously, the sample size would be too small. The **questioning technique** may also have a bearing on whether the results are usable. A survey, for example, may ask whether a college student has ever been treated for a sexually transmitted disease, and 38% may have answered, "Yes." In a debate round, an advocate may present the results as, "38% of the students on our college campuses have a sexually transmitted disease." Obviously, that number is inflated because many of those who affirmed that they had been treated may have been cured; thus, they may no longer have the disease. The questions themselves may be flawed, as well. A survey on dreams and dreaming may ask respondents if they have ever *floundered* in their sleep. That question is vague because the word *floundered* could be defined any number of different ways. Therefore, any results compiled from that question would be useless.

Over and under representation may also take place and should be guarded against. **Over representation** takes place when people surveyed wrongfully include themselves in the category being explored. For example, if asked the question "Did you vote in the last election" many people may answer "yes" even if they did not vote. This is because voting is seen by many as an important civic duty, which they might not want to admit ignoring. **Under representation** takes place when people surveyed wrongfully exclude themselves from a category being explored. For example, suppose individuals who are married are asked if they ever had an extramarital affair. Clearly, many individuals may answer "no" to this question even if they have had such an affair. The best way to combat both of these sampling problems is to stress the need for an honest answer and to ensure anonymity.

The third common concern voiced about statistics is the means employed to determine central tendency. There are three ways to determine central tendency in a group of numbers: mean, median, and mode. Each of these methods may render a completely different result, so choosing one over another may benefit the arguer. Certainly, as consumers of argument, we must be aware of the differences.

Mean refers to the mathematical average. This is the same as the averaging that you did in elementary school. You take the sum total of a group of numbers and divide by n. Median seems to be the most preferred by statisticians for providing the most accurate picture of central tendency. Median is merely the number that falls in the middle of a group of numerically listed numbers. If you have an even amount of numbers, you use the mathematical average of the two middle numbers. For instance, for the list of numbers, 2, 3, 4, **5**, 6, 7, 10, the median would be 5. There are seven numbers total, three numbers less than *five* and three numbers greater than *five*. Hence, *five* is the median, falling in the middle of that group of seven numbers. Mode seems to be the least preferred method of generating central tendency. Mode is simply the number appearing most often in a group of numbers. For list of numbers, 1, 2, 3, 4, 5, 6, 7, 7, 7, obviously the mode would be 7. The undesirable nature of the mode becomes apparent in this example because *seven* is no where near the "center" of that group of numbers.

The cost of housing is a good example of where methods of discovering central tendency are misused. As a simplified example let's say that we had a neighborhood with the following housing values:

$600,000	Mode:	$600,000
$600,000		
$600,000		
$300,000		
$250,000	Mean:	$214,000
$ 98,000		
$ 89,000		
$ 85,000		
$ 78,000	Median:	$ 87,000
$ 76,000		
$ 67,000		
$ 55,000		
$ 53,000		
$ 45,000		

In this example, the mean is $214,000; the median is $87,000; the mode is $600,000. Clearly, there is a marked difference between the three outcomes. If you were deciding whether to move into a particular neighborhood, it would be difficult to decide that if you were given the Figure of $600,000 or even $214,000 as the cost of housing. However, for a person minimally qualified to buy a home, the $87,000 median Figure is much more palatable, and much more representative of the cost of the housing listed. Nine of the fourteen houses listed are under $100,000. Although this example is hypothetical, it does represent the characteristics of many numerical factors, such as annual income, auto prices, professional athletes' salaries, or the yearly intake of pork fat.

A final consideration is that numbers in themselves do not often tell the entire tale. Yet, our culture has taught us that numbers do not lie. So, we are caught between what we do not know and what we have been taught. The rule of thumb is that a single number usually needs to be compared to something else. For instance, if someone were to argue that your college student population has too many people on academic probation and they give the proof that 150 students are currently in such a situation. 150 students certainly seem like a lot. However, 150 compared to what? If your college has 15,000 students, 150 is only 1% of the student body. What if the national average were 3% of a given student body on academic probation? If so, the 150 figure may actually be low, not high. As well see in Chapter 10, claiming significance where there is none is called *a fallacy of significance.*

Toulmin analysis for statistical argument is problematic because the tests and rules for statistics fill volumes. So to say that the warrant assumes the argument meets the key tests would make the warrant for any statistical argument volumes long. To simplify matters simply list the warrant as an assumption that the statistical methodology is sound. If the study is a survey, you may want to indicate that the sample size is sufficient and the sample was randomly produced. If the study is an experiment, you may want to indicate that the study is externally valid and so on. On the other hand, if you are making an inference from the statistical information, then the warrant is easier. Then, you simply state that the statistical information is a good indication of what you want to know. For instance, an argument could be built using the above housing information:

> The average price of a home in this neighborhood is $214,000. Therefore, I probably can't afford to buy a home here, unless the median price is a better indicator.

The Toulmin analysis might proceed as follows:

Claim:	I can't afford to buy a home here.
Data:	The average price of a home is $214.000.
Warrant:	The mean price of a home is a good indicator of ability to pay.
Qualifier:	Probably.
Reservation:	Unless the median price is a better indicator.
Backing:	None.

ANALOGY ARGUMENT

An **analogy** is a comparison of two things to make a descriptive or argumentative point. A **figurative analogy** is used to make a descriptive point. A figurative analogy may not be used as an argumentative tool because the instances compared are too different to establish a high level of probability. Comparing our membership in the United Nations with getting a car repaired is an example of a figurative analogy. The two items, membership in an international organization and repair of a car, are items from different classifications. The key to identifying a figurative analogy is that the items are just that, from different classifications. Figurative analogies are effective tools for explaining a difficult point. In fact, some of the greatest public speakers throughout history have used figurative analogies to convey complex concepts. However, the first rule in determining valid analogy reasoning is to exclude all figurative analogies from consideration.

Literal analogies, on the other hand, may be used to establish a high level of probability. Literal analogies compare items from the same classification. College *A* and college *B* for instance are items from the same classification: colleges. Therefore, a comparison of college *A* and college *B* would provide the framework necessary for a literal analogy. Any two items within the same classification provide the same framework: two trees, two houses, two cars, two hot air balloons, two cities, two countries, two military campaigns, two advertising blitzes, two argumentation courses, and so on.

The simple fact that the analogies are from the same classification of things alone does not guarantee a sound argument. The analogies must also be similar in significant detail. You may argue for instance that the type of student government at Maple College would work well at Oakwood College. Obviously, comparing two colleges meets the first test of ensuring a literal analogy. However, in order to meet the second test, you would need to establish that Maple and Oakwood were similar in detail: private, 5,000 or fewer students, well funded student government, etc. If this is true, you may move to the third test for analogy reasoning.

The third test asks the advocate to determine whether there are critical differences that deny the comparison. For instance, you may compare the world court to the US Supreme Court. Certainly, the analogy meets the first test: they are both courts and thus are in the same classification. They are also similar in significant detail: both have justices, both render decisions, and both promulgate their decisions to their respective constituencies. However, when you apply the third test, you find a critical difference that denies the comparison: the US Supreme Court's decisions are binding; the world court's decisions are advisory. So if you were to argue that what works for the US Supreme Court would work for the world court, you may be committing a fallacy of analogy reasoning.

To review, the tests for analogy reasoning are as follows:

1. Are only literal analogies used?
2. Are the instances similar in significant detail?
3. Are the differences non-critical?

An analogy warrant, of course, would assume the argument meets these tests. Notice also that the questions are progressive. In other words, if you answer "no" to any of them, there is really little need to continue to the next test; the analogy must be considered invalid if a *no* answer to but one question appears obvious.

An argument may be presented as follows:

> The Gotham City program to reduce rat infestation should also likely work in the city of Oz. The Gotham program reduced rat sightings by 50%. Both cities have about the same population and socio-economic conditions. Of course, if it turns out the rat population in Oz breeds quicker than those in Gotham then all bets are off.

The Toulmin analysis should proceed accordingly:

Claim:	The Gotham City program to reduce rat infestation should also work in the city
Data:	The Gotham program reduced rat sightings by 50 percent
Warrant:	Gotham and Oz are similar in significant detail and have non-critical differences
Qualifier:	Likely
Backing:	Both cities have similar population and socio-economic conditions
Reservation:	Unless the rats in Oz breed faster than the rats in Gotham.

CAUSAL ARGUMENT

Causal argument suggests that some instance or event forces, gives rise to, or helps produce a particular effect. Note the root-word "cause" in this type of argument. So it is pronounced "cause" + "ull" (as in the word *full*). A careless reader may accidentally substitute "casual." In class discussions over the years, your authors have noticed some students being embarrassed at their oversight, which is why we're mentioning it here. When a careless reader begins to ask us in class whether there is a "casual" relationship, we explain that, with the changes in recent civil law, we're really not supposed to discuss the private lives of our students. Of course, what the reader meant to say was "causal" relationship, two forms of which are discussed fully in this section.

There are two types of causal argument. **Cause-to-effect argument** occurs when the advocate knows the cause and is projecting what the effect will be. Usually, this is a present-to-future argument. Many arguments on quasi-policy topics are cause-to-effect. On the nuclear-freeze-is-desirable topic, advocates argued that the known cause (nuclear freeze) would produce desirable, but unknown, effects (peace, reduced threat of nuclear war, etc.). Through fiat power (the power of the affirmative to implement policies hypothetically so that they may be evaluated by the advocates), the nuclear freeze occurs hypothetically during the debate round (the present). The debate focuses on what the effects (the future) of that policy change would be.

Effect-to-cause arguments, as the name suggests, are the exact opposite of a cause-to-effect argument. Here, you look at a present effect which is known, and you project into the past to try to determine an unknown, but suspected, cause. You may also work from a past effect (World War II) to an earlier cause (the suspected cause or causes of World War II). If there were a worldwide catastrophe tomorrow, you can bet that the world's leaders would all be engaged in effect-to-cause argument, trying to determine how such an event could have occurred.

Regardless of which type of causal argument employed, the tests for both are the same:

1. Does the alleged cause precede the effect?
2. Is the cause relevant to the effect?

3. Is the cause a consistent factor in producing the effect?
4. Can other possible causal explanations be ruled out?
5. Are there any counter-causes that may prevent the effect?

The first question, does the alleged cause precede the effect, is an obvious one, yet one that is not always easy to answer. Clearly, if someone maintains that "A" causes "B," then "A" must happen before "B." While this is obvious, it is not always easy to prove. For example, in the 1970s two conditions in the public high school system were observed. First, there seemed to be increasing drug usage among students. Second, the overall test scores of students seemed to be declining. Some saw a connection between the two and maintained that the increased drug usage was causing the lower scores. This led to the "Just Say NO!" drug campaign that was spearheaded by Nancy Reagan during the 1980s. The idea was that if drugs could be eliminated from the schools, then scores would begin to rise. Others, however, argued that the exact opposite was true. They argued that lower grades among students actually were the cause while increased drug usage was the effect. They maintained that as the economy had become worse students felt more pressure to get good grades and when they failed to achieve those grades they turned to drugs to escape the pressure and fear of an uncertain future. Still, others maintained that a third variable actually was the cause. These people argued that the increasing breakup of the family structure lead to both poor grades and increased drug usage among students. In other words, drug usage did not cause poor grades and poor grades did not cause increased drug usage. Instead, the disintegrating family structure was the real cause of both declining academic performance and increased drug usage. So which came first? Drug usage, lower grades, or decreased parental involvement? Clearly, the advocate for either of these positions has a burden to demonstrate that their causal variable came before the effects.

It is important to understand that, while it is required in a causal argument to prove that the alleged cause preceded the effect, simply establishing such a chronology is not sufficient. Just because "A" occurred before "B," it does not follow that "A" caused "B." Obviously, just because a school bell rang and then five minutes later it started to rain, it is does not follow that the ringing of the school bell caused the rain. To claim a causal connection between two events, based simply on the chronology of those events, is to commit what is known as a *post hoc ergo propter hoc* fallacy. (This fallacy is discussed in Chapter 10.) However, while establishing a chronology between two events (that "A" preceded "B") is not sufficient to prove a cause-effect relationship between them, such a chronology is nonetheless a necessary condition of any causal argument. Once a chronology has been established, then the second question can be asked.

The second question is also on the most basic of levels: Is the cause relevant to the effect? Many people read horoscopes because they believe that the position of the stars at birth causes one to have a certain disposition and destiny. However, scientific data reject such a causal relationship. The position of the stars at birth has absolutely nothing to do with a person's fate. The cause is not relevant to the effect. Similarly, some people believe that walking underneath a ladder will bring bad luck. Again, a person's physical position *vis a vis* a ladder really is irrelevant to the effect, bad luck. It may not be intelligent to walk under a ladder, since something may fall on you, but, beyond that, there is no relevancy. Some people have held that the stock market crash in 1929 caused the Great Depression. In answering whether the crash and the depression are relevant, one may have to say, "Yes." At least, it is possible that the one caused the other. Both instances are economic in nature. Both instances had global repercussions.

The third consideration is whether the cause is a consistent factor in producing the effect. That is, when "A" is present does "B" normally follow? In the hard sciences, it is often maintained that to establish a true causal argument, it must be the case that, under the same circumstances, when "A" is present "B" always exists. For example, we know that if water is put into a temperature of 32 degrees or lower at sea level, the water will freeze. It happens every time. However, in the social sciences, it is not possible to be so stringent. For instance, numerous studies (and common sense) reveal that when a person studies for an exam they tend to do better than if they did not study at all. Further, we find this is tendency is consistent among most individuals. Further validation occurs when an increase in "A" leads to an increase in "B." For example, if more studying (three hours vs. one hour) tends to lead to better scores, there is a stronger reason to believe that the cause effect relationship exists.

The fourth test asks if all other possible causes can be ruled out. For example, many people believe that plea bargaining in criminal cases should be eliminated. They argue that it is unjust to give criminals a lighter sentence than they really deserve. Those in favor of plea bargaining argue that if plea bargaining is banned the courts will become extremely overcrowded. In support of this, some point to the state of Alaska which briefly banned plea bargaining in state criminal cases. Statistics showed that during that period the number of criminal trials did increase. This they argued showed that elimination of plea bargaining does lead to clogged courts. However, opponents of plea bargaining usually countered by arguing that while it was true that trials did increase during this period, it had nothing to do with the ban on plea bargaining. They maintained that the increase in trials was due to the increasing population of Alaska during that same time. They argued that the percentage of increased trials was in direct proportion to the increased population. In order for pro plea bargaining advocates to establish the link between banned plea bargaining in Alaska and the increased trials, they would have to be able to rule out this other causal possibility.

If, however, the advocates are able to demonstrate that their causal mechanism is the only relevant change that has occurred they are on very strong ground. For instance, California has instituted a law known as "Three Strikes and You're Out." This law gives mandatory prison sentences of 25 years to life for criminals convicted of a third felony who also have been previously convicted of one or two violent crimes. Proponents claim immediately following the law's enactment violent crime in California decreased by 2%. Advocates of the Three-Strikes Law maintain that this decrease can only be attributed to the new law since it is the only relevant change that took place prior to the decrease in violent crime. Of course, opponents challenge this assessment.

The final test asks whether any counter-causes exist to prevent the effect. Suppose you argued that a unilateral nuclear freeze would lead to world peace. However, the opposing team in turn argued that a unilateral freeze would leave other countries with no incentive to negotiate with us. Therefore, in the long run, a freeze may postpone important arms negotiations and actually fuel the arms race. You would need to argue that no such counter-cause would exist, and that a more likely scenario would be for other countries to cure any economic woes by similarly freezing production and deployment of nuclear arms.

For the purposes of a Toulmin analysis, a causal argument might run something like this:

> There probably will be a great depression in the next decade, unless we do something now. Economic disparity between the rich and the poor has increased. The distancing has become greater. The greater the disparity, the greater the chance for economic catastrophe.

The Toulmin analysis would look something like this:

Claim:	There will be a great depression in the next decade.
Data:	The economic disparity between the rich and the poor has increased.
Warrant:	Economic disparity is a relevant, inherent, and sufficient cause of depression.
Qualifier:	Probably.
Reservation:	Unless we do something now.
Backing:	The greater the disparity, the greater the chance for economic catastrophe.

SIGN ARGUMENT

Sign argument is inferring the existence of a secondary (unknown) variable as the result of observing a primary (known) variable. Sign argument serves as the basis for the medical profession. When you have a cold, you don't see the cold virus; you see the symptoms or signs of the virus: clogged sinuses, runny nose, sore throat, nagging cough, and aching head. When a doctor diagnoses someone with A.I.D.S., the doctor does not see the A.I.D.S. virus, but rather he or she runs a test to determine whether the patient has the antibodies for the A.I.D.S. virus. The presence of the A.I.D.S. antibodies is a sign that the person has A.I.D.S. The legal profession also relies to some extent on sign or circumstantial argument. You are sitting in your car on the side of the road at 2:00 am with a blood alcohol level of .20, and your engine is hot, keys in the ignition, and there are no empty bottles of alcohol for miles around. A police officer stopping by would surely arrest you for driving while under the influence of alcohol. All of the circumstances in which that officer finds you serve as signs that you had been driving while intoxicated.

In a debate round, sign argument plays an important role as well. A sign argument is an argument in which two variables are linked, so that if one is present, the other is also likely to be present; if one is missing, the other is also likely to be missing. Many events or circumstances serve as signs that some other event or circumstance exists. Conversely, the absence of certain events or circumstances serves as signs that some other event or circumstance is absent. The tests for sign argument are as follows:

1.   Is the known variable relevant to the unknown variable?
2.   Is the sign relationship inherent?
3.   Are complimentary signs present?

The first test, relevancy, asks whether the sign relationship is merely possible. If the US sent a large regiment of soldiers to Honduras, it would be possible that we were going to attack a bordering country. Therefore, the variables are relevant to each other. However, if we applied the second test to determine if the sign relationship were inherent, we would find that it is not. The presence of additional US troops in any given country usually does not mean attack. We simply may be performing military maneuvers or merely deterring a bordering country's possible aggression. Therefore, the sign relationship is relevant, but not inherent. Other sign relationships might be inherent. For instance, if we observe it snowing outside we can be certain that the temperature is less than 32° F. That is because the temperature must be that cold before it will snow. Inherent sign relationships are very rare.

The third question asks if other complimentary signs are present. If the unknown variable is not inherent to the known variable then finding other signs which compliment, or support, the first sign will make the argument stronger. For example, say you are driving down the road and all of a sudden traffic becomes extremely congested. You surmise that there must be a traffic accident. The known variable (congested traffic) is certainly relevant to the unknown variable (a traffic accident). It is not an inherent sign however as other reasons for the backed up traffic could exist. For instance, there could be road construction occurring. However, let's suppose that you also see an ambulance speed by. That would be a complimentary sign and would strengthen the position that the traffic congestion is due to a traffic accident and not to road construction.

On the other hand, say an advocate were to argue that North Korea did not plan to attack South Korea. As proof, the advocate read evidence explaining that the North Koreans have not crossed the border since the end of the Korean War, and that the North Koreans have recently withdrawn many soldiers from the North-South

Korean boarder. These signs certainly are relevant to the suspected variable that the North Koreans do not plan to attack South Korea. But is the sign relationship inherent? The answer is "yes." If a country were planning an attack, it certainly would not withdraw troops from the future front. If anything, that country would amass troops on the border. Let's evaluate a sign argument using the Toulmin analysis:

It definitely is going to rain tomorrow. There is a rainbow ring around the moon, and the crickets are chirping wildly.

Claim:	It is going to rain tomorrow.
Data:	There is a rainbow ring around the moon, and the crickets are chirping wildly.
Warrant:	These datum, ring and crickets, are relevant and inherent to the claim, rain.
Qualifier:	Definitely.
Reservation:	None.
Backing:	None.

ARGUMENT BY DEFINITION

The **argument by definition** is basically a deductive argument. This type of argument determines whether something should be included within the realm of a particular definition or classification. The argument by definition argument then may make inferences about that classification. The tests for argument by definition are as follows:

1. Is the definition clear?
2. Is the definition the accepted definition?
3. Does the phenomenon under evaluation fit within the scope of the definition?

The first question asks if the definition is clear. This obviously is very important. For instance, a definition of drunken driving that read "the operating of a motor vehicle after having consumed too much alcohol" would be too vague. The first question one would ask is "what does too much mean?" This definition is simply not clear. On the other hand, defining drunken driving as "Operating a motor vehicle with a blood alcohol level of .08% or greater" is pretty specific.

The second question asks if the definition is the accepted definition. In some situations there will be a clear answer to this and sometimes there won't. In California the .08 blood alcohol level is the legally stipulated definition. It was what the courts will use to determine if one is intoxicated. In other situations the definitions will not be stipulated and the advocates must debate over which definition should be used. Again, the Bill Clinton saga over the term "sexual relations" serves as a good example of this. Both parties had to argue before the judge over which definition should be used in the court case. In academic debate, having debates over definitions are quite common.

The final question asks does the phenomenon under evaluation fit within the scope of the definition. Assume one is pulled over for driving erratically by the police, taken down to the station and given a sobriety test that ultimately shows a blood alcohol level of .08. The police would have a fairly strong case that you fit the definition of drunken driving. You might, if you had very good toxicologists, be able to argue that yes, you did drink some alcohol and yes the tests did show a .08 blood alcohol level. You might maintain however that while you were actually driving your automobile your blood alcohol level had not yet reached .08 and that the test that was conducted at the police station, a half hour after being pulled over, does not necessarily prove you were at .08 while driving. If a reputable toxicologist testified that given the type and amount of alcohol consumed, your blood alcohol level would not have had time to rise to .08 when you were pulled over, you might be able show that you don't fit the definition of drunken driving. Let's apply a similar example to the Toulmin model.

> The driver had a blood-alcohol level of .20 while driving in the state of California. Therefore, the driver almost certainly is guilty of driving while intoxicated, unless the breath meter was not functioning.

In completing a Toulmin analysis, the definition of *driving while intoxicated* becomes the warrant:

Claim:	The driver is guilty of driving while intoxicated.
Data:	The driver had a blood alcohol level of .20.
Warrant:	Driving while intoxicated in California is defined as having a blood-alcohol level of .08 or higher while operating a motor vehicle.
Qualifier:	Almost certainly.
Reservation:	Unless the breath meter was not functioning.
Backing:	None.

SUMMARY

The Toulmin model was used to reveal the structure of an argument and to discover the underlying assumptions of it. There are six components that make up the Toulmin model. Data, claim and warrant are the three basic components and are present in all arguments. The claim is the conclusion to the argument, the data are the supporting reasons and the warrant, which is normally implied, is the assumption that must exist in the audience's mind in order to connect the data to the claim. In addition to these three basic components are three auxiliary components that may or may not be present. The qualifier is the degree of certainty attached to the claim, the backing is additional support for the warrant and the reservation is a possible exception to the claim. Armed with this information, it should be easier for advocates to construct their own sound arguments and to find weaknesses in opponent's arguments.

Next, this chapter covered the various forms of argument: testimony, example, statistical, analogy, cause, sign, and definition. An argument from testimony is an argument that uses as its support the authority of another person. There are four questions that are asked to determine the strength of such arguments: 1. Is the source an expert? 2. Is the expertise relevant on the subject being discussed? 3. Is the source unbiased? 4. Is support available?

Argument by example is examining the particular instances in a classification or population in order to find the patterns or similarities within the grouping. The tests for example argument are as follows: 1. Are the examples relevant to the claim? 2. Are there a sufficient number of examples? 3. Are the examples typical? 4. Are counter examples insignificant? 5. Is the claim qualified?

Statistics involve the use of numbers: conclusions to studies, results of opinion polls, or total numbers of people or objects within a certain classification. When utilizing statistics it is important to determine if a sufficient and representative number has been collected. It is also important to understand how statistics are reported. The mean is the average, the median is the middle number in a series of numbers and the mode is the number that repeats itself most often.

Causal argument suggests that some instance or event forces, gives rise to, or helps produce a particular effect. The tests for causal argument include: 1. Does the alleged cause precede the effect? 2. Is the cause relevant to the effect? 3. Is the cause a consistent factor in producing the effect? 4. Can other possible causal explanations be ruled out? 5. Are there any counter-causes that may prevent the effect?

An analogy is a comparison of two things to make a descriptive or argumentative point. The tests include: 1. Are only literal analogies used? 2. Are the instances similar in significant detail? 3. Are the differences non-critical?

Sign argument is inferring the existence of a secondary variable as the result of observing a primary variable. The tests for sign argument are as follows: 1. Is the known variable relevant to the unknown variable? 2. Is the sign relationship inherent? 3. Are complimentary signs present?

Argument by definition determines whether something should be included within the realm of a particular definition or classification. The tests for argument by definition are as follows: 1. Is the definition clear? 2. Is the definition the accepted definition? 3. Does the phenomenon under evaluation fit within the scope of the definition?

CHAPTER 10

EXPOSING FALLACIES

The purpose of this chapter is not to give you a complete picture of all of the fallacies ever discussed. That could fill volumes. The purpose of this chapter is to provide the advocate with a brief description of the most common fallacies confronted during a debate. Advocates must avoid using fallacies and must be able to expose fallacies committed by their opponents.

THE FALLACY OF EXAMPLE ARGUMENT

The **fallacy of example argument** is a fancy name for a misused inductive argument. This fallacy is also called a *hasty generalization*. A fallacy of example reasoning occurs when an advocate violates one of the key tests for example argument. Those key tests are as follows:

1. Are there a sufficient number of examples?
2. Are the examples typical?

Remember that these tests are not objective scientific litmus tests; nevertheless, if you feel that your opponent may have insufficient or atypical examples, it may be worth your while to press the point. Say that your opponent argues that people have their medical privacy violated due to unprotected computer data banks. Your opponent argues further that this violation of privacy is harmful. For proof, your opponent offers a single example of Mr. Magoo who lost his job because his company's management discovered, through unprotected medical data banks, that he had been treated for a serious disease. While that is a compelling example, it is only one instance, and it may be atypical. You must challenge your opponents either to provide additional examples or to read general testimony evidence that indicates that the problem is significant. While asking for additional proof, point out that the example, as presented, is insufficient and atypical; thus, your opponent has committed a fallacy of example reasoning. Additionally, you can strengthen your position by reading evidence denying that the problem is widespread.

THE FALLACY OF COMPOSITION

The fallacy of composition holds that what is true of the parts is true of the whole. However, this is not always the case. For instance, a collection of the greatest National Basketball Association players on one team would not ensure that that team would be a great team. It might turn out that all of the players have big egos and want to be the star of the team. No one may be willing to do the "dirty" work, like rebounding and diving for lose balls, which is necessary to have a successful team. Similarly, milk, Pepsi, orange juice, and beer may taste great individually, but it does not mean that if you mixed them all together the outcome would be an even better tasting beverage. In fact, the outcome would probably taste quite bad. Likewise, the ingredients that go into making a cake (flower, raw egg, oil, etc.) individually may taste quite bad, but when combined the outcome is quite tasty. The saying that the "whole is greater (or worse) than the sum of its parts" applies to this fallacy.

THE FALLACY OF DIVISION

The fallacy of division holds that what is true of the whole is true of the parts. It is thus the opposite of the fallacy of composition. Of course, what is true of the whole is not necessarily true of its constituent parts. The team that wins the Super Bowl is generally considered to be the best team in professional football. That does not mean, however, that the Super Bowl champions have the best players at each position on their team. In fact, it is possible that they might not even have one of the best players at any position on their team. Just because a movie wins "Best Picture" it does not follow that all of those responsible for its production are the best at their jobs.

THE FALLACY OF MISTAKEN CAUSATION

A **fallacy of mistaken causation** is a causal argument that fails to meet the key tests for causal reasoning. To review the tests for causal reasoning, they are listed here:

1.   Does the alleged cause precede the effect?
2.   Is the cause relevant to the effect?
3.   Is the cause an inherent factor in producing the effect?
4.   Can other possible causal explanations be ruled out?
5.   Are there any counter-causes that may prevent the effect?

Should your opponent argue that the President's administration's domestic policies caused third world countries to turn to communism, you would need to argue that your opponent is guilty of a fallacy of mistaken causation. In asking the first question, about whether the cause is relevant, you would have to say, "no." Without any compelling evidence to the contrary, US domestic policy rarely affects a third world country's choice of political philosophy. If your opponent's argument dealt with US foreign policy, then that may be a different matter altogether.

A specific causal fallacy is the fallacy of *post hoc ergo propter hoc,* which means literally "after the fact therefore because of the fact." This **post hoc fallacy** occurs when chronology becomes confused with causation. For example, Shortly after Ronald Reagan's inauguration in 1981, the Iran Hostage Crisis ended. However, just because the inauguration occurred before the hostages' release does not mean that the inauguration caused the release. To believe so would be to fall victim to the *post hoc* fallacy. It may be true that the captors were waiting for Carter to leave office; even so, the inauguration did not cause the release. Advocates commit the *post hoc* fallacy whenever they try to demonstrate a causal link based solely on the chronology of the events. While chronology is necessary to establish a causal connection, chronology by itself does not prove causality. Chronology merely makes causality possible.

THE FALLACY OF SIGNIFICANCE

The fallacy of significance refers to the use of statistics. As mentioned in a previous chapter, an advocate must compare a single statistic to another number in order to determine whether that statistic is significant. To charge that the single statistic is significant without the comparison often leads to the fallacy of significance. Recall the example from the previous chapter: 150 students on academic probation is not necessarily a lot of people on academic probation. It could be the lowest percentage ever achieved by a college in the history of post-secondary education. But of course, you cannot know that until you compared the 150 Figure to other colleges past and present.

THE FALSE ANALOGY

The false analogy occurs when the tests for analogy reasoning are not followed. The tests are,

1.   Are only literal analogies used?
2.   Are the instances similar in significant detail?
3.   Are there are any critical differences that deny the comparison?

Remember that that there are two types of analogies. Literal and non-literal analogies. Non-literal analogies can never be used for a basis of critical comparison. Non-literal analogies may be figurative in nature. Comparing marriage to a roller coaster: both have a lot of ups and down, twists and turns, and highs and lows is a figurative analogy. They are poetic in nature but don't prove anything. Non-literal analogies may also be informative in nature. A parent telling a child that a good breakfast provides energy to the body like gasoline provides energy for a car may help the child to understand why eating a good breakfast is important. But once again, it can't be used as any type of proof. If someone advances a non-literal analogy as a form of proof, it is a logical fallacy.

Literal analogies are the only type of analogies that can be used to advance an argument. Literal analogies involve comparing two items that fall within the same classification scheme. For example, those who advocate socialized medical care in the US often use Canada's socialized medical system as a comparison. This then would be a literal analogy and worthy of critical analysis. The key now is to ensure that there are no key differences between the two.

Say your opponents argue that a homeless program works in the US; therefore, it will work in Ethiopia. Obviously, there are critical differences that deny comparing the US to Ethiopia. The governmental structure in Ethiopia and the high percentage of Ethiopians living in poverty may preclude a US style program from working there. If these differences are not accounted for in the argument, then a false analogy exists.

A Priori Fallacy

An *a priori* **fallacy** is an inability to adjust our major premises to disconfirming information. All of us have a set of values and beliefs called a world view. Each belief and value in that world view could be formed into a major premise of a syllogism. For instance, a person may have a major premise which says that "everything our country does is wrong." Then, if our country should do something right, like secure the release of a hostage, that person, rather than evaluate the event for rightness or "wrong-ness," would immediately assign evil motives. This type of reaction relates directly with the *a priori* fallacy. Closed mind, opinionated, dogmatic, intolerant, or even naive are all descriptive terms that could easily apply to a person who constantly commits the *a priori* fallacy.

When one enters the world of intercollegiate debate, often an advocate must rethink some issues. A communist takeover of a country for instance is not considered automatically evil. If you were to argue that US policies are bad because they enhance the risk of communist takeover of third world countries, your opponent may ask you to provide a concrete harm from communist takeover. Many novice debaters are hard pressed to answer that question. Our society drills us with propaganda about how evil communism is, but that same society fails to arm most of us with the information or critical thinking skills necessary to fill a one-minute speech against communism.

The following statement illustrates the *a priori* fallacy:

> John couldn't have been convicted of hit-and-run driving. He's not that kind of person. He's responsible.

In this example, the person speaking has a major premise about John that precludes John's illegal behavior. It is an *a priori* fallacy; because the arguer's <u>prior</u> beliefs prevent the arguer from even considering the new disconfirming information.

BEGGING THE QUESTION

The statement, "abortion is wrong because abortion is murder," is an example of the **begging the question** fallacy. The question that is being begged . . ."is abortion really murder?" is unanswered by the statement. In order to propose the above argument, you would need to first prove that human life begins at conception and that the process of terminating a pregnancy meets the legal definition of murder. Otherwise, abortion cannot be considered murder. This type of fallacy uses one unsupported claim to prove another. The above argument looks like this:

Unsupported claim number one: Abortion is wrong.
Unsupported claim number two: Abortion is murder.

ARGUING IN A CIRCLE

Like begging the question, **a circular argument** also employs two unsupported claims. Circular argument differs, however, because its claims reverse rolls. The following conversation demonstrates the circular nature of this fallacy:

Mary: Jesus is really God.
Joan: How do you know that?
Mary: My preacher says so.
Joan: Why does your preacher say so?
Mary: Well, because Jesus is really God, pure and simple.

The following schematic shows what is happening here:

Claim: Jesus is really God.
Data: Because my Preacher says so.

Claim: My preacher says so.
Data: Because Jesus is really God.

If your opponents become entrenched in a circular argument, you must point out that fact, and you must explain that the first unsupported claim still lacks sufficient proof. Without additional data, your opponents must lose that particular argument.

OVER-RELIANCE ON AUTHORITY

As discussed earlier, one key fallacy is the over-reliance on authority. It is not a fallacy to rely on authority. That is something we must all do at times in this complicated society. However, it is a fallacy to overly rely on authority. This fallacy is committed when a reason for a claim cannot be provided when requested. The above example in the fallacy of circular argument shows why this is so. Even if your preacher is highly credible in both expertise and objectivity, it is still a fallacy if he cannot provide a reason for his opinion that Jesus is really God when requested. Why? Because an over-reliance on authority leaves the listener with no reason to adopt the assertion as a belief, value, or plan. This fallacy is a fallacy because it is merely the illusion of reason: nothing but an assertion by an alleged expert.

In order to avoid relying too much on authority, an advocate should be able to include the "reason given" by the expert if requested. Therefore, had the arguer in the Jesus-is-really-God argument above provided the reasoning behind accepting the divinity of Jesus, then it would not be a fallacy of this type. For example, in the above argument, the Christian could have provided the preacher's reason, such as,

> Jesus Christ is perfect in all things. Human beings are not perfect. Since only God is perfect, then Jesus Christ must have been one with God, as Jesus Christ says in the *New Testament*.

You may disagree with the evidence and/or reason given, but once a reason is provided then it is not an over-reliance-on-authority fallacy. The over-reliance-on-authority fallacy occurs therefore when an expert is quoted making an assertion: in other words, no reason is given by the expert or the advocate to support the expert's claim.

This fallacy is important to watch for in both parliamentary and cross-examination debate. In either debate format, one may make a claim like, "Henry David Thoreau believes 'that government is best which governs not at all . . .'" If no reason is given to accept Thoreau's conclusion, whether it's Thoreau's reason or the advocate's reason, it is merely an assertion and therefore a fallacy of over-reliance on authority. In a debate, you should challenge the expert's claim, by saying that it is merely an assertion, that no reason is given, and therefore it is a fallacy of over-reliance on authority.

This fallacy could be made by cross-examination advocates when their opponents merely read a pile of quotations. If this were to happen, in a questioning period, you may ask your opponents about the pile of quotations. If your opponents are unable to articulate the reasons given when asked, then you can expose your opponents for being guilty of the over-reliance on authority fallacy. In this case, although the reasons may have been articulated by the experts, this is still an over-reliance on authority fallacy because the advocate has relied too heavily on the pile of quotations and too little on the articulation of reasons. Remember, argumentation is "reason giving." If there are no reasons, there is no argumentation. Period.

Reductio Ad Absurdum

Reductio ad absurdum is a Latin phrase, that means literally, "reducing to the absurd." Also called the fallacy of extension, the *reductio ad absurdum* fallacy has become entrenched in intercollegiate debate. Occasionally, a debater will argue something like, "if we raise the price of milk, nuclear war will result." That argument would go something like this:

I. If we raise the price of milk, catastrophic consequences will result.
    A. U.S. milk prices affect the overall food-price picture.
    B. A significant rise in food prices adversely affects the world's economy.
    C. When the world's economy is harmed, revolutions are triggered.
    D. Revolutions give rise to a means-to-end mentality.
    E. The means-to-end mentality will lead to nuclear war.

This argument is nothing but a series of cause-to-effect arguments. The more links that are added the more unlikely the final result. Unfortunately, such an argument cannot be dismissed by simply saying that it is a fallacy. Many debate critics accept this type of argument. When refuting the fallacy of extension, focus on the weakest links. And, if you cannot destroy the links, at least show that the initial cause (in this case a rise in milk prices) is not a unique or important factor in the end result. You may also ask for examples. For instance, ask the other team to give an example of sub-point "C": "Tell me one revolution that was started solely because of a faulty world economy." If your opponents cannot answer, you have strengthened your case. If they do give an example, ask why we haven't had a nuclear war yet.

A related fallacy is **the slippery slope fallacy.** Instead of evidence supporting each link as in the fallacy of extension, the progression or slippery slope toward catastrophe is asserted. The metaphor implies that, once you take a first step, you will automatically slide all the way down the hill. A common example of the slippery slope fallacy is the warning sometimes mentioned about drugs: If you inhale one lung full of marijuana, soon you will be taking and selling hard drugs. Additionally, some Supreme Court decisions commit this fallacy, when they assert that, once a freedom is limited, sooner or later the freedom will be destroyed completely. Implication of the slippery slope fallacy does not mean that the eventual catastrophe will not occur; it just means that the conclusion is unproved. A marijuana user may very well end up a drug pusher, but the same user also may never smoke again. Slippery slope is a fallacy because the conclusion is pure speculation.

THE *AD HOMINEM* FALLACY

Ad Hominem means literally "against the man." This fallacy substitutes the person for the argument. If one were to dismiss arguments made by Howard Stern about the need for stronger Affirmative Action polices by simply stating that "Howard Stern is a long haired freak" then one would be committing the *ad hominem* fallacy. Attacking the Hair style of Howard Stern is in no way a logical response.

Through desperation of not being able to respond to a particular argument, a frustrated debater may falsely accuse his or her opponents of fabricating the evidence. Not only would that be a highly serious charge, but it would also be an instance of an *ad hominem* attack. The debater focused on the person (opponent) rather than the argument. Obviously, you should never accuse your opponents of anything for which you don't have concrete proof. However, if your opponents did actually fabricate evidence, would the accusation then be an *ad hominem* attack? The answer is "no." If the accusation is germane to the issue and true, then it is not a fallacy.

A fine line divides a justified credibility attack from an *ad hominem* attack. In each case, whether evaluating opponents or the experts they cite, be sure to determine if the credibility attack is relevant to the claim. If your opponent cites Joseph Stalin, the late Soviet dictator, on the nature of his regime, obviously a statement about Stalin's character would not be an *ad hominem* attack. Stalin killed millions of Soviet citizens in the guise of political necessity, and his name has been all but erased from contemporary Soviet culture. Any statement Stalin made about his regime must be considered in light of his character. A good rule of thumb is to combine a credibility attack of sources with other arguments as well. In that way, you can't be accused of *substituting* the person for the argument.

THE FALLACY OF FALSE CONSOLATION

Many contemporary debate rounds boil down to which position has the least risk and the most benefits. **The fallacy of false consolation** takes that position to an extreme by confusing a least harmful situation with a completely desirable situation. When you console someone, you tell them that things are really okay. When you falsely console someone, you tell them things are okay when they really are not. Look at the example of a false consolation fallacy:

> I guess that I have no reason to complain. I mean I know my well has been polluted with toxic waste and I'll probably die of cancer in 30 years. However, I really don't have a problem compared to people in Africa that have no water at all and will die of dehydration tomorrow.

The fact that toxic waste has contaminated this person's drinking water <u>is</u> a problem. Just because people suffer greater harm elsewhere does not negate her problem. She needs to confront her problem while others in the world need to confront theirs. Merely because some people are better off than others does not justify maintaining an undesirable status quo.

THE FALSE DILEMMA FALLACY

The prefix "di" means "two." A true dilemma forces an advocate to make a choice between <u>two</u> alternatives. A **false dilemma** attempts to force the same choice; however, the difference is that, with the false dilemma there are two other possibilities not accounted for. First, both choices may be able to exist simultaneously. For instance, many fundamentalist theologians argue that either Evolution is true and no God exists or evolution is false and God exits. Many religious scientists point out this is a false dilemma as God and evolution may both exist. That is, they argue God could have created the natural universe in such away to allow evolution to occur.

Secondly, a false dilemma occurs when two choices are given but more alternatives exist. When former President Ronald Reagan was accused in the Iran-Contra affair, the media tried to put him into a true dilemma: Either Reagan did not know what happened and he was incompetent, or he did know and he was corrupt. When defending himself against the accusation, Reagan tried to prove that the dilemma actually was false. Reagan suggested that his management style involved giving general directions to subordinates then allowing them to carry out the specifics, which explains why he might not have known what happened. Therefore, Reagan presented a third option not mentioned by the media: He did not know what happened, but he was still a competent manager. While there is still much doubt in many American's minds, Reagan's remark represents the correct strategy to use when advocates are pinned to a dilemma.

The phrase, "America: tolerate it or leave it," is another example of a false dilemma. There are other options besides the two undesirable ones listed. You could "change it" or "love it," for instance. When forced into a dilemma, simply show the critic that there is a desirable third or even fourth option not mentioned by your opponents. Thus, you prove the dilemma false and escape losing the particular point.

THE FALLACY OF IGNORING THE ISSUE

Normally, the **fallacy of ignoring the issue** occurs in the cross-examination period of a debate. If the respondents fail to answer directly the questions posed to them, they may be guilty of this fallacy. An occurrence of this fallacy may transpire as follows:

Questioner: Isn't it true that the McCabe study's conclusion contradicts your position here?

Respondent: We cite many other studies with the same inference.

Questioner: You mean you misrepresent many other studies, too?

Respondent: For instance, the Jones and Johnson study read in 1AC clearly demonstrates what we're trying to say.

Questioner: Look, I don't care about that. I want to know about the McCabe study you just read. Doesn't McCabe's conclusion contradict your position here?

Respondent: Will you let me answer the question my way? I need to explain the Jones and Johnson study.

Obviously, the respondent fails to address the question about the McCabe study. Instead of answering the question, the respondent ignores the issue and instead talks about another study altogether. If you find yourself in the position of the questioner, you need to make it clear in cross-examination or in your team's next speech that the other team failed to answer that particular question. You are also free to speculate as to why the respondent failed to respond: Perhaps you were correct in observing that the McCabe study's conclusion contradicted the team's position.

THE FALLACY OF THE LOADED QUESTION

A **loaded question** assumes a premise that has yet to be established. If you answer a loaded question, you tacitly concede that the premise is true. "When did you stop sniffing glue?" is an example of a loaded question. That question assumes the premise that you once sniffed glue and that you have stopped. If you were to answer "Yesterday," you would be conceding to that premise.

When confronted with a loaded question, immediately point out that it is a loaded question and then address the premise, not the question. In answer to the "glue" question above, you should say (and hopefully with some degree of honesty), "that is a loaded question. I have never sniffed glue, and I don't appreciate the insinuation." Even asking the questioner to rephrase the question might be a good option to exercise. A loaded question, after all, is a thinly disguised accusation.

THE *AD POPULUM* FALLACY

Occasionally, the non-policy debate advocate will support a position with an opinion poll. If that is done to show how people feel about a particular issue, then that is a legitimate approach. However, if an opinion poll is used to support a particular position, then that may be an ***ad populum* fallacy.** *Ad populum* literally means "of the people." Just because people believe something to be true does not make it true. At one time, much of the world believed that the earth was flat. Obviously, people's beliefs did not make the earth flat. If your opponent argues that abortion is justified because the majority of Americans favor it, simply point out that your opponent is guilty of an *ad populum* fallacy.

Ultimately, democracy is founded upon this type of fallacy. Voting makes right whatever the majority feels is right. That is why it is not only important for us to vote, but it is also important for us to make an informed choice when we do so. Democracy's success depends upon having a knowledgeable voting public. Additionally, the popular opinion has sometimes stood against what in retrospect many of us view as truth. Socrates, Jesus of Nazareth, Copernicus, Thoreau, Darwin, Freud, Mahatma Gandhi, Susan B. Anthony, Martin Luther King, Jr., and others suffered unjust criticism because they espoused beliefs that differed from the popular opinion of their time.

THE FALLACY OF PSYCHOLOGICAL LANGUAGE

A technique enjoyed by numerous novice debaters is the fallacy of psychological language. This fallacy includes both baiting an opponent and using loaded language. **Baiting an opponent** involves insulting an opponent or rudely criticizing an opponent's argument. Whereas the *ad hominem* fallacy concerns attacking a person's character, baiting an opponent simply means attempting to anger the other person. This fallacy usually assumes that the instigator of the baiting does so consciously. However, more often than not, the novice debater does it unknowingly. After a debate round, someone might mention to the debater that he or she was rude, and that debater may not have realized it. If an opponent angers you, you must try to keep your cool. There is little worse for a critic than watching two novice debaters verbally assault one another.

The fallacy of loaded language involves using emotionally laden words rather than sound logic. Someone may argue that "the evil and tyrannous Democratic Party should be curtailed from its dictatorial operations in the US congress before the world explodes into nuclear holocaust and kills all of the angelic Republicans." This argument has not a shred of proof in it, yet it seems rather compelling. After all, who is going to argue against angels and in support of evil and tyrannous dictators? When confronted with an opponent who tends to sound good, but lacks evidence, be sure to mention the lack of proof to the critic.

THE FALLACY OF EQUIVOCATION

Many words can have more than one meaning. As we saw in Chapter 2, clarity of terminology used in an argument is of utmost importance. The **fallacy of equivocation** occurs when the meaning of a word changes during the course of an argument. Suppose you pick up the morning newspaper and read a headline that says "President of the United States shot while visiting China." You think "what a tragedy" and perhaps fear that a war might even occur. As you rapidly read the article you find that while visiting China the President had his picture taken. Clearly, the word "shot" has taken on a different meaning than you first thought.

Another example occurred in a recent debate on whether television is harmful. An affirmative student presented a definitive stock issue that "drugs are harmful." To support this first value stock issue, he gave information about how drugs can lead to addiction, health problems, and death. Then in the designative stock issue, he argued that television is a drug. His support for this second of two value stock issues was that TV has the same sedating and addicting effect as do many drugs. Then, later in the debate, the negative advocate correctly pointed out that the affirmative had equivocated on the word *drug*, using it literally in one case and metaphorically in another. The affirmative debater thus lost the debate, solely due to committing this fallacy.

Hopefully, you, too, will be able to spot equivocation when it occurs.

THE FALLACY OF THE STRAW PERSON

The **fallacy of the straw person** involves ignoring the real issue and arguing a similar but less threatening issue instead. The metaphor, *straw person*, refers to a physical fight in which a person decides to wrestle the easy-to-beat straw person rather than the tough-to-beat real person. In a debate on air pollution, you might argue that diesel engines pose a great health risk. Your opponent, lacking evidence on diesel exhaust, might respond with evidence proving that smog devices on gasoline engines work well. While gasoline engines pose a similar pollution problem as do diesel engines, gasoline engines are only tangentially relevant. Therefore, you would need to point out that your opponent has committed a straw argument and explain that your original argument about diesel effects still stands.

THE FALLACY OF TRADITION

The **fallacy of tradition** occurs when someone equates the best way to do something with the way it traditionally has been done. An opponent may argue, "For nearly a century the US government has generated revenue through income taxes, so that must be the best way to finance national expenditures." However, just because it has been done that way does not make it the best way. If you hear such a fallacy of tradition, you need to explain that your opponent committed the fallacy and that the issue in question thus remains unsupported.

THE FALLACY OF SIGN REASONING

This fallacy is often referred to as a non sequitur which literally means, "it does not follow." In a sense, however, the name non-sequitur is misleading because all fallacies are really non-sequiturs in that no conclusion necessarily follows from any type of fallacious reasoning. Therefore, it is best to think of this as **the fallacy of sign reasoning.** Remember that a sign argument contains two parts. The first is the known variable and the second is the unknown variable. From the known variable we infer the existence of the unknown variable. This fallacy of sign reasoning occurs when a conclusion does not follow from the premises or the evidence. For instance, someone might argue, "He must be a moral man since he has nice clothes." In this case the known variable is the nice clothing and from this the conclusion is made that he must be moral. This is a fallacy of sign reasoning because clearly the unknown variable of being moral does not follow from the known variable of having nice clothes. After all, Adolf Hitler was a very nice dresser but we would hardly consider him to be a moral person.

THE FALLACY OF SHIFTING THE BURDEN OF PROOF

One of the basic tenants of argumentation is that he or she who asserts a claim has the burden of proving that claim. In Chapter 1 it was noted that an argument is a claim supported by reasons. **The fallacy of shifting the burden of proof** occurs when the advocate of a claim maintains they have proven the claim simply because their opponent has not or cannot provide evidence to deny the claim. Let's suppose that your friend states that she believes in extra terrestrial life from another planet and when asked why, she responds because no one has proven that it doesn't exist. In this case, she would be guilty of committing the fallacy of shifting the burden of proof. Just because no proof is given that extra terrestrial life doesn't exist is hardly proof that it does exist.

This fallacy commonly occurs during periods of cross-examination. During their speech party "A" will maintain that a claim is true and not provide any supporting evidence. During cross-examination, party "B" will ask if they read any evidence to provide support for the claim. Party "A" will respond, not by answering the question, but instead by asking Party "A" they have read any evidence that denies the claim. Party "B" will then say "no," sit down, and start searching for evidence to disprove the claim. Party "A" will then act as though they have just proven their point. Don't let this happen to you. If your opponent makes a claim, insist that **they** provide support for it. Don't let them shift the burden of disproving the claim on to you. Of course, if they do provide support, it would then be incumbent on you to either point out flaws with their support and /or to read contrary evidence.

SUMMARY

In this chapter, some of the more common fallacies were discussed. In order to become proficient at identifying fallacies, however, you need to do more than merely read a chapter explaining fallacies. You really need to make identification of fallacies an ongoing effort. Some texts even suggest trying to identify at least one fallacy a day. Advertisements, newspaper articles, network news broadcasts, classroom lectures, interpersonal conversations, books, letters, group discussions, speeches, debates, etc. are good sources of fallacies. Critical thinking is something that requires more than mere knowledge acquisition. You need to make critical thinking a habit or even a philosophy by which to live.

CHAPTER 11

REFUTING AND REBUILDING ARGUMENTS

Debates do not take place in isolation. Debates involve two **hostile parties** who disagree over whether a claim should or should not be adopted. In a court of law the hostile parties would be the prosecution and the defense; in a Presidential debate the hostile parties would be the Republican and Democratic candidates (and perhaps even some third party candidates); in Parliamentary debate they would be the Government and the Opposition and in cross-examination style debate they would be the affirmative and the negative. By hostile parties, we do not mean that the two parties dislike each other personally. We have all had debates with family members and friends who we like and respect. To say that two parties are hostile simply means that the two parties have opposing views on an issue.

Since debates involve a hostile party, debaters will be introduced to arguments with which they disagree. The process of confronting these arguments is known as refutation. **Refutation** can be defined as the process of responding to opposing arguments in order to eliminate or weaken them. Refutation is a necessary component of any debate. As we mentioned earlier in this textbook, in debate, silence means consent. That is, if a debater fails to refute an argument raised by the opposition, then that argument is in essence granted or agreed on. Therefore, it is vital that debaters have a solid understanding of the various refutation techniques that are available.

PREPARING FOR REFUTATION

The first step in the refutation process is to be prepared to engage in refutation. This means that the debater must have a comprehensive understanding of the issues both for and against the resolution. The more knowledge the debater has about the resolution, the more effective the refutation will be. Most beginning debaters tend to spend much time researching material that supports their side of the debate. This is a very good start. However, it should not stop there. Effective debaters also become keenly aware of the issues that might be raised by their opponents and develop arguments to counter those positions before the debate even begins. Obviously, one cannot anticipate every argument that might be raised. However, in almost every debate there are obvious areas of attack that one can anticipate their opponent advancing. For example, if debating the resolution "Resolved: That the US should substantially reduce its reliance on nuclear energy" the affirmative should anticipate that the negative will argue that such a policy will lead to higher energy prices and increased reliance on and consumption of fossil fuels. The affirmative should be prepared to effectively deal with these arguments before the debate begins. Similarly the negative could probably anticipate that the affirmative might argue that nuclear energy creates radioactive waste that is dangerous or that the nuclear power plants have a risk of exploding. The good negative team will have anticipated and prepared for these likely affirmative arguments well before the debate. Of course, until the debate actually begins, the debaters cannot be sure what arguments their opponent will in fact raise. However, the more prepared one is prior to the debate, the easier the refutation will be during the debate.

The Three "Ds" of Refutation

There are three strategies of refutation. They are Deny the argument, Diminish the argument and Disbar the argument. We refer to these as the "Three D's" of refutation. They are presented in order of their effectiveness. In other words, it is best to deny an argument, if that cannot be done, then it is next best to diminish the argument, and finally, one can attempt to disbar the argument.

Deny the Argument

The most effective refutation technique is to simply deny the truth of the argument. In a legal proceeding, the defendant might claim that he is not guilty of the alleged crime, a politician might argue that he did not take a bribe or a husband might contend that he is not having an affair. If your opponents argued that Iraq is expansionary, a good argument would be to directly deny it.

There are three steps involved in this strategy. First, the debater must deny the truth of the argument. This is as simple as saying 'I completely disagree that capital punishment is not a deterrent, I will argue that capital punishment is a deterrent."

The second step is to provide evidence, proof or analysis for the counter claim. You might, for instance, cite a criminal expert who says capital punishment does deter future murders. But what if your opponents also provided support for their contention that capital punishment is not a deterrent? In this situation we have two contrary claims both with support. At this point the audience might not know who to believe. Imagine that you are a juror on a murder case. The prosecution calls Dr. Jones who testifies that in his professional opinion the defendant was sane when the killing took place. Also, suppose the defense calls Dr. Smith who testifies that in her professional opinion the defendant was not sane when the killing took place. Who do you believe? It is because of this dilemma we must conclude with step three.

The third step is to provide a reason why your support should be preferred over your opponent's support. Perhaps your source is more qualified, has more educational background, more experience or is less biased. Or perhaps your evidence is more recent, or summarizes the consensus of opinion on a subject. What ever the reason, you should be prepared to show why your support is superior to that used by your opponent.

Diminish the Argument

As we have just seen, the most effective refutation technique is to simply deny the truth of an argument. But what if that is not possible? What if Iraq really is expansionist? What do you do then? Well, life has not ended. One thing that you will learn in debate is that there is an argument against everything. If an argument cannot be directly denied, it might still be diminished. This simply means that while the argument is not denied, it is shown to have little if any effect on the debate. There are numerous ways to diminish an argument, they include turning the argument, showing that the argument is not relevant, mitigating the argument, pointing out contradictions, showing a lack of impact to the argument and arguing there are no links to the argument.

Turn-around Arguments

Perhaps the most effective way to diminish an argument is to argue a **turn-around,** which is defined as taking what seemed to be an opponent's argument and using it to support your position. Some common arguments used during the military support topic should give you an idea of how to approach this. Affirmatives would argue that the Soviets were by nature expansionist. (Remember; this topic was debated prior to the end of the Cold War.) Negatives responded, however, by turning around that argument. They argued that merely believing that the Soviets were expansionist was problematic and gave rise to an unnecessarily aggressive US foreign policy. The nature of US foreign policy had caused the Soviets to be extremely defensive. An outgrowth of their defensiveness was that they were more expansionary than they would have been otherwise simply because the US tried to involve itself in every part of the world that the Soviets had an interest. The Soviets feared being forced out of the resource picture by the aggressive US, so they used military solutions to protect their interests. So what had been an affirmative argument (US military support to other countries was necessary to prevent Soviet expansion) became a negative argument (the Soviets were forced to appear expansionist due to an aggressive and misguided US foreign policy).

Show the Argument Is Irrelevant to the Resolution

Another technique is to show that while the argument raised by your opponent might be true, it is irrelevant to the issue at hand. For instance, let's assume the resolution "Resolved: That the evolutionary theory of life on Earth is true." This is a factual resolution. Either evolution is true or it is not. Let's suppose the negative argues against the resolution by arguing that the chances of life beginning on Earth by itself using only natural processes is nearly impossible. They maintain that a supernatural force must have played a role in the origin of life on Earth. The affirmative could respond to this argument by granting out the argument. They could maintain that this argument is absolutely true but then point out that the question of how life began on Earth is irrelevant to the question of if life evolved on Earth, however it originated. The affirmative could point out that evolution has nothing to do with explaining how life originated on Earth. Evolution only maintains that life changes over time, i.e., decent with modification. Life could have started by natural processes, been divinely created by a higher power, or been dropped off by extraterrestrial beings. The bottom line is, whether life started by natural process or by divine intervention, the question of how life originated on Earth is completely irrelevant to whether evolution is true or not. Origins of life and evolution of life are arguably completely unrelated concepts.

Mitigate Arguments

If you cannot directly deny an argument, you can bring in facts that help weaken the argument. Perhaps a good argument against Iraq being expansionary is that it does not have the economic means to be expansionary. In other words, maybe it is expansionary in theory, but in practice, it has not the means. The not-so-covert war against the Kurds, the economic embargo, and the two wars with the U.S.-led forces have drained Iraq of its economic means to expand elsewhere. While Iraq may want to expand, currently it cannot.

Another way to mitigate an argument is to show that the argument is being overly impacted. For instance, perhaps your opponent argues that college speech codes violate the 1st Amendment. As support they read evidence which says "some Constitutional scholars maintain that college speech codes are unconstitutional." You could point out that the evidence implies that not all scholars agree with the claim since the evidence says "some." Also, you could point out that we don't even know how many "some" are. It could be just two.

Finally, one can mitigate quantitatively. If your opponent argues that the unemployment rate is at 10 percent, you might be able to show that it is really only at 3 percent. While this would not deny unemployment exists, it would show that it is not nearly as bad as it is being portrayed.

Point Out Contradictions

Another problem may involve contradictions. Debate resolutions concern complex issues. Often debaters, when trying to deal with those complexities, accidentally contradict themselves. If you detect an apparent contradiction you ought to point it out and ask your opponent to resolve them. In addition, ask the critic to discount both sides of the contradiction until it is resolved.

For example, in debating the proposition "Resolved: That the United States federal government should increase regulations requiring industries to substantially decrease the domestic production and/or emission of environmental pollutants" some affirmatives argued that industries should be required to eliminate dioxin emissions. They maintained that dioxin emissions cause numerous health diseases and eventually death. Some negatives argued that dioxins were not dangerous and therefore did not need to be regulated. They also argued that increased regulations would cause these industries to flee the United States and relocate in nations with very benign environmental regulations. This, they maintained, would lead to even higher levels of dioxin emissions, resulting in the deaths of even more people. Many affirmatives maintained that this was a contradiction. If dioxin levels really were not dangerous as the negative maintained then how could dioxin emissions cause death to people in other nations? Clearly, the negative could not have it both ways.

Demonstrate a Lack of Impact

Another logical flaw often included in a case is the lack of an impact. An advocate may argue that something is true, but gives no reason why we should care. If there is no reason to care or no impact, you ought to mention that. For example, someone may argue that millions of people in the United States have lawns outside of their houses. The question left unanswered by that statement is whether lawns are good or bad. You could simply say, "They argue lawns. I say, so what? There is no impact given by the affirmative as to whether lawns are good or bad. The argument is therefore irrelevant."

There may be plenty of reasons for believing lawns are bad: pesticides, fertilizers, highly-polluting lawn mowers, etc. However, until your opponents make some of those arguments, you should not let them get away with failing to spell the impacts out. In fact, you should press further for quantification of how many people are harmed by lawn pesticides, fertilizers, and mowers. Pressing for quantification, even in Parliamentary debate, is a good way to show the critic how much your opponents don't know about their arguments.

Argue No Links

Another logical flaw commonly committed in debate is faulty cause-to-effect reasoning. Therefore, you should always look for weak causal links in your opponent's presentation. Be especially wary of a case that argues that the world will end if we act or believe a certain way. Often, such drastic argumentation includes a faulty causal link somewhere. You simply need to point out where the weak links are and offer some possible alternative explanations. For example, on the nuclear freeze topic, debaters tried to argue that unless we freeze now, there will be a nuclear war within five years. If this happened to you, you should simply offer some other plausible interpretations of the future. You could also suggest that the lack of a freeze will make people even more scared to use the advanced weapons in the future, or you could show that a balance of power, regardless of the number of weapons, is what maintains peace.

Disbar the Argument

A third refutation strategy is to disbar the argument. Disbarring an argument involves showing that the support for the argument is defective or of questionable integrity. Using this strategy, the advocate maintains that his or her opponent's claim should not be accepted because of the suspect evidence on which it is based. Notice how the advocate is not saying the argument is not true or that even if true is of little importance to the dispute. Rather they are maintaining that the burden of proof for acceptance of the argument has not been met. There are many ways to disbar an argument, they include denying the connection between the claim and the evidence, questioning the authority of the evidence, questioning the recentness of the evidence, and questioning the logic used by your opponent.

Question the Connection between the Claim and the Evidence

Occasionally, advocates will issue a claim and then cite evidence which does not even come close to supporting that claim. For example, your opponent may claim that the US army is ill-equipped to carry out an invasion of Burma. Assume, however, that the supporting evidence which is read refers to the navy and not the army being ill-prepared for such an invasion. You could point out that the navy being ill-prepared does not prove that the army is ill-prepared. This happens more frequently in novice division. Your first response, then, in refuting that claim is simply to point out exactly what the evidence or proof did say. To do that, simply quote the crucial part of the evidence to jog the critic's mind. Then mention the claim statement to reveal the discrepancy. If it's parliamentary debate, and you know more about a historical fact or critical publication, then you may simply point out that the issue in question is irrelevant to your opponent's claim. In order to become good at this type of analysis, you need to listen carefully to evidence and proof while it is being alluded to by the other team.

Question Authority

Another thing that you can do is question the authority of the evidence. If the authority is a person, be sure his or her credentials are related to the claim. For example, on the nuclear freeze topic, affirmatives often quoted Hans Bethe, a Nobel Prize winning physicist, who advocated a unilateral freeze. Although apparently a credible source, his credentials (physicist) were not related to the claim (foreign policy). Besides relevance to the claim, also look for whether the source of evidence is biased. On the United Nations topic, many teams quoted the Heritage Foundation, a conservative political organization. Opponents quickly took issue with that source, due to its conservative bias. Of course, not all information from biased sources should be discarded; however, it is a point of contention that should be raised. While relevance to claim and bias are important elements of source credibility, sometimes opponents will not qualify a source at all. If questions in cross-examination do not establish a source's credibility, then you can indict the source on the grounds that he or she could be the janitor at the *New York Times* for all you know. Furthermore, you should argue that the unqualified evidence should be discounted in the debate.

In parliamentary debate, if your opponents use an intensive reading background as proof for some arguments, you should feel free to raise points of information (discussed at length in Chapter 4) to question the sources. For example, let's say your opponents cite Henry David Thoreau in his famous essay, "On Civil Disobedience." You could argue that Thoreau had no training in psychology or political science, and that any success using his theories (Gandhi and Martin Luther King) are atypical. Perhaps your opponents will have an answer for you, and you may want to pick and choose which sources you challenge. However, failure to press for information about questionable sources could hurt your cause.

Question the Recentness of Evidence

There are other things that you can argue, as well. One is to argue the recentness of the evidence. The Recentness of evidence is always important in debate. Depending on the argument, if the evidence is not recent (for example, not within the last two or three years as a rule of thumb), it may be of questionable validity. An effective way to argue against outdated evidence is to point out that something has happened in the interim to make your opponent's argument of dubious value. In other words, one possible justification for postdating opponent's evidence is because the issue under scrutiny has changed radically in the last few years; what was once true of that issue is true no longer. For instance, say your opponent reads a 1976 piece of evidence indicating that most states have shoddy drunk driving laws. You can point out that legislation dealing with this problem has changed drastically since then due to the activities of groups like Mothers against Drunk Driving (M.A.D.D.). Therefore, your opponent's evidence clearly is outdated.

Question Opponent's Logic

While the source is important to scrutinize, so is the logic of your opponent's argumentation. Often, novice debaters will attempt to prove a general claim statement with only one example. For instance, in Parliamentary debate it is common practice to give a single example to support each claim statement. A negative speaker, in this case, should question whether the government is using correct example reasoning.

Example reasoning is a form of argument that moves from specific instances to a more general claim. As discussed in Chapter 9, two of the tests for example reasoning are to ask whether sufficient examples have been provided and to ask whether those examples are typical. If either of these tests are violated the government is guilty of a **hasty generalization.** A Leader of the Opposition can simply argue that one example is not sufficient and challenge the Government to come up with more examples. Another option is to provide proof that documents counter examples. The reason for providing counter examples is because a third test for example reasoning is to be able to account for negative instances. If the government cannot do that, the opposition will probably win the argument. Example reasoning is only one type of logic to be questioned. Chapter 9 of this text outlines the tests for sign, analogy, causal, etc. Use them.

Four-step Refutation

In order to refute successfully, the advocate should follow a clear organizational format. Regardless of how good the refutation is, it will be wasted if it is presented in a disorganized manner. For this reason, the advocate should utilize **four-step refutation**.

Four-step refutation asks the debaters to use the following four steps: first, to briefly identify the opponent's argument; second, to briefly introduce your argument; third, to give evidence or analysis; and, fourth, to offer an impact or summary statement. Using this style, the advocate needs to argue the heading of each contention, the logic of each contention, and/or every sub-point of each contention. Usually, you do not skip any sub-points. Argue each sub-point in the order that it was presented by the resolution-proponents. Most importantly, when restating your opponent's argument, be sure to state the substructure of their case. You will actually say things like, "in terms of contention I, sub-point 'B,' where my opponent argues . . ." If you need to save time, often it is fine to *group* arguments. For instance, if there are two sub-points in a contention that are similar, you may be able to refute both of them at the same time. For instance you might say "Group contention I sub-point A and B. Notice how they both rely on Dr. Smith as support. I will argue that Dr. Smith is a biased source." Be careful not to group dissimilar sub-points; a good team will quickly point out that you left one of its arguments unanswered, even though you made it appear as though you argued it. Luckily, for parliamentary debaters, the substructure of the government case is usually not as detailed. Nevertheless, you should refer to whatever form of signposting was used by the government, even if it were as simple as "my first example, my second example, etc."

Four-step refutation can be mastered quickly with a fair amount of practice. Figure 8.1 gives an example of four-step refutation. This type of refutation provides a formula approach to answering arguments. As mentioned the formula starts with the first of four steps, which is to **briefly restate your opponent's argument** that you are refuting. That means a number of things. One thing it means is that you should only *briefly* state the argument. Do not help your opponents by completely arguing their argument over again. Simply repeat their claim statement. The reason you do this is to tell the critic and your opponents exactly which argument you are refuting so that they can keep an accurate record of it on their flow-sheets. Another thing that this means is that you need to state the letter or number of the sub-point each time you move to the next of your opponent's arguments. Failure to do the latter may muddle the debate. Additionally, if the critic does not know which sub-point you are arguing, he or she may not be able to record your arguments, which could affect whether you win or lose the round.

Throughout the debate you need always to state clearly which sub-point you are arguing. This is not merely a requirement of first negative, but it is a requirement of every debater throughout a debate.

The second step of four-point refutation is to **briefly state the claim statement for your argument.** A common mistake frequently made by novice debaters is that they forget this step, but it is very important. Often, novice participants will make argument after argument, without ever giving an introductory claim statement for those arguments. One reason for having claim statements is so that those recording your speech can write down the claim statement and then listen to the evidence/proof/example. If you fail to introduce your evidence or analysis, often those listening will not understand what you are trying to get out of it. The third step is to **give the evidence or analysis** to support your claim. When referring to specific publications, be sure to give full source citations, when possible. Traditionally, most critics expect at minimum the following: name of expert, the credentials of the expert, the title of the book or document, and the full date of the citation. At least, be prepared to defend the credibility of the sources you use, even in parliamentary debate. The norm for cross-examination-style debate now is to give the last name and date, and if pressed by the other team to give the rest of the citation. The final step of four-point refutation is to **give the impact to your argument.** Impact statements are brief summary statements of the evidence or analysis. These statements usually indicate why you think you should win a particular argument.

In the example in Figure 11.1 notice the use of full source citation, the reference to affirmative case substructure, and the brevity of steps 1, 2, and 4. Emulation of this style will help you win numerous debates. However, a formula is not all that you need; you also need to be able to formulate lines of argument.

PREPARING FOR COUNTER-REFUTATION

When you engage in a debate, whether as an affirmative or negative, you must not only anticipate what arguments your opponent will likely bring up so that you may prepare for your refutation, but you must also expect that your arguments will be refuted by your opponent. In other words, you must prepare for counter-refutation. The process of refutation and counter-refutation is a continuous process in a debate.

1. They said in Contention II, Sub-point A, that religious groups will enact federal legislation to suit their own whims.

2. We say that the federal courts would strike down any religiously inspired legislation.

3. Documentation for this comes from J. Phillip Wogeman, professor of Christian Social Ethics at Wesley Theological Seminary, in *The American Academy of Political and Social Science Annals*, November, 1979. Wogeman says, "And religious groups, when they go lobbying for (their own theological views) must expect them to be struck down eventually by the courts even if they are enacted into law."

    (Parliamentary debaters would merely paraphrase this source because prepared materials are prohibited in most forms of parliamentary debate.)

4. The impact to this evidence is that our government has checks and balances, such as the courts, to prevent a single interest from dominating the legislative process.

FIGURE 11.1

Example of Four Point Refutation

You must not only be aware of what you are refuting but you must also pay close attention to what your opponents are refuting and then counter-refute accordingly. As you prepare for the debate you should also be preparing for what you will say in response to your opponent's refutation. This is somewhat analogous to chess. In chess, you must look into the future and anticipate your opponent's future moves. You must not only try to attack your opponent you must also defend from counter attacks he or she may make. When you construct your arguments, you need to keep in mind how you plan on defending them for the remainder of the debate. Unless you are very lucky and run into an opponent who concedes the debate, you can expect that your arguments will be refuted by your opponent.

Preempting Potential Arguments

One way to refute your opponent is to build refutation into your original argument. This is known as **preempting** an argument. Either the affirmative or negative can do this. For instance, you might say "I know my opponents are going to get up in their next speech and argue that a policy of banning the private ownership of hand guns violates the Second Amendment of the US Constitution. I want to argue however that that is not true." The affirmative could build counter-refutation into their opening case. The negative could build counter-refutation into their prepared positions such as topicality arguments, counterplans, disadvantages, value objections etc.

Is it a good idea to preempt arguments? There is no clear answer. However, a good rule of thumb is as follows. If you are sure that your opponent will raise a particular argument, then preempting might be a good strategy. Similarly, if you are sure that the audience or critic will be raising this argument in their own minds, even if your opponent doesn't raise it, then it is also probably a good idea to preempt it. This is especially true when debating in front of a lay audience. However, if you are not sure that your opponent will raise the issue or sure that the audience will think of it, then you are probably better off not preempting the argument. No need to plant seeds of doubt where none existed before. Of course, you cannot preempt every argument. Even if you could, it doesn't mean that your opponent would not raise the argument anyway. At some point in the debate your arguments will be attacked. You must be prepared for the counterattack.

Rebuilding Original Arguments

To begin with, the subsequent speakers must be able to refute the opposition's attacks and rebuild the original positions. In order to do that the second speaker will need evidence and ideas to support the exact same sub-points from the first speaker. Therefore, when preparing the affirmative/negative case, debaters should simultaneously prepare for the rest of the debate. Often, debaters may want to set up their opponent by planting a weaker argument in the first speech, and, in their second, allude to much stronger evidence to make the negative argument look foolish in retrospect. Be careful using any kind of strategy, though. CEDA and NPDA have both tried to avoid the game playing that could so easily plague the activity. Strategy can backfire, as well. In the illustration just given, a few critics expect the first speech in defense of the resolution to contain the best arguments. Putting the weaker argument first may incite those few critics to look unfavorably toward your position. However, for the most part, as long as there is not a major shift in your argumentation, such a strategy will most often, for most critics, help your position.

What is clearly necessary, though, is for the second speaker to have at least one evidentiary idea for every sub-point in from the first speech. In other words, you are really writing the first speech twice, just with slightly different proof. Try to use as many different sources as possible too. In CEDA and NDT, one reason that you need so much evidence is because of the preponderance of evidence standard borrowed from the law courts for debate purposes. Preponderance of evidence merely says that the weight of evidence on a particular issue has a bearing on who wins that issue. The quantity of evidence can sometimes influence the "weight" of argumentation. For example, if ten psychiatrists testify that the defendant was insane at the time he or she committed the crime and only two psychiatrists testify that the defendant was not sane, then the preponderance of expert testimony supports the finding of insanity. If the affirmative reads five pieces of credible evidence from separate sources on a particular sub-point and the negative two, the affirmative in CEDA and NDT will almost always win that point on preponderance of evidence alone. Therefore, it is important for the subsequent speakers to be able to read evidence to rebuild their case.

When engaging in counter-refutation, it is important that the speaker **extend** the original position and not simply repeat the original position. Extending an argument means that the debater shows how the refutation made against the argument is erroneous in some manner and therefore the original argument is still valid. For example, suppose the affirmative argues that increased US military presence in the Middle East is necessary to prevent Iraq from being expansionary. In response, the negative refutes this argument by arguing that while Iraq would like to be expansionary, they lack the military strength to expand. In meeting this objection the second affirmative speaker should not simply read more evidence saying how Iraq wants to expand. This would simply repeat the original argument without refuting the objection raised by the negative. Instead, the affirmative should be prepared to read evidence showing how Iraq does have the military strength to expand. Perhaps the negative evidence is two years old and since then Iraq has rebuilt its military. If so, then this should be demonstrated.

Five-step Counter-refutation

The second speaker should always begin his or her refutation by briefly restating the original point from the first speech. This should be done by referring to any signposting used by the first speaker. For instance, you should say something such as, "In terms of our original argument in observation one, sub-point 'A,' where we said that human life is the highest value, our opponents said . . ." After reminding the audience of your original argument, then tell us what your opponents argued on that point, next give your claim, proof, and summary of that proof.

Using this format, you are performing **five-step counter-refutation style**. This is how it looks:

Step 1:   Briefly state your original argument.
Step 2:   Briefly remind your audience about your opponent's refutation.
Step 3:   Briefly give your counter-refutation.
Step 4:   Give proof, read evidence, or give explanation.
Step 5:   Summarize your position.

Second speakers should do the same thing for every single sub-point making up their original position, even where an opponent missed a sub-point. In that case, you should simply note that you're winning that point due to your opposition dropping the argument. You should also tell the critic why that dropped argument is important to the debate.

The job of the second speaker is twofold, however. Not only must you rebuild your own case, but you must also refute all attacks. You must remember to do both refuting and rebuilding. A common error made by novice debaters is that they frequently do one but not the other. A rule of thumb to follow is to argue one sub-point at a time and refute the attacks first, and then rebuild with new proof last. Often re-explaining your original evidence can be an effective way of refuting negative attacks. Then when offering further proof, you will make your argument look even stronger. Remember, you must be sure to extend your original arguments. Do not simply repeat the argument, but give some new insights or new analysis as to why your position is best.

POINT OUT ERRORS IN OPPOSING REFUTATION

One good way to help yourself as a second speaker is to remember a few tricks of the trade. Remember the three D's of refutation, Deny, Diminish and Disbar, can also be used in counter-refutation.

Arguing **no threshold** when the negative makes an argument can be a good way to defeat an argument. Let's say the negative argues that the affirmative value of equality is going to move us into a tyrannous government and society. You could simply argue that the negative did not provide a threshold: once society passes that threshold, tyranny results. In other words, ask the judge how much "equality" is needed before tyranny occurs. You could point out that the negative or opposition never proved what that threshold would be.

You may also argue that your opponent's refutation is **non-unique.** If society already has the exigency (causal situation) present in the *status quo*, then the second speaker may argue that the argument is "non-unique." Take the example above. You could say that "equality" already exists as a value in the status quo, and we don't have tyranny now; therefore, the affirmative case adds nothing uniquely harmful to the status quo. Additionally, if the effect already exists in the status quo, then you have an even stronger argument. Let's say the negative is trying to argue that your emphasis on equality will lead to people trying cases in civil court. That's an argument crying for a "non-unique" response. As the second speaker, you could just argue:

> We have equality now and we have proliferation of civil suits now; therefore, the affirmative case is NOT going to uniquely cause civil suits. The negative argument is non-unique.

Next, you may argue that a negative argument has **no impact.** Perhaps the negative team successfully proves the above argument: the affirmative case uniquely causes an increase in civil suits. You might say, "so what, there's no impact or harm argued by the negative." In fact, you might point out to the judge that the right to sue for damages is a good thing, and that your case may actually be increasing rights. If someone is truly harmed, in say an industrial accident, then an increased emphasis on equality would be good if it stops a company from maltreatment of workers or prevents future continuation of unsafe working conditions. The lack of impact by the negative team thus allows the affirmative team to show that the civil-suits argument has no impact that would force dismissal of the affirmative case.

In fact, you could show through the use of the **turn-around** that it may actually have an affirmative advantage, as the worker safety argument demonstrates. In other words, you have turned an argument from initially favoring the negative to an advantage for you. Lack of impact and turn-around strategies can also be used by the negative against the affirmative.

Finally, you could show that your arguments are of a **conditional** nature. This means that you are arguing an either/or position. For instance, earlier in this chapter we mentioned how some negative teams seemed to be contradicting themselves by arguing first, that dioxin emissions were not dangerous and then arguing that if regulated, companies would relocate to third world countries, leading to increase dioxin emissions and therefore increased death in those nations. Many affirmatives argued this was a contradiction. However, some negatives countered that this was a conditional argument. In other words, the negative maintained that dioxin emissions were not dangerous, but even if they were dangerous regulations would lead to the industries relocation into other nations and the subsequent death of the citizens of that nation.

SUMMARY

In this chapter, we examined how to engage in effective refutation. Effective refutation requires that the advocates have an in-depth understanding of both sides of the resolution. Advocates should anticipate the likely arguments to be raised by the opposition and to develop responses to them well before the debate begins.

There are three overall refutation strategies. They are denying the argument, diminishing the argument and disbarring the argument.

Four-step refutation was discussed. Four-step refutation involves first, identifying the opponents argument; second, briefly stating the claim statement for your argument; third, providing the support for your claim; and fourth, showing the impact to your argument.

Finally, techniques for counter-refutation were discussed. Debaters should consider preempting arguments and learn how to successfully extend their original arguments when attacked. When engaging in counter-refutation, debaters should utilize the five-step counter-refutation organizational format which is similar to four-step refutation.

The techniques discussed in this chapter apply to all forms of debate. There are many other approaches that you can take. The lines of argument discussed in this chapter are merely suggestive of the ways that an advocate can refute and counter-refute the arguments made by their opponents.

CHAPTER 12

CROSS-EXAMINATION

THE NATURE OF CROSS-EXAMINATION

Many forums of debate make use of cross-examination. In Presidential debates, the candidates are usually asked questions that they must respond to by a panel of journalists. In some cases, the candidates are even able to ask one another questions. In courts of law, attorneys call witnesses to the stand and question them to ascertain their knowledge about certain aspects of the case. In sports, the manager of a team may hold a press conference to announce a major trade. During this conference the manager will have to answer all kinds of questions from the media. In a business meeting, the presenter of a new business idea is likely to be asked many questions during the presentation. In academic debate, debaters also have the chance to question one another following their constructive speeches or sometimes even during their speeches.

Cross-examination is a very dynamic part of any debate. While a proponent may be able to smoothly deliver a carefully prepared and crafted speech, it may be more difficult to answer the tough questions that follow, especially when there is limited time to formulate a response. While it is important to be able to respond to questions in stressful situations, it is just as important to be able to ask good questions. Cross-examination is a focal point of most debates because it is the only time that the two advocates have the chance to directly interact and challenge one another.

THE QUESTIONER

The questioner is the person who is asking the questions. The questioner needs to remember that they will be questioning a hostile party. That is, the person they are questioning will not want to give them favorable responses. In a court of law, when an attorney calls his or her own witness, the witness is considered a friendly witness. This is known as direct examination. The attorney in this instance has probably talked to the witness beforehand and knows what the witness will say. Because the witness is friendly, the attorney can ask open ended questions and allow for narrative style responses. However, when the opposing attorney questions the same witness, the witness is now considered a hostile witness. This is known as cross-examination. The attorney must take great care to control the questioning process as the testimony could be damaging to his or her case.

During debates, your opponent is a hostile party. They will not want to give you information that will be harmful to their case or beneficial to yours. Cross-examination is a skill that must be practiced. You should have a strategy and purpose in mind when engaging in cross-examination.

Most tournament and classroom formats limit the cross-examination period to a few minutes. During that time, the questioner should attempt to accomplish a number of goals. These goals include clarifying points, exposing opposition weaknesses, and setting up future arguments. In order to accomplish the goal, questioners should use controlling questions. Controlling questions are questions which attempt to limit the respondent's answers.

Clarify Points

When you are the questioner, the first order of business must be to clarify any points of which you are unclear. Don't be afraid to ask the opposition to define a term you are not familiar with or to explain an argument that is unclear to you. Failure to clear up cloudy areas will usually result in problems later in the debate. Simply ask direct, **open questions,** such as, "What is the thesis of your case?" or "Explain the essence of the disadvantage" or "Could you summarize why it is you don't think we are topical?" Ask these questions with the tone of voice of already knowing the answer, as if you are probing for a flaw in their case. Avoid appearing confused or overwhelmed.

Another advantage of clarifying a point is to get the opposing team to commit to a position or to be more specific in the details of their argument. This information could be valuable as you plan your refutation. For instance, if the other team has argued that Euthanasia should be made legal you need to understand if they are referring to passive euthanasia (turning off a respirator) or active euthanasia (injecting a poison) or both. If this point is unclear, you could spend a lot of time arguing that the active process of taking someone's life, even if they are in great pain, is wrong. The other side might then agree with all of those arguments but then contend they were not discussing active euthanasia, only passive euthanasia, and therefore the arguments raised are irrelevant. Had you clarified the type of euthanasia they were referring to in cross-examination, then you could have better focused your arguments.

Expose Opposition Weaknesses

Pointing out the flaws in the other's position serves as the second purpose for the questioner. There are many potential flaws that can be exploited. The lack of a threshold (e.g., failure to show when we cross the threshold from insignificant to significant hand gun restrictions), the lack of harm, the lack of strong evidence, the commission of fallacies, or the failure to establish a causal link all consist of possible flaws to be explored.

For example, you might ask "You claim that handguns cause significant harm to society, but doesn't your evidence only say that handguns are harmful, not significantly harmful?" Or you might ask "Doesn't your evidence only say that that handguns MAY be harmful, not that they have proven to be harmful?" Or you might ask "Considering that your source was the victim of a handgun crime doesn't that make their testimony a bit biased?" Or "Your evidence that says handguns are harmful to society is three years old and therefore is not reflective of the impact handguns are having on society right now, isn't that correct?" Or "Isn't it true that the study you are citing (about handguns being harmful to society) had been indicted since it only studied the effects of gun violence in a few locations and then tried to generalize those results to the entire nation?" Or "Doesn't your study actually take into account all gun problems and not just those from handguns?" All of these questions would tend to point out weaknesses in the argument advanced by the opposing team. Remember that it is not important to get your opponent to agree with your question. They will probably disagree. The point you are trying to make is with the critic, not the questioner.

Set Up Future Arguments

Additionally, as questioner you may want to set up future arguments. In order to do that, try to pin your opponents to a position. For instance, assume the following resolution "Resolved: That the Federal US federal government should significantly increase restrictions on the sale of hand guns." The questioner might attempt to set up a disadvantage on what would happen if criminals began purchasing longs guns (rifles, sawed-off shot guns, etc.) instead.

Negative:	"You claim that many people are killed or seriously injured by handguns during crimes. Is that correct?"
Affirmative:	"Yes, in fact we read two pieces of evidence on that point"
Negative:	"Did people commit crimes before the advent of handguns?"
Affirmative:	"Of course."
Negative:	"If your policy were to go into effect, wouldn't people still commit crimes?"
Affirmative:	"Yes, but they wouldn't be able to shoot people anymore"
Negative:	"Your policy only makes it harder for people to get hand guns, correct?" I mean it doesn't regulate long guns, right?"
Affirmative:	That is correct. But handguns are used much more often by criminals than are long guns"

Negative:	"And that is because handguns are so easy to purchase right? I mean that's why you want to make them harder to purchase, correct?"
Affirmative:	"That is correct."
Negative:	"And your plan makes it a lot harder for people to get guns, correct?
Affirmative:	"Yes, our plan makes it much harder to purchase handguns."
Negative:	"So, isn't it logical to assume that people who want to commit crimes will purchase long guns instead of handguns?"
Affirmative:	"Well, I don't know about that."
Negative:	"Well, if I'm a criminal and I want to commit a crime and I want a gun to use in the commission of that crime and I can't get a handgun because your policy is very effective and makes it all but impossible for me to get a handgun doesn't it make sense that I am going to get a long gun if they're still easy to purchase?"
Affirmative:	"Well, I guess that would make sense, but."
Negative:	"By the way, isn't someone who is shot by a long gun more likely to be seriously injured or killed than is someone who is shot by a handgun?"
Affirmative:	"Well, again, I am not sure about that. Maybe . . .
Negative:	"That's fine, thanks"

Use Controlling Questions

Since you will be questioning a hostile party, you will need to take care to control the cross-examination period. To do this, you will need to ask questions that limit the type and range of answer the respondent can give There are some techniques that help the questioner to control the cross-examination which are illustrated in the above hypothetical interaction.

First, know the answer to the questions you ask. Notice how the questioner already knows what the answers are to the questions that are asking. Unless you are asking for clarification, you should already know what the answer will be. Try never to ask a question, except for clarification purposes, to which you do not already know the answer.

Second, try to ask **closed questions.** A closed question limits the respondent's answer. It can be a yes or no question but it need not be. For example asking someone "Is your GPA over 3.0?" is a closed question. But so is asking someone "What is your GPA?" Unless clarifying points ask closed questions whenever possible.

Third, ask a series of closed questions. This allows you to set up the premise of the argument (in this case that criminals will switch to long guns). Later, you can establish the logical connection from the premise.

Fourth, always start with the less threatening questions to establish the premise. Notice that the earlier questions are easier for the respondent to answer.

Fifth, try and use the respondent's answers to build your own case. Notice that the questioner used the affirmative's own solvency position to set up their disadvantage. The affirmative had to admit that their policy would make it harder for people to purchase handguns. If they answered "no" to this question, they would undermine their solvency. By answering "yes," the affirmative provided the link to the disadvantage.

Sixth, follow up on arguments made by the respondent. For example, the respondent tries to be evasive as to whether or not criminals will purchase long guns if handguns are made harder to obtain. However, the questioner skillfully follows up on this issue, asking a fairly long question that points out the logic in this assumption.

Seventh, link the questions to future arguments. The questioner's last question plants the seed in the critic's mind that long guns are more lethal than handguns. The evidence to support this point would be provided when the first negative constructive develops the "long gun" disadvantage. Finally, the first negative constructive can use admissions made by the respondent to establish the link to the disadvantage. The first negative constructive should say something like "remember that during cross-examination the affirmative admitted that their policy will make it much harder for criminals to get handguns. And remember they also admitted that people will still want to commit crimes post plan implementation. This gives us the link to the disadvantage that under the affirmative plan, criminals will simply switch to using long guns. And this is harmful because as we will prove long guns are much more lethal than are handguns."

Remember, as a questioner you must always phrase your ideas in the form of a question. Avoid making statements or speeches. Making statements usually causes your opponent to argue with you. The entire cross-examination then may become a shouting match. Also, avoid being argumentative or rude. Simply ask questions the way you would ask a friend. If the respondent becomes angry or rude, try to maintain your poise. If your questioning fails to move forward as planned, do not force the issue; simply, start another line of questioning.

Most importantly, be sure to maintain control. In other words, do not allow the respondent to ask you a question (except to clarify a question you asked). If the respondent asks you a question, kindly say, "This is my cross-examination, please answer *my* question." Also, avoid allowing the respondent to talk beyond a reasonable amount of time. If the respondent begins to speak too long, simply say, "Thank you, that's fine." If he or she continues to speak, say the same thing a couple of additional times progressively more forcefully until you receive compliance. Sometimes, appealing to fairness can also be helpful. While they still are talking, say, "I only have a short time, and I'd really like to ask a number of other questions," or "You still have another speech to say all of this; let me use my questioning time now please." Another tactic is to simply begin asking your next question. Again, avoid becoming frustrated or rude.

THE RESPONDENT

The respondent is the person who is answering the questions. As the respondent you must keep in mind that the questioner will be asking you questions with the intent of exposing weakness in your case or trying to set up their future arguments. Even the most benign question can prove harmful. Remember, they would not ask the question if they didn't think it was important. You need to be on guard at all times and think your answers through. Before answering, ask your self "why would they want to know this?" The respondent's goals include answering questions in a knowledgeable fashion, avoiding possible traps, and gaining control of the questioning period.

Know the Issues

The most important objectives for the respondent are to know the issues surrounding the topic and to know their arguments and evidence for the particular debate. Knowledge of the topic is important for all aspects of debating, but especially for the role of the respondent. The questioner can ask you any question on the topic. The more you read about the topic, the better a debater you will be and the better you will handle cross-examination. Of particular importance is for you to know your affirmative case if you are an affirmative respondent or to know your negative arguments if you are a negative respondent. For instance, a questioner may ask you about the methodology of a particular study you cite. Ideally, you should be able to answer that question without looking at your notes. If you do not know the answer, try to avoid having your partner prompt you or shuffling through books or evidence not yet read in the debate. It may hurt your credibility. If you do not know the answer simply try to answer as best you can using information from your previous arguments. Simply admitting that you do not know the answer to a question is also an option. Such an admission probably will not lose you the debate, but answering a question incorrectly could get you into trouble. Suggest confidently that you will clear up the issue later in the debate if it becomes important. Whatever you do, never make up an answer. This can only come back to hurt you. The best options are to study the topic and memorize your arguments so you can answer all questions accurately and to your advantage.

Avoid Traps

A second goal for the respondent is to avoid getting trapped. There are a number of things you can do. First of all, before the debate, discuss with your partner potential traps that you want to avoid. Decide the safest position to take, and be ready to argue that position later. Second, during the cross-examination, avoid being pinned down to a dubious position. For instance, the questioner may ask, "If we prove that the Iraqis are warmongers, we should win the debate, right?" Avoid answering such questions "yes." Instead, just say "no," or say something like, "First of all the Iraqis are not warmongers, and, even if you could prove that, you would not necessarily win the debate." Third, destroy the premise of the question before answering the question. When doing so use specific evidence from your speech. For instance, in the example given above, you might say, "The Iraqis are not warmongers; I proved that with my response on contention one, 'B,' the Jones evidence, that showed that Kuwait had been waging an economic and covert war with Iraq. Iraq's invasion was totally justified." The more specific you can be in citing your evidence, the better.

Finally, avoid answering tricky yes/no questions with a simple *yes* or *no*. Give your explanation first. Otherwise, your opponent may not allow you to give an explanation at all, and you will appear rude trying to give one. For instance, a questioner may ask, "Have the Iraqis been involved in any military action in the past twenty years?" Obviously, the answer to that question is yes, but a simple *yes* answer will allow your questioner to build a premise to a line of questioning that may get you into trouble. You should answer, "Any aggressive action by the Iraqis is purely defensive and protective; I read you that evidence in my last speech. So yes, they have been involved in military action, but they are not expansionist." In a sense, you are predicting where the line of questioning is headed and trying to stop it before it bears fruit.

Try to Control the Cross-Examination Period

While being knowledgeable and avoiding traps are important for the respondent, important also is trying to take control of cross-examination if possible. One way to do that is to continue answering as long as your questioner allows you to speak. Continue summarizing evidence and points that you have made earlier in the debate. However, when the questioner does stop you, be polite and let him or her pose the next question. Another thing you can do is ask a question of your questioner. If he or she answers, you have just taken control of the questioning period. Continue asking questions politely until your opponent discovers the error or the cross-examination ends. Additionally, if your opponent makes a statement, rather than asks a question, attempt to converse with him or her. A conversation is much less of a threat than if the questioning were to continue. However, avoid getting into an emotional argument with your opponent. A conversation is one thing; an emotional argument is a completely different issue.

As the respondent, try to remain poised and calm. Do not ever act frustrated or as though your opponent's question has upset you. There will always be a question or two that will baffle you. Try to use arguments that you have already made in order to compensate for what you may not know, but be honest. Lying can only get you into trouble. Furthermore, understand debate theory and use it when answering questions. For instance, it is helpful, at times, to point out to affirmative questioners that it is they, not you, who have the burden of proof. Additionally, know all of the answers to generic questions on the topic. Whether debating in an argumentation class, on the intercollegiate circuit, or in a public forum, a number of questions usually become standard. Know and rehearse answers to those questions. Finally, whether you are the questioner or the respondent, feel free to use humor when appropriate. Being facetious, for instance, can be a way out of a difficult situation. Humor is one way to help accomplish that goal, and cross-examinations are the most likely place to incorporate a funny line or two.

SUMMARY

Cross-examination is an integral part of many types of debate ranging from political, to legal to academic forums. Cross-examination is a very dynamic part of the debate because it is the only opportunity the two debaters have to directly confront one another.

The questioner's goals include clarifying points, exposing opposition weaknesses, and setting up future arguments. This is accomplished by using controlling questions. The respondent's goals include answering questions in a knowledgeable fashion, avoiding possible traps, and gaining control of the questioning period.

CHAPTER 13

DEBATING

RESOLUTIONS OF FACT

Recall from our earlier discussion that a factual resolution determines truth or falsehood, existence or non-existence of occurrences or things. Factual resolutions have occasionally found their way into a semester of old-style CEDA debate. However, the most relevant application of factual argumentation in CEDA would be in defense of minor claims under the umbrella of a value or policy resolution.

On the other hand, parliamentary debate is much more likely to have a resolution of fact. As mentioned earlier, proverbs and clichés (culturally-assumed truths) are sometimes used as topics of choice for parliamentary rounds. Learning how to argue both sides of a factual resolution may be one of the best ways to prepare for an in-class assignment or a debate tournament.

Remember that *affirmative* and *government* are synonymous terms. We will use the terms interchangeably in this chapter. When there is a distinction to be made, we will try to make that distinction clear. Additionally, *negative* and *opposition* are synonymous terms.

Everyone respects facts. People may like or not like a particular fact, and may or may not act on the facts they know, but everyone respects "facts." Science sets out to find them. Lawyers try to prove them. Students try to learn them. Books are full of them. The two little kids argue over them. And sometimes debaters debate them.

So what is a "fact?" The answer is more complex than it may seem. There is an entire branch of philosophy that deals profoundly with this issue. It is called "epistemology," from the Greek words *epi histani* meaning "to place before." It concerns how the world is "placed before us" and why we think we "know" what we know. In quantum physics, the observer becomes part of the observed fact, so that the distinction between perception and reality is blurred.

THE NATURE OF FACT

For our purposes, a fact is an empirically verifiable phenomenon. A fact may be distinguished from an opinion, the truth of which is not empirically verifiable. A statement of opinion involves a larger degree of subjectivity. This subjectivity means that different observers can hold different opinions of the same phenomenon and both be justified.

Empirical verification means that the phenomenon is as objective as humanly possible and that any two observers making the same observation should reach the same conclusion. It is a "fact" that 1+1=2. Anyone anywhere should reach the same conclusion. Scientists keep repeating experiments that others have performed to make sure that results are objectively verifiable by any observer. After a certain number of repetitions, the observations will be accepted as "facts."

It is not a "fact" that "2" is a "good" number. Two different observers, both looking at the same math problem could reach different opinions. If the numbers are the score of a ball game, the score is a fact while our opinion of the score depends on which side we are on.

Empirical verification means that it is subject to proof through our senses. Someone someplace can, or did, or will, see the phenomenon, hear it, touch it, taste it, or smell it. If a phenomenon is not, at least theoretically, empirically verifiable it is not a fact.

The fact that we may not be able to empirically verify something ourselves does not change it from being a fact. You may never have seen the earth from space, but someone else has and reported that it was round. The shape of the earth was a "fact" even before someone saw it from space because "in theory" it was objectively, empirically verifiable.

People may hold opinions about facts. Some people believe that ghosts exist. Some do not. These beliefs are opinions based on the different experiences various observers have had and the information available to them. Theoretically, the existence or non-existence of ghosts can be empirically proven or disproved. We just haven't done it yet to everyone's satisfaction.

Cross-cultural Considerations

Other times and other societies have used different criteria to determine "facts." For example, in the Middle Ages, if a scholar wanted to know whether a male horse or a female horse had more teeth he reasoned: the male is the superior of any species (it was a sexist society), possession of a greater number of teeth is a mark of superiority. Therefore, a male horse must have more teeth. The scholar did not look in the horse's mouth. The reason was that he didn't trust his senses to tell him the "truth." The Devil might be deceiving him into thinking he saw what was not really there. His standard or criterion for "truth" was logical consistency. If his senses told him something that was logically inconsistent his senses were wrong. However, any similarly-placed scholar who knew the rules of logic would reach the same conclusion based on logical consistency.

It was against this idea of "truth" that the Renaissance rebelled. Other societies have used everything from revelation to dreams as a measure of "facts." In order to extend the concept of a fact to the cross-cultural level, we need a more complex definition.

A fact is the existence or non-existence of a subject, condition or predicate, or relationship in accordance with an agreed upon objective criterion. The key word is "objective." Whatever standard any society has used it is a standard that the members of that society believe will produce the same results for any similarly placed observer.

Fortunately for you it is not necessary to unravel the mysteries of the universe in order to debate a resolution of fact. So long as you stay within twentieth-century Western culture you can use empiricism as the test of "truth." Furthermore, you'll have to. This concept is so deeply imbedded in modern consciousness that you couldn't dislodge it if you wanted to. Consider how difficult it would be for you to accept the number of teeth a horse has based on logical consistency rather than observation.

RESOLUTIONS OF FACT

For our purposes, a resolution of fact has to have as its object the proof or disproof of a fact. This means it is tied to empirical proof. Therefore, *a resolution of fact is a resolution that is, at least in theory, empirically provable.*

A resolution of fact may be thought of as describing what is, was, or will be. It may be distinguished from a resolution of value in that it does not propose an attitude toward anything, and may be distinguished from a proposition of policy in that it does not propose an action. Thus if no other criterion is stated, we may reasonably presume that when someone tries to prove a "fact," he or she is trying to prove something that is, at least in theory, empirically provable. Unless a contrary criterion is presented, a resolution of fact is a resolution that, at least in theory, may be proven with empirical evidence.

The Convertibility of Resolutions

A common situation is to begin debating a resolution of value but for the affirmative to define its criterion in such a way that it becomes empirically provable. Consider the following:

Resolved: that Bing Crosby is the best singer in American recording history.

The affirmative then defines "best" at "largest selling." The number of records sold can be empirically proven (one could, at least in theory, count them going over the counter). If this definition of "best" is allowed, the proposition of "value" becomes, in reality, one of fact. We call this "the convertibility of propositions."

The reverse can also happen. Assume the resolution above started out as "Resolved: that Bing Crosby is the best selling artist in American recording history." If the affirmative defines "best selling" as "most popular" the resolution has been converted into a resolution of value because "most popular" cannot be determined by counting records.

As always, the judgment will be not on the resolution but on the resolution as defined. A resolution may start out in one status and be defined into another. As a general rule, affirmatives would prefer proving facts over values and values over policies. Negatives prefer the reverse.

The *Prima Facie* Case Elements for a Resolution of Fact

There are either two or three elements to prove for any resolution of fact.

I.   Definitions.
II.   Evidence.
[III.]   Inference.

If the evidence one is using is direct, there are two. If the evidence is indirect, then a third element of Inference is added. This is the simplest structure for any status of resolution.

Definitions

The affirmative must provide sufficient definitions to make clear any unclear terms in the resolution. The affirmative should also define any terms not in the resolution that would not be readily understood. If no definition is given, the judge should assume that the common usage definition is intended. If the terms are still not clear based on common usage, the context of the case as a whole may be used to determine meaning. If the terms are not clear from context, the affirmative has not met its burden.

There are no special terms singled out in Fact resolutions as a special burden of affirmative definition. In Value debate the evaluatum and criterion almost always require definition, even if other terms are clear. In Policy debate, the Plan requires special clarification. However, it would be inaccurate from this to assume that definitions are unimportant in Fact debates. It is just that there is no regularly-occurring type of term that can be singled out for special mention.

A criterion may also be important. For example, if you're going to try to prove that human beings evolved from lower forms of life, then you may need a standard by which to judge evidence. Carbon dating, location a fossil was found, completeness of artifact, etc. could all become standards of inclusion/exclusion. In other words, what evidence are you going to allow in the debate? Additionally, you may use a criterion to evaluate the evidence that you decide to include.

Evidence

Evidence is a reason for believing that something is true. As such, it will form an enthymeme with the resolution. Therefore if one states the resolution (keeping in mind the way it has been defined) and says "because," what follows is a reason.

Since facts are empirically verifiable, the reason will be an empirical observation or an opinion about something that is empirically provable. Evidence is an opinion or empirical observation offered to support a claim.

Evidence may be direct or indirect. If it is direct evidence there are no further elements and the debate shifts to the relevance and reliability of the evidence. If it is indirect, the evidence requires the drawing of an inference to support the claim.

To determine whether evidence is direct or indirect use the following *test: evidence is direct if one cannot simultaneously believe the evidence to be true and the claim to be false. If one could believe the evidence to be true and the claim to be false, then the evidence is indirect. If the evidence submitted is indirect, then a third element is required. Any proof involving indirect evidence requires an inference.

Inference

An inference is an assumption necessary for the evidence to support the resolution. Many facts we wish to prove are not resolutions but other kinds of claims. The above definition of inference would, in such cases, be reworded as an assumption necessary for the evidence to support the claim. This is the same as stating or explaining the suppressed premise in an enthymeme.

The inference must at least be explained to demonstrate that the evidence reasonably supports the claim. The inference may have to be proven evidentially to show that a reasonable person could accept the evidence given in element II and conclude that the resolution or other claim is justified.

Chains of Inference

It is common for inferences to extend in "chains" between the piece of evidence you have and the claim you're trying to prove. Consider the following case. To prove:

A Sample Case

Resolved: that extraterrestrial intelligent life exists.

I. Definitions and Criteria

You may decide to define *intelligent* and *life*. (Definitions of those terms could be done from a field context. In other words, you may find some leverage using the definitions of those who are actually searching for life now. This could also feed the analysis on a criterion, such as the one below.)

A criterion by which you may judge the evidence may involve looking for *signs* of intelligent life, rather than for a direct observation of the life itself. (In other words, look for patterns in the astronomical surroundings that could only be ordered by unnatural configuration, rather than by natural. Professionals searching for signs of intelligent life are doing just that, looking for a sign. If they were looking for anything else, unless you're the real-life version of Fox Mulder, from the TV show *X-Files*, you probably would be deemed slightly crazy. Also recall our discussion about sign argument, that an inherent sign relationship can reveal unseen or previously unknown variables.

II. Evidence (a reason which is an empirical observation)

"Astronomer Smith reports in her article in last month's News magazine that she is receiving regular radio signals from Star X that may be produced by an extraterrestrial civilization."

This is indirect evidence. Smith is reporting an empirical observation (receiving signals) but one can believe this without believing the resolution. It is therefore indirect. Also notice how this corresponds with the criterion of *signs*.

III. Inference (the affirmative might explain)

Regular radio signals are not a natural phenomenon, and thus they indicate some kind of being has built a radio transmitter. What the affirmative really means is a good deal less definite. The inference here is at least a seven step chain, all of which a judge must be willing to fill in. Detailed, the chain is:

1) Smith has watched the needles on the equipment move in a certain way. This is the only direct evidence in this chain. By itself, it wouldn't prove much except that the needles moved in a certain way. It is indirect evidence for the claim of extraterrestrial life because it involves the following inferences:

2) (Inference) The movement of the needle indicates certain kinds of signals reaching the instrument. This is an inference, but a very safe one. Most judges wouldn't even think of this as an inference.

3) (Inference) The regular nature of the signal makes it unlikely that it was produced naturally.

4) (Inference) If this type of signal is not natural it must be unnatural. This divides all phenomena into the natural and unnatural. If it's not one it must be the other.

5) (Inference) An unnatural radio signal indicates beings capable of building a radio transmitter.

6) (Inference) Building a radio transmitter is a sign of intelligent life.

7) (Inference) The intelligent life that built the signal is still there. Remember, the resolution says "exists," and a radio signal from a distant star would take many years to reach Earth.

So here we have seven beliefs, or inferences, necessary to connect the evidence to the claim. In inferential chains, as in any other chain, you look for the weakest link. Somewhat simplified the chain is shown here:

E.T. life, builds trans., sends signal, signal reaches machine, moves needle

Despite the number of inferences involved, most of us would take regular radio signals as a possible sign of life. The weak link would probably be inference 7 (that the life is still there). The question would be whether or not this single piece of such evidence makes the sign relationship "probable." The test of how well it proves its claim would in large part depend upon whether or not other claims could be drawn from the same evidence.

Something very much like the above debate happened a few years ago when astronomers picked up signals of the kind described. The weakest link proved to be inference 3. Upon further investigation it was concluded that the regularity of the signals was indeed a natural phenomenon caused by a star rotating on its axis at incredible speed. In this case, therefore, the sign relationship would be relevant, but not inherent (or probable).

IV. Opinion Evidence

If Smith had said "I believe that extraterrestrial life exists," we would have opinion evidence supporting the claim. This would require the inference that Smith's opinion is a subjective assessment of empirical data. She has made observations and reached to judgment based on those observations.

Opinions are usually indirect evidence unless the fact that they are held is the issue. if we were debating "Resolved that most scientists believe that extraterrestrial life exists" it would be direct proof of such a claim.

Sign Argument. An astute reader may note the similarity between the use of inference in proving claims of fact and the use of sign argument from our discussion in Chapter 9. Essentially, the radio signals in the above example serve as signs of intelligent life. The tests for sign argument apply. In this case, the sign relationship is possible: extraterrestrial intelligence may be evident from a repeated radio signal. However, the relationship is not inherent. Natural objects, in this case, a fast spinning star was the cause of the signal.

NEGATIVE STOCK ISSUES FOR A RESOLUTION OF FACT

The negative strategy on a resolution of fact is directed toward element III, the inference. As you have seen above, this is the weakest part of proving a fact. Since inferences only have to be presented when the evidence (element II) is indirect, the key is to show that the evidence does not directly prove the resolution.

With this overall strategy in mind, we will consider three stock negative issues: burdens and standard of proof, the "on case" elements, and "off case" arguments. As with all negative positions, the negative on a resolution of fact can show 1) that there is not a *prima facie* case established and/or 2) that even if there is a *prima facie* case, the off case arguments outweigh the on case analysis. Before attacking the on case and off case issues the negative may wish to posit an observation on the burdens and standards of proof.

Standards and Burdens

A good starting point for the negative is to remind itself and the judge of the affirmative's burden. To do so is not really an argument but just a correct statement of debate theory.

The affirmative has the burden to prove the resolution true to the level required by the standard of proof for the resolution (see Chapters 2 and 3). Normally this will mean that the affirmative must show the resolution is "probably" true. Thus, unless the resolution allows the affirmative to show that something is "possible," mere "possibility" is not enough. The affirmative is expected to show that the resolution is "more likely than not" a true statement.

A negative should also remind itself that this is, or is supposed to be, a proposition that is empirically provable. If the affirmative definitions would not allow for empirical proof, the affirmative may have defined itself into a proposition of value. The best negative response is then to thank the affirmative, and point out that now a criterion must also be proven since one can no longer use empiricism.

On-case Arguments

Remember that an affirmative on a proposition of fact has three elements to establish: I. Definitions, II. Evidence and (if the evidence is indirect) III. Inference.

On-case Issue I: Definitions

Obviously a negative should be aware of possible definitions an affirmative might use, which are good for the affirmative and which are good for the negative. If the terms are defined unreasonably, attacks that they are unreasonable per *se* are appropriate. If the affirmative definitions are reasonable, the negative will wish to offer alternative definitions that are better. These same comments could be made for any negative on any resolution. There are two special grounds for challenging definitions in a fact debate.

1. Empirical Definitions. Since facts are empirically provable the definitions should lend themselves to empirical proof. If an affirmative defined "intelligent" as "what seems to humans to be intelligent," the term is defined subjectively. If a negative could offer an alternative definition based on an objective standard, such as "having produced tools," it could argue that the negative definition is better because it is better in accord with the empirical nature of fact resolutions.

2. Literal Language. In a fact debate it is particularly important terms be taken literally and not metaphorically.

You may recall the overly emotional anti-abortion resolution "Resolved: that the butchering of unborn babies should be stopped." The term "butchering" is used here metaphorically. If literally defined, the resolution would be untrue. In a resolution of value, where attitudes are at stake, the metaphoric language would simply imply an attitude and might be acceptable. In a fact debate it is out of place.

On-case Issue II: Evidence

The affirmative evidence will be either an observation or an opinion (or several of each). It will be either direct of indirect.

The standard attacks on any evidence are that 1) it is not relevant, 2) it is not reliable (this includes issues of competence, bias, and hearsay or second-hand evidence), or 3) it is relevant and reliable but it has little weight (the technical phrase is "has low probative value").

The strongest affirmative proof is the direct observation, the "eye witness." Direct observations are always relevant, and thus would have to be attacked as unreliable or of low probative value (it doesn't prove what the affirmative wants it to prove).

It is rare for a single piece of evidence by itself to prove a complex resolution. A negative should therefore argue that the evidence, while direct, is not sufficient to prove the claim. It is only a partial proof, and actually carries the inference that a more complete proof would repeat its finding.

The best case is the single laboratory experiment. By itself, it is direct evidence, and relevant, but it is not a complete proof. The technical term is that the evidence is "over-claimed." "Over-claiming" means that the advocate claims the evidence proves more than it reasonably does. It is a standard debate challenge to evidence. In an earlier chapter, we considered over-claiming as a part of relevance.

If the evidence is clearly direct, the only recourse is to attack it as unreliable. A negative will certainly want to cite other observers who studied the same phenomenon but did not reach the conclusion the affirmative source reached. Here is a good place to distinguish the on case attack from the off case. If the negative observer simply did not find what the affirmative source found (Jones says his observatory hasn't detected regular radio signals), it is an on case attack on reliability. If the negative source has another explanation (Brown says the regular signals are caused by a natural phenomenon), it is an off case attack based on an alternate inference. This is a fine point of theory, and in practice the attacks can be run together.

The next strongest type of affirmative evidence is the opinion. Since opinions are weaker than observations, a negative will want to stress the opinions present in almost any empirical observation. For example, it is Smith's observation that the needles on his instruments moved, but it is her opinion that regular radio signals mean life.

The weakest type of affirmative evidence is indirect evidence. Since this is the weakest type of evidence, a negative will want to show whatever inferences are present in supposedly direct evidence.

You will remember that the test for direct evidence is that you cannot simultaneously believe the evidence to be true and the claim to be false. The negative will therefore want to show that one can indeed believe that the evidence as stated represents somebody's observation, but that even if this is accurately reported the claim is not proven.

If alternative inferences can be shown the evidence must be indirect. If the evidence is indirect, it should be possible to show alternative inferences. Either way one thinks of it, it opens the best negative attack on a resolution of fact, the alternative inference. If the evidence can be shown to be arguably indirect, the inference is now at issue.

On-case Issue III: Inferences

There are two basic attacks on inferences, one on case and one off case. The on case attack is to break the inferential chain. The negative should do for the judge what we did above in examining Smith's statement. The negative should make the chain seem as long as possible and look for the weakest link. If a weak link can be found and defeated, the chain breaks, the inference fails, and the resolution is not supported. Also, if the resolution must be "probably" true, each link in the chain must be a least a "probable." The probative value of an inferential chain can be no greater than the probative value of its weakest link. And neither does water rise higher than its source.

Off-case Attacks

The major off-case attack on a resolution of fact is to show that the evidence can be explained in alternate ways: that alternate inferences are reasonable. The lovely feature of this attack is that the negative can run several alternate inferences. The negative does not have to say one of these is correct, that's another resolution. The negative need only show that the existence of one or all of these alternative explanations makes it less than probable that the affirmative inference is correct, and therefore the resolution is not probably true.

Attacks on the Evidence will show that the evidence is over-claimed or indirect. Attacks on the inferences will show that either the offered inference is unwarranted or that alternate inferences are more justified. While any element can be attacked, for fact debates, the off case will usually center on the alternative inferences that can be drawn from the affirmative's evidence.

A Sample Case of a Resolution of Fact

Assume that George is being tried for the murder of Martha. Assume that Gertrude, a friend of Martha and enemy of George, was watching through the keyhole and says that she saw "everything." She testifies that George drew a gun, pointed it at Martha, and killed her in "cold blood." The resolution implicitly under discussion is Resolved: that George murdered Martha.

Standards and Burdens.   Both the prosecution and the defense would realize that George's guilt must be proven in this case not just to probability, but beyond a reasonable doubt. The defense is much more likely than the prosecution to draw this to the jury's attention.

Prima Facie or On-case Elements

I. Definitions.   The terms "George" and "Martha" would seem self-explanatory, although of course "George" would be "defined" as the defendant. "Murder" would be defined as "the killing of one human being by another with malice." "Malice" has been defined in many ways, but we will take it to mean a "hardness of heart not respectful of the value of human life."

II. Evidence.   Gertrude's observations through the keyhole would be direct evidence. One cannot simultaneously believe the accuracy of the testimony and also believe that George did not shoot Martha.

Gertrude's statement that this was "in cold blood" is an opinion and represents an opinion drawn by the witness. Normally, the opinion would not be admissible and the court would ask for the observations she made that allowed her to form this opinion. She might report that George had a "stern and sober look on his face, and was staring directly at Martha." In a sense, these too are "opinions," but they place the jury one step closer to the scene. One way to think of the purpose of testimony is that it is given to let the jury "borrow" the eyes and ears of the witness.

The defense counsel would now try to show that Gertrude's testimony was inaccurate. This could be done by indicting her on grounds of bias (because she liked Martha and didn't like George) and on grounds of competence (because keyholes do not give a very good view of the room). It is important to realize that these questions go to the weight of the evidence, not to its nature. It's still direct, but it may be wrong. The prosecutor would still not have direct evidence of "malice." The malice must be "assumed" and is therefore "inferred."

III. Inference.   The prosecutor would argue that one does not point and fire a gun at another person unless one has no respect for life. If George had been in an irrational rage when he fired, he might not have felt "malice" but only passion (and the crime would be manslaughter). But, there is no evidence of rage here and his malice may be reasonably inferred.

Off-Case Arguments: Alternative Inferences.   The defense can argue that even if Gertrude reported accurately what she saw (which isn't certain) her observations about George's mental condition are open to other interpretations. He may have been "stern and sober" because he was afraid of Martha and he was "wary." He may have been temporarily insane. He may have been in a drugged state and not known what he was doing.

AN ALTERNATIVE *PRIMA-FACIE* FORMAT
BASED ON SYLLOGISMS

In *Critical Thinking through Debate*, we try to describe methods of debating that directly employ the theories and practices of critical thinking. To further this goal, we would like to introduce an alternate way of looking at fact stock issues: through the backdrop of the conditional (if/then) and disjunctive (either/or) syllogisms. Please recall our discussion of syllogisms from Chapters 7 and 8. One of our justifications for using disjunctive and conditional syllogisms as determiners of fact comes from the field of technology and the field of biology.

In technology, most if not all computer systems are binary in nature, running off of a series of bits. Bits are essentially the basic "on-off" components of computers, and bytes are a series of eight of these "on-off" switches. The "facts" of what you see in the virtual world of your computer boil down to an essential "either it's on or it's off" question of zeros and ones: A one signifies it's on; a zero signifies it's off. Additionally, computer programming languages are little more than intricate series of "if/then" propositions. Therefore, virtually the entire factual world of computers is based on nothing more than "either/or" and "if/then."

Additionally, for many in the biological sciences, the factual framework of all of life is based on the same disjunctive and conditional premises. According to Gary Marcus in his book, *The Birth of the Mind: How a Tiny Number of Genes Creates the Complexities of Human Thought,* genes, the building blocks of all life on Earth, work almost exclusively on dilemmas and conditions. Genes determine in the human womb, for instance, whether a cell will become part of the liver or a part of the brain by turning on and off the correct functions. Further principles of "if/then" added into the equation guide the development, as well as the day-to-day operations of the genes. Marcus writes:

> Rather than acting in absolute isolation, most genes act as parts of elaborate
> networks in which the expression of one gene is a precondition for the expres-

sion of the next. The THEN of one gene can satisfy the IF of another and thus induce it to turn on. In this way, a single gene that is at the top of a complex network can indirectly launch a cascade of hundreds or thousands of others, leading to, for example, the development of an eye or a limb. (p. 61)

It seems that our technological and biological worlds are based on virtually nothing but binary and conditional information. In fact, according to *Time Magazine*, February 17, 2003, the proteins that operate the interaction of the genetic material in human beings comprise roughly five exabytes of information. An exabyte is 1,152,921,504,606,846,976 bits. Five exabytes is equivalent to every word estimated to have been spoken by every human being over the past 150,000 years. While the Human Genome Project is an exceptional scientific landmark, it is merely a scratch on the back of the real data. Theoretically, when computers are invented that can process that much information, the virtual world could very possibly become synonymous with the real. Until then, genetic cloning and experimentation will be rife with mistakes. No human can possibly process all the information that comprises life, but with the help of super computers we may someday be able to do more than merely understand.

Essentially, the factual determination of our world comes in the form of either/or and if/then components. Within this backdrop, it seems more than justified to use disjunctive and conditional syllogisms as the basis of stock issues for proving propositions of fact.

If you recall from our discussions earlier in this chapter, the original stock issues of fact were definition, fact and inference. The necessity of definitions is a constant and should be considered an integral part of any fact or value case. We will thus not include a discussion of definitions in our explanation of this experimental format. Excluding definitions, the original stock issues translate fairly well into the conditional syllogism. Inference is equivalent to the major premise. Fact is equivalent to the minor premise. The conclusion is equivalent to the resolution. Here is what it would look like:

> Stock Issue One: Inference (major premise): If constant radio waves originate from outside Earth's galaxy, then intelligent life other than from Earth exists.
>
> Stock Issue Two: Fact (minor premise): Constant radio waves originate from outside Earth's galaxy.
>
> Resolution: (Conclusion): Intelligent life other than from Earth exists.

Here the affirmative team would need to prove the major premise (the first stock issue), as well as prove the minor premise (the second stock issue). If a factual determination to prove the minor premise were to be found, obviously you would have a fairly compelling argument in favor of the resolution. However, that would be contingent upon the major premise also being proven probably true within the rhetorical situation of a given debate round or event.

The disjunctive syllogism would work well in situations where there are only two options. For example, take the dilemma that President Bush the Elder faced when confronting Saddam Hussein prior to the first Persian Gulf War. Saddam's troops were amassed on the Saudi-Kuwait border. The resolution might have read as follows: Resolved: That Saddam Hussein's troops are amassed on the border for offensive purposes. The syllogism would be worded thus:

Stock Issue One: Either Saddam's army is amassed on the border for offensive or defensive purposes.

Stock Issue Two: Saddam's army is not amassed on the border for defensive purposes.

Resolution/Conclusion: Saddam's army is amassed on the border for offensive purposes.

Even though this syllogism is valid, you need to prove the truth of both stock issues. In the first stock issue, an affirmative would need to prove that those two options are mutually exclusive and that they are the only two options available. For example, can troop deployment be both defensive and offensive in nature? The answer is probably, yes. So even though this syllogism passes the unconditional validity test, you still need to prove, in a debate, that these possibilities are mutually exclusive in this particular situation: either the troops were protecting newly acquired territory or preparing to invade Saudi Arabia. Additionally, you would need to preclude the possibility that Saddam's troops were just on leave or on military training. The last two options and others are pretty easy to dismiss since he had just invaded Kuwait.

In the second stock issue, you need to prove that the defensive possibility is untenable. At the time that Saddam had taken over Kuwait and lined up on the Saudi border, it looked very positively as though he were about to attack Saudi Arabia next. His troops moved directly to the Saudi Border. Of course, it could have also been possible that Saddam simply wanted to protect his newly acquired, oil-rich asset of Kuwait. We therefore would have needed other evidence to prove this stock issue.

During experimental debates held by your authors among their students, these stock issues, in syllogism format, have worked well. We encourage you to experiment with them, with approval from your debate coach or argumentation teacher. In a future edition of the book, look for updates of our efforts to expand the relationship between critical thinking and debate practices.

Summary

Resolutions of fact are based on the belief that our senses are the way we determine "truth." Facts do not require that we "like" them, only that we acknowledge and believe them. Facts are based on evidence. Evidence might take the form of opinions or observations, or both. If the evidence is direct, only the quality of the evidence is at issue. If evidence is indirect, it requires an inference and the inference must be presented so that it can be objectively examined. Negatives should routinely hold the affirmative to its full burden and standard of proof. Any *prima-facie* element is subject to attack, and off case a negative can show alternative inferences.

CHAPTER 14

DEBATING
RESOLUTIONS OF VALUE

Our society is composed of many differing views on issues of values. Some of them are very serious and some of them are not overly important. Consider the following: Is abortion moral or immoral? Is Michael Jordan the greatest basketball player of all time? Does the welfare system do more harm or good? Is television programming more beneficial or detrimental to society? Is Affirmative Action a desirable or undesirable policy? Was M*A*S*H the greatest television show of all time? Is assuring economic growth more important that assuring protection of the environment?

These are all issues that we debate about on a regular basis. Values permeate our society. It is therefore important that both proponents and opponents of value resolutions know how to argue their cases effectively.

THE AFFIRMATIVE/GOVERNMENT CASE

In order to debate the affirmative side of a topic, debaters need to prepare a presentation, called an affirmative case. The first affirmative speaker makes that presentation as the first order of business in a debate. In Parliamentary debate, the first person to speak is the Government's Prime Minister. Remember; *affirmative* and *government* are synonymous terms. We will use the terms interchangeably in this chapter. When there is a distinction to be made, we will try to make that distinction clear.

An affirmative case in non-policy debate is a highly structured argument, fulfilling both the definitive and the designative stock issues. In a policy debate, the affirmative team will write a case that follows the motive (ill), blame (inherency), cure, and cost stock issues discussed in-depth in the next chapter. The first affirmative speaker usually presents the case in outline form. Each stock issue becomes an extended argument. For instance, he or she actually says things like, "observation one, dioxins harm human life; sub-point A, Dioxin causes cancer in humans." Exactly how to substructure a case is discussed later in this chapter. A typical case is divided into stock-issue segments. A value case will have a section for definition of terms (the first part of the definitive stock issue), another for criteria (the second part of the definitive stock issue), and a final section for the application of the criteria (designative stock issue).

Additionally, an affirmative case needs to have anywhere from ten to twenty quotations, with full source citations, included in the text. Therefore, writing a good case often involves doing a sufficient amount of research first. Earlier, we discussed how to find and evaluate evidence. Now it's time to write the arguments.

We'll start with the value affirmative case.

How to Construct a Value Affirmative Case

Definition of Terms

As indicated earlier, a non-policy affirmative case is usually broken down into three separate sections. The definitive stock issue includes two of those sections: the definition of terms and the criteria for the case. The third section involves the designative stock issue, which is the application of the criteria. First, you need to find adequate definitions for the key terms of the resolution. Defining the terms correctly can have a direct bearing on whether you win or lose a debate round. Non-policy debate encourages debaters to take middle-of-the-road approaches to the topic. Jack Howe (1985) writes that debaters should "explore the main issues of a problem and not the peripheral ones" (p. 20). Therefore, the novice debater should not try to be tricky by defining terms of the resolution in obscure ways. Look at the historical context of the resolution. Usually, debate topics concern contemporary controversies. The controversy as dealt with by the major media is usually the best hint as to how to analyze the resolution, and, hence, define its terms.

Topicality also becomes an issue when defining terms. The affirmative is required to be topical, i.e., discuss the resolution and not go beyond it. If the affirmative goes outside of the resolution, it will lose the debate if the negative can adequately prove that the affirmative is non-topical. It is only logical that no matter how good an affirmative's arguments are, if the negative successfully argues a topicality argument (proving that the affirmative is not within the boundaries of the debate resolution), an affirmative cannot win the debate. As a beginning debater, it is only important to understand the concept of topicality and to try to use definitions that will guarantee the topicality of your presentation. Some judges will not base their decision on whether the affirmative is topical, but that is not a chance a beginning debater should take.

Criteria for Judgment

Once you have defined the key terms of the resolution, you need to establish the criteria for judging the debate. In order to get started finding a criteria for the case you have chosen, take another look at the evaluative phrase of the resolution. If the phrase says, "is beneficial," ask yourself what is beneficial about the subject. Make sure that you form this benefit in the abstract. You are looking for overall benefits, such as economic, political, or social. For instance, in the nuclear freeze topic, the overall benefit would be political; in this case, world peace and security would be the specific political values. If your resolution has no word synonymous with the words "good" or "bad," then it is NOT a value resolution. Remember, as we discussed earlier, a value resolution is really a resolution that evaluates. If your resolution is not evaluating (saying something is either good or bad), then you must look to policy or fact as the correct classification.

Another source of overall standards is the values outlined by Milton Rokeach (1973). Figure 14.1 lists the terminal values spelled out by Rokeach. Kelley (1981) even suggests that debaters be required to read the works of Rokeach. Rokeach lists abstract values universally held by all people. If any of these values apply, it certainly would qualify for the type of criteria for which most judges look. Not all of Rokeach's list can be used for the purposes of debate, but much of it can. Many critic expect debaters to use these kinds of abstract values in non-policy debate. That expectation arises from the idea that values play a big part in non-policy decisions, especially in value decisions.

Another possible way to locate a criterion for your case is by perusing works of philosophers, especially political philosophers. Dictionaries or anthologies of philosophy are often helpful to the debate student with little background in philosophy. These can help the student locate certain philosophies more easily than reading original texts. The advantage to using philosophers as support for your criterion is that they often give supporting analysis for use of a certain value or standard. Plato, St. Thomas Aquinas, Thomas Hobbes, John Locke, David Hume, Thomas Jefferson, John Stuart Mill, and Henry David Thoreau are examples of the more predominantly used philosophers in academic debate. A common idea of J.S. Mill, often used in affirmative cases, is that idea that people should be allowed to exercise freedom as long as their actions do not harm others. The famous categorical imperative, by Immanuel Kant,

1)	A comfortable life	10)	Inner Harmony
2)	An exciting life	11)	Mature love
3)	A sense of accomplishment	12)	National Security
4)	A world at peace	13)	Pleasure
5)	A world of beauty	14)	Salvation
6)	Equality	15)	Self-respect
7)	Family security	16)	Social recognition
8)	Freedom	17)	True friendship
9)	Happiness	18)	Wisdom

FIGURE 14.1

Terminal Values

says that people should not use other people as a means to an end; thus, the categorical imperative is often used as the standard by which to judge particular issues.

More concrete standards are also acceptable in value debate. For instance arguing that having a strong military is good could have served for the standard in the national conscription resolution. Of course, implicit in the more concrete standard are abstract values such as peace and security. By using concrete standards, you are simply putting the emphasis on the more specific. Your criteria contention would simply argue that the team which can demonstrate the best path to a strong military would win the debate.

A final source of criteria is United States' documents such as the *Constitution*, the *Bill of Rights*, or the *Declaration of Independence*. Encased in these documents are the values and standards on which our society is based. If anything does not match up to these standards, it is fairly easy to call that "thing" detrimental. On the other hand, anything that facilitates American political values would almost assuredly be deemed beneficial. The American political value of the sanctity of human life, as outlined in the *Declaration of Independence,* is often the most supreme of all standards (although there are arguments to the contrary). Anytime you can link your case to the loss or maintenance of human life you are usually on fairly solid argumentative ground. Few things in our culture or political heritage outweigh the value placed on life. Realize in your search for a criterion that it is fine to have more than one criterion if you feel it would be advantageous.

It has also become quite popular in intercollegiate debate to argue that values contrary to the United States heritage are superior values. In the process of its manifest destiny, it is argued, the United States all-but destroyed dozens of native cultures which were and are ecologically superior to the capitalistic mindset of the United States. While many reading this book may wonder why such arguments may be efficacious in the process of debate, you'll need to remember that academic debate is a critical-thinking activity in which all ideas may be questioned, including the very rules for the debate activity itself. Just because the present eco-political system has a certain philosophy (capitalism and representative democracy) does not mean that that philosophy is automatically superior to any alternative. Recall our definition of argument: a claim backed up by reasons. Also recall that assuming our heritage superior to all others would be considered a fallacy of tradition.

Once you have found the best criterion for your case, the next step is to write a contention supporting that standard as the best standard for judging the resolution at hand. The contention will probably involve two to four sub-points. Figure 14.2 lists an outline of the criterion contention of a case that was written by Cindi Sellinger and Dorise Gray of CSU, Chico. In this example, Cindi and Dorise secured their criterion from the Supreme Court decision of *Shenck v. the United States*.

The case argued that restrictions on media coverage of terrorism were justified. The standard of the Court was to determine whether there exists "a clear and present danger" to US security or to US citizens. If such a danger existed then restrictions on media coverage would be justified. Also important in outlining the criterion is dem-

Contention I. The criterion for today's round is the Clear and Present Danger Doctrine.

> **Sub-point A.** First Amendment press freedoms are not absolute.
>
> **Sub-point B.** Protection of National Security and human life always outweigh free press and speech.
>
> **Sub-point C.** Through application of the Clear and Present Danger Doctrine, the Supreme Court has recognized this hierarchy of life over freedom of the press.
>
> **Sub-point D.** Restrictions on media coverage of terrorism are a legitimate application of the Clear and Present Danger Doctrine.

FIGURE 14.2

Criterion Contention Establishing a Value Hierarchy

onstrating that your value is more important than competing values. In other words, you need to establish a **hierarchy of values.** In Cindi and Dorise's case this is done by arguing that national security and human life are more important than press freedom. Additionally, the contention establishes that the first amendment protections of speech and press have never been absolute. A *clear and present danger* has always provided an exception to the first amendment. Here, a clear hierarchy of life over freedom has been established.

Establishing this type of hierarchy is not always necessary. However, some critics feel that such a hierarchy is important in every affirmative case. In a value topic that asks the affirmative to prove that one thing is more valuable than another, such as the energy and environment topic, it may be important to always establish this hierarchy. In other cases, developing the hierarchy may simply serve as an effective preemption to negative arguments. Every good value debate should come down to a clash on an abstract level, whether or not the affirmative attempts to develop the hierarchy originally. In the debate over restrictions of terrorism coverage, the value clash almost always dealt with life versus freedom. It became easy, therefore, for the affirmative to predict the negative stance and establish the hierarchy in their first speech. As mentioned earlier, political philosophers discussed values, and the focus of their work often established a hierarchy of values. Referring to political philosophers can thus facilitate your argument. Judith A. Best (1980), in her book, *The Mainstream of Western Political Thought*, states:

> The history of political philosophy is in itself evidence that there are a variety of ends or values for [people] and that these ends or values are fre-

quently in conflict. On the other hand, the history of political philosophy indicates that there is a hierarchy of values. From Socrates, who saw a conflict between two very high things, philosophy and the law, to Nietzsche, who saw conflict between truth and life, each philosopher has ultimately agreed that there is a hierarchy of values. And so, though Socrates taught moderation and attempted to reconcile or mitigate the tension between philosophers and the city, he found philosophy to be higher than the law. So Nietzsche found life to be higher than truth. So Locke and Rousseau declared freedom to be the highest value. So Tocqueville and Aristotle preferred excellence to equality.

   While the philosophers of the Western political tradition have differed in the precise placement of values in a hierarchy, they have agreed that there is and must be a hierarchy. (p. 13, 14)

Clearly, using a philosopher's arguments can be an effective means to support a particular hierarchy.

Application of the Criterion

   After completing the criterion contention it becomes necessary to apply that value or standard in the subsequent contention(s). Advocates should argue those contentions, or arguments, on a more specific level than the criterion itself. Assume a debate is taking place over the desirability of a unilateral freeze on nuclear weapons and a criterion of world peace is advanced. In that case the contention(s) must demonstrate how a unilateral freeze would enhance world peace. To do that often sub-arguments are needed to help develop the larger issue. The contentions should set up the big picture while the sub-points should consist of the Figures within that picture. Usually the last sub-point for every contention gives the impact to the contention and the link to the criterion. Figure 14.3 shows an outline of a designative contention on the military-support-to-non-democratic-nations topic. Notice the first two sub-points do not even discuss US military support or world peace. Those sub-points serve only as sub-arguments to help reach the conclusion found in sub-point "E." That final sub-point also links the criterion of world peace both to military support and to Iraqi expansion, thus serving as a strong conclusion to the contention and strong support for the resolution. Remember, each of these sub-points needs to be supported by at least one piece of credible evidence.

   It is also possible to argue what are called **independent contentions.** A case with independent contentions is similar to policy debate's version of the alternative justification case (which is described in the next chapter) which is a strategy that allowed policy affirmatives to win the debate if they won any one of a number of different plans. Often debaters of value topics will do something similar by presenting two or three independent contentions. In such a case debaters may need to present the respective number of separate criterion as well. Those criteria are usually out-

Contention II. Military support to non-democratic nations deters Iraqi aggression and prevents war.

> **Sub-point A.** Iraq has been expansionist in the past and has a religious doctrine of dominance.
>
> **Sub-point B.** Iraq is expansionist now.
>
> **Sub-point C.** US military support can deter Iraq.
>
> **Sub-point D.** The lack of military support would encourage Iraqi expansion.
>
> **Sub-point E.** Iraqi expansion almost always involves war; hence, the criterion of world peace is maintained through US military support.

FIGURE 14.3

Outline of a Designative Contention

lined in the first couple of sub-points within the contentions themselves or they can be outlined in the beginning of the case. The advantage to running a case with independent contentions is that, theoretically, you only need to win one contention to win the debate. There is some controversy as to whether independent contentions are valid, but many critic accept the concept and many more allow the legitimacy of independent contentions be argued by the debaters. A note of caution is that you must be sure that your contentions truly are independent. Do not use the same piece of evidence or analysis for independent contentions and do not have the concept of one contention depend on a sub-point in another. If either is true, you should reconsider using the independent structure.

The Categorical Syllogism

Perhaps a better way to look at the definitive and designative stock issues would be to look at them through the filter of the categorical syllogism. For example, let's take the resolution "Resolved that: the welfare system is bad." Once we have the resolution we know that we also have the conclusion to our argument. Therefore, we need to back up the syllogism to find the premise. Since we also know that a valid syllogism has three parts, once we have the conclusion, we further know that we have two of those parts. The "C" and the "B" terms as mentioned in previous chapters. (You may want to review that discussion at this time.)

Thus, "the welfare system" is the "C" term, and "bad" is the "B" term. We would then use X as the "A" term. X will become any of the values or criteria previously discussed. The syllogism would look like this:

X is bad.
The welfare system is X.
The welfare system is bad.

You may do this with almost any value resolution. Let's say for the purposes of our discussion that X is "causing dependency." The syllogism now looks like this:

Major Premise (Definitive Stock Issue):	Causing dependency is bad.
Minor Premise (Designative Stock Issue):	The welfare system is causing dependency.
Conclusion (Resolution):	The welfare system is bad.

In this case, you have created your basic case outline using the categorical syllogism as a guide. You may also see now a theoretical justification for the two stock issues. Technically, if you can prove "probably" true the two premises, then you have "forced" the resolution true. Recall our discussion from previous chapters.

Any value topic may be manipulated in this fashion. All three of your instructors have used this format to help their students brainstorm case ideas for value debate, and all three have seen students excel with this method. Take the following resolution: Increased environmental regulations, requiring industries to reduce pollution, would be desirable. Again, this resolution is equivalent to the conclusion of the categorical syllogism as discussed in Chapters 7 and 8. You may thus create the syllogism, as suggested above:

Major premise (Definitive/Criteria): Improving human health would be desirable.
Minor premise (Designative/Application): Increased environmental regulations, requiring industries to reduce pollution, would be improving human health.
Conclusion (Resolution): Increased environmental regulations, requiring industries to reduce pollution, would be desirable.

The important point is that the phrase "improving human health" may be substituted in both places you find the "A" term above. Any logically consistent phrase logically will do. For example, a debater and his/her partner might brainstorm the following list of possible "A" terms:

Improving human health
Saving human lives
Improving quality of life
Improving the economy
Improving foreign relations

Reducing cancer cases
Preventing further harm to the ozone
Reducing the greenhouse effect

Each one of these possible "A" terms would represent a completely separate categorical syllogism and a completely separate case. For example, "preventing further harm to the ozone" is substituted for "improving human health," as follows:

> Major premise (Definitive/Criteria): Preventing further harm to the ozone would be desirable.
> Minor premise (Designative/Application): Increased environmental regulations, requiring industries to reduce pollution, would be preventing further harm to the ozone.
> Conclusion (Resolution): Increased environmental regulations, requiring industries to reduce pollution, would be desirable.

The important point to note is that each of the premises requires argumentation; that is, reasons for accepting the premises. Too often, in value debate, the debaters assume that the criterion is fine as an assertion. However, as the example above illustrates, the major premise definitely needs evidentiary support because not everyone believes that ozone fluctuations are necessarily a problem.

Additionally, for parliamentary debate, in which the government's case is constructed in a short 15 minutes, this brainstorming method may be a way to generate dozens of viable cases in a very brief period. Additionally, once put into the format of a syllogism, the parliamentary debaters will then have a workable outline for the case. Let's take the above argument as an example. The government may outline a case as follows:

Outline of a Government's Case

[An Introduction in your own words.[
Observation One: Definitions
>   (These are in addition to the syllogism)
>   *Ozone:* a protective layer around the earth's atmosphere which protects the health of all life.
>   *Industries:* we'll be focusing on industries, like the auto industry and the power industry, which require the burning of fossil fuels.

Observation Two: Criterion (Major Premise)
>   Preventing further harm to the ozone would be desirable.
>   The ozone is needed for protection.
>   Further harm to the ozone would increase skin cancer deaths.

Observation Three: (Minor Premise)
> Increased environmental regulations, requiring industries to reduce pollution, would be preventing further harm to the ozone.
>> Eliminating methyl bromide would protect the environment.
>> Eliminating release of ozone depleting pollutants would protect the environment.

Notice that this case follows the categorical syllogism as a guideline. A parliamentary debater may use more than one criteria and more than one application; thus, the government could advance independent contentions.

NEGATIVE STRATEGIES IN VALUE DEBATE

In debating against the affirmative, the negative's or opposition's minimal burden is simply to show reasonable doubt concerning the affirmative's case. Technically, the negative/opposition need not prove or establish anything. Remember, those supporting the resolution have the **burden of proof,** which means that they have to prove the resolution true. The opposing debaters, on the other hand, have no resolution to uphold and thus have a wider range of argumentative options open to them.

There are numerous methods to use to disprove the affirmative/government: *prima-facie* arguments, definitional arguments, topicality challenges, point-by-point refutation, and off-case arguments. Some of these approaches are necessary and some of them are optional. What is important to remember is that the more you prepare and practice, the more proficient you will become. Debating on this side of the resolution has some unique difficulties. For instance, you rarely know what the other team is going to argue until the debate begins. That's why preparation is so important. This chapter will address these approaches and difficulties in order to help you handle the negative or opposition side of the debate.

REFUTING THE DEFINITIVE STOCK ISSUE

The first or second speaker may attack the substance of the affirmative/government case. There are exceptions to this which will be discussed later. For now, it is important to explain what case attacks look like.

Prima-Facie Argumentation

First, you should consider whether the case supposedly justifying the resolution is *prima facie. Prima facie* literally means "at first look." In simpler terms, your opponents need to have satisfactorily fulfilled all of the stock issues for value debate or they are not *prima facie*. Technically, if the affirmative fails to fulfill even one of the stock issues or any other major issue, they should lose the debate.

If you conclude that either of the two value stock issues are missing from the affirmative case, you may then issue a *prima-facie* challenge. To do that, demonstrate to the critic that this necessary component is missing from the support of the resolution. A common mistake made by beginning debaters is to leave out a criterion, which, of course, is part of the definitive stock issue.

Once you make the challenge, if your opponents cannot adequately explain the absence of a criterion, their position will be weakened considerably, and they will more than likely lose the debate. If, on the other hand, they are able to come up with some kind of criterion when pressed for it, at least their credibility will be hurt. Moreover, the challenge, which caused the affirmative or government to come up with a criterion, will also make it easier for the negative or opposition to clash with the value position.

Definitional Arguments

Often resolution-proponents will choose tricky definitions that that attempt to sidestep anticipated challenges. Unfortunately, sometimes the implications of these "tricky" definitions do not become apparent until the end of the debate when it is too late to argue them. At that point the opposition/negative will have probably lost the debate due to lack of foresight. To avoid this problem, it is important to take issue with any definition that seems suspect of being non-standard.

Another common non-standard definition used by resolution-proponents is a narrow definition. Often a narrow interpretation of a very complex word will be used. When you hear an extremely short or narrow definition, you may want to take issue with it. Again, you need to note first that the definition is narrow. However, narrowness is not in itself bad, so you also need to give a reason why the narrow definition is unreasonable. Second, you need to provide a longer, more general definition.

Other unreasonable definitions may include definitions which are too broad or take the word out of context of the resolution. What is important to understand from this discussion is that if you hear a questionable definition, you need to take issue with it. First, suggest why it may be unreasonable and, second, offer an alternative definition. If you fail to do either of these things, most critic will allow the original definition to stand. Failing to show why the original definition is unreasonable gives the critic no reason to accept your definition over theirs. Additionally, failing to offer an alternative definition leaves only one definition for that term in the debate, that belonging to the affirmative or government. While that definition may be inappropriate, it is the only one, and it will stand. Most critics feel that something is better than nothing.

Debate in general predominantly uses the reasonable-definition standard discussed thus far. However, another overall standard can be used as well: the best-definition standard. When using this standard, you need not prove that the resolution-proponent's definition is unreasonable, but you merely have to prove that your definition is better. In order to prove that your definition is best, you can do a number of things. First, you may argue that your definition better takes into consideration the historical context of the resolution. Second, you can argue that, in the context of the wording of the resolution per se, your definition makes more sense. Third, you may even argue that your definition allows for more "clash" and hence is best for debate purposes.

Nevertheless, whichever standard you use, be sure to issue any definitional arguments in leader of the opposition's speech or 1NC. Many debate judges see definition arguments as operational issues that must be addressed in the first speech; 2NC or the member's speech is too late.

Topicality Arguments

While examining definitions, you may note that the affirmative/government is not topical due to a misused or unreasonable definition. Recall that topicality arguments question whether the resolution-proponent's case is within the bounds of the resolution.

Topicality in CEDA: For example, on the religious activism topic, the affirmative was required to prove that religious activism in politics harmed the American political process. Some affirmatives ran cases that argued that religious groups told their followers how to vote. The harm was that large numbers of puppet voters put the political process in the hands of a few fundamentalist religious leaders. Many negatives, however, questioned whether telling people how to vote was actually "activism in politics." Consequently, a topicality argument grew out of a definitional concern with that phrase. If this were the case, the negative would have to word the complaint in the form of a structured topicality argument. If the negative was to win that argument and prove to the critic that telling people how to vote was not "activism in politics," then technically the negative ought to win the debate on the topicality argument alone. Jan Vasilius (1980) argues, "In value debate . . . the affirmative case stands as the sole interpretation of the resolution. It is, therefore, not a partial issue. If the negative succeeds in winning topicality there is a total victory" (p. 53). Figure 14.4 gives an example of how the activism topicality argument might be phrased. Notice how the argument is arranged: first, standards or definitions; second, violations of those standards; and, third, impact of the violations. There are two different ways to argue topicality: one, you can use the affirmative's definition against them; or, two, you can argue that the affirmative's definition is unreasonable and suggest an alternative. Figure 14.4 looks at the first way of arguing which is preferable when possible.

Regardless of the approach taken, topicality arguments are an effective way to argue in academic debate. As a negative/opposition debater, you should always ask yourself whether the affirmative/government case is on the topic or not. If there is

Sub-point A Standards. The affirmative defines *activism* as political activism by people who go beyond normal citizenship to try to change existing political norms.

Sub-point B Violations. The affirmative violates their own definition on two levels.

    1. Voting. The affirmative argues that religious groups tell their followers how to vote, yet they define activism as "going beyond normal citizenship." To the extent that voting is not beyond normal citizenship, the affirmative is non-topical by their own definition.

    2. Telling people how to vote is not quite political activism. Telling people how to vote is religious propaganda, with dubious political implications. After all, how do we know whether these people vote as they are told?

Sub-point C Impact. The affirmative debaters are non-topical on two counts. Unless they resolve this discrepancy, they should lose the round.

FIGURE 14.4

Sample Topicality Argument

any question whatsoever, you should consider running a topicality argument. Many critic expect topicality arguments to be run in 1NC. The reason is that they feel definitional issues such as topicality are operational issues that should be resolved as early in the debate as possible. Second negative constructive may not get away with running a topicality argument. If you are debating team debate, you need to be aware of this requirement.

Often, topicality arguments are difficult to think of while preparing the 1NC speech. Often, novice debaters will finish with a debate and say to themselves "We should have run a topicality argument; that case was clearly non-topical." To avoid resorting to such hindsight make a conscious effort to consider topicality before every first negative presentation.

Recall from our discussion in an earlier chapter how to make points of order in parliamentary debate. A topicality argument in parliamentary debate looks substantially different than the one described in the previous section. In CEDA, topicality is argued throughout the debate, and at the end the judge makes a decision. In parliamentary debate, there is no need to wait. The judge should rule immediately on the topicality of the government's argument. If you hear something that does not seem to be in line with the resolution, stand up and say "point of order." Wait for the Speaker of the House (debate critic) to acknowledge you. Then explain why the government is not topical.

Let's take the example of the following topic: "The House believes that 'that government is best which governs least.'"

Let's say the government argues that a private college is best when it allows the students freedom to pursue individualized educational goals. At that point, you could stand up. This is what might follow:

Leader of the Opp:	Point of order.
Speaker of the House:	Yes.
Leader of the Opp:	The Prime Minister is not discussing the resolution. A private college is not a government, nor is it run by the government.
Prime Minister:	It is a form of governance. We don't need to discuss a government.
Speaker of the House:	The opposition's point is well taken.

Let's break down this exchange. Let's say you are the leader of the opposition. You may make a point of order at any time, even while the Prime Minister is speaking. In other words, you may interrupt. Once the Speaker of the House (remember, the Speaker of the House is the judge) acknowledges you, you have, according to many, 15 seconds to make your case. You notice also that the Prime Minister makes a quick justification. It is your authors' experience that even though such a statement is not written into the rules, most speakers/judges allow the advocate a quick statement. Here the speaker of the house rules in your favor, and does so by saying, "point well taken."

This means that for the rest of the debate, the Prime Minister's argument about private schools will be disregarded by your Speaker of the House. The Prime Minister may do a number of things at this point. First, the PM can change the hypothetical example to correspond with the Speaker of the House's interpretation. For example, the PM could say, "all right, it's a public school, run by the government." A second option for the PM is to forget the educational example altogether.

Topicality in either permutation, CEDA or Parliamentary, is an important weapon to keep in your arsenal. You can refute a lot of otherwise problematic arguments with a simple argument of classification. Furthermore, topicality is extra important in value debate because definitions are a part of the stock-issue framework: hence, the lengthy discussion here.

Argue Criteria

When arguing criteria, there are at least four approaches that you can take. The first approach consists of the *prima-facie* requirement discussed earlier. This approach can only be used if the resolution-proponents lack a criterion. The second approach is to accept the criterion, but to show that it is not fulfilled or applied. For example, on the military-support-to-non-democratic-nations topic the criterion of preventing an aggressor's expansion was given in support of the resolution. One way to argue that criterion would be to accept it as the standard for judgment, but to show that U.S. military support does not prevent such expansion. You could argue that non-democratic countries change leaders regardless of support and that various leaders choose for themselves which alliances, if any, they will form. When using this technique of arguing criteria, you could have used the historical example of the Samoza regime in Nicaragua. The US supported him for years, but he was overthrown in spite of US aid (or because of it). Before the end of the cold war, the Soviets had significant influence in Nicaragua, and we had little. If you could prove, in Nicaragua and overall, that US military aid does not prevent aggressive expansion, you could win the debate.

A third approach to arguing criteria is to demonstrate the flaws of the criterion itself. For example, an argument against the criterion of the sample case discussed earlier in this chapter was that the clear-and-present-danger standard only applies in time of war, not during terrorist activities. Of course, the second affirmative had evidence demonstrating that terrorism is analogous to war; however, the negative could still win this argument through effective extensions in its rebuttal presentations. Demonstrating that the criterion is flawed is a good first step toward winning a debate.

The fourth approach is to argue that your negative/government criterion is superior to the resolution-proponents' criterion. All you need to do is to establish the hierarchy of your value over your opponents'. If the resolution-proponents' value is the sanctity of human life, you might offer the value-criterion of individual freedom. You would simply give your critic(s) and audience some reason(s) to prefer your criterion.

The latter three approaches to arguing criteria are not mutually exclusive. You could feasibly argue that the affirmative criterion is flawed, that it is inferior, and "even if" it is not flawed or inferior, it does not apply anyway. When you use this type of "even if" argument, be sure that the critic and your opponents understand that it is a conditional argument. In other words, when you argue that the criterion does not apply, that does not mean that you forfeit your arguments that it is flawed or that your value-criterion is superior. Simply make your intentions clear to the critic and your opponents.

REFUTING THE DESIGNATIVE STOCK ISSUE

When refuting the designative stock issue, the negative maintains that the claims are not true, that the arguments are irrelevant or have little weight, or that the evidence on which the arguments rest is suspect. The negative must listen closely to the evidence and analysis used by the affirmative. If flaws are detected they need to be pointed out to the critic. Counter evidence challenging the truth of the affirmative claims can also be read. The negative should be ready to point out why their evidence is better than the affirmative's evidence. For a much more detailed discussion of refutation techniques refer to Chapter 11. When facing an affirmative, the negative will either be addressing a case based on dependent or independent contentions. Both types of cases call for different negative approaches.

Arguing against Dependent Contentions

The first thing the negative should do is determine if the contentions advanced by the affirmative are dependent or independent. As discussed earlier dependent contentions rely on one another while independent contentions stand by themselves. Many affirmatives may argue that their contentions are independent when in fact they are not. If you believe the contentions are dependent then point this out to the critic.

If the contentions are dependent, then the negative has a few strategies. Just like a chain is only as strong as its weakest link, so an affirmative case relying on dependent contentions is only as strong as their weakest contention. If one dependent contention can be proven to be false, then the whole case will fall. For example, assume the affirmative is arguing in support of the resolution "Resolved: that television is harmful to American society." To support this resolution the affirmative offers the following two contentions. The first contention argues that Political Apathy is harmful to a democratic Society and the second contention argues that television causes political apathy. In this instance the affirmative would have to win both contentions.

First, the negative can concentrate all of their attacks on just one of the contentions. The negative could simply argue that apathy is not harmful, so even if television does cause apathy, it is irrelevant. Or the negative could grant that apathy is bad but argue that television does not cause apathy. Of course, by just arguing against one of the dependent contentions, the negative debaters put all of their eggs in one basket. If they fail to disprove or turn the contention then they will lose the debate unless they are winning on a definitive stock issue. Therefore, the second option is for the negative to argue against both affirmative contentions and hope they just win one. In the above example the negative would argue that apathy is not necessarily bad and that television does not cause apathy anyway.

Another option for the negative would be to try to turn the argument. For example, the negative could grant that apathy is bad but then argue television actually decreases apathy. When turning dependent contentions the negative must be careful not to turn both contentions because if they do they will be double turning themselves. For example, suppose the negative argues that apathy is good (turn) and that television decreases apathy (turn). Now the negative has just proven that television stops (in fact decreases) a good thing from happening. The affirmative in this case would just grant both turns and thank the negative for proving the resolution true. Clearly, if television stops a good thing from happening to society it should be viewed as harmful.

Arguing against Independent Contentions

If the contentions are truly independent, then the negative debaters must be sure that they argue both contentions if their aim is to simply deny the truth of the arguments. Let's assume the same resolution as discussed above. This time the affirmative offers two independent contentions. The first contention argues that television causes increased violence in society while the second contention argues that television promotes sexual promiscuity. If the negative only argued against the first contention, the affirmative could, at least in theory, ignore that contention and simply point out that the second Contention had been granted and further maintain that the second contention independently proves the resolution true.

A second negative strategy is to try to turn both contentions. The negative could argue that television decreases violence (turn) and that television decreases sexual promiscuity (turn). Unlike when facing dependent contentions, the negative does not have to worry about double flipping themselves when turning both contentions. Notice how these two turns don't end up proving the resolution true.

Finally, a riskier strategy is for the negative to attempt to turn one of the contentions and show that the impact of the turn outweighs the impact of the other contention. For example, the affirmative may concede that television causes increased violence in society, but then argue that television actually decreases sexual promiscuity (turn). They could then claim that the advantages of decreased sexual activity outweigh the harm of increased violence. Therefore, on balance, television is more beneficial. This last strategy is a risky one and should be utilized with great care.

Deny Applications to the Criterion

Regardless if you are facing an affirmative case based on dependent or independent contentions the negative should look carefully at the affirmative criterion to make sure that the designative issues filter through the criterion. If there is no affirmative link to the criterion, then the affirmative should not win that argument. For example if the affirmative criterion is "apathy is bad," but the designative arguments say "TV causes violence," then the affirmative should not win. In the independent contentions illustration above, in order for the affirmative to win, a criterion argument needs to be imbedded within each independent contention. The bottom line is this: the affirmative needs to filter arguments through a criterion. If it's not filtered through a criterion, then it cannot count in the debate.

OFF-CASE ARGUMENTS

Most often, the negative team in a value debate will want to begin off-case arguments in their first speech. Off case arguments are those that do not directly address the resolution-proponents' case, but rather simply advance the cause of the negative. For example, let's say that their case was built around the following syllogism:

> Causing dependency is bad.
> Welfare causes dependency.
> Welfare is bad.

In this case, the first negative speaker may want to provide an alternate criterion through which an alternative case could be filtered. In the above syllogism, the resolution-proponents are requiring you to discuss economic dependency. Any other discussion by the negative will not filter through the affirmative criteria (causing dependency is bad) and thus should not be allowed by the critic. In this case, the negative may want to provide "economic security" as its criteria. Thus the first negative speaker may "shell out" a position arguing that welfare is good because it provides economic security for those who need it. The second negative speaker will then expand upon that idea with a structured and in-depth argument, including statistics on how many children benefit from the food, clothing, and housing provided with welfare benefits. This type of off-case argument could best be described as a counter-warrant or counter-example of the resolution. Since in this example, the resolution-proponents did not discuss security, the off-case attack mentioned above rests upon the validity of the criteria debate: that is, whether the judge is going to allow the negative to present an alternative criterion on economic security.

A better way to go may be through the use of value objections. Value objections, as currently practiced in value debate, are general attacks on the values implied by the affirmative case. More and more critic are requiring that value objections apply to the resolution-proponents' case. General attacks upon the resolution usually do not have much affect, unless they can be linked to case side. The best way to approach off-case arguments from the perspective of a novice competitor is to look at the resolution and develop a few sound arguments against it. Look at the underlying values implied in refutation of the resolution. Remember, that when you use these general arguments in a debate you are going to have to link them somehow to the affirmative cases that you hit, but that is not so difficult. The key, again, is to look for values.

On the UN-membership-is-no-longer-beneficial topic, second negative speakers had a significant amount of success running value objections that talked about the value of world cooperation. Affirmatives were asked to show that the UN was no longer beneficial to the US, implying that the worth of the UN should be determined by each nation separately. Negatives objected to that value of nationalism and offered value objections supporting a world government. All second negatives had to do in order to link that V.O. to the affirmative case was to simply find a place in the affirmative argumentation that supported the concept of nationalism.

Ideally, however, once the beginning debater has had some experience debating in intercollegiate competition, he or she can begin to compile a list of opposing cases. With that list, he or she can develop specific value objections for each of the different types of cases. CEDA, more and more, is beginning to require on-point value objections. The general ones, even when linked to case, are seen as weaker arguments than the more directly responsive ones.

Value objections (VOs) are delivered in outline form in the same manner as the affirmative/government case. You need to do a number of things in each VO. A suggested method of structuring VOs is to include 4 steps: introduction, link to the resolution-proponents' case, implications of their value, and the impact of those implications. Figure 14.5 lists the outline of a sample value objection that employs this structure.

When you are writing the value argument, make the "A" sub-point of the VO the introduction of your value. In the "B" sub-point, try to find a specific sub-point on case to which you can link the value objection. For instance, if the case talks about giving military aid to El Salvador and other right-wing dictatorships, you can link a dictatorship VO to that type of case. Therefore, in the "B" sub-point of that VO, you would state something to the effect that "the affirmative supports the value of giving military aid to right wing dictatorships as they indicate in Contention II, sub-point A of their case." Sub-point "C" of the value objection "objects" to the value of giving military aid to dictatorships. Arguments may include the fact that dictatorships use

---

I) We object to our opponents' value of supporting dictatorships with US Military Support.

    A) (Introduction of your value.) The negative/opposition advocates the value of sanctions for dictatorships.

    B) (Link to the resolution-proponents' case.) They support the value of giving military aid to dictatorships, as they indicate in Contention II sub-point A, of their case.

    C) (Implications of the resolution-proponents' value.) The support of repressive regimes is bad.

        1) Dictatorships use US aid to subjugate their people.

        2) Common people from these countries hate the US.

        3) Marxist influence grows in a country that resents the US.

    D) (Impact.) If Marxists are successful, the US may never have influence over that country again, and such a victory for communism may threaten the post-Cold-War, democratic resurgence.

FIGUE 14.5

Outline of a Value Objection

US military support to subjugate their people. Other arguments may try to show that, because the US supports dictatorships, citizens from those countries hate the US. Another argument may try to prove that Marxist revolutionaries become more influential in a dictatorship supported by the US. After developing the argument, the fourth step in a value objection is to give an impact statement. In the example given above, a possible impact statement would be that if the Marxists are successful, the US may never have influence over that country again. That type of impact statement would be especially effective if the resolution-proponents' criterion were maintenance of US relations with all dictatorships in order to prevent Marxist influence.

In summary, VOs should be linked to case, should develop analysis through sub-points, and should give impact. The format offered here is only suggestive. Experiment with various formats to see what works best for you. Some value topics are easier than others for developing off-case arguments. The best place to start looking for ideas is the resolution itself. Just be sure to make the best out of the second negative speech. It can often make the difference in a debate round. Also, be sure to work closely with your partner, so that your value objections do not contradict the arguments from your first speech.

SUMMARY

In this chapter we have looked at ways to research and analyze a value debate topic. Techniques for writing an affirmative case were discussed. With regard to writing the case, this chapter outlined methods to define terms, establish criteria, and application of the criterion. Affirmative cases may utilize either dependent or independent contentions. The categorical syllogism was introduced as a model for constructing affirmative cases. This chapter also discussed negative strategies.

CHAPTER 15

DEBATING
RESOLUTIONS OF POLICY

Policy debate grows out of the same instinct that says "Don't just stand there, do something!" When a problem presents itself one sooner or later feels compelled to act. It is the proposal of a manifest act that distinguishes policy debates from debates of fact and value. If the debate is a public debate, adopting the resolution means doing something. If the debate is academic it is judged on the basis of whether or not the critic would support the action proposed by the resolution.

Policy debate seems to be the predominate type of intercollegiate debating as academia moves into the twenty-first century. Should the welfare system be reformed? Should your taxes be increased to build new schools? Should your neighborhood be rezoned to allow for commercial development? These are all important issues with which our society struggles. It is therefore important to have an understanding of how policy disputes can be effectively advocated and opposed.

This chapter will examine the nature of policy disputes. Initially, the traditional stock issues will be examined, next the affirmative strategies will be explored, and then the negative responses will be considered. Finally, the words *should* and *fiat* as they apply to policy debate will be examined.

TRADITIONAL POLICY STOCK ISSUES

Policy debate asks the advocates to debate whether a specific change in the present system (of government, of education, of foreign policy, etc.) is necessary. In order for a society to justify change there has to be a significant reason for change. Our major institutions do not make major changes in policy without a serious and compelling reason. Change always involves a certain amount of risk. One key difference that separates policy debate from fact and value debate is the inherent risk involved in adopting the resolution. We know what things are like under the status quo. When things are good we want to maintain the status quo. When things are bad we want to change the status quo. However, while we hope that our proposed changes to a flawed *status quo* will lead to improvement, we can never be certain that our changes will have the desired results. In fact, our changes may backfire and things may end being worse then they were before. We can all probably remember taking some action that at the time seemed like a good idea but that we later came to regret. The more extensive the proposed change, the greater the risk involved. Unlike fact or value, policy is a risky business. Beliefs or attitudes can be held, and no risk incurred, until we act on them. It is an internal matter whether we consider the earth flat or round, until we try to sail around it.

Policy debate is the most focused of all the forms of debate. Since an action is to be taken and a risk incurred, everything in the debate focuses on that action. The overriding issue is always: is the proposed action expedient? Expediency simply means that the resolution's agent is better off taking the action than not taking it. If the answer is yes, then the action should be taken. If the answer is no, then the action should not be taken.

In order to demonstrate that taking the proposed action is expedient and to compensate for the risk inherent in taking that action, the affirmative is required to prove a number of contingent factors. These factors are called **stock issues.** The stock issues for policy debate are **Motive, Blame, Cure, and Cost.** The negative of course will try to refute one or more of these stock issues. For further explication of the policy stock issues, a **medical analogy** can be helpful.

Motive

Motive (sometimes referred to as Ill) is the requirement to prove that a significant need for change exits. The medical analogy suggests that you do not have surgery unless you are confronted with fairly serious health concerns. In the same way, our institutions should not make major policy changes unless justified. Motive actually contains two requirements that the affirmative must establish. The first requirement is to prove a harmful condition exists. The second is to show that the harm is significant. For instance, assume that at a particular intersection one person every five years is hit and killed by a car. Clearly this is a harmful condition. But would this justify putting up a stoplight at that intersection? Probably not. While harm exists it is probably not considered to be significant enough to warrant such a measure. However, if one person were killed every month at an intersection then the harm would probably be considered significant enough warrant a stoplight. What constitutes a significant harm from an insignificant harm is subjective and open for debate. How many people have to die on a yearly basis before it becomes significant enough to warrant a stoplight? This is an answer that the affirmative must be able to answer. Obviously, the affirmative is going to contend for a low number while the negative is going to argue for a high one. While we break down motive into harm and significance we normally think of them as one combined idea (i.e., a significant harm).

The negative obviously has two strategies when refuting the motive issue. They can argue first that harms do not exist. Second, they can argue that even if harms do exist they are not significant enough to warrant a policy change. If a negative advocate were able to prove that there is no harm or that the harm is insignificant, the negative should win the debate. The affirmative must win all of the stock issues in order to win a debate; the negative only need win one. Back to the medical analogy, should a second opinion prove to you that your health is not threatened, you may decide against a surgical procedure. Any undesirable situation must be quantitatively and/or qualitatively significant in order to justify a major change in the *status quo.*

Qualitative significance refers to the erosion of significant human values such as freedom or equality. Think of the root word in qualitative: *quality.* When the quality of life is adversely affected then that is a qualitative harm. For example, perhaps not many Americans die from terrorist attacks; however, many Americans do not feel free to travel to some parts of the world. The lack of freedom is significant qualitatively; our quality of life (perceived freedom) is affected adversely by international terrorism.

Whereas qualitative significance refers to the harm to our value system, quantitative significance refers to quantity or numbers. Again, think of the root word here: *quantity.* Usually, quantitative significance looks for the amount of financial loss, human injury, and human death.

Let's look at the policy topic, "Resolved: That the Federal Government should increase the number of shelters for victims of domestic violence." In order to help justify that topic you would have to prove that domestic violence is significant enough to demand an increased number of shelters. If you could show that millions of people are seriously injured and thousands are killed during incidents of domestic violence, you would go a long way toward proving quantitative significance. Of course, since the topic refers to "increasing the number of shelters," among other things, you also would have to prove that there is not nearly enough shelter space to fill the need. You might also have to prove that, because there is inadequate shelter space, a significant number of family members are forced to remain in a dangerous environment. Furthermore, you would have to show causality in terms of the number of family members that suffer worse fates because of the lack of refuge. The bottom line is that your critic needs to know that additional shelter space is needed.

Qualitative and quantitative justification may be used separately or together. Qualitative alone, however, is sometimes looked upon as a weak justification. You may need to justify to your critic the sole use of qualitative significance. Quantitative harm alone is hardly ever a problem. The best approach, of course, is to use both qualitative and quantitative.

Let's look at the policy topic, "Resolved: The Federal Government should ban industrial practices that are harmful to the ozone layer." An affirmative advocate could argue the quantitative harm of the number of injurious and fatal skin cancer cases due to increased ozone depletion. The Environmental Protection Agency (EPA) estimates that a one percent drop in ozone causes an additional 43,000 cases of skin cancer annually in the United States. EPA's worst case scenario involves an additional 261 million skin cancer cases and 5.6 million cancer deaths during the next 80 years. Darrel Rigel, Associate Professor of Dermatology at New York University, says "that would mean that virtually everyone in the country would get skin cancer. And it wouldn't be from lying out in the sun. The radiation would be so intense it wouldn't take much more than walking around in the street." Obviously, the Figures from the EPA and the interpretation of those Figures by Rigel paint a pretty ominous picture of the quantitative effects of ozone depletion. An advocate using these statistics would prove easily that something needs to be done. Additionally, an affirmative advocate also could argue the qualitative results of ozone depletion: People would not be as free to spend as much time out of doors. Among other things the freedom to enjoy nature would be impeded. Of course, with the above topic you would have to indict "industrial practices." However, if it were possible to find evidence indicating that US industrial practices cause localized decreases in ozone totaling at least one percent, you would have a fairly compelling link.

Blame

Blame is the second stock issue. This requirement asks the debaters to prove that the status quo is inherently responsible for the present harms or lack of advantages. Inherency can mean, at the simplest level, the causes of the condition. A discussion of blame assumes that if the status quo is not inherently flawed there is then no reason for major changes. The affirmative in a policy debate is required to show that the status quo is inherently flawed, thus justifying a major change of policy.

There are two components that make up the blame stock issue. They are cause and permanence. The first requirement is that the affirmative isolate the cause of the undesirable situation (what is causing the problem in the status quo, preventing the status quo from obtaining an advantage or preventing the status quo from achieving a desired goal). Without knowing the cause, it is very difficult for any policy advocate to have confidence that their policy will solve the undesirable situation. If you had knee problems but the doctors were unable to isolate the cause of those problems, it would be very difficult for the doctors to prescribe, with any degree of confidence, a particular medical procedure to cure your ailment. At most they might be able to treat the symptoms by giving you pain relief pills, but to cure your knee they would need to know the cause.

Take the example of health care inequality. Why is it that people who live in the inner cities generally lack the same degree of health care attention compared to those who live in the suburbs? There may be various causes of this situation. For example, the high cost of medical treatment; the general lack of medical benefits offered by inner city employers compared to benefits offered by larger corporations; lack of qualified health care professionals willing to work in the inner cities because they believe they can make a more lucrative (and perhaps safer) living practicing in the suburbs; parents unwilling to spend their limited funds on a trip to the doctor when the condition does not seem serious, inner city tax revenues being too limited to afford the latest hospital equipment.

Along with isolating the cause of the problem, blame also requires that the affirmative demonstrate that the cause of the problem (and hence the problem itself) is an inherent feature of the status quo. That is, the undesirable condition cannot simply be a temporary situation, but one that is a recurring and persistent feature of the status quo. Let's extend the medical analogy. If the cause of your knee pain is simply a sprain, then no action is likely to be required. The cause of the pain is not a permanent feature. Given a few days, the knee will fix itself and you will soon be as good as new. However, if the cause of your knee problem is that you tore your anterior-cruciate ligament (like one of your authors did), then the cause of your knee problems is of a permanent nature. The torn ligament will not fix itself. An action, in this case surgery, is required.

In the health care example the affirmative would have to show that the present causes of health care inequalities are inherent in the status quo. That is, the causes will not simply stop existing. The expense of medical attention will not suddenly drop. Employers will not in the foreseeable future be able to offer adequate medical benefits to their employees. Individuals will not suddenly be able to afford to purchase health coverage from private insurance providers. Health care professionals will not suddenly become altruistic and start flooding to the inner cities to set up their practices. The budget of hospitals located in the inner cities will not suddenly increase. Parents' attitudes of not spending their limited resources on non-severe medical situations will not suddenly change.

Some debate theorists have argued that because it is often very difficult, if not impossible, for policy advocates to isolate and/or treat the root cause of a problem, then policy advocates should not be required to either identify the root cause nor offer polices that eliminate the root cause. Instead, they argue that polices that merely treat the symptoms should be acceptable. Certainly, even if doctors were unable to diagnose and/or fix the cause of your knee pain, taking the pain relief medication might still be a wise course of action.

Take the example of health care inequalities. It is certainly easier to propose actions to address the symptoms of health care inequalities (offering free vaccines at inner city schools, setting up free clinics, providing incentives for medical professionals to practice in the inner cities, offering government subsided health insurance, giving employers tax advantages for offering health benefits, etc.) than it is to address the root cause (fixing the economic plight of inner cities).

In policy debate, the concept of inherency has been grouped into three classifications: structural, attitudinal, and existential. The three types of inherency are given in the order of affirmative preference. An affirmative should always try to establish structural inherency. If it can't the affirmative can try for attitudinal inherency. Existential inherency should be reserved for the situation in which neither structural nor attitudinal inherency is present.

Structural inherency, as its name suggests, deals with the structure of existing conditions that govern society. Structural inherency can be thought of as the incapability of the status quo to solve the harm or gain the advantages without the adoption of the resolution. Structural inherency may come in the form of a barrier or a gap. A *structural barrier* is the existence of a policy that causes or allows an undesirable condition to exist. For example, anti-abortion advocates often point to the Supreme Court decision in Roe vs. Wade as the structural reason why abortion exists. For abortion to be abolished, Roe vs. Wade must either be overturned or substantially modified. A *structural gap* refers to the absence of a policy which causes or allows an undesirable condition to exist. For example, many political reformers argue that the lack of term limits is responsible for the present state of political corruption. As long as politicians are allowed to serve numerous terms in office, it is argued, they will be more concerned about pleasing special interest groups than serving their constitutes. The institution of term limits is viewed as the solution to this condition.

Attitudinal inherency refers to the notion that people's attitudes are responsible for many of the undesirable conditions that exist. Attitudinal inherency can be thought of as the unwillingness of the status quo agents to take action to solve the harm or gain an advantage even though no structural impediment exists. For example, one may argue that an inherent reason why women are not hired to coach National Basketball Association teams is perhaps because of the chauvinistic attitudes of the NBA owners and players.

Existential inherency is an undetermined condition in the status quo, the existence of which is inferred from the presence of the undesirable condition. In some situations it might be argued that a harmful condition exists but the cause is not known. The problem with existential inherency should be obvious. If the cause of the problem cannot be identified it is difficult to have confidence that the proposed solution will fix it.

Cure

Cure is the third stock issue. It is here that the advocate lays out the plan and shows that it can work. A plan is a concrete, specific proposal that serves as an example of the proposition. The elements of a plan usually consist of two required planks (the agency and mandates,) and three conditional planks (enforcement mechanism, funding, and an addendum). Figure 15.1 shows an example of a basic plan. Affirmative advocates may create virtually any plan that they see fit.

The reason that the affirmative has such latitude is due to academic debate's notion of fiat. Fiat in this context is not a small car that breaks down all the time. Rather, **fiat** is the power to put something hypothetically into existence for the purposes of debating its worth. In other words, the debater does not have to prove that something *will* happen only that something *should* happen. Fiat power precludes the policy debater from having to prove that congress and the president will support the affirmative plan. Fiat power makes the pragmatics of politics as such irrelevant to the academic debate. The debaters and the judge take on governmental power to implement whichever plan they see fit. The focus of the debate should be on the merits of a given plan, not on whether some brain-dead politician will vote for it. You may fiat the existence of a new administrating body, a new law, a new penalty, a new branch of the military, or a new branch of the government. You must still prove the worth of those items, but you need not prove that the items *will* become part of the status quo. There are however limitations to fiat power. You may not fiat an attitude change, and you may not fiat impossible technologies. For example, you may not fiat into existence a device that will render all radioactive materials inert. Fiat power is limited to the political nature of policy adoption. Fiat power simply allows the debaters to become legislators for the day. Whatever is within the power of the government is also within the purview of the debate round. Fiat power, however, does *not* include the ability to go beyond present human capabilities. Fiat power will be discussed in more detail later in the chapter.

All policy propositions call for a change to take place. As a result, the affirmative must specify the **agency** that will administer the program. That agency could be an existing agency, such as the Environmental Protection Agency, or it could be a new agency created for the purposes of the debate. In the **mandates** the affirmative must state what action is to be taken, for example lowering the levels of allowable dioxin emissions by 50%. These two planks are also critical as they determine if the affirmative is topical. If the plan utilizes a different agency than that specified by the resolution and/or implements different mandates than those specified by the resolution, the affirmative plan is deemed to fall outside the boundaries of the resolution.

To be topical, the plan must stick to the words of the resolution. Think of the resolution as a playing field. If you go outside the boundaries of the field your play does not count. If you stay within the field, then you may win or score a point. The same is true with debating. If the affirmative stay within the topic, only then can they win. Going outside of the topic may not only cause the affirmative plan not to count, but it also may result in them losing the debate altogether. Let's consider the topic "Resolved: That the US government should provide economic aid to non-democratic nations." If an affirmative team offered a plan for Canada to give military aid to England, the negative could claim that the affirmative team is not topical on three points. The affirmative team would be non-topical because, first, the resolution said *US*, not *Canada*; second, the resolution said *economic,* not *military* aid; and third, the resolution said *non-democratic nation,* not *democratic* nation. If the negative team advanced a topicality argument on one, two, or all three of these issues, the affirmative should lose the debate. The affirmative must be very careful to advance only topical plans. The negative should pay close attention to the affirmative plan and stand ready to offer a topicality argument if they believe the affirmative has strayed beyond the scope of the resolution.

Along with the agency and mandate planks, many, but not all, policies will require either an enforcement, funding, or addendum plank. The **enforcement mechanism** is usually a penalty for non-compliance with the mandates. For example, an enforcement mechanism to compel companies to comply with lower dioxin admission levels could be to hire more inspectors, have more inspections, and to assess significant financial fines to those companies found to be in violation. The *funding* plank describes how the policy is going to be paid for if it costs money. For example, where is the government going to get the money to pay for the increased number of inspectors? Is the affirmative going to increase taxes, cut existing programs or use some other procedure? The *addendum* plank allows the affirmative to specify any miscellaneous procedures that might be necessary to carry out the policy. For example, the affirmative might specify that the plan does not apply to the military.

Besides being topical, the affirmative plan must also be workable. **Workability** means that the technical aspects of the plan must be able to operate as intended, without any glitches. For plans advocating a new law, often workability issues deal with enforcement. For example, workability problems arise in an affirmative plan mandating that sexist people change their attitudes about women. There would be no way to force people to alter sexist views; therefore such a plan would not be workable. However, it might be possible to force people not to engage in sexist behavior. The plan in Figure 15.1 may fall victim to a negative workability argument. The enforcement section mentions criminal prosecution. The negative could argue that most lumber companies are corporations. The negative also might be able to find evidence that says that it is nearly impossible to apply a criminal prosecution to a corporation. If that were so, the affirmative plan may be unenforceable, thus unworkable.

Plank One: Agency: The Department of the Interior will oversee the project. The department will create an agency to insure the mandates are carried out. The agency will be entitled The Old-Growth Preservation Commission.

Plank Two: Mandates: A. The states will set aside all old growth timber. B. All old-growth timber harvesting will be prohibited. C. The federal government will supply corporations with subsidies for the set-aside land. The subsidy program will be similar to the farm subsidy program, but the payments will take place over a twenty-year period.

Plank Three: Enforcement: A. Under this plan, harvesting of old growth timber will be felonious. Criminal prosecution will result in the minimum sentence of 6 months in jail and a $10,000.00 fine. B. States that fail to comply with the mandates may lose eligibility in any of a number of federally-funded programs.

Plank Four: Funding: Funding will come from federal and state general revenues.

Plank Five: Addenda: Exemptions will include the following: A. Removal of trees when necessary for fire protection or control. B. Removal of trees as a part of general forest management. C. Applications for other exemptions may be filed with the commission for review. All exemptions must entail a compelling state interest.

FIGURE 15.1

Policy Debate's Version of a Plan

As in all stock issues, the negative only need neutralize one to win the debate. If the negative wins either the topicality or workability argument, the negative should win the debate. The affirmative must win this and all other stock issues. Recall the medical analogy; if a patient were given an appendectomy for cancer of the larynx that would certainly not help the cancerous condition. The cancerous larynx would still be in the body. The operation to remove the appendix would be unhelpful and, in debate terms, unworkable and non-topical.

Cost

Cost is the fourth stock issue. In this section the affirmative must show that their plan will solve the undesired condition as outlined in the motive section without accruing any significant disadvantages. There are thus two components to the cost issue which the affirmative must meet. These two components are referred to as solvency and advantages. Likewise, the negative could attempt to demonstrate that either or both of these requirements have not been met.

This term is often misunderstood by beginning debaters. Novice debaters tend to think of *cost* as dealing with how much the plan will cost monetarily to implement and how it will be funded. This is not the case. As we just saw, funding for the plan falls under the stock issue of *cure*. Cost in this context refers to the detrimental consequences of the plan. For example, the cost of undergoing radiation treatment for cancer might be loss of hair and nausea. The patient would have to determine if these harmful side effects (costs) are outweighed by the benefits of the treatment. In ones personal life the *cost* of cheating on one's spouse may mean having that person divorce you. Do not confuse cost with funding.

Solvency is the requirement to prove that the affirmative plan can correct the current undesirable situation. Referring to the medical examples discussed in the motive section, if a proposed surgery would not solve the ailment then the surgery would not be justified.

Solvency can also be quantified. For instance, say an affirmative team was to argue that the US should fund family counseling programs for domestic violence cases. And say the affirmative were able to locate evidence that indicates that in 80% to 90% of the cases, counseling prevents further abuse. The 80-to-90-percent evidence thus provides the quantification for the solvency requirement. Eight out of ten violent family members never resort to violence again. Through implementation of the plan, the affirmative would prove that a significant part of the problem could be solved. Of course, much of the domestic violence will continue. It is not the job of the affirmative to prove 100% solvency. The affirmative need only prove that a significant part of the problem will be corrected.

Sometimes it is not possible to provide quantification. In that case, testimony evidence, cause-effect evidence, or even analogy evidence can help to prove solvency. An affirmative advocate might be able to locate a quotation from an expert that attests to the validity of a similar plan. Similarly, one might be able to find cause-effect evidence. The *cause* would be your plan; the *effect* would be the correction of ills. Finally, analogy evidence is a great way to provide solvency. If you could prove that somewhere else in the world a similar plan solved related problems, you could go a long way toward proving your plan solvent.

It is not enough, however, for the affirmative to simply show that the plan will solve the undesirable condition. The affirmative must also be able to demonstrate that no major disadvantages will occur as well. If an operation would better one's vision but at the cost of permanent severe headaches, then one would probably not opt for the surgery. This second component of the cost issue is referred to as the **advantage section.** What advantages or disadvantages will result from plan implementation? The affirmative debaters themselves are not required to list the disadvantages; however, when the negative argues disadvantages, the affirmative must be able to prove that the advantages from the plan outweigh the disadvantages. If the negative can convince the critic that the disadvantages to the plan outweigh the advantages to the plan, then the negative should win the debate.

In addition, the advantages have to be accrued directly and uniquely from the topical aspects of the plan. They cannot be derived from anything else. For example, assume the following resolution "Resolved: That the US should significantly lower the levels of dioxin emissions." If the affirmative is able to prove that cancer rates will decrease if less dioxins are emitted, this advantage would be legitimate since it stems directly from the topical requirements of the resolution. However, suppose the affirmative had a plank in their plan that stated that the money collected from fines levied on companies not complying with lower dioxin levels will be used to feed starving children. The advantage of feeding starving children would be illegitimate as it does not stem directly from topical planks of the resolution.

POLICY CASE STRATEGIES

With an understanding of the stock issues, it is now possible to discuss affirmative case strategies. There are four primary strategies that the affirmative may utilize depending upon the nature of the resolution: the Needs Analysis Case, the Comparative Advantage Case, the Goals Case, and the Alternative Justification Case. Regardless of the type of case selected, the affirmative advocates in a policy debate must present a *prima-facie* case in the first affirmative speech. The case must include reference to the stock issues of motive, blame, cure, and cost.

Needs Analysis Case

The first type of case is known as the Needs Analysis case. Utilizing this strategy, the affirmative argues that there are significant harms inherent in the status quo which can best be solved by implementing the affirmative's plan. Harms are commonly thought of as present harms or potential harms. A present harm is an existing problem: such as, *presently the economy is bad.* A potential harm is a future problem: such as, *the economy is going to become bad.* Of course a harm can be both a present and potential harm at the same time: *the economy is bad now and is going to get even worse in the future.*

Once the brainstorming is done, debaters would need to research each point to see whether there exists any evidence of support. Each of the sub-points in the first, second, and fourth contention would require documentation. The third major argument, the plan, may or may not be evidenced. Because the affirmative has fiat power, the plan need not be documented. Notice how each major argument in Figure 15.2 concerns itself with a stock issue. Contention one deals with the ill stock issue. Contention two addresses blame or inherency. The third major argument involves an explanation of the affirmative's plan (cure). And the fourth major argument addresses the cost stock issue: solvency, advantages vs. disadvantages. Please review the following brainstormed policy case:

Brainstormed Policy Debate Outline

Resolved: that the federal government should significantly increase its commitment to education.

I. **Poor education causes economic and social problems (ill).**
    A. Schools are not retaining students.
        1. Adolescents who drop out early become a burden on society at a significant cost annually (quantitative harm).
        2. Adolescents who drop out early are more likely to become involved in criminal behavior.
        3. Crime by dropouts results in significant harm (monetary loss, injury, and murder) to other members of society (quantitative harm).
    B. Schools are not training the needed workforce.
        1. Increased vocational training is needed to keep our economy afloat.
        2. The lack of vocational training may be a key contributing factor to a future recession.
        3. Quality of life will be adversely affected in a recession (qualitative harm).

II. **The problem is inherent (blame).**
    A. Schools are not equipped to retain students.
        1. There are inadequate resources to retain students (structural).
        2. School personnel do not care about the dropout problem (attitudinal).
    B. Schools are not equipped to offer vocational education.
        1. By the end of the next two decades, 80% of the jobs will require at least two years of advanced training.
        2. Schools simply are not prepared to handle the sheer numbers of people who will require vocational training (structural).

III. <u>Plan (Cure).</u>

    Plank One, <u>Agency</u>: The program will be run through the Dept. of Education. A Retention and Voc. Ed. Commission will be established.

    Plank Two, <u>Mandates</u>: The program will mandate retention and vocational educational programs for K-14. Goals will be established as follows: one, half of those now dropping out will be retained; two, the number of students currently in vocational programs will be doubled.

    Plank Three, <u>Enforcement</u>: Schools who fail to reach established goals may be denied further funding.

    Plank Four, <u>Funding</u>: The program will be funded by a national lottery.

IV. <u>Advantages (Cost).</u>

    A. Higher retention of students reduces crime (solvency).

    B. More vocational education will enhance the economy (advantage).

Comparative Advantage Case

The second strategy is known as the **comparative advantage case.** Advantages might be thought of as "potential goods." Utilizing this strategy the advocate maintains that adoption of the resolution is necessary to gain a desirable condition which the status quo does not have. For example, the advocate might argue that adoption of the policy would make a decent economy even better.

A comparative advantage case uses the following structure: first, show that the advantages do not now exist; second, show that the status quo is inherently incapable of achieving the desired advantages; third, offer a plan; and fourth, show that your plan will result in the comparative advantages. To organize such a case, you would follow a similar format as the one detailed above. However, instead of a contention dealing with harms you would develop a contention explaining that the desired advantages do not now exist. The second contention would still concern itself with inherency, but it is inherency of a slightly different kind. This type of inherency deals primarily with proving that the status quo is inherently incapable of producing such desirable effects. The third major argument, the plan, follows the same format as do all plans. And finally, the fourth major argument, cost, is also the same as the traditional case, except there is usually no reference to solvency. You simply list the comparative advantages.

Whether one thinks of problems and plans as involving harms or advantages is largely a matter of perspective. It can equally well be said that to solve a harmful condition is to gain an advantage or that not gaining an advantage is harmful. If someone suffers from an awful disease, is curing the disease an advantage to be gained or is eliminating the pain a harm to be solved? The answer seems to be that it may be thought of either way, but sometimes it is easier to think one way and sometimes it is easier to think the other way. Figure 15.2 shows a continuum with harm at one end and advantages at the other. A needs analysis case eliminates a *harmful* condition to

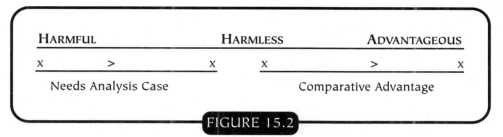

FIGURE 15.2

Harm-Advantage Continuum

reach a *harmless* or slightly advantageous position on the continuum. A comparative advantage case starts at the *harmless* part of the continuum and moves society to an extremely *advantageous* position.

The Goals Case

The goals case is a third option in arguing a policy resolution. The goals case is very similar to the definitions-criteria-application format of non-policy debate. In fact, the goals case is also called the criterion-satisfaction case. Usually, this type of case follows a four step process similar to the comparative advantage. The first step of the goals case is to outline a goal of the status quo. To do that, you could quote a governmental official, such as the current US President. Perhaps the President has set goals for an area of your topic in which you have an interest. You would need to locate an official government document outlining that goal, or you could find a goal statement issued by the President or the White-House staff. Additional data in contention one could support the worth of such a goal. Perhaps the goal is to land a human on planet Mars. Along with the official or semi-official acknowledgment of such a goal, you would need to prove to your critic why such a space mission is needed. In the second contention, you must show why the goal cannot now be achieved. Again, this is inherency in a slightly different form; you argue that the status quo is incapable of achieving the stated goal. The third major argument is, as usual, the plan. The fourth major argument lists the key advantages from adopting the plan and fulfilling the goal.

The Alternative Justification Case

Alternative justification is another variation of a policy case. Alternative justification involves the affirmative offering more than one case. The theory is that if the affirmative wins but one of the cases, the affirmative should win the debate. This is different from the stock issue analysis discussed at the beginning of this chapter. Essentially, if the affirmative wins one of its cases, it *has* won all of the stock issues;

albeit, only one complete version. The affirmative may also offer alternative plans for a single case. In other words, major arguments one (motive), two (blame), and four (advantage) would remain the same. Alternative plans would be offered to complement the case. The same theory holds true for the alternative plans. The affirmative only needs to justify one of the plans to win the debate.

NEGATIVE STRATEGIES

Having discussed affirmative strategies, it is time to examine how the negative can argue against policy topics. First negatives in a policy debate *traditionally* introduce topicality arguments, minor repairs, counterplans, and disadvantages. Second negatives usually extend on these arguments as well as refuting the motive and blame. Workability and solvency issues are also argued by the second negative speaker.

There are four strategies that the negative can call upon. They are defense of the present system, minor repair of the present system, counterplan, and reliance on presumption. In addition, the negative may wish to advance a disadvantage to the affirmative policy or claim that the affirmative's plan is not topical.

Defense of the Present System

The negative uses the strategy of *defense of the present system* when they maintain that the status quo is good and that no changes are required. When using this strategy the negative should be able to identify the essential features of the status quo policy and be able to illustrate their importance and value. All policies have two components. The first is the plan's underlying goal and the second is the plan's administration. It is possible to agree with the goal of a policy while disagreeing with how that goal is being carried out. When advocates use a *defense of the present system* strategy they defend both the status quo goals and the administration.

For example, many people under the age of 21 argue that the drinking age should be lowered to 18. They maintain that it is inconsistent to allow 18-year-olds to vote in elections and fight in wars, yet not be able to drink. Opponents maintain that the goal of the present drinking age is to protect lives and that protecting lives transcends the loss of any social liberties of which young adults may feel deprived. Opponents then use evidence to demonstrate that the status quo's present policy of requiring an individual to be 21 before they can legally drink does in fact save many lives which otherwise would be lost. It is thus maintained that the 21-year drinking age policy is extremely desirable and that to enact legislation to lower the drinking age would be harmful.

The defense of the present system strategy is psychologically the most appealing position that the negative can adopt. Using this strategy the negative focuses on explaining to the critic the benefits of the present policy rather than pointing out flaws in the affirmative proposal. From this perspective, the affirmative is completely wrong. The status quo is not something to change, but it is something to maintain.

Minor Repair

In our previous discussion of the defense of the present system strategy, we noted that there are two elements to any policy. The first is the goal of the policy, and the second is the administration of the policy. One can agree on the goal of a policy, but believe that the administration of the policy is flawed. That is essentially the strategy employed with a minor repair strategy. The negative maintains that no new structural changes are required. They contend that by better administration (usually by better education, funding or enforcement) of present policies, the undesirable situation articulated by the affirmative can be solved.

On the gun control topic, affirmative teams attempted to prove that the status quo was dangerously flawed. They argued that thousands of people needlessly die from accidents and crimes. A lack of tough legislation and a misinterpretation of the US Constitution contributed to much of the problem. On the surface, the harms seemed inherent.

However, many negative teams countered with a minor repair of education and enforcement. The negative advocates argued that another gun control regulation was not needed. Negatives maintained that there were already numerous gun control laws on the books and that simple enforcement of those laws as well as education about the laws would solve the affirmative's claimed harms. They argued that education would prevent accidents, and they argued that vigorous enforcement of existing laws would keep convicted criminals from getting guns. Education, in this context, was a minor repair because it did not alter the structure of existing institutions; it simply informed people about them. An educational campaign would merely inform people how to use a gun. Enforcement of existing laws was a minor repair because it also did not significantly change the status quo. In fact, enforcement was actually an endorsement of the status quo; what enforcement did, according to the negative advocates, was make the status quo regulations work.

Recently, many religious organizations have argued for a Constitutional amendment allowing prayer in public schools. They maintain that Supreme Court decisions banning school prayers have created an environment that infringes on students' religious rights. They cite examples where teachers and administrators have told students they cannot even say grace before lunch. Opponents to the Constitutional amendment argue that the harms cited by the affirmative are not inherent in the present policies. They point out that the Supreme Court rulings only prohibit mandatory, state sponsored prayers. They point out that present laws and court rulings already give students the right to engage in personal prayers during the school day (before lunch, before a test, etc.). They maintain that if teachers and administrators are unaware of these laws and are under the false impression that all prayers in public schools—public and private—are unconstitutional, then all that is needed is to educate school officials of the present laws allowing private prayers and to enforce those policies if necessary. As a result, no new structural change, in this case a Constitutional amendment, is required to solve the alleged harms.

Let's consider the following analogy. You're trying to decide what to do about your car. It does not run. You ask yourself, "Do I need a new engine?" The implied resolution is "Resolved: That I should get a new engine for my car." In order for you to adopt the resolution, you will need to prove to yourself that the major, costly repair is justified. If you have cracked the engine's block, thrown a rod, and frozen your engine from running it with no oil, your engine would have the structural flaws needed to justify getting a new one. The current engine is useless. No mechanic in town could repair a cracked block. However, if the problem is from simple neglect of the recommended service of your car, and if the car could be fixed by simple maintenance (routine oil changes, new spark plugs, etc.) then purchasing a new engine would not be needed. By simply adhering to the manufacturers suggested service policy, already part of the status quo, your engine problems would be solved.

Counterplan

A third strategy open to the negative is to argue a *counterplan*. Using this strategy the negative maintains that a better solution than that offered by the affirmative exists that should be utilized to solve any existing problems. As such, the negative offers a different policy that is completely independent of both the affirmative policy and the status quo. The counterplan is perhaps the most complicated strategy open to the negative but if utilized correctly can be quite effective. To utilize the counterplan strategy effectively the negative advocate should understand the requirements of the counterplan as well as the different types of counterplans.

Requirements of the Counterplan

Let's start with the requirements of the counterplan. There are four traditional standards that a counterplan must meet before it can be adopted. Counterplans must meet the affirmative motive for change, be non-topical, be competitive with the affirmative proposal and be preferable to the affirmative policy.

The first requirement of the counterplan is that it must meet the affirmative's motive for change. Consider the following resolution "Resolved: that the US should increase its military support to NATO." Suppose that the affirmative argues that the former Soviet Union is very unstable and that a military *coup d'etat* is likely. The affirmative team in this scenario also argues that such a coup would threaten the post-Cold-War peace, and that present NATO forces have been downsized so much that they are incapable of handling such a threat effectively. Thus they claim that the increased military build up of NATO is crucial to handle any such threat. Using the counterplan strategy, the negative might concede that such a military coup is likely.

The negative would disagree however that the way to solve the problem is to have the US build up NATO. Instead, the negative would offer an alternative plan. Whatever this plan is, it must alleviate the threat pointed out by the affirmative. This should make logical sense. If the negative counterplan did not deal with the post *coup d'etat* threat, then the affirmative policy that addresses the threat would need to be adopted.

When presenting a counterplan the negative must also make sure that its proposal is *not* topical. If it were topical, the affirmative could claim it as its own. Using the same NATO resolution, assume that the affirmative argues that the US should give more naval ships to NATO. The negative cannot offer a counterplan of giving more missiles to NATO. This is because missiles are also a form of military support. If the negative were to offer such a counterplan, the affirmative could simply grant the counterplan as it validates the resolution under consideration. The negative could offer a counterplan of giving military support to a non-NATO country, or reducing the current levels of military support to NATO. These two counterplans would clearly be non-topical.

The third requirement of this strategy requires the counterplan to be **competitive** with the affirmative proposal (that is, the critic must be forced to choose between the affirmative policy and the negative counterplan). One test for competitiveness is whether the counterplan is **mutually exclusive** with the affirmative's suggested policy. Mutual exclusivity means that it is impossible for both the affirmative plan and the negative counterplan to be adopted. Using the above example, if the affirmative is arguing to increase military aid to NATO and the negative offers a counterplan to decrease military support to NATO, the counterplan would clearly be mutually exclusive and thus competitive. Logically, it is impossible to increase military support to NATO while decreasing military support to NATO.

A second way to show competitiveness is to demonstrate net benefits. Here the negative maintains that while both plans could logically be done, it is "net" beneficial to do only the counterplan. For example, suppose the negative offers a counterplan of giving increased military support to China instead of to NATO. The negative contends that a better way to contain any Soviet military aggression is to build up China and make the Soviet military face a two-front war. In theory, both the affirmative and negative plans could be done (and thus there is no reason not to vote for the resolution). However, the negative might contend that while both could be done it is desirable to do only one. It might be argued for instance that it would cost too much money and be too large of a drain on the economy to build up both NATO and China and that just building up China is adequate to contain any soviet threat if a military coup were to take place.

Assume that the negative presents a counterplan and is able to demonstrate that it solves the affirmative harm, is not topical, and is competitive. Would this be reason to reject the affirmative policy for the negative counterplan? The answer is no. This is because the last requirement of preference has not yet been demonstrated. The negative must also demonstrate that their plan is more advantageous than the affirmative policy. Let's assume that the negative offers a counterplan of providing military support to China in lieu of building up NATO and let's suppose that both plans decrease the Soviet military threat. If both plans work equally well then there is no reason to vote against the affirmative. However, suppose that the negative plan more effectively contained the threat, and/or reduced the chances of the US being dragged in by treaty to a war. Then an advantage for opting for the counterplan is established.

Types of Counterplans

There are different ways which the negative can utilize the counterplan strategy. The first is known as the traditional counterplan. When using this option the negative agrees with the affirmative on the motive and blame stock issues. That is, the negative concedes that there is a significant problem and also concedes that the status quo is inherently incapable of fixing the problem. However, the negative maintains that the affirmative plan is not the correct course of action that should be followed to solve the problems and offers instead their own policy.

The second option is to argue a **conditional counterplan.** With this option the negative does not concede the motive and blame issues. The negative will first contest the motive and/or blame stock issues. The negative will then argue that even *if* a problem were present and inherent the affirmative's plan would not be a good way of solving the problem. The negative then offers their counterplan as a way to solve this harm. In other words, the negative is arguing that the harms do not exist, but even if they did exist the counterplan would be a superior course of action to take. When using this option the negative should make it very clear that they are arguing conditionally or else they will appear to be contradicting themselves. After all, offering a counterplan to solve a nonexistent harm arms the affirmative with too much ammunition. Simply clarifying the conditional nature of the counterplan allows the negative to offer what seem to be contradictory positions.

A third counterplan option is known as the **alternative justification counterplan** strategy. As its name suggests this is similar to the alternative justification affirmative strategy. When using this strategy, the negative offers more than one counterplan and argues that any one of them is preferable to the affirmative policy. These counterplans may be either traditional or conditional in nature.

Fourth, the negative may choose to use the **studies counterplan** strategy. Using this strategy, the negative team maintains that not enough information is known about the problem and that the best course of action is simply to study it more in-depth and then decide at a later time what, if anything should be done.

Finally, the negative might decide to argue what is known as a **utopian counterplan.** With this option, the negative maintains that the very fabric of society is inherently flawed and thus a complete societal restructuring is required. For instance, the negative might maintain that the existence of independent nation states is what is to blame for the alleged problems. The negative thus maintains that only through implementing a world government can the problems be solved. At first glance the utopian counterplan may seem to have very little application to the "real world." This is not necessarily so. The major social and political revolutions are grounded in the utopian view. For example, the Bolshevik Revolution that overthrew Czarist Russia during World War I was based on a utopian assumption. The Bolsheviks believed that capitalism was the root cause of societal harms. The only way to have a "good" society was to completely overthrow capitalism and implement a communistic system.

As is evident, the counterplan is a very complicated negative strategy and should be utilized only by the debater who has a clear understanding of all of its requirements. Remember however, that basically the negative is just saying, "We might agree that there is a problem, but we feel that there is a better solution than those provided for by the resolution and the affirmative team." In academic debate, counterplans are run in the 1NC.

Reliance on Presumption

The last negative strategy is the *reliance on presumption strategy*. When the negative uses this strategy they are simply trying to convince the critic that the affirmative has failed to prove their case. It is analogous to a defense lawyer who simply attempts to poke holes in the prosecution's case without putting on their own defense and then simply hopes that the jury will find that the prosecution has failed to meets its burden of proof.

Utilizing this strategy the affirmative points out possible flaws in the affirmative's analysis and evidence. The negative might question the recentness of some evidence, whether a source is biased or the methodology of a study. The negative simply contends each of the stock issues by arguing that while they may be true, they may not be true and the affirmative has simply failed to offer sufficient evidence to prove their claims. The negative offers no positive reason to vote against the resolution, but instead just questions whether the affirmative has given sufficient reasons to vote for it.

In essence, the negative debaters are simply relying on presumption. If they can cast enough doubt on the affirmative case, even if they don't prove that the affirmative is wrong, they in theory should win the debate. However, many critics may find this to be a weak strategy. Many critics prefer that the negative defend a specific policy. Also, many advocates confronted with a problem may decide that any action is better than no action. However, the negative advocates who meet an affirmative case for which they are unprepared may find this option to be their best and perhaps only strategy.

Disadvantages

An additional negative argument is the disadvantage. In a disadvantage, the negative team argues that the affirmative plan will produce harmful impacts. To win a debate based on the disadvantage, the negative must prove that the disadvantage links to the affirmative mandates, that it is unique, that it meets the brink test, that it has an appropriate time frame, and that it outweighs affirmative advantages.

The first requirement of the disadvantage is that it must **link** to affirmative mandates. If the affirmative debaters were to argue that the federal government should ban all nuclear power, for example, the negative team should argue the most obvious disadvantage: the lack of power will cause blackouts, increase power rates, and increase use of fossil fuel. An affirmative defense is to demonstrate there is no link to the mandates. However, with the nuclear power ban, it would be difficult to prove that those harms would not occur.

The second requirement of the disadvantage is that it must be **unique** to the affirmative mandates. Uniqueness means that the harms do not now exist but will exist if the affirmative plan is adopted. In the above example, the negative could try to claim a "greenhouse effect" impact off of the increased use of fossil fuels. However, the affirmative could respond by contending that the "greenhouse effect" is going to happen regardless of whether the affirmative plan is adopted. Perhaps there are other causes of the "greenhouse effect." Therefore, the greenhouse impact is not unique to the adoption of the affirmative case. In the end, a non-unique disadvantage is NOT a reason to reject the affirmative plan. After all, why condemn the affirmative debaters for something that is going to happen anyway? In other words, why condemn the affirmative for a non-unique disadvantage?

The third requirement for a disadvantage is that it must meet the **brink** test. In other words, does the affirmative plan "push us over the brink" to suffer whatever the disadvantage is? If so, then the affirmative plan is suspect and should be rejected. However, if the affirmative plan is not proven to push us into the disadvantage, then the negative has not provided enough proof for a brink. For example, suppose that in order for the greenhouse effect to take effect, fossil fuel emissions would have to increase by 12% over current levels. If the negative can demonstrate that the affirmative's plan will increase fossil fuel emissions by at least 12% then they will have met the brink test. Conversely, if the affirmative can prove that fossil fuel emissions will not increase by at least 12% then the disadvantage would be non-existent.

The fourth requirement for a disadvantage is that it must occur in an appropriate **time frame.** If it were proven that the greenhouse effect would occur but that it would not take place for one thousand years, then the affirmative can claim that the negative impacts are too futuristic to be considered. Many things could happen over the course of time that could make the disadvantage irrelevant. For instance, future technology may find a way to effectively combat the greenhouse effect.

The final requirement of the disadvantage is that the impact must **outweigh** the affirmative advantage. Let's assume the affirmative proves that storage of hazardous nuclear waste is inherently flawed, that leakage will occur, that people will be exposed to the waste, and that in the next fifty years approximately three hundred people will die as a result of this exposure. The affirmative thus claims as an advantage the saving of three hundred lives. Now let's assume the negative can demonstrate that the greenhouse effect will occur as a result of the affirmative's policy, in an appropriate amount of time, and that it will cause the death of millions of people. In this case the negative would have clearly shown that the disadvantage outweighs the advantage. A policy that causes the death of one million people while saving only three hundred people is clearly a flawed policy. However, if the greenhouse effect would only cause the death of one hundred people then the disadvantage would not outweigh the advantage.

Jurisdictional Arguments

Debates occur on two levels. There are the substantive issues and there are the jurisdictional (or procedural) issues. While substantive issues deal with those arguments that go to supporting or opposing the resolution, jurisdictional issues deal with creating the framework which decides what those substantive issues are. Jurisdictional issues are therefore *a priori,* that is, jurisdictional issues must be decided before the substantive issues can be decided. Think of a court of law. The prosecution may try to introduce evidence which the defense attorneys believe should be excluded because they believe it was obtained by the police during an illegal search. The defense would raise an objection, and the judge would then halt the trial and hear arguments by both the defense and the prosecution on the issue, usually at a sidebar or when the jury is not present. After hearing the arguments, the judge would then rule immediately whether to sustain or overrule the objection. If sustained, the evidence would be excluded, and the prosecution would have to continue with its case without introducing the evidence. If overturned, the prosecution would be allowed to introduce the evidence. This type of legal objection is similar to jurisdictional arguments made in academic debate.

In Parliamentary debate, the opposition may raise a point of order and then, like in a court of law, the speaker of the house would make an immediate decision and the debaters would then continue based on that ruling. Unfortunately, in cross examination style debate, the judge does not rule on the jurisdictional issue until the end of the debate. Therefore, the affirmative and negative must continue arguing the jurisdictional issues, as well as the substantive issues, throughout the debate. Following the debate, the judge would decide the jurisdictional issues first, and then move on to the substantive issues if required. There are three major jurisdictional issues that are normally raised in a policy debate. They are **topicality, effects topicality,** and **extra-topicality.**

As discussed earlier in this chapter, topicality assesses whether or not the affirmative plan adheres to the debate resolution. The plan agency and the mandates are the focus of the topicality argument. If the negative can demonstrate that either the affirmative's agency or mandates as designated in their plan are different than those specified by the resolution, then the affirmative should lose. For example, the debate resolution may read: "Resolved: that the federal government should require the timber industry to stop cutting old-growth forests." If the affirmative were to argue that the State of California should require PALCO not to cut the headwaters, the negative could point out that a federal government requirement was needed by the affirmative in order to be topical. Since the affirmative chose instead to use a state as its plan agent, the affirmative should lose the debate. Similarly, if the affirmative plan required the Department of the Interior to require PALCO to plant a tree for every old-growth tree that they cut down, the negative could again maintain that the affirmative plan was not topical. That is because while the resolution requires the halting of the cutting down of old-growth forests, the affirmative mandates allow for continued cutting of old-growth forests. It is important to remember that the negative need only show that either the affirmative's plan agency or mandates are outside the resolution in order to win the topicality argument.

Some affirmatives will try to argue that they are topical by effects. This is known as effects topicality and it is a misunderstanding of what it is to be topical. To be topical, the agency and the mandates must be directly related to the resolution. When someone says they are topical *by effect* they are saying, that, while their agency and/or mandates might not be topical, the effects of their plan end up nonetheless doing what the topic requests. For example, consider the resolution "Resolved: That the United States should substantially reduce its reliance on nuclear energy." The affirmative mandates are to significantly increase the safety regulations on nuclear power plants. They then argue that the effect of these tougher regulations is that some nuclear power plants won't be able to meet the new safety requirements and will be shut down. Thus they argue we will end up relying less on nuclear energy under their plan just as the resolution requires. This is a non-topical plan. Notice how the affirmative's mandate of "tougher safety regulations on nuclear power plants" is not a mandate to reduce our reliance on nuclear energy. It is possible those nuclear power plants could meet the new regulations or that safer plants could be built. In no way does the affirmative's mandate *require* the US to reduce its reliance on nuclear power. As such this is a non topical case even if it is true that some power plants would get shut down. It is an error to think that topicality is evaluated by the effects of the plan. Topicality is evaluated by the direct adherence of the mandates and the agency to the resolution.

The negative must also be on the alert for affirmatives who try to sneak extra-topical planks into their plan and then try and claim advantages off of them. Extra-topical planks are planks that go beyond the scope of the resolution and thus are non-topical. In other words, some affirmatives will have the required planks that make them topical, but then they will add extra non-topical planks as well. The only advantages the affirmative may claim are off of mandates that are required by the resolution. For instance, consider the resolution "Resolved: That California should abolish plea bargaining in all criminal cases." The affirmative mandates are to:

1) End plea bargaining, and
2) Segregate non-violent criminals from violent criminals.

They claim the advantage that by segregating the criminals in this manner, the non-violent criminals will not be corrupted by the violent criminals and will be able to be more effectively rehabilitated. In meeting this case, the negative should point out that while plank one is topical, plank two is extra-topical. Clearly, segregating non-violent from violent criminals, while perhaps being a good idea, is not germane to abolishing plea bargaining. California could do the second plank without ever adopting the resolution of ending plea bargaining. This advantage is therefore illegitimate. Remember, the affirmative can only claim advantages off of topical planks. In this case, the negative should force the affirmative to sever the second plank and its associated advantage.

Sometimes the affirmative will try to gain non-topical advantages by directing the spending of revenues created by their plan in an advantageous way. This would also be an extra-topical advantage. For instance, consider the resolution "Resolved: That the United States should reduce its military commitment to NATO." The affirmative claims that by reducing our military commitment to NATO we can then save five hundred million dollars annually. The affirmative then designates that this money will be spent on education. Better education they thus claim as an advantage to their plan. Clearly, the spending of this money on education (or anything) is extra-topical. The adoption of the resolution does not inherently cause better education, and thus better education would be an illegitimate advantage that the negative should force the affirmative to sever. This works both ways. The negative could not claim that the government will spend this extra revenue in a bad way, perhaps to start building an even larger nuclear arsenal, and then claim a disadvantage off of it. That is because, like the advantage, the disadvantage would be a result of an extra-topical plank and thus not inherent in the adoption of the resolution.

Likewise, the affirmative could not claim an advantage off of a funding plank that results in positive side effects. For example, assume the resolution "Resolved: that the United States should significantly increase its commitment to higher education." In order to pay for more colleges, better equipment and more faculty the affirmative claims that 10 less B-2 bombers will be built each year and the savings redirected to higher education. This certainly is a legitimate funding plank as the affirmative may raise the funds in any way it chooses. However, the affirmative could not claim as an advantage a decreased risk of war. That is because the decreased risk of war that comes with the elimination of 10 B-2 bombers is not directly related to the resolution. Clearly, the advantage could be gained by just eliminating the 10 B-2 bombers without adopting the resolution of having the US increase its commitment to higher education. However, in this case the negative could claim a disadvantage off of the funding plank. If the negative could prove that eliminating the B-2 bombers would actually reduce the United States' ability to maintain it presence in critical areas of the world, they could claim it as a disadvantage. Notice, in this case, the negative's disadvantage is an inherent effect of the affirmative's plan, not necessarily the resolution. While the resolution per say is not being rejected by this disadvantage, the proposed plan that would implement it is.

The Meaning of *Should* and
Fiat in Policy Debate

Just about all policy propositions contain the word *should*. The word should, in policy debate, suggests that the proposed action would be in the best interest of society. *Should* means *ought to,* but not necessarily *will.* This means that the resolution's agent should perform the proposed action. It does not mean the action will be performed, only logically that it ought to be performed. As a result, affirmatives do not have to prove that the resolution's agent would in fact pass the resolution, only that he or she should.

The fact that a proposed resolution may go against current public opinion or even violate a law or the Constitution is normally irrelevant in an academic policy debate. For example, most people are opposed to raising taxes, but this does not mean that raising taxes, if shown to be advantageous, should not be done. Presently most polls tend to show that the majority of people are opposed to extending marital rights to homosexual partners. This fact does not necessarily mean that such legislation should not be implemented. Additionally, if a proposed resolution would violate the law or the Constitution, it does not mean that it should not be adopted. At one time it was unconstitutional for women to vote. However, when advocates for change were able to demonstrate good reasons why women should be allowed to vote, the Constitution was amended via the passing of the 19th Amendment. Today, many people argue in favor of very restrictive gun control legislation. Many who oppose such legislation often claim that it violates the 2nd Amendment. This is irrelevant even if true. The question simply becomes, should the Constitution be amended to allow for more restrictive gun control measures than the 2nd Amendment currently allows?

Thus, in fact debate and in value debate, there is no affirmative "fiat power" to implement the resolution because there is no action to fiat. Fiat power is a fictional power given to the affirmative team to implement the resolution if it is decided that the resolution should be adopted. Fiat power allows the affirmative to dismiss "would" arguments and to focus the debate on "should" arguments. Fiat power is limited to the "should" question. The affirmative cannot fiat, for example, people's attitudes. The affirmative team might be able to fiat that taxes will be raised; it cannot, however, fiat that people will like it. The affirmative can fiat that a commission will be established to oversee some measure, but they cannot fiat that the individuals on the commission are incorruptible.

Negative Fiat Power

Fiat power has also been extended to the negative in policy debate. This is necessary to allow the negative to implement counterplans without worrying about the "would-should" debate described above. For example, take the resolution "Resolved: That the US should substantially increase its security assistance to Southeast Asia." The negative might argue a counterplan saying that the US should increase its assistance to NATO and not to Southeast Asia. This seems to be a reasonable extension of negative fiat power. Just as the affirmative should not be required to prove that Congress will increase security assistance to Southeast Asia, only that Congress should, the negative should not have to demonstrate that Congress will increase security assistance to NATO instead of Southeast Asia, only that it should.

There are however competing views as to the extent and range of negative fiat ability. The first view is "the division of ground" theory. According to this view the affirmative's ground for the debate is limited to that provided by the resolution. The negative is then provided all ground that falls outside the scope of the resolution. This theory thus allows the negative to fiat all agents and/or mandates not specified in the resolution.

For example, on the US increased security assistance to Southeast Asia topic, the affirmative fiat power would be limited by the resolution to include only the US government as its agent of action. The negative would have fiat over all other agents not mentioned in the resolution. The negative could contend that the United Nations, Japan, Australia or England should increase its security assistance to Southeast Asia instead of the US doing so. Simply put, this theory allows the negative to argue that agents other than those specified in the resolution should carry out the mandates dictated by the resolution.

Additionally, the "resolution as division of ground" theory also allows the negative to fiat mandates not specified in the resolution. The negative could have a counterplan that uses as its agency the US government but with non-topical mandates. For example, the negative might argue that the US should decrease its security assistance to Southeast Asia; or increase its security assistance to a non-Southeast Asian country; or increase its non-security assistance to Southeast Asia. In all of these counterplans the negative is fiating the resolution's agent (the US government) but using non-topical mandates.

There are objections to the "resolution as division of ground" theory as it applies to negative fiat power. First, some maintain that if the resolution really does divide fiat ground, then the negative should not have fiat power over the agent specified in the resolution. In the above example, the affirmative would have fiat power over the US government while the negative would have fiat power over all non-US agents (such as the United Nations or any foreign nation). Yet, current practice seems to give the negative fiat over both the resolution's agent as well as agents not specified in the resolution. Some maintain that this practice is not consistent with the "resolution as division of ground" theory, as the affirmative only has fiat power over the resolution's agent while the negative ends up with fiat power over both the resolution's agent and all other possible agents.

Second, some argue that the "resolution as division of ground" theory tends to divorce academic policy debate from real world policy debate. All public policy debates tend to bind both the affirmative and the negative to the same national boundaries. For example, assume that the Republican Congress was trying to advance legislation that would increase US security assistance to Southeast Asia and that the Democrats opposed this policy. In the real world the Democrats could not argue that England should increase its security assistance to Southeast Asia instead of the US and then claim that they will fiat England into doing so even if England has no inclination to take such action. Both parties have jurisdiction only over the US Government.

Finally, it is argued that giving the negative fiat power over all agencies not contained in the resolution can lead to extremely abusive and almost magical-like counterplans. For example, on the increased US security assistance to Southeast Asia topic, some affirmatives argued that the United States should increase its security assistance to the National League of Democracy (the democratically elected government of Burma which was in exile after being overthrown and replaced by a military dictatorship) to help overthrow the military government which allegedly was engaging in gross violations of human rights. Some negative teams advanced a counterplan calling for the Burmese military government to lay down their arms, endorse democratic reform and halt all human rights abuses. They claimed this was a superior plan to sending in US military troops, as the affirmative favored, because their plan would not lead to war and death. When affirmatives would object to this by arguing that the Burmese government would never take such action, the negative responded by saying "we don't have to prove the Burmese government WOULD do such a thing, only that they "SHOULD" do such a thing. We will fiat this action." Clearly, this is an abuse of negative fiat power which can occur when the negative, unlike the affirmative, is not required to have boundaries created by the resolution, placed on their fiat ability. Fiat power was established in academic debate so that the debate could focus on the "should" and not the "would" of the resolution. It was never intended to be a magic wand.

For the above reasons, another view of negative fiat power is that the negative, like the affirmative, is bound to the agent specified in the resolution. For example, assume the resolution "Resolved: that the US Navy should carry out bombing raids against Iraq." The negative could argue that the US Airforce, instead of the Navy, should carry out air-raids against Iraq. The negative would not be allowed however to argue that the United Nations or France should carry out bombings against Iraq instead of the United States. The negative would also not be allowed to fiat that Iraq will voluntarily halt from engaging in the actions which are prompting a US military response.

Negative fiat power is a very dynamic and ever changing paradigm in the academic debate community. Normally, critics will side with the team that best argues for its theoretical position in the debate. We believe it is important for debaters to understand the basic perspectives on negative fiat power so they will be prepared to defend or refute negative fiat positions when they are raised in a debate.

SUMMARY

This chapter discussed the parameters of policy debating. The stock issues of motive, blame, cure and cost were introduced. It was pointed out that the affirmative advocate must win all four of these stock issues while the negative need disprove just one of them. Next, four affirmative case strategies were then discussed. These included the needs analysis case, the comparative advantage case, the goals case, and the alternative justification case. The four negative counter strategies of defense of the present system, minor repair, counterplan and reliance on presumption were explained. The disadvantage and the topicality argument were also discussed. Finally, the meanings of the word *should* and the term *fiat* were explained as they pertain to policy debate.

ATTENDING A DEBATE TOURNAMENT

Some argumentation students are fortunate to have the opportunity to compete in an intramural or intercollegiate debate tournament. Many colleges have forensics teams that travel regularly to multi-school events, and even more colleges host annual or semiannual intramural debate tournaments. At intramural events, students in the various speech and argumentation classes from one campus compete against one another. Still, other students may have the chance to compete in an intercollegiate debate tournament attended by many different colleges and universities. This chapter will focus on how an intercollegiate debate tournament operates. However, intramural debate tournaments are very similar.

THINGS TO BRING

Before you head off to that first debate tournament, you will want to make sure you have the proper supplies. This is a relatively short list, but all of the items are very important.

1. **Flow paper.** You will need this to flow the arguments that you, your partner and the other team make. A flow is simply an outline of what is said during the debate. There are many different types of a paper you can use. Art pads are nice for the beginning debater because they are large and give you a lot of room to write on. They can be a little cumbersome however. Lots of students like to use 8.5" × 14" legal pads. These are less awkward than art pads and take up less room. They are also lined, which is helpful to some. Still others like to use 8.5" × 14" blank paper. It doesn't really matter what you use. Find a type of paper that works well for you.

2. **Different colored pens.** You will need these to flow the arguments with. Debaters tend to use different colors so they can color code the arguments. Usually, the affirmative arguments are flowed in black or blue ink and the negative arguments in red. Bring a few pens of each color in case you lose one or one breaks. Some students like to use the four-colors in one pen. This way they don't have to keep switching pens during the debate. Also, this makes it possible to flow each debater with a different color. Usually the first affirmative speaker is flowed in black, the first nega-

tive speaker in red, the second affirmative speaker in blue and the second negative speaker in green. It doesn't really matter though. The nice thing about this is that one can tell not only which side made an argument by just looking at the color of the ink, but actually which speaker made the argument.

3. **A stop watch.**   You will use this for timing your speeches and for keeping track of your preparation time. Most judges will have a stopwatch and keep track of speaking time and preparation time during the debate. However, many students like to time themselves, especially when they are speaking. It is not uncommon for judges to be so involved in listening to the debate and flowing the debate that they forget to give a time signal. Also, many judges will give only visual time signals, so if you are not looking at them at the exact time that they give the signal you will miss it. It is nice to have a stop watch with you so that as you are speaking you can monitor your time yourself. However, while you may choose to monitor your opponents' speaking time (which we recommend against) you should never say, "that is time," or some equivalent, just as time expires.

4. **A dictionary.**   This is especially important in Parliamentary style debate where a different topic is handed out for each round. You will obviously want a general reference dictionary (like *Websters*), but it also is a good idea to have specialized reference dictionaries that cover areas such as politics, the law, etc.

5. **A file system for your evidence.**   Don't bring in a stack of articles under your arm and expect to be able to find the exact article you need during the debate. You will need to have your articles at least semi organized before the debate. During the debate you don't have much preparation time, so you need to be able to find your information quickly.

6. **Post-it notes and post-it tape.**   The post-it notes are used to write notes on that can be stuck to your flow pad. The tape is used to pre-flow your affirmative case, as well as your pre-created negative arguments such as topicality arguments, counterplans, and disadvantages. By flowing these arguments on flow tape, it is possible to simply reapply these tapes in subsequent rounds without having to pre-flow the information again and again.

7. **Extra copies of your affirmative case (if doing CEDA/NDT).**   You will be debating at a minimum three times as the affirmative. You therefore need to have copies of your affirmative case. You want more than one copy for a few reasons. First, in case you lose or misplace one copy, you will have another one. It is also a good idea to keep the copies in different locations. Second, during the debate, the negative can ask for a copy of your affirmative case. You are obliged to give them one. If you don't have a copy, then you will have to give them the one you read. This leaves you without a copy of your case for the debate which can be problematic if you need to refer to it. Also, make sure you get your copy back after the debate if you give it to the other team. A smart thing to do is to put your affirmative case on colored paper so you can easily identify it.

8. A snack.   Debates, especially on Fridays, are often scheduled three or four rounds in a row with little to no break in between. Also, since many rounds are scheduled in the evening time the campus cafeteria is often closed. There are often no food sources close to the campus, and even when there are there simply is not enough time to patronize them. As a result, students can get very hungry. Having a small stack can go a long way towards giving you extra energy to get through those later rounds as well as easing those nagging hunger pains.

9. A positive attitude.   This should be an educational and fun experience. It is normal to be a little nervous. Remember; if it's your first tournament, you will be in novice division and so will everyone against whom you will be debating. You will not be debating against some school's best debate team in open division, so relax. Just remember what Abraham Lincoln told General McClellan who was reluctant to engage his army in battle because his soldiers were not experienced in combat. Lincoln allegedly said, "Our soldiers may be green, but so are the Confederate's . . . we are all green together." No matter what happens, the sun will rise tomorrow. So go with a positive attitude. This is going to be fun! Of course, McClellan's men were soundly defeated later, but that's not important now. The good news is that you're not going to die even if you suffer a tough defeat in a debate, and much can be learned if you keep a positive attitude.

GETTING ORIENTED

Once you arrive at the site of the tournament, you are entering the debate equivalent of the twilight zone. There are many things happening at once at a tournament: many people rushing from one place to another, students practicing speeches by literally talking to walls, debaters digging through piles of briefs and evidence to find the perfect argument, first affirmative speakers armed with stopwatches reading through their cases quickly, and hundreds power eating donuts as though the adrenaline rush isn't enough to fuel the day. It can, at first, seem a little overwhelming. However, with just a little information you should be able to handle the situation with ease, as long as you don't mind a little trans fat, craziness, and sugar in your diet occasionally.

Learning Your Code

Intercollegiate debate tournaments are attended by numerous colleges and universities. Some schools will have many two-person debate teams, and some schools may field only one team. The current practice is normally to list each two-person team by its school name, followed by the first initial of each student's surname. For example, a team from Santa Rosa Junior College consisting of students Cara Doyle and Krista Hamilton might be coded as "SRJC DH." An alternative to the norm is to assign each college and in turn each two-person team its own code. Some tournaments may give schools alphabetical symbols and students numerical codes. For example, Santa Rosa Junior College may be given the code "A," and the above-mentioned students may be coded as follows: Cara Doyle: 1, Kristen Hamilton: 2. Thus, that Doyle-Hamilton duo's code will be A $\frac{1}{2}$ for the remainder of the event. Obviously, once you arrive at the tournament you will want to quickly learn your debate code from your coach or postings area.

Finding Your Room

Once you know your debate code you will need to find the room in which your debate is to take place. To do this you will want go to the postings area. At the postings area you will find signs, usually taped to a wall, which identify the different debate formats. For example if you are in Policy debate you will want to find the sign that says POLICY. Once you find the appropriate sign, you will want to find your division. A debate tournament will usually have different levels of competition. Novice division is for beginning debaters, Junior Division is designed for students with 1–2 years of experience and Senior Division, sometimes called Open Division, is designed for students with 3–4 years of experience. All debaters need to know in what division they are entered.

Debate tournaments usually consist of six preliminary rounds. Students will be required to debate three times as the Affirmative/Government and three times as the Negative/Opposition. To find what side you will be debating on for a given round and where you will be debating, you need to check the debate postings.

The debate postings will identify which round is taking place, which team is competing against which team, which side of the motion/resolution each team has been assigned, the room in which the debate will take place, and who the critic will be (Figure 16.1). Students should write all of this information down so they won't

Round 1	Division: Novice	Time: 10:00 am	
Aff/Govt	Neg/Opp	Room	Critic
SRJC DH	Modest KL	Burbank Hall 254	C-O'Keefe
SFSU AZ	Chico NP	Burbank Hall 260	A-Babin
Berkeley VS	Davis FT	Emeritus Hall 1518	F-Hayward
Sacramento BG	Cal Poly CR	Emeritus Hall 1601	K-Hendrickson

FIGURE 16.1

Novice Division Debate Posting Sheet

forget it. If you check the postings and don't find your code recheck the postings and make sure you are looking at the correct debate postings (are you looking at the POL-ICY postings by mistake, when you are in Parliamentary debate?) and the correct division (are you checking junior division when you are in novice?).

If you are sure you have checked the correct postings and division and are positive you are not listed, don't panic. Simply find your coach and let him/her know of the situation; they will take care of the problem or tell you what to do to resolve it. If you cannot find your coach, then go to the tabulation room, and let the tournament staff know of the situation. You should plan to get to your room as soon as possible. Many tournaments have a forfeiture rule, usually 10–15 minutes. If you show up late, you might find that you have forfeited your debate.

Getting Your Topic

If you are competing in CEDA/NDT style of debate you will obviously know your topic, as the topic is the same for the entire academic year and never changes from tournament to tournament. However, if competing in NPDA style of debate you will obviously not know your topic in advance, as every round of a particular tournament will utilize a different topic. There are normally two ways that tournaments will disseminate the topic to students. The traditional way is to give the topic to judges. Normally the topic will be attached to the debate ballots so when the judges pick up their ballots they will have the topics. The judges, upon reaching the room where the debate is scheduled, will then tell the students what the topic is. From that point on the students will leave the room and have fifteen minutes to prepare. The second approach, and one that is gaining favor, is to have a **mass announcement.** Utilizing this approach, all of the students gather together at a meeting place twenty minutes before the round begins. At this point a member of the tournament tabulation room will announce the topic to everyone at the same time, hence the term mass announcement. If this approach is used, then students normally have twenty minutes of preparation time opposed to the fifteen minutes allowed in the first approach. The five extra minutes are allotted to give students time to walk to their rooms.

Setting Up

At this point we will assume you have checked the postings and have found the room. Great! But what if no one else is in the room? Don't worry; your opponents and the critic will be in shortly. It is very common for a debate tournament to get behind schedule. If you are sure you are in the correct place, go ahead and start setting up. Traditionally, if you are affirmative you will set up on the judge's left, and if negative on the judge's right. This is not a rule so please don't tell your opponents to move to the other side of the room if they set up differently in the advent that they get to the room first.

Next, if you are competing in CEDA/NDT, write your code and your names (first and last) on the board and also indicate the order in which you will be speaking. The judge will need this information for the debate ballot. If you are participating in parliamentary debate, depending on how the topic is disseminated, you may not yet know in what order you will be speaking, as sometimes the topic will influence the speaking order. You will normally write this information on the board when you come back from your preparation time. Figure 16.2 illustrates a typical chart as it would appear on a classroom blackboard indicating the team code and speaking order. The same format is used for both NPDA and CEDA/NDT debates.

If you are participating in policy (CEDA/NDT) debate, you will want to set up your evidence files. Double check to make sure everything is where it should be. If you are going affirmative, make sure your affirmative case is in order. It is generally a good idea to have multiple copies of your affirmative case in case one gets lost. Your opponents are likely to request a copy of your case to use during the debate. Although all cases and evidence should be respectfully returned at debate's end, sometimes inadvertently that does not happen.

When your debate judge or critic enters the room he/she will take a seat somewhere in the room. Don't expect a lot of other people to be there. Usually the critic will be the only other person besides the debaters in the room. In some cases though there may be a few other people: perhaps other students from the participants' college team, members of a student's family, or even anonymous students from an argumentation course there to observe the debate as a class requirement or for extra credit. If you make it to an elimination round (which we hope you do) you can count on there being a small audience. (An elimination round, also called an "out-round," is a debate that occurs after the preliminary six rounds are completed; normally, a two-person team earns the right to participate in "elim" rounds by being successful in the first six rounds. Usually, 25% to 50% of the original field advances to such

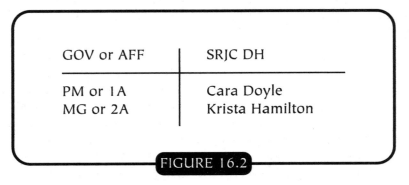

FIGURE 16.2

Team Code and Speaking Order

rounds. How many teams advance is subject to the nature of the field and the tournament rules used to determine "breaks," that is which teams advance.) Before any debate begins, the judge will generally give you his/her judging philosophy. This is simply a list of the things that the critic likes and dislikes. It is fine to ask judges for a judging philosophy if it appears they are not going to give one. It is also fine to ask the judge any specific questions before the debate begins. Listen carefully and try to incorporate the critic's comments into your debating style. For instance, if the critic says that the use of humor is important, then lighten up a little. If the critic expresses a dislike for topicality arguments, you might think hard before advancing one. However, at the novice level, it is best just to be yourself. Don't overanalyze the situation.

EVALUATING THE DEBATE

Debates are a win/lose proposition; there can be no tie. This is because, in theory, as a result of presumption, the negative wins all ties. The debate critic has a ballot on which she or he must indicate a winner. At the end of a six round tournament then, the best win-loss record a team can have is 6–0 (6 wins and no losses), and the worst record a team can have is 0–6 (zero wins and 6 losses). Due to the way debates are scheduled during a tournament, the vast majority of teams have a win-loss record somewhere in between.

As well as assigning a win/loss to each two-person team, critics also independently evaluate the effort put forth by each individual participant. In order to do this, at the end of the round, the critic assigns speaker points to each debater (usually on a 30 point scale, with 30 being the best). Ties are permitted. In fact, it is not unheard of for some critics to give 30 points to all four debaters! Hence, in a typical tournament the most speaker points that a debater can accumulate is 180 points (30 points × 6 rounds = 180 total points). Usually, debaters receive between 20 and 28 points per round. These speaker points are important for two reasons. First, the debaters who accumulate the most speaker points for the tournament are usually given special "speaker awards." Second, the total speaker points accumulated by a team for a tournament (that is, you and your partner's total points) are used to help determine which teams are advanced into the elimination rounds and what the seeding will be. The most team speaker points that can be accumulated in one debate round total 60 points (if both you and your partner are awarded 30 points each). Obviously then, the most points that can be accumulated by a single team for an entire tournament is 360 points (60 points per round × 6 rounds = 360 points).

The critic must also rank the debaters 1–4. That is, the critic must decide who did the best job of debating, who was second best, then third best, and then fourth. No ties are permitted for these rankings.

Therefore, the best possible individual rating a debater can receive is 30 points and a #1 ranking. It follows that the second best rating available is 30 points (ties permitted) and a #2 ranking (remember, no ties are permitted for rankings). Normally, the team winning the debate will also receive the most team speaker points. However, it is possible for the team winning the decision to have fewer total team speaker points than the losing team. This is called a "low point win." A low point win is assigned often when a less-skilled team happens upon an argument or set of arguments to which the more skilled team has at best an inadequate response.

The critic will also write comments to both teams on the debate ballot. These comments consist of advice to all of the debaters about how they can improve along with an explanation as to the win-loss decision. The debate ballots for all six preliminary rounds (along with elimination round ballots, more on that later) will be put into that school's tournament packet and released to that school's official coach after the tournament is over.

At one time it was traditional for debate critics not to disclose their decisions to the debaters. Over the last few years however, that has been changing. This is truer in policy debate than in parliamentary debate although it is becoming more the norm in parliamentary debate as well. In fact, recently policy debates have been extended to two-and-a-half-hour blocks to allow time for an oral critique by the judge. Remember that critics are not required to disclose their decisions. If critics do not wish to disclose their decisions, do not pressure them to do so. If they do disclose their decisions do not argue with them about their decisions when they go against you. Remember that critics have to vote for one side in each debate, and they have based their decisions on how they perceived the round. Simply listen to their critiques, and try to learn from what they have to say. If you have a question or comment, ask it in a friendly and respectful manner. For instance you might ask, "You obviously did not agree with our topicality argument. Do you have any suggestions on how we could argue it better?" Critics in general want to see you improve and want to help you in that endeavor. Also, if you are going to be debating on a regular basis, it just makes no sense to act rudely towards critics who vote against you, as you will more than likely have them judging you in future rounds, maybe even in an elimination round that very afternoon.

ELIMINATION ROUNDS

Elimination rounds (often called "out rounds") take place in each division after the preliminary rounds are completed. Elimination rounds are the equivalent to the playoffs in basketball or any other similar sport. The teams that do the best in the preliminary rounds are then advanced to the elimination rounds for the chance of winning the tournament in that particular division. In general, approximately one-third to one-half of the total participating debate teams in a given division is advanced to the elimination rounds. The criteria for determining which teams advance are twofold: The first criterion is win-loss record, and the second criterion is team speaker points. These criteria are also used for the purposes of seeding the teams that do advance.

Team	Record	Team Points	Advanced	Seeding
A 1/2	6-0	330	yes	1
B 3/4	5-1	340	yes	2
A 3/4	4-2	315	yes	3
E 1/2	3-3	317	yes	4
C 1/2	3-3	316	no	N/A
H 1/2	2-4	300	no	N/A
D 5/6	1-5	295	no	N/A
B1/2	0-6	280	no	N/A

FIGURE 16.3

Novice Division Preliminary Standings

Figure 16.3 shows how the teams entered in novice division in a hypothetical tournament might have faired (for simplicity, school alphabetical and student numerical codes were used instead of school names and student initials). Because there were eight debate teams entered, four of them advance to the elimination rounds. (Had there been sixteen or more teams, then eight would have advanced; 32 or more teams would allow 16 to advance, etc.)

There are formulas in many leagues that allow for slightly more than 50% to advance. (Check any tournament's published documentation for that information, usually available online). In this hypothetical novice division it took a win-loss record of 3–3 with 317 points to advance. Notice that the win-loss record is used as the first criterion and team speaker points as the second criterion. As a result, team "A1/2" is the highest seeded team because they were the only 6–0 team, even though team "B 3/4" had more speaker points. Also notice that it is possible to have more than one team from the same school advance into the elimination rounds. In this case, school "A" has advanced two teams.

As table 16.4 illustrates, based on this seeding, the elimination brackets for novice division would have team "A1/2" debating team "E 1/2" (seed #1 versus seed #4), and team "B 3/4" debating team "A3/4" (seed #2 versus seed #3). The winners of each of these rounds would advance to face one another in the final round (there would be separate elimination brackets for Junior and Open divisions). During elimination rounds there are usually three critics (although there can be more, as long as there is an uneven number) who decide who wins. The three critics independently decide which team they believe won the round. Thus, a team can win by gaining all

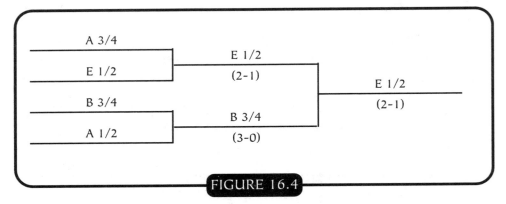

FIGURE 16.4

Novice Division Elimination Bracket

three of the critics' ballots (3–0 decision) or by gaining two of the critics' ballots (2–1 decision). In elimination rounds, speaker points are not usually awarded. As Figure 16.4 shows, in this mock tournament the number-four seeded team (E1/2) upset the number-one seeded team (A 1/2) in one of the semifinal rounds on a 2–1 decision. In the other semifinal round, the number-two seeded team (B3/4) beat the number-three seeded team (A 3/4) on a 3–0 decision. That set up a final round between the number-four seeded team (E1/2) and the number-two seeded team (B 3/4). The team E 1/2 won the final round on a 2–1 decision and thus are considered the novice tournament champions (there would be a junior champion and an open champion as well) even though they began the elimination rounds as the lowest seeded team.

SUMMARY

This chapter was intended to help the debater who may be attending her/his first academic debate tournament. Intercollegiate debate tournaments are competitions that are held between numerous schools. Students will want to make sure they have brought the necessary items. There are three divisions of competition: novice, junior and open. Each team normally debates six. Three times they will be the affirmative and three times the negative. The teams with the best records and highest combined speaker points after six rounds advance into single-elimination rounds (meaning that it only takes one loss to be eliminated). Teams are seeded by their preliminary record. The elimination rounds are usually judged by three critics. The team that wins the final round is considered the champion for that tournament. Oh yeah, tournaments are a lot of fun. We hope to see you at a tournament soon.

GLOSSARY

Advantages: In policy debate, arguments made by the advocates of change which attempt to prove that their plan, if implemented, will have desirable effects, other than solvency. See also *cost* and *solvency*.

Affirmative: The advocates that support a resolution. For example, on the topic, "Resolved: that continued military involvement in the Bosnia area would be undesirable," affirmative advocates would support that statement. In other words, the affirmative debater answers "yes" to the question implied by the proposition, "Is military involvement undesirable?"

Alternative Justification: An affirmative/government strategy in policy debate wherein multiple mini-cases are offered. Any one of the mini-cases fulfills all of the stock issues for policy debate. Thus the advocates of change may win the debate by successfully proving just one of the mini-cases. Theoretically, the resolution's advocates could lose all but one mini-case and still win the debate. However, the negative/opposition may be able to convince the debate critic that the lost mini-cases should be considered counter warrants and thus the affirmative/government may lose.

Argument: A claim supported with reasons.

Argumentation: The justification of facts, values, beliefs, or policies through oral or written advocacy. Also, the theory used to evaluate such advocacy.

Assertion: An unsupported claim.

Blame: See also inherency.

A Burden of Proof: A necessity to prove an assertion. The indefinite article, *A*, indicates that this is a burden that applies to any advocate who presents a claim in a debate.

The Burden of Proof: The requirement for the resolution's advocates to demonstrate the desirability or validity of their proposed fact, value, or policy. The definite article, *THE*, indicates that this is a specific burden that affects only the resolution's advocates.

The Burden of Rebuttal: The requirement of advocates to respond to arguments raised by their opponents. In academic debate a failure to respond to an opponent's argument usually means the granting of that argument (also known as the burden of rejoinder or the burden of clash).

Case: The arguments chosen by an affirmative team to support a given resolution. Those arguments are presented in an six-to-ten minute speech as the first order of business in a debate round. In the course of a debate, advocates refer to those affirmative arguments as *case, case side, on case,* or *the affirmative case.*

C.E.D.A.:   An acronym for *Cross Examination Debate Association,* the intercollegiate debate organization that sponsors non-policy debate topics.

Claim: A declarative statement.

Contradiction: Conflicting claim statements where no reasons are provided.

Claim Tree: A diagram that illustrates the requirements of a debatable proposition. The claim tree indicates that, in order to be debatable, a claim must have clarity, jurisdiction, and controversy.

Comparative Advantage: An affirmative/government strategy in policy debate. In this strategy, the advocates of change do not necessarily have to prove that the *status quo* is harmful, but rather prove that their plan would be better than the *status quo.* In other words, the *status quo* might be mediocre; but, with the plan, society would be significantly improved.

Constructives: In team debate, the first four speeches in which advocates build arguments for and against the resolution and against each other.

Contention: An extended argument supporting an advocate's position. A contention usually contains at least two different pieces of evidence in support of an issue. Debate contentions are delivered in outline form, and each sub-point in the outline is supported by evidence.

Cost: A stock issue in policy debate which requires the advocates of change to prove that their plan will solve the harms and/or produce advantages. See also disadvantages.

Counterplan: A strategy in policy debate in which a plan is offered by the negative/opposition. The counterplan must be non-topical, be competitive, address the affirmative's motive, and be preferable to the resolution advocate's plan.

Counterwarrants: General resolutional attacks by the negative. Rather than link arguments to the affirmative position, the negative instead refutes various examples of or warrants for the resolution. The negative usually justifies counter warrants by demonstrating that the affirmative interpretation of the resolution is in some way unreasonable or narrow.

Cross Examination: A series of questions asked by an opposing debater of the most recent constructive speaker in cross-examination style debate.

Cure: A stock issue in policy debate for the advocates of change, which requires the presentation of a plan. That plan must be workable and topical. Planks in the plan usually include an agency, mandates, staffing, funding, and enforcement.

Debate: Debate is the process of logically evaluating a claim by entertaining arguments for and against the claim, and then adopting or not adopting the claim as a reasonable resolution of a dispute. Academic debating involves serious inquiry on a resolution and advocacy both for and against that resolution. Advocates attempt to persuade a third party that their arguments are superior.

Deduction: An argument where given the truth of the premises, the conclusion must be true.

Defense of the Present System: A strategy by the negative/opposition debaters in policy debate wherein they maintain that the *status quo* does not need to be changed at all.

Definitive Contention: An argument or series of arguments in which the affirmative attempts to establish the standard, value, or criterion for a particular resolutional interpretation. A definitive contention may or may not involve specific definitions of terms.

Designative Contention: Affirmative arguments in a non-policy debate that evaluate an issue based on the standards or values set in the definitive contention.

Disadvantages: In policy debate, negative or opposition arguments which attempt to prove that the resolution-advocate's plan, if implemented, will have deleterious effects.

Evidence: In this textbook, evidence is defined liberally, including lay opinion and observation. Evidence is a form of proof used to justify a claim. Evidence includes expert opinion and observation, studies and consensus of studies. The latter is usually viewed as the most credible form of evidence.

Fact Proposition: A claim or proposition which asks advocates to determine the truth or falsehood, or the existence or non-existence, of subject, condition, or relationship, according to some agreed upon criterion.

Fallacy of Reasoning: A flaw or error in reasoning.

Forensics: Intercollegiate speech and debate competition.

Goals Case: A policy case that sets a future objective as the standard by which to judge the affirmative plan. The future objective is usually one endorsed by the status quo, either with a statement from the US President, or some other official representative of the federal government. However, in order to be inherent, the affirmative must prove that the status quo is now incapable of reaching that goal.

Government: The side in parliamentary debate which is charged with the responsibility of supporting the resolution.

Induction: An argument where given the truth of the premises, the conclusion is probably, but not necessarily, true.

Inherency: A stock issue in policy debate (also referred to as *blame*). Inherency refers to why the problem exists and why the present system in not capable of solving those problems. In a needs-analysis affirmative case, the affirmative team must prove that the harms are inherent, meaning that the status quo institutions are flawed and in need of major repair. There are eight institutions that may contain those structural flaws: military, family, education, economy, religion, government, law, and medicine. Inherency may also be attitudinal in nature, meaning that the disposition of the people causes the harm. Civil rights violations are usually harms with attitudinal inherency.

Leader of the Opposition: In parliamentary debate, the first speaker for the Opposition. The *Leader* gives the only rebuttal speech for the Opposition.

Member: In parliamentary debate, the term *member* is used to identify the second speaker of each team. The Member of the Government and the Member of the Opposition give a constructive speech, but do not give a rebuttal speech, for their respective sides.

Minor Repair: A negative position in policy debate that maintains the harms identified by the affirmative can be solved without adopting the resolution by simply improving what already exists in the present system. The phrase *minor repair* is best understood as an analogy to car repairs. The affirmative has to prove the resolution, which is analogous to getting a new engine. The negative may change anything short of that, like spark plugs. The logic is that you don't get a new engine if you only need a minor repair. Negative ground for minor repair includes additional staffing, funding, enforcement, or training, as long as no new policies or laws are added in the process. Once a new law is enacted, it is not a minor repair.

Motive: A stock issue in policy debate, which requires the advocates of change to show a reason or reasons for implementation of a new policy. This is done by showing that the present system is flawed or that a better system is available.

N.D.T.: *National Debate Tournament* is an annual tournament (and activity) sponsored by the American Forensic Association that traditionally uses propositions of policy.

Needs Analysis: An affirmative position in policy debate that maintains there are significant harms in the status quo.

Negative: That party which opposes the resolution under debate. Negative teams or advocates usually refute the affirmative case and offer constructive arguments that deny the validity of the resolution.

Non-Policy Debate: Consists of a formal educational activity in which two to four participants contend over propositions which are not policy-oriented or legislative in nature. Usually, non-policy debates dispute the nature and application of values (values such as freedom and the sanctity of human life).

NPDA: National Parliamentary Debate Association is the national organization which sponsors parliamentary debate.

On Case: The affirmative case and subsequent arguments for and against it. Also, *case side*.

Off Case: Any arguments initiated by the negative or opposition which does not directly refute the affirmative or government stock issues. (Refutation of stock issues would be on-case argumentation.) Off-case arguments include the following: counterplan, topicality, value objections, counterwarrants, disadvantages, *etc.* Off-case arguments would also include the subsequent arguments for and against these negative/opposition arguments.

Opposition: The side in parliamentary debate which is charged with the responsibility of refuting the government's case and/or negating the resolution.

Plan: See cure.

Point of Information: In parliamentary debate, advocates may ask an opponent questions while he or she is speaking. To do this, the advocate rises during the speech of his or her opponent and says, "Point of Information." The opponent will say "yes" or "no thank you," depending on whether he or she is willing to take a question at that moment of his or her speech.

Point of Order: In parliamentary debate, advocates may directly address The Speaker of the House (debate judge) to question whether the practices of their opponents violate the procedures of the House. For example, in the Prime Minister's rebuttal, the opposition may rise to make a point of order about new arguments. These are analogous to objections made in a court of law.

Point of Personal Privilege: In parliamentary debate, advocates may directly address The Speaker of the House (debate judge) to question the personal nature of the advocacy of their opponents. If an advocate feels offended or personally attacked, that is when a point of personal privilege may be made. For example, if a Prime Minister were to naively utter a racist statement, the Leader of the Opposition may rise to make a point of personal privilege.

Policy Proposition: A proposition which proposes taking some kind of action.

Presumption: The assumption that the present system will remain in effect until desirable and sufficient reasons are found to change it. In non-policy debate, presumption is not well established but usually lies with the negative. In policy debate, presumption also lies with the negative and against the affirmative policy change.

Prima Facie: A complete affirmative or government case, which, at first glance, fulfills all of the stock issues for the type of proposition being debated. A case that would convince a reasonable person to adopt the resolution.

Prime Minister: In parliamentary debate, the first speaker for the government. The Prime Minister is the leader of the government and gives the only rebuttal speech for the government.

Proposition of Fact: See Fact Proposition.

Proposition of Value: See Value Proposition.

Proposition of Policy: See Policy Proposition.

Rebuttals: Speeches in which advocates are expected to refute the most recent opposing arguments and rebuild their own position. Rebuttals should summarize constructive arguments and provide a clear focus for the debate.

Reliance on Presumption: A negative/opposition strategy in debate, which maintains that the resolution's advocates have failed to meet the burden of proof. See also *The Burden of Proof* and *Presumption.*

Significance: Qualitative and/or quantitative impact on the status quo of the harm isolated by the advocates of change. Qualitative significance refers to the impact on values like freedom and privacy. Quantitative significance refers to the numbers affected. Usually quantitative significance concerns itself with the number of people injured or killed, or the amount of money or property lost. The requirement to prove significance also applies to any solvency, advantages, and/or disadvantages raised during a debate.

Solvency: In policy debate, arguments made by the advocates of change which attempt to prove that their plan, if implemented, will fix the problems within the *status quo*. A good way to remember the definition of solvency is to note the root word *solve*. Solvency is concerned with whether the plan *solves* the harms outlined in the resolution advocate's case. See also *cost* and *advantages.*

Sound Argument: A deductive argument that is both true and valid.

Speaker of the House: In parliamentary debate, the Speaker of the House is the debate critic who rules on points of order and points of personal privilege, and who renders a decision for the government or opposition at the conclusion of the debate.

Status Quo: The way things currently are.

Stock Issues: The standard arguments that must be proven by affirmative advocates.

Strong: An inductive argument which has a high probability of being true.

Syllogism: Three part, explicit statement, which includes a general rule (technically called a major premise), a statement concerning the present case (the minor premise), and a conclusion based on these premises.

Topicality: The requirement that the advocates of the resolution must conform to the wording of the resolution. Also, an argument made by the negative in a cross-examination format debate which contends that the affirmative case is not relevant to the resolution. In policy debate, the plan is the sole determiner of topicality. In parliamentary debate, a topicality challenge is raised as a point of order by the opposition.

Valid: A deductive argument which is constructed in such a manner that the conclusion must follow.

Value Proposition: A subjective statement. Usually, a proposition of value will include a words like justified, detrimental, better, etc. The term *value* may be a misnomer, because values need not be discussed. More accurately, these propositions should be called *propositions of evaluation.*

Workability: Part of the plan-stock issue in policy debate and a requirement for the advocates of change to prove that the mechanics of their plan are sound. For example, generation of adequate funding or enforcement provisions for specified mandates must be feasible. Note the root word, *work.* The plan must *work,* as outlined.

SELECTED REFERENCES

Bartanen, M. D. (1982). The role of values in policy controversies. In Don Brownlee (Ed.), *C.E.D.A. Yearbook 1982* (pp. 19–24). Long Beach, CA: C.E.D.A.

Bartanen, M. D. (1988). *C.E.D.A. Report.* Tacoma, WA.

Best, J. A. (1980). *The mainstream of western political thought.* New York: Human Sciences Press.

Berube, M. (1984). Debating hasty generalizations. In Don Brownlee (Ed.), *C.E.D.A. Yearbook 1984* (pp. 54–59). Long Beach, CA: C.E.D.A.

Biggers, T. (1985). A single swallow and other leaps of faith. In Don Brownlee (Ed.), *C.E.D.A. Yearbook 1985* (pp. 32–38). Long Beach, CA: C.E.D.A.

Brey, J. (1989). A descriptive analysis of CEDA judging philosophies part I: Definitive acceptance or rejection of certain tactics and arguments. In Walter Ulrich (Ed.), *CEDA Yearbook* (pp. 67–77). Dubuque: Kendall/Hunt.

Brownlee, D. (1980). Advocacy and values. In Don Brownlee (Ed.), *Perspectives on Non-Policy Argument* (pp. 43–47). Long Beach, CA: C.E.D.A.

Brownlee, D. (1981). In search of topicality. In Don Brownlee, (Ed.), *Contributions on the Philosophy and Practice of C.E.D.A.* (pp. 32–35), Long Beach, CA: C.E.D.A.

Brownlee, D. (1982). Debating value propositions. In Carolyn Keefe, Thomas B. Harte, Laurence Norton. (Eds.), *Introduction to Debate.* (pp. 287–292). New York: McMillan.

Brownlee, D. (1982). The consequences of quantification. In Don Brownlee, (Ed.), *C.E.D.A. Yearbook 1982* (pp. 29–31). Long Beach, CA: C.E.D.A.

Brownlee, D. (1986). *C.E.D.A. Report #12,* Long Beach, CA.

Brydon, S. R. (1984). Judging C.E.D.A. debate: a systems perspective. In Don Brownlee, (Ed.), *C.E.D.A. Yearbook 1984* (pp. 85–88). Long Beach, CA: C.E.D.A.

Brydon, S. R. (1986). Presumption in non-policy debate: In search of a paradigm. *Journal of the American Forensic Association, 23,* 15–22.

Church, R. T., Wilbanks, C. (1986). *Values and policies in controversy: An introduction to argumentation and debate.* Scottsdale: Gorsuch Scarisbrick.

Cirlin, A. (1984). On negative strategy in value debate. In Don Brownlee, (Ed.), *C.E.D.A. Yearbook 1984* (pp. 31–39). Long Beach, CA: C.E.D.A.

Cirlin, A. (1986). Evaluating cross-examination in C.E.D.A. debate: On getting our act together. In Brenda Logue (Ed.), *1986 Yearbook Cross Examination Debate Association* (pp. 43–50). Towson, MD: C.E.D.A.

Darley, J. M., Gross, P. H. (1981). A hypothesis-confirming bias in labeling effect. *Journal of Personality and Social Psychology*, 28.

Davies, P. (1983). *God & The New Physics*. New York: Simon and Schuster.

Dixon, T. S., Leslie, C. R. (1984). Propositional analysis: A need for focus in C.E.D.A. debate. In Don Brownlee (Ed.), *C.E.D.A. Yearbook 1984* (pp. 16–23). Long Beach, CA: C.E.D.A.

Ehninger, D., Brockriede, W. (1963). *Decision by debate*. Toronto: Dodd, Mead, and Company.

Ehninger, D., Brockriede, W. (1978). *Decision by debate*. New York: Harper and Row.

Eisenberg, A. M., Llardo, J. A. (1980). *Argument: A guide to formal and informal debate*. New Jersey: Prentice-Hall.

Freeley, A. J. (1981). *Argumentation and debate: Reasoned decision making*. Belmont: Wadsworth Publishing.

Freeley, A. J. (1986). *Argumentation and debate: Critical thinking for reasoned decision making*. Belmont: Wadsworth Publishing.

Fryar, M., and Thomas, D. A. (1979). *Basic debate*. Skokie, IL: National.

Gergen, K. J., Gergen, M. M. (1981). *Social psychology*. New York: Harcourt.

Gross, W. (1984). A case for debating propositions of policy. In Don Brownlee (Ed.), *C.E.D.A. Yearbook 1984* (pp. 7–10). Long Beach, CA: C.E.D.A.

Henderson, B. (1980). Theoretical implications of debating non-policy propositions. In Don Brownlee (Ed.), *Perspectives on Non-Policy Argument* (pp. 1–12). Long Beach, CA: C.E.D.A.

Howe, J. H. (1981). C.E.D.A.s objectives; lest we forget. In Don Brownlee (Ed.), *Contributions on the Philosophy and Practice of C.E.D.A.* (pp. 1–3). Long Beach, CA: C.E.D.A.

Howe, J. H. (1982). Debate should be a laughing matter. In Don Brownlee (Ed.), *C.E.D.A. Yearbook 1982* (pp. 1–3). Long Beach, CA: C.E.D.A.

Howe, J. H. (1985). It's time for open season on squirrels. In Don Brownlee (Ed.), *C.E.D.A.Yearbook 1985* (pp. 14–20). Long Beach, CA: C.E.D.A.

Ingalls, Z. (1985). Resolved that competition in collegiate debate is as fierce as in a basketball play-off game. *The Chronicle of Higher Education, 29, 30.*

Jensen, V. J. (1981). *Argumentation: Reasoning in communication*. New York: D. Van Nostrand Company.

Jones, A. M., Crawford, S. W. (1984). Justification of values in terms of action. In Don Brownlee (Ed.), *C.E.D.A. Yearbook 1984* (pp. 11–14). Long Beach, CA: C.E.D.A.

Kahane, H. (1984). *Logic and contemporary rhetoric: The use of reason in everyday life*. Belmont: Wadsworth.

Kaplan, A. (1964). *The Conduct of Inquiry*. Chicago: Chandler.

Kelley, B. M. (1981). An alternative to N.D.T. debate. In Don Brownlee (Ed.), *Contributions on the Philosophy and Practice of C.E.D.A.* (pp. 8–14). Long Beach, CA: C.E.D.A.

Marcus, G. (2004) *The Birth of the Mind: How a Tiny Number of Genes Creates the Complexities of Human Thought.* New York: Basic Books.

Matlon, R. J. (1978). Debating propositions of value. *The Journal of the American Forensic Association. 14*, 198–204.

Matlon, R. J. (1988). Debating propositions of value: An idea revisited. In Brenda Logue (Ed.), *CEDA Yearbook* (pp. 1–14). Dubuque: Kendall/Hunt.

Miller, T. H., McVay, K. R. (1984). An audience analysis curriculum: Its theory, practice and implications. In Don Brownlee (Ed.), *C.E.D.A. Yearbook 1984* (pp. 65–73). Long Beach, CA: C.E.D.A.

Millsap, S., Millsap, S. (1985). Reflections on solvency in quasi-policy propositions. In Don Brownlee (Ed.), *C.E.D.A. Yearbook 1985* (pp. 29–31). Long Beach, CA: C.E.D.A.

Patterson, J. W., Zarefsky, D. (1983). *Contemporary debate.* Boston: Houghton Mifflin Company.

Podgurski, D. T. (1983). Presumption in the value proposition realm. In Don Brownlee (Ed.), *C.E.D.A. Yearbook 1983* (pp. 34–39). Long Beach, CA: C.E.D.A.

Ray, J., Zavos, H. (1966). Reasoning and argument: Deduction and induction. In Gerald R. Miller and Thomas R. Nilsen, (Eds.), *Perspectives on argumentation.* Chicago: Scott Foresman and Company.

Rieke, R. D., Sillars, M. O. (1984). *Argumentation and the decision making process.* Glenview: Scott, Foresmen and Company.

Rokeach, M. (1973). *The nature of human values.* New York: The Free Press.

Sanders, G. H. (1983). *Introduction to contemporary academic debate.* Prospect Heights: Waveland Press Inc.

Sayer, J. E. (1980). *Argumentation and debate: Principles and applications.* Sherman Oaks: Alfred Publishing Company.

Scott, R. J., Wynn, T. (1981). Avoidance of the false claim: Some considerations for debating and judging propositions of value. In Don Brownlee (Ed.), *Contributions on the Philosophy and Practice of C.E.D.A.* (pp. 20–31). Long Beach, CA: C.E.D.A.

Sheckels Jr., T. F. (1984). *Debating: Applied rhetorical theory.* New York and London: Longman.

Simon, J. E. (1980). *Argumentation and debate: Principles and applications.* Sherman Oaks: Alfred Publishing Company.

Sproule, J. M. (1976). The psychological burden of proof: On the evolution of Richard Whately's theory of presumption. *Communication Monographs. 43*, 115.

Sproule, J. M. (1980). *Argument, language and its influence.* New York: McGraw Hill.

Thompson, W. N. (1971). *Modern argumentation and debate: Principles and practices*. New York: Harper and Row.

Tolbert, G., Hunt, S. (1985). Counter warrants: A method for testing topical justification in C.E.D.A. debate. In Don Brownlee (Ed.), *C.E.D.A. Yearbook 1985* (pp. 21–28). Long Beach, CA: C.E.D.A.

Ulrich, W. (1983). Philosophical systems as paradigms for value debate. In Don Brownlee (Ed.), *C.E.D.A. Yearbook 1983* (pp. 22–28). Long Beach, CA: C.E.D.A.

Vasilius, J. (1980). Presumption, presumption, wherefore art thou presumption? In Don Brownlee (Ed.), *Perspectives on Non-Policy Argument*. (pp. 33–42). Long Beach, CA: C.E.D.A.

Whately, R. (1963). *The elements of rhetoric*, (Ed.) Douglas Ehninger, 7th ed. (p. 124) Carbondale: Southern Illinois University Press.

Whillock, R. K. (1988). The practice of theory: A controversy in current debate. *The Forensic of Pi Kappa Delta, 73*, 6–15.

Zeuschner, R., Hill, A. (1981). Psychological presumption: its place in value topic debate. In Don Brownlee (Ed.), *Contributions on the Philosophy and Practice of C.E.D.A.* (pp. 20–31). Long Beach, CA: C.E.D.A.

INDEX

NOTE: *Italicized* page numbers refer to figures and illustrations.

A

academic debate, 11–12, 67–69, 89. *see also* cross-examination debate; parliamentary debate
    benefits of, 13–14
    interscholastic forensics, 14–17
accuracy, compurgation and, 122–124. *see also* evidence
"A" claims, 149, 156. *see also* moods
addendum plank, *274*, 274–275
ad hominem fallacy, 202, 205
ad populum fallacy, 205
advantage section, 276
affirmative, 9–10, 70
    clarification by, 21
    cross-examination debate, preparation time, 87–89, *88*
    defined, 10
    "defining the affirmative out of the round," 22
    descriptors, *10*
    in value debate, 247–248
    in value debate, case construction, 248–256, *249*, *251*
age, of books, 102–105
agency plank, 40, 273–275, *274*
alternative justification, in policy debate, 276, 279–280
alternative justification counterplan strategy, 284
American Civil Liberties Union (ACLU), 110
American Debate Association (ADA), 17
analogy
    as argumentative tool, 183–185
    as definition, 27, 183
    false, 197–198

antecedent (P), 138
appeal to authority, 120–121
application, as value debate stock issue, 36–38
approval, shown by audience, 77, 81
a priori fallacy, 198–199
a priori issues
    jurisdiction as, 287
    procedure as, 21
arguing in a circle, 199–200
argument, 171, 192–193
    analogy, 183–185
    causal, 185–188
    defined, 3
    by definition, 190–191
    example, 176–179
    future, setting up, 225–226, 227
    sign, 188–190
    statistical, 179–183
    testimony, 174–176
    Toulmin analysis, 171–174, *172*, *173*
argumentation, 18
    argument *vs.*, 3
    debate and, 8–10
    study of, 1–5
Argumentation and Advocacy (National Communication Association), 100
argument by definition, 190–191
Aristotle
    means of persuasion and, 5–8
    The Rhetoric, 5, 26
artificial presumption, 52–53
assertion, 2, 115–116, 127–128
attitudinal inherency, 271, 272
authority
    appeal to, 120–121
    over-reliance on, 121, 200–201
    questioning, 214–215
authors
    of books, 103
    of web sites, 111

B

backing, in Toulmin analysis, *173*, 173–174
Bacon, Francis, 143
baiting an opponent, 205
begging the question fallacy, 199
Best, Judith A., 251–252
best-definition standard, 257–258
Bethe, Hans, 214–215
bias, 12, 124–125
 in evidence, 118–119
 of resolutions, 64
 testimony argument and, 176
biology, 242
Birth of the Mind, The (Marcus), 242–243
blame, as policy debate stock issue, 39–40,
 268
Book Review Digest, 104
books
 classic, 92, 104–105
 for research, 101–105, *102*
Boolean logic, 108
brainstorming, 255
briefs, 87
brink test, 286
bubble burst theory, 56
burden of clash, 57
burden of proof, 53–57
 assignment of, 55–56
 burden for proof, 54–55
 burden of clash, 57
 evidence and, 116
 initial burden met in, 56
 resolutions of fact and, 238, 241
 shifting of, 207–208
 in value debate, 256
Bush, George H.W., 244
Bush, George W., 30
by-lines, in newspapers, 106

C

case refutation arguments, 74, 75
categorical syllogisms, *134*, 134–138, 169
 claims, 149–151, *151*
 distribution, 156–157, *157*
 figures, *154*, 154–156
 moods, 153
 standard form, *151*, 151–153
 validity, 135–138, 157–158
 validity, matching mood and figure for,
  161–162, *162*
 validity, rules and, *158*, 158–161
 validity, Venn diagrams for, *136*,
  136–138, 162–168, *163–168*
 in value debate, 253–255
causal argument, 185–188
 arguing no links, 213–214
 non-unique refutation, 221–222
causation, mistaken, fallacy of, 196–197
cause-to-effect argument, 185–188
central tendency, 181
certainty, as standard of proof, 59–60
chains of inference, 235
Christian Science Monitor, 106
circular argument, 199–200
circular fallacy, 120
claims
 categorical, 149–151, *151*
 enthymematic connection to reason,
  6–8
 evidence and, 214
 Toulmin analysis, 171–174, *172*, *173*
claim tree, 19, *20*
 clarity, 19–27, *23–24*
 controversy, 28–29
 jurisdiction, 27–28
clarification
 in cross-examination, 224, 226
 in parliamentary debate, 77, 80
clarity, 19–25
 definitions, evaluation standards for,
  27
 definitions, methods for, 25–27
classic books, 92, 104–105
Clinton, Bill, 22–23, *23–24*, 36, 190–191
closed questions, 226–227
common knowledge
 of evidence, 127, 128
 standard of, 92
 violations of, 79
Common Law, 116

comparative advantage, in policy debate, 276, 278–279, *279*

competence, 118–119, 120
    external tests of, 122–124
    internal tests of, 120–121

competitiveness, in counterplan strategy, 283–284

completeness, 42

composition, fallacy of, 196

compurgation, 122–123

computer searches, for research, 101, *102*, 105–106

conclusion, of categorical syllogisms, 134, 152, 161

conditional counterplan strategy, 284

conditional nature, of arguments, 222

conditional syllogisms, 134, 138–139
    "pure," 139, *139*
    structure of, *138*

Conduct of Inquiry, The (Kaplan), 145

Congressional Digest, 107

Congressional Quarterly, 107

cons, defined, 9–10

consensus
    of expert opinion, 127, 129
    of lay opinion, 127, 129
    of studies, 127, 129–130

consequent (Q), 138

"conservative," 159

contradiction
    assertion and, 2
    for refutation, 212–213

controversy, 28–29, 45

copula, of categorical syllogisms, 150–151, *151*

Corcoran, Joseph, 15

cost, as policy debate stock issue, 40, 268, 275–276

cost-benefit analysis, 38

counterplan strategy, 282–285

counter refutation
    five-step style, 220–221
    preparing for, 217–220

credibility. *see* compurgation; evidence

criteria
    arguing, 260–261

denying applications to, 263
    as value debate stock issue, 36–38, 248–252, *251*

critical thinking, 45. *see also* argumentation; debate
    cross-examination debate and, 82–83
    defined, 4–5

Critical Thinking Through Debate (Corcoran, Nelson, Perella), 12–13

critics. *see* evaluation; judgment; Speaker of the House

cross-examination, 223, 230
    questioner in, 223–228
    respondent in, 228–230

cross-examination debate, 10, 13, 67–69
    advantages, disadvantages of, 81–83
    development of format, 85–87
    parliamentary debate compared to, 69–70
    preparation time for, 87–89
    shifting the burden of proof, 207–208
    speaker responsibilities for, 83–85
    time constraints for, *68*
    typical format of, *86*

Cross-Examination Debate Association (CEDA), 16, 67, 69, 70, 81, 82, 85
    on-point value objections, 265
    preponderance of evidence, 219–220
    topicality in, 258–260

cure, as policy debate stock issue, 40, 268, 272–275

current event policy topics, 71–72

D

Darden, Christopher, 35

Darley, J.M., 145–146

data, in Toulmin analysis, 171–174, *172, 173*

debatable claims
    claim tree, *19*, 19–29
    classification of, 29
    prima facie case, 40–43
    propositions, 29–33 (*see also* resolutions of fact; resolutions of policy; resolutions of value)
    stock issues, 33–40

debate, 18. *see also* cross-examination;
    evaluation; parliamentary debate;
    resolutions of fact; resolutions of
    policy; resolutions of value
    academic, 11–17, 67–69, 89
    argumentation and, 8–10
    defined, 4–5
    printed, for research, 101, *102*, 105–106
    study of, 1–5
    theory of, 12–13
    tournament, 67, 86, 295–304, *300*, *303*,
        304
decision making, presumption and, 49
Declaration of Independence, 250
deductive reasoning, 133–134, 144, 169. *see
    also* syllogisms
    categorical syllogisms, *134*, 134–138
    conditional syllogisms, *138*, 138–139,
        139
    disjunctive syllogisms, 139–143, *140*, *141*
defense, defined, 10
defense of the present system strategy,
        280–281
"defining the affirmative out of the round,"
        22
definitions
    disputes about, 22
    as element for resolutions of fact, 234,
        238–239
    for factual debate, 36
    methods for, 25–27
    for value debate, 36–38, 257–258
definitive stock issue, 36–38, 256–261, *259*
Delta Sigma Rho-Tau Kappa Alpha, 16
demonstration
    of competence, 124
    hearsay and, 126–127
denying an argument, 210–211
dependent contentions, 262
descriptive statistics, 179
descriptors, *10*, 108
designative stock issue, 261–263
dialectic process, 8
dictionary definitions, 25
diminishment, of an argument, 211–214
direct evidence, 235

direct examination, 223
disadvantage, policy debate based on,
        285–287
disapproval, shown by audience, 77, 81
disbarring an argument, 214–216
disjunctive syllogisms, 134, 139–143, *140*,
        141
distribution, of categorical claims, 156–157,
        157
division, fallacy of, 196
division of ground theory, 291–292

E

"E" claims, 149, 157. *see also* moods
effects topicality, 287, 288
effect-to-cause argument, 185–188
elementary Venn diagrams, *136*, 136–138.
        see also Venn diagrams
elimination rounds, 302–304, *304*
emotional language, 124–125, 230
empirical study, 129
empirical verification, 232, 233, 239
enforcement mechanism, 40, 273–275, *274*
English Common Law, 53
enthymeme, 6–8, *7*, 173, 234
epistemology, 231
equivocation, fallacy of, 206
ethos, 5–6
etymological definitions, 26–27
evaluation
    criteria, in value debate, 248–252
    of research materials, 103–106 (*see also*
        evidence)
    of tournament debate, 301–304, *303*, *304*
    win-loss decisions, 82, 301–304
evidence, 92, 113, 115, 131. *see also*
        argument
    claim and, 214
    defined, 93
    as element for resolutions of fact,
        234–235, 239–240
    for factual debate, 36
    fact *vs.* opinion, 130
    hierarchy of, 127–130
    interpretation of, 116, 117

library research, 91
library research, genres of material,
    101–112
library research, levels of material,
    99–101
need for, 115–116
preponderance of, 219–220
recentness of, 92–93, 215
relevance of, 116–118
reliability of, 116, 118–127
sources of, 93–99
verifiability of, 71
example argument, 176–179
example argument fallacy, 195
exclusive disjuncts, *141*, 141–143
existential import, 158, *168*
existential inherency, 271, 272
expert opinion
    in hierarchy of evidence, 127, 129
    testimony argument and, 175–176
extending an argument, 220
extension, fallacy of, 201–202
external tests
    of bias, 124–125
    of competence, 120–121
    for research material accuracy, 104–105
extra-topicality, 287–289

F

fact, defined, 231–233
factual debate, 36. *see also* resolutions of
    fact
factual propositions. *see* resolutions of fact
fallacies, 3, 195, 208
    ad hominem, 202, 205
    ad populum, 205
    appeal to authority, 120–121
    arguing in a circle, 199–200
    begging the question, 199
    circular, 120
    composition, 196
    division, 196
    equivocation, 206
    example argument, 195
    false analogy, 197–198

false consolation, 202–203
false dilemma, 203
ignoring the issue, 204
loaded question, 204
mistaken causation, 196–197
over-reliance on authority, 121, 200–201
a priori, 198–199
psychological language, 205
reductio ad absurdum, 201–202
shifting the burden of proof, 207–208
significance, 197
of significance, 182
sign reasoning, 207
straw person, 206
tradition, 206–207
false analogy, 197–198
false consolation, fallacy of, 202–203
fiat power, 272–273, 290–292
field-specific authorities, 26
figurative analogy, 183
figures, of categorical syllogisms, *154*,
    154–156
    matching moods and, 161–162, *162*
    standard form, 154–156
fill factor, 115–116
first affirmative constructive (1AC), 69, 83
first affirmative rebuttal (1AR), 84–85
first negative constructive (1NC), 83, 259
first negative rebuttal (1NR), 84
first principals, 116
five-step counter-refutation, 220–221
flowsheets, 69, 88
forensics, 14–17. *see also* tournament debate
    organizations, 16–17
    teams, 14–15
four-step refutation, 216–217, *218*
framers, of resolution, 48–49, 61–63
Freud, Sigmund, 143
Fuhrman, Mark, 35
funding plank, 40, 273–275, *274*

G

generalization
    hasty, 195, 216
    stereotyping and, 145–146

genre, research materials by, 101–102, *102*
    books, 101–105
        computer searches, 107–112
        government publications, 106–107
        newspapers, 101, 105–106
        periodicals, 101, *102*, 105
        printed debates, 107
Gergen, K.J., 146
Gergen, M.M., 146
glossary of terms, 305–311
goals, in policy debate, 276, 279
Goldman, Ron, 35
government, 10, 70. *see also* parliamentary
    debate
government publications, 101, *102*, 105–107
Gray, Dorise, 250–251
Greenhaven Press, 107
Gross, P.H., 145–146
grounds, 172. *see also* data, in Toulmin
    analysis

H

harm-advantage continuum, *279*
hasty generalization, 195, 216
hearings, Congressional, 106–107
hearsay, in evidence, 118–119, 120, 125–127
heckles, 77, 80
Hinkley, Richard, 55–56
hostile parties
    cross-examination of, 223–224
    defined, 209
Howe, Jack, 248
Hussein, Saddam, 30, 36, 244
hypothetical syllogisms, 134. *see also*
    conditional syllogisms

I

"I" claims, 149, 157. *see also* moods
"if-then" arguments. *see* conditional
    syllogisms
ignoring the issue, fallacy of, 204
impact, refutation and, 213
implicit resolution, 48
inclusive disjuncts, *140*, 140–141, 142–143

independent contentions, 252–253, *253*,
    262, 263
indexes
    of individual journals, magazines, 105
    of literature reviews, 99
    to periodicals, 105
indirect evidence, 235, 240
inductive reasoning, 133–134, 143–146, 169
inference
    as element for resolutions of fact, 235,
      237–238, 240
    for factual debate, 36
inferential statistics, 179
inherency, 270–272, 278. *see also* resolutions
    of policy
innocence, presumption of, 53
inoculation theory, 180
insanity plea, 55
internal tests
    of bias, 124–125
    of competence, 120–121
    for research material accuracy, 103–104
Internet, for research, 101, *102*, 105–106
internet service providers (ISPs), 111
interpretation, of evidence, 116, 117. *see also*
    argument
investigation, evidence and, 94
Ito, Lance, 42

J

Jones, Paula, 22
judges. *see* judgment; Speaker of the House
judgment
    criteria, in value debate, 248–252
    of tournament debate, 301–304, *303,*
      304
judicial knowledge, 127, 128
judicial system, Protagorean model and, 9
Junior Statesmen of America (JSA), 17
jurisdiction, 27–28, 287–289

K

Kahane, Howard, 134
Kant, Immanuel, 249–250

Kaplan, Abraham, 145
Katz, Bill, 105
Katz, Linda Sternberg, 105
Kelley, B.M., 249

L

lack of impact, as refutation, 213
language, literal, 239
lay opinion, 127, 128, 129
Leader of the Opposition. *see also*
        parliamentary debate
        preparation time by, 72–74
        rebuttal by, 76–77
        speaker responsibilities of, 74–75
legal debate, stock issues for, 34–35
Lewinsky, Monica, 22–24, 36
libel, 103
"liberal," 159
libraries, for research
        genres of material in, 101–112
        levels of material in, 99–101
        preparation for using, 91
Lincoln/Douglas debate
        defined, 68–69
        time constraints for, *68*
links to affirmative mandates,
        disadvantage and, 286
literal analogies, 183–185
literature reviews, 99
loaded language, fallacy of, 205
loaded question, fallacy of, 204
logic. *see* categorical syllogisms
logical thinking, 4–5
Logic and Contemporary Rhetoric (Kahane),
        134
logos, 6
Los Angeles Times, 106
low point win, 302

M

magazines. *see* periodicals
Magazines for Libraries (Katz, Katz), 105
Mainstream of Western Political Thought, The
        (Best), 251–252

major premise, in categorical syllogisms,
        134, 154–156, 159
major terms (P), 152, 163–168, *164*, *168*
mandates, in policy debate, 40, 273, 286
Marcus, Gary, 242–243
mean, 181–183
median, 181–183
Member of Government (MG), 75
Member of Opposition (MO), 76
Michelin Guide to Magazines, 105
middle terms (M), 152, *154*, 154–156,
        160–161
Mill, J.S., 249
minor premise, in categorical syllogisms,
        134, 159, 165–156
minor repair strategy, 281–282
minor terms (S), 152, *165*, 165–168, *168*
misconstruing an opponent's arguments,
        violations of, 79–80
mistaken causation, fallacy of, 196–197
mitigating an argument, 212
modalities, 58, 173
mode, 181–183
modus ponens, 138
modus tollens, 138
Mondale, Walter, 12
moods, 153
        matching figures and, 161–162, *162*
        standard form, 154–156
moral-ground abuse, 75
motive, as policy debate stock issue, 35,
        38–39, 268–270, 282
mutual exclusivity, in counterplan strategy,
        283

N

Napoleanic Code, 53
National Communication Association, 100
National Debate Tournament (NDT), 16,
        67, 70, 81, 85, 219–220
National Educational Debate Association
        (NEDA), 17
National Forensics League (NFL), 16
National Parliamentary Debate Association
        (NPDA), 16–17, *67*, 70

needs analysis, in policy debate, 276–279, *279*

negation, 25–26

negative, 9–10, 70
    cross-examination debate, preparation time, 87–89, *88*
    defined, 10
    descriptors, *10*
    fiat power, 290–292
    no impact, 221–222
    policy debate strategies, 280–287
    in value debate, 256
    in value debate, off-case arguments, 263–266, *265*
    in value debate, refuting definitive stock issue, 256–261, *259*
    in value debate, refuting designative stock issue, 261–263

negative claims, 159–160

negative stock issues, for resolutions of fact, 237–238

Nelson, Mark, 15, 21

net benefits, 38, 283

new issues in rebuttals, violations of, 79

newspapers, for research, 101, *102*, 105–106

Newspapers for Libraries, 106

New York Times, 106

no impact, of negative argument, 221–222

non-party evidence, 97

non sequitor fallacy, 3, 207

non-standard form, of syllogisms, 151–153

non-unique refutation, 221

no threshold, refutation and, 221

"not topical," 21

O

observations, defined, 93

"O" claims, 149, 157. *see also* moods

off-case arguments, 74, 75
    evidence for, 116
    in value debate, 263–266

off-case attacks, resolutions of fact and, 240–241

on-case arguments, resolutions of fact and, 238–240

open questions, 224

operational definitions, 25

opinions. *see also* evidence
    defined, 93
    resolutions of fact, 240

Opposing Viewpoints (Greenhaven Press), 107

opposition, 10, 70
    admissions by, 96–97
    errors in refutation by, 221–222
    exposing weaknesses of, 224–225
    questioning logic of, 215–216

"or," as inclusive disjunct, *140,* 140–141, 142–143

out rounds, 302. *see also* elimination rounds

outweighed impact, as requirement of disadvantage, 286–287

over-claiming, 239

over representation, 181

Oxford University Press, 104

P

parliamentary debate, 10, 13, 67–69, 89
    advantages, disadvantages of, 70–71
    cross-examination debate compared to, 69–70
    evaluation of, 302
    evidence for, 92, 94–95, 115, 117, 118
    jurisdictional arguments, 287–289
    parliamentary procedure, 77–81
    preparation time for, 72–74
    refutation used in, 215
    speaker responsibilities for, 74–77
    time constraints for, *68*
    topics for, 71–72
    in value debate, 247, 255, 259

parliamentary procedure, 77–81

pathos, 5–6, 26

"Pat" (*Saturday Night Live* character), 142

patterns
    distribution, of categorical claims, 156–157, *157*
    in inductive reasoning, 143

Perella, Jack, 15

perfect induction, 176–177

periodicals
    Argumentation and Advocacy (National Communication Association), 100

for research, 101, *102*, 105
personal experience, as evidence, 94–96
persuasion, Aristotelian means of, 5–8
Phi Rho Pi, 16
Pi Kappa Delta, 16
plaintiffs, 10
plausibility, as standard of proof, 59
plea bargaining, 187
points of clarification, 77, 80
points of information, 77–78, 215
points of order, 77–79, 118
points of personal privilege, 77, 80
policy propositions. *see* resolutions of
        policy
popular press, for research material, 99–100
possibility, as standard of proof, 58–59
post hoc ergo propter hoc fallacy, 186, 197
predicate, of categorical syllogisms,
        150–151, *151*
preempting an argument, 218–219
preparation time
        for cross-examination debate, 87–89, *88*
        for parliamentary debate, 72–74
preponderance of evidence, 219–220
presumption, 49–53, 285
prima facie case, 34, 40–43, 83
        alternative format, based on
                syllogisms, 242–244
        assertion, 127–128
        elements for resolutions of fact,
                234–235, 241–242
        evidence for, 116
        in value debate, refuting definitive
                stock issue, 256–257
Prime Minister (PM), 69, 247
        preparation time by, 72–74
        rebuttal by, 77
        speaker responsibilities of, 74
printed debates, for research, 101, *102*,
        105–106
probability, as standard of proof, 59
procedural arguments, 74–75
procedural issues, 21
proof. *see* burden of proof; standards of
        proof
propositions, 29–33, 47. *see also* debatable
        claims; resolutions of fact;

resolutions of policy; resolutions of
        value
        factual topics, 30–31
        policy topics, 32–33
        value topics, 31–32
pros, defined, 9–10
prosecution, 10
Protagoras of Abdera, 8–9
Protagorean model of debate, 8–10, *9*, 29
psychological language, fallacy of, 205
public debate, 11–12
public speaking, in parliamentary debate,
        71
publishers, 103–104
pure conditional syllogisms, 139, *139*

Q

qualifiers, 58, *173*, 173–174
qualitative/quantitative significance,
        269–270
quality, of categorical syllogisms, 150–151,
        151
quantifier, of categorical syllogisms,
        150–151, *151*
questioner, in cross-examination, 223–224
        clarification by, 224
        future arguments set up by, 225–226
        opposition weaknesses exposed by,
                224–225
        questions controlled by, 226–228
questions
        closed, 226–227
        control of, in cross-examination,
                226–228, 229–230
        defined, 47
        open, 224
        technique, 181
        yes/no, 229
quotations, 98, 248

R

Ray, J., 133–134
Reader's Guide to Periodical Literature, The,
        105
Reagan, Nancy, 186

Reagan, Ronald, 12, 56, 197, 203
reason, enthymematic connection to claim, 6–8
reasonable-definition standard, 257
reasoning, 133, 147
    deductive, 133–134, 144
    deductive, categorical syllogisms, *134*, 134–138
    deductive, conditional syllogisms, 134, *138*, 138–139, *139*
    deductive, disjunctive syllogisms, 134, 139–143, *140*, *141*
    inductive, 133–134, 143–146
rebuilding, of original arguments, 219–220
rebuttals. *see also individual types of debate*
    in parliamentary debate, 76–77
    in parliamentary debate, violations, 79
    Toulmin analysis, *173*, 173–174
reductio ad absurdum, 201–202
refutation, 209, 222–223
    counter-refutation, 217–220
    of designative stock issue, 261–263
    five-step, 220–221
    four-step, 216–217, *218*
    opposition to, 221–222
    preparing for, 209–210
    three "D's" of, 210–216
    in value debate, of definitive stock issue, 256–261, *259*
relevance
    diminishing an argument and, 211–212
    of evidence, 116, 117–118 (*see also* argument)
reliability, of evidence, 118–119. *see also* argument
    bias, 118–119, 120, 124–125
    competence, 118–119
    dimensions of, *119*
    hearsay, 118–119, 120, 125–127
reliance on presumption strategy, 285
reporters, newspaper, 106
representative samples, 180
research, 81, 82. *see also* evidence
reservation, in Toulmin analysis, *173*, 173–174
resolution, 10, 45–46
    burden of proof in, 49, 53–57
    defined, 47–48, 68–69
    as division of ground theory, 291–292
    framers of, 48–49
    implicit, 48
    irrelevancy of argument and, 211–212
    origin of, 46–47
    for parliamentary debate, 73
    presumption in, 49–53
    standard of proof in, 49, 58–63
    wording of, 63–65
resolutions of fact, 30–31, 36, *37*, 231, 244
    on claim tree, *20*
    convertibility of, 233–234
    evidence and, 130
    fact, cultural considerations about, 232–233
    fact, defined, 230–231
    fact, nature of, 231–232
    negative stock issues for, 237–238
    off-case attacks, 240–241
    on-case arguments, 238–240
    for parliamentary debate, 73
    presumption for, 51–53
    prima facie, alternative format based on syllogisms, 242–244
    prima facie case elements for, 234–235
    sample cases, 235–237, 241–242
    standard of proof for, 60–61
    standards, burdens of proof, 238
resolutions of policy, *31*, 32–33, 234, 267, 293
    affirmative strategies, 276–280, *279*
    on claim tree, *20*
    evaluation of, 302
    "fiat power," 290–292
    harm-advantage continuum, *279*
    jurisdictional issues, 287–290
    negative strategies, 280–287
    for parliamentary debate, 73
    presumption in, 50–51
    sample brainstormed outline, 277–278
    "should," 290–292
    standard of proof for, 61
    traditional stock issues, 267–276
    version of a plan, *275*

resolutions of value, 31–32, *39*, 247, 266
    affirmative/government case, 247–248
    affirmative/government case,
        construction of, 248–256, *249, 251*
    on claim tree, *20*
    evidence and, 130
    hierarchy of values, *251*, 251–252
    negative strategies, 256
    negative strategies, off-case arguments,
        263–266, *265*
    negative strategies, refuting definitive
        stock issue, 256–261, *259*
    negative strategies, refuting
        designative stock issue, 261–263
    for parliamentary debate, 73
    presumption for, 51–53
    sample outline, 255–256
    standard of proof for, 60–61
    terminal values, *249*, 249–250
respondents, in cross-examination, 228
    control of, 229–230
    knowledge of, 228
    traps avoided by, 229
restatement, of opponent's argument,
    216–217
Rhetoric, The (Aristotle), 5, 26
rhetorical argument, 5–8
Rokeach, Milton, 249
rules, of the syllogism, *158*, 158–161

S

sample size, 181
Saturday Night Live, 142
scholarly periodicals, 105
scholarly press, 99–101
second affirmative constructive (2AC),
    83–84
second affirmative rebuttal (2AR), 69, 85
second negative constructive (2NC), 84
second negative rebuttal (2NR), 85
self-interest, 124–125
Sellinger, Cindi, 250–251
shells, 87
Shenck v. the United States, 250–251
shifting-presumption theory, 56

shifting the burden of proof, fallacy of,
    207–208
"should," in policy debate, 290–292
sign argument, 188–190
significance
    example argument and, 177, 178
    fallacy of, 182, 197
    motive and, 267
sign reasoning, fallacy of, 207
silence, consent and, 57
simple random samples, 180
Simpson, O.J., 35, 42
slippery slope fallacy, 201–202
solvency, 275
sophists, 8
sources. *see* evidence
Speaker of the House, 78, 79
    evidence rulings by, 92
    speaker responsibilities of, 74
speaker responsibilities
    for cross-examination debate, 83–85
    for parliamentary debate, 74–77
specialist press, 99, 100
speed, of speaking, 82
standard form statements, *151*, 151–153
standards of proof, 58–63
    certainty, 59–60
    plausibility, 59
    possibility, 58–59
    probability, 59
    resolutions of fact and, 238, 241
statement against interest, 125
statistics
    in argumentation, 179–183
    fallacy of significance in, 197
status quo, 49–50, 267–268
stereotyping, 145–146, 178
stock-issue analysis, 34–35
stock issues, 33–34, *37*
    defined, 268
    for fact debate, 36, *37*, 237–238
    for legal debate, 34–35
    for policy debate, 35, 38–40, *41*,
        267–276
    for value debate, 36–38, *39*, 256–257,
        256–263, *259*

stratified random samples, 180–181
straw person, fallacy of, 206
"strong" arguments, 144
structural barrier, 271–272
structural gap, 272
structural inherency, 271–272
studies counterplan strategy, 284
subject, of categorical syllogisms, 150–151,
    151
sufficiency, example argument and, 177–178
suppressed premise, 6
Sweeny, Julia, 142
syllogisms, 134
    categorical, *134*, 134–138
    conditional, *138*, 138–139, *139*
    disjunctive, 139–143, *140*, *141*
    four possible determinations for, *135*

T

tag team cross-examination, 86
team debate, 68
team speaker points, 301–304
technology, 242
temporal-displacement case, 73
testimony argument, 174–176
text book publishers, 104
third-party sources
    published, 98–99
    unpublished, 97
three "D's" of refutation
    denying an argument, 210–211
    diminishing an argument, 211–214
    disbarring an argument, 214–216
"Three-Strikes Law," 187–188
time, for preparation, 72–74, 87–89, *88*
time constraints
    for academic debate formats, *68*, 78
    in cross-examination debate, 86
time frame, as requirement of
        disadvantage, 286
Time Magazine, 243
time-warp case, 73
titles, validity of, 122–123
topical issues, 21–22
    assigned in tournaments, 299

knowledge of, for cross-examination,
        228
    in policy debate, 283
    in value debate, 248, 258–260, *259*
topicality
    for parliamentary debate, 71–72
    in policy debate, 287–288
    resolution and, 47
Toulmin, Steven, 58, 171. *see also* Toulmin
        analysis
Toulmin analysis, 171–174, 192–193. *see also*
        argument
    analogy argument, 184–185
    argument by definition, 191
    causal argument, 188
    example argument, 178–179
    fully diagrammed, *173*
    primary components of, *172*
    sign argument, 190
    statistical argument, 183
    testimony argument, 174–176
tournament debate, 67, 295, 304. *see also*
        Cross-Examination Debate
        Association (CEDA); forensics;
        National Debate Tournament
        (NDT); National Parliamentary
        Debate Association (NPDA)
    code for, 297–299, *300*
    evaluation of, 301–304, *303*, *304*
    items to bring to, 295–297
    orientation for, 297–301
    speaking order, *300*
    time constraints of, 86
tradition, fallacy of, 206–207
traditional counterplan strategy, 284
traps, in cross-examination, 229
truth, in syllogisms, 135–138
turn-around arguments, 211, 222
typical internal tests, 121
typicality, example argument and, 177–178

U

under representation, 181
uniqueness, as requirement of
        disadvantage, 286

universal examples, defined, 95
unpublished sources, as evidence, 96–97
URLs (Uniform Resource Locators), 108–112
U.S. Congress
    Congressional Digest, 107
    hearings, 106–107
U.S. government documents, as debate
        criteria, 250
utopian counterplan strategy, 284–285

V

validity, in syllogisms, 135–138, 157–158
    matching mood and figure for,
        161–162, *162*
    rules for, *158*, 158–161
    standard form and, 151–153
    Venn diagrams for, 162–168, *163–168*
value debate, 36–38, 234. *see also*
        resolutions of value
value objections (VOs), 264–266, *265*
value propositions. *see* resolutions of value
Vasilius, Jan, 258
Venn diagrams, *136*, 136–138, 162–168,
        163–168
violations, in parliamentary debate, 79–80

W

Wall Street Journal, 106

warrant, 6
    analogy, 184
    Toulmin analysis, 171–174, *172, 173*
Washington Post, 106
"weak" arguments, 144
web pages. *see* World Wide Web
win-loss decisions. *see also* evaluation
    in cross-examination debate, 82
    record, 301–304
wire services, 106
Wise, Helen, 14
witnesses. *see* cross-examination
workability, 274
world view, *a priori* fallacy and, 198–199
World Wide Web, 101, *102*, 105–106
Wright, Susan Webber, 22, *23*

X

"x," placement of in Venn diagrams,
        165–168, *166–168*

Y

yes/no questions, 229

Z

Zavos, H., 133–134